ART *of* EMBROIDERY

History of Style and Technique

ART of EMBROIDERY

History of Style and Technique

LANTO SYNGE

*Theo,
with all best wishes
from Lanto —
Nov. '01.*

THE ROYAL SCHOOL OF NEEDLEWORK

Antique Collectors' Club

©2001 Lanto Synge

World copyright reserved

ISBN 1 85149 359 X

The right of Lanto Synge to be identified as author of this work has been asserted by him in accordance with the Copyright, Designs and Patents Act 1988

All rights reserved. No part of this publication may be reproduced, stored in a retrieval system, or transmitted in any form or by any means electronic, mechanical, photocopying, recording or otherwise, without the prior permission of the publishers.

British Library Cataloguing-in-Publication Data
A catalogue record for this book is available from the British Library

Designer: Peter Butler

Half-title. Detail of an early 18th century English coverlet with silk chain stitch embroidery and false quilting, a true fusion of Asian and European technique and design.

Frontispiece. A canvas work panel, probably French, c.1750, with both real and exotic flowers and birds.

Origination by Antique Collectors' Club
Woodbridge, England
Printed and bound in Italy

Dedicated to
Her Majesty Queen Elizabeth the Queen Mother,
Patron of the Royal School of Needlework,
with her gracious permission

*The Robe of Estate made for the coronation of
King George VI and Queen Elizabeth in 1937 was
designed and embroidered by the Royal School of Needlework*

... not a rag in it under forty, fifty or a thousand years old
HORACE WALPOLE DESCRIBING DRAYTON HOUSE

*4. An Elizabethan silk purse
decorated with gold and silver thread, seed pearls and spangles.*

Contents

Preface 9

Introduction 10

Chapter One
Early Needlework 32

Chapter Two
The Mediaeval Period 40

Chapter Three
The Post-Mediaeval Period 66

Chapter Four
A Note on Heraldry 100

Chapter Five
The Seventeenth Century 110

Chapter Six
A Note on Costume 160

Chapter Seven
The Eighteenth Century 170

Chapter Eight
A Note on Furniture 226

Chapter Nine
The Nineteenth Century 250

Chapter Ten
China: A Long Heritage of Silk 286

Chapter Eleven
Indian Export Needlework 310

Chapter Twelve
The Twentieth Century 324

Notes 334
Glossary 340
Bibliography 344
Acknowledgements 347
Index 348

PREFACE

It is nearly twenty years since I completed *Antique Needlework* and that book has now gone into the past. This work is a completely new version, considerably expanded, newly illustrated and correcting some howling errors of omission and prejudice of my younger enthusiasm. There are also some new chapters in this book, notably on China and India which have contributed so greatly to the decorative arts in Europe and America.

I have always tried to illustrate with pictures that are not the already familiar old favourites but have included this time some indispensable touchstones together with many less well-known wonders of needlework and embroidery. Studying antique textiles is largely a matter of looking at interesting pieces and the great joy is that it is now so much easier to reproduce a wide selection of fabulous examples.

LMS 2001

5. Birds, flowers and animals, both wild and domestic, are assembled here with typical English charm in out of scale proportions. c.1720.

INTRODUCTION

*Pray, sir, take the laudable mystery of embroidery
into your serious consideration.*

THE history of decorative needlework is intriguing and diverse, with a world-wide richness and broad, human implications. A study of it takes us into many periods and facets of social history, since embroidery is one of man's oldest skills, referring us to each branch of the fine and decorative arts and pointing to fascinating interplays of inspiration and design generally. The antiquity of the art has given it a unique depth while the simple occupation of making patterns and images with needle and thread provided the humble origin for the creation of many objects of great beauty.

We are fortunate to be living at a time when, as students or collectors, we have easy access to a vast range of historical pieces and can consult scholars and experts with wide or specialised areas of knowledge. Museums and country houses display many wonders of needlework, while the antiques trade and salerooms still offer opportunities to view and handle a considerable variety of pieces. However, the essence of both making a study and building a collection is selection, and this book attempts to guide readers to focus on and enjoy fine examples of needlework, pointing to special qualities within an outline history of the subject. Equally, it is hoped it may encourage modern embroiderers to undertake new projects inspired by timeless qualities.

The Bible tells us that Adam and Eve sewed fig leaves together at the beginning of time, and in *Exodus* XXXV there is a remarkable description of how Moses furnished the Tabernacle with curtains 'embroidered with needlework, of fine twined linen; with cherubim skillfully worked'. Whether it was sewing or weaving that was first

*6. A silk cope of about 1300 depicts the genealogy of Christ. Here the harpist
King David is in a vine stem leading from the prophet Jesse.*

Introduction

developed is largely a matter of conjecture. Textile scholars are divided on this question; both techniques were practised long before the invention of thread or its application to other pliable materials, and they differ distinctly, with contrasting methods of manufacture.[1] There is some confusion between tapestry weaving and needlework; we are concerned here with the latter, sewing, for though weaving is related, and woven materials usually provide the fabric on which needlework is done, the method of workmanship is entirely different. Weaving, as in the making of tapestries, is done on a loom with many threads being bound together as in basketwork, while needlework, as the word implies, is carried out with a needle and a single thread. The word tapestry is often loosely and, strictly, incorrectly applied to canvas needlework. The tapestry weaving process is complex and expensive and was chiefly employed for making large pictorial hangings. Needlework, on the other hand, is based on the simple craft of sewing, with at times a wide variety of stitchery. Although some of the finest embroidery was made professionally, much is domestic in character and workmanship, reflecting homely uses and personal designs.

The earliest needlework was of a plain, practical nature, done with strong fibrous materials such as hair, to join skins and furs for clothing, and embroidery was used to strengthen parts subject to greater wear. From this basic necessity a sumptuous decorative art gradually emerged. The words needlework and embroidery are nearly synonymous. The former is general, embracing in its widest sense ordinary work such as knitting, darning and seam making, but it also includes embroidery, which more specifically suggests decoration or ornament. In old records, 'embroidery' normally refers to work in silks, but nowadays 'needlework' can equally refer to decorative stitchery. The term 'needlepoint' is applied in America to canvas work; earlier it referred to the sewing of lace made with a needle rather than bobbins. It may also be noted here that metal threads were 'wrought' while wools, in crewel embroidery or tent stitch, were 'worked'.

Left. 8. A 14th century French mitre depicts the Coronation of the Virgin in silk and gold.

Below. 9. Cope from Averbode Abbey. Bands of embroidery illustrate the life of St Matthew. Southern Netherlands, 1554.

Opposite. 7. The Kiss of Judas, c.1320. The best English mediaeval embroidery, opus anglicanum, *is finely drawn and executed with extraordinary expression. (See also Plate 49 for another section.)*

The Art of Embroidery

The primarily practical nature of needlework has held a disciplinary brake on decorative fantasies, curbing it within useful strictures. Its first purpose was always to provide clothing, both plain and ceremonial:

> *No surplice white the priest could wear*
> *Bandless the bishop must appear*
> *The King without a shirt would be*
> *Did not the needle help all three.*
> MARY MILLER'S SAMPLER, 1735

From this arose opportunities for very elaborate costume, reaching especially glorious heights in mediaeval religious and secular garments, in Tudor court dress and in eighteenth century costume. The early use of quilting for protection and warmth developed into intricate decorative work and the need for personal colours for identification in mediaeval military encounters led to magnificent heraldic embroidery for the battlefield and court functions. The seventeenth century witnessed the use of fine needlework for newly sought household comforts, hangings and upholstery. New forms of fashionable costume and formal dress developed rapidly throughout the seventeenth, eighteenth and nineteenth centuries. Additional sewing in the form of samplers, pictures and objects was related to the general delight in making personal and domestic articles of either a utilitarian or a decorative nature. Despite the perishable nature of textiles, pieces were made, at least sometimes, with the hope of preservation for posterity, a hope that continues today.

10. A corner of a fine linen tablecloth with squares of darned net, filet or lacis, derived from pattern books. Signed IAC and dated 1638.

Every country and race, and both rich and poor, have enjoyed traditions of needlework, some very sophisticated, some naïve but charming, and some with ancient roots. There is a unifying strand of charm conjured up in the fusion of traditional techniques and forms with adaptations brought about by the availability of new materials or influence from other crafts. A certain humorous naïvety is often a notable feature together with a characteristic language of motifs, as is the slightly angular drawing of figures or foliage, emphasising the problems of stitching over regularly woven materials, all becoming conventional aspects and all part of the engaging language of needlework.

Over the last five centuries Europeans have been able to draw upon materials from world trade and these have naturally shaped local production. From early times high quality wool and linen was readily available. In the meantime,

Introduction

11. Portrait of Elizabeth Vernon, Countess of Southampton, c.1620, showing examples of fine embroidered costume, accurately portrayed.

The Art of Embroidery

Above. 12. A late 17th century English crewelwork curtain worked in shades of blue green with elegant curling leaves.

Opposite. 13. A French bed hanging, c.1690, embroidered with silk and wool on linen to a design attributed to Daniel Marot (1661-1752). 10ft. 10¼in. x 3ft. (330.7cm x 91.4cm).

silk was one of the earliest traded commodities; dye was another. Italy's pre-eminent trading through Mediterranean and Adriatic ports preceded more general oriental imports and created a basis for supremacy in making high quality textiles, but for a long time imported silks and dyes remained precious commodities.

Often erroneously thought of as a humble and homely craft, needlework was in fact expensive, requiring costly materials, and was practised by queens and those from the highest ranks of society. The professionals of the craft were highly rewarded. In a Greek poem of the twelfth century Theodorus Prodromos says that if he had followed the embroiderers' trade his cupboard would have been full of bread, wine and sardines.[2] Henry III paid an embroideress the large sum of £11 for a chasuble and altar-piece and clearly held her in high regard as he subsequently paid her a visit when she retired to Bury St Edmunds.[3] Four women worked for him for three and three-quarter years making an altar frontal for the high altar of Westminster Abbey.

Contrary to Tennyson's epithet, 'Man for the sword and for the needle she', much mediaeval English needlework was done by men in workshops. Their craft was highly organised, exceptionally skilled and, above all, artistic in design and execution; the work became famed as *opus anglicanum* throughout Europe and was widely exported.

In France and Italy similar workshops were established; the use of materials and designs followed a predictable formality appropriate to both those countries' aristocratic patronage. English needlework, however, followed trends relatively independent of the continent. In the Middle Ages England produced vestments of unparalleled beauty but later products never attained such elevated style or originality. There was, however, a continued tendency to soften influences of formal design and a delight in variation. Less prestige was attached to domestic embroidery and fashions are seen to have been slow-moving, partly bound to adaptation of old conventions but also subject sometimes to whims of the moment, and generally full of variety and life.

Inevitably, the styles of ecclesiastical vestments were continuously influenced by architecture. Romanesque arches and roundels formed the basic framing for hierarchic figures. Later a Tree of Jesse motif (Plate 6) and elements of Decorated Gothic were adopted from architectural tracery (Plate 7). The finest artists drew out the designs, and cross-currents of mood can be noted in illumination, stained glass, metalwork,

Introduction

carving and enamels. After the fourteenth century English vestments were past their best and fine fabrics from continental Europe, such as velvets, damasks and brocades, relegated embroidery to smaller areas on orphreys, bands and roundels. Amongst painters who made designs for embroiderers were Sandro Botticelli (1440-1510) and Albrecht Dürer (1471-1528). A drawing by the latter for the hood of a cope is in the Victoria and Albert Museum. It depicts the Assumption of the Virgin and her Coronation. Later the nobility employed artists to design amateur works for them. Catherine de Medici, for example, had an attendant designer called Frederico di Vinciolo; he was author of an influential pattern book, *Les Singuliers et Nouveaux Pourtraicts et ouvrages de Lingerie* (1587), that had ten editions.

Fearful plagues, which devastated the craftsmen's communities, and the political and religious upheaval of the Reformation brought the flowering of English ecclesiastical needlework to a close. In the meantime, the Field of the Cloth of Gold tournament in 1520, proudly depicted in paintings, shows a great transition to new materials. At this historic event Henry VIII and François I met *en fête* with huge supporting forces of courtiers and militia. The tournament took its name from the impressive spectacle of a dazzling mass of cloth of gold fabric, the ultimate of extravagance and worldly show. By now woven fabrics were pre-eminent, and seem to be a symbol of the Renaissance.

Opus anglicanum had undoubtedly been one of the great peaks in needlework history. Another of roughly the same time was Chinese embroidery, magnificent survivals of which have come to light recently from the sacred safe-keeping of Tibetan monasteries. Tudor costume and seventeenth century domestic furnishings are certainly further high points. Eighteenth century canvas work and costume embroidery has outstanding charm and elegance while revivals and experimentation in the last two hundred years is also full of interest, occasionally remarkable, but perhaps not of equal stature to these earlier achievements.

The so-called Renaissance period saw a development of outlook marked by several key features: a new respect for, and desire to imitate the ancients, a new interest in science and a feeling for involvement in the real world rather than superstition.

Paintings show how the Tudor period was especially rich in costume and domestic embroidery. Occasionally it was well documented. The 'Inventair of the Queenis [Mary Queen of Scots] Movables, November 1561, at the Palace of Halerudehous' enumerates twelve 'beddis maid in broderie' of extraordinary richness. Beds were indeed an important symbol as the setting of the great events of life. It is recorded that in 1582 at Sheffield Castle the Earl of Shrewsbury had eighty-two feather beds. Another invaluable descriptive record was made by Paul Hentzner, giving details of his travels in the 1590s. On visiting the Tower of London, for example, he saw all sorts of embroidered beds, garments and items of which we now have little knowledge such as 'sadles of velvet of different colours'.

17

The Art of Embroidery

14. One corner of a very large Portuguese rust-coloured bed cover, probably late 17th century and influenced by Bengali floor spreads.

Elizabeth I was given an embroidered saddle amongst the customary New Year gifts in 1588-9. Despite the magnificent costumes worn it is interesting that even as late as 1598 a foreign visitor remarked on the lack of floor coverings, saying that even the Presence Chamber of Queen Elizabeth at Greenwich was 'strewn with hay'.[4] The full luxury of domestic furnishing was yet to come.

Following the Renaissance other countries produced patterned silks but England did not, leaving extra requirements for embroidery. Many late sixteenth and seventeenth century needlework designs were in the form of neat scrolling curls, hoops, or tendrils comparable with, for example, illuminated manuscripts and metalwork patterns as on Gothic church doors. The style is derived from Chinese floral patterns though the origin seems to have been Egyptian. It is equally seen in *opus anglicanum* and Christian Orthodox needlework. Open-ended roundels were filled with foliate sprigs, incorporating flowers and insects in bright silks and metals or were in 'cole black silks'[5] as worn by the Miller's wife in Chaucer's *Canterbury Tales*. Flowers in contrasting moods indicate swings of taste and fashion. Tudor and Stuart flowers were derived from accurately depicted representations of specially cultivated specimens, and were increasingly worked into scrolling patterns, the formation of which became as important as the individual depiction. In the late seventeenth

Introduction

century, real flowers were still portrayed, and again deliberately as specimen 'slips', or sprigs, and in sprays and group arrangements. Unreal, exotic foliage and blooms of oriental origin were a feature of crewelwork at the end of the century, and during the first half of the eighteenth. From the 1730s floral needlework, in tent and cross stitch on canvas, depicted natural garden blooms in controlled groupings. This was suited to carpets, chair seats and to other furniture. By the end of the century many more arrangements were embroidered, with precision and naturalism, in fine silks; these were gathered in baskets, vases, or neat posies tied by a ribbon. Further exotic and unreal chinoiserie flowers and fruit were depicted in late Georgian and Regency designs but all were overtaken in the nineteenth century by garish and blowzy blooms of canvas stitched Berlin work. Throughout three centuries, however, gardening and

15. A large 17th century picture, including raised stumpwork, the motifs embroidered on a satin background. c.1660.

The Art of Embroidery

Right. 16. The silk embroidery of this Queen Anne bed cover, with a quilted background, shows garden flowers laid out in a quartered pattern derived from Persia.

Opposite. 17. One of a set of Indian bed hangings finely embroidered in cotton, and imitating Chinese lacquer and wallpaper, for the European market. c.1725.

needlework reflected comparable joys, in layout, colouring and selection; the two pastimes were frequently discussed in similar terms:

> *What greater delight is there than to behold the earth apparelled with plants, as with a robe of imbroidered works, set with orient pearles and garnished with great diversitie of rare and costly jewels.*
> JOHN GERARD'S *HERBAL* 1597

Fashion generally, having reached certain conventions, changed slowly, and most needlework followed traditional forms, without startling novelty or originality. The Oxburgh hangings (Plate 84, page 94), for example, worked by Mary Queen of Scots and Elizabeth Shrewsbury, are amongst our rarest treasures, though the designs and the technique were far from new. Their great charm rests in a combination of good drawing and colouring with interesting shapes, curious subjects and engaging emblems, and especially charged with their historical associations.

Significant injections of influence came to England with the arrival of the Houses

The Art of Embroidery

18. This Viennese chasuble of about 1700 is decorated with rich and colourful embroidery noticeably refraining from religious imagery.

of Orange and Hanover in 1688 and 1714. Queen Mary, who ruled with William III, was, it is said, more often seen with a skein of thread about her neck than attending to State affairs; among a number of hangings worked by her was a set for a bed at Hampton Court referred to by Daniel Defoe as 'of her own work, while in Holland, very magnificent'.[6]

At the French court, Madame de Maintenon was equally passionate about needlework and is said to have done it while travelling in her carriage. Buildings in Paris and at Versailles were carried out for Louis XIV to a scale and excellence never before attempted and architecture influenced every element of the decorative arts in

Introduction

France and throughout Europe. The Baroque period was one of grandeur and formality, with confident and passionate expression in all the arts and with general magnificence elevating the status of those in power. The French king's taste is seen to have been transformed from Italian baroque to the theatrical frivolities of Bérain. Charles Le Brun supervised the mammoth schemes of interior decoration, and sumptuous textiles added both richness and softness to the monumental apartments. In England and France, luxurious comfort was achieved in the warmth of hangings, noble beds and rich upholstery. French craftsmen with a wide variety of needlework

19. A French crewelwork bed hanging, more formalised than English ones, with flower posies reminiscent of Indian marble inlay. c.1720.

23

The Art of Embroidery

skills were well ordered in guilds pertaining to their roles, and these co-ordinated high standards. They included *chasubliers, brodeurs, tailleurs, lingères* and *tapissiers* (upholsterers). The Broderers' Company in London incorporated most of these departments including the last, especially important suppliers, and was a powerful organisation. The haberdasher who supplied materials, equipment and contacts with professional designers was a significant link in all the businesses, and we note in *The Canterbury Tales* that the haberdashers, weavers and dyers were all wealthy merchants. Political and trade rulings, enforced through legal restrictions, were made from time to time but were usually short-lived attempts to encourage or curb fashions and crafts. These included a limitation on imports of inexpensive oriental needlework and the forbidding of the manufacture of embroidered and cloth-covered buttons, to boost the trade of metal button makers.

20. This early 18th century English wing chair retains its original rococo needlework worked in wools highlighted with silks.

Introduction

Eighteenth century needlework, especially on clothes, was often bright and delicate, with clarity and line like a Mozart tune. Likewise the ancient skill of quilting was adapted to wonderfully decorative effects especially on coverlets or 'counterpanes', a word derived from the quilting stitch *contre pointe*. Samplers, originally samples of patterns, became essentially quaint and decorative exercises bridging a gap between costume and pictures, and less rigorously associated with learning the skills of sewing. Later ones are now more generally familiar than the finer early ones which are rare; many later ones have, however, a pleasing charm and alluring sentimental qualities. Most have texts indicating the combination of learning moral lessons alongside stitchery, as in Mary Cole's of 1759:

> *Better by Far for Me*
> *Than all the Simpsters Art*
> *That God's Commandments be*
> *Embroider'd on my Heart.*

Much eighteenth century canvas work has come down to us and has made a particularly lasting impression in panels and on furniture. The progression of

Above. 21. A mid-18th century tent stitch picture, possibly for a firescreen, with large blooms in an 'oriental' vase, standing in a hillocky landscape.

Left. 22. Also English and with bucolic elegance, an eastern bible story is represented with oak trees and oriental birds. Jacob at the Well is embroidered mostly in wool in satin stitch, unlike the more familiar canvaswork, as Plate 21. c.1750. 25¼in. x 20¾in.(64cm x 53cm).

The Art of Embroidery

23. This French panel is entirely worked in silk chenille, a twisted 'caterpillar' thread, producing a velvety texture, c.1780. Note the tones in the table carpet.

pictorial motifs arrived at a significant format around the 1730s. Mediaeval embroidery had been largely narrative but since then the depiction of human activities, animals and scenes has been in the form of isolated figures. 'Spot' motifs without link or relationship were a characteristic feature of amateur seventeenth century needlework while professionals embroidered scenes derived from engravings. But in the eighteenth century there was a general delight in pictorial composition, together with a profusion of flowers. Rustic scenes with stylised shepherds, shepherdesses and sheep were amongst the most popular subjects (Plates 22 and 151) as well as new renderings of the ever-suitable but more ponderous myths, fables and Bible stories. All these found their way on to needlework upholstery. Each developed ultimately into silk and wool pictures, depicted in less appropriate neo-classical terminology. Human faces always presented a major challenge to needleworkers and latterly the struggle was abandoned in favour of painting in the finer details and backgrounds.

Introduction

Much needlework of the late eighteenth and nineteenth centuries was unremarkable; it tended to imitate the *mètier* of painting and engraving rather than have its own character, but some pieces have considerable charm and in every period there are always interesting and unusual exceptions. Sometimes woven fabrics and carpets mirrored embroidered designs and even copied the look of stitchery. Locally produced and imported rugs, Axminster and Bessarabian for example, were successfully based on needlework patterns and a sewing tradition was carried on alongside these with a tendency to coarser, densely textured workmanship.

Berlin woolwork was the first main innovation of the nineteenth century, being established in Germany and then brought to England around 1820. It was a further form of needlepainting. Thousands of printed and coloured patterns, mostly in the form of pictures, some after old masters or popular modern painters, were produced on squared paper that indicated each stitch for canvas embroidery. Originally published in Berlin, they were available at Mr Wilks' shop in Regent Street, London

24. A wool embroidered version of George Stubbs' painting of a great tiger, worked from an engraving in about 1800.

The Art of Embroidery

by 1831, together with soft, brightly coloured merino wools, also imported from Germany. There was on the whole little artistry in this embroidery, although in some cases ladies invented ingenious tasks with greater originality, normally for 'useful' household items, and sometimes on a large scale.

The other kind of needlework massively produced in the first half of the nineteenth century was Ayrshire whitework. Tens of thousands of impoverished women in Scotland and Northern Ireland were employed in their own homes at the organised industrial production of children's clothes, aprons, bonnets and other garments of light cotton muslin elaborately 'flowered' with white embroidery. Much of the work was exported to England, Europe and America. The central co-ordinating workshops and businesses were comparable with the needlework industry that exported vestments in the Middle Ages.

This book cannot, of course, cover every aspect of historical needlework and embroidery. I shall be limited to a discussion of decorative work chiefly concentrating on Great Britain but with consideration also of prominent influences from other European countries, developments of techniques taken to America and the interplay of textile trade between Europe and the Orient. Indian needlework was for a considerable period linked in design and technique with Western embroidery and Mughal embroidery ranks with some of the finest in the world. There was a similar interplay with certain aspects of Chinese textiles but the most famous Chinese embroidery, as on court robes, is not closely reflected in European design. It encompasses a world of its own, culturally distant from Western styles. It fascinated early travellers and successive merchants but European reflections had a distinctive character, never seriously adopting the philosophical grammar of Chinese forms and symbolism, or attempting to emulate the minuteness of workmanship. As early as the second century the Chinese were a source of wonder for 'precious figured garments resembling in colours the flowers of the field, and rivalling in fineness the work of spiders'. Over many centuries Chinese styles and techniques have changed relatively little; a classical idiom had emerged early on and, being an entirely satisfactory and matured form, it was on an elevated plane not subject to much variation. It was certainly wholly independent of European fashions, apart from items specially made for export. A Chinese chapter must however be included here, especially as there has been a significant increase of interest in Chinese robes and other textiles within an international context.

Introduction

I have not included lace, a subject in itself, but certain aspects, especially needlepoint lace, are partially considered. Venetian 'gros-point' lace is clearly related to embroidered whitework and to other needlework in both design and technique.[7] Influences of bobbin lace on needlework are also noted.

It was in reaction to the tired unambitious nineteenth century mainstreams and the technical complacency of the Great Exhibition of 1851 that William Morris and other craft-orientated designers broke away from the inevitable mechanisation of needlework. They sought wholly handmade, individual, even idiosyncratic hallmarks in both technique and design. In doing this they first turned to a revival of mediaeval forms as well as adapting elements of Persian design. Huge leaf patterns were tried out alongside colourful Gothic constructions. They were heavily graceful and laden with ornate detailing, quite unlike the elegant mediaeval originals or Georgian revivals from which they were derived or bypassed respectively. Other designs were supplied by leading painters, often rich but sometimes becoming over-complex.

Too busy a combination of decorative elements, or too many stitch varieties, or colours, weakens design. It was in this respect that much Victorian needlework failed to have significant lasting qualities. Earlier and finer pieces show how a certain simplicity and control are crucial factors of success. In the twentieth century a sense of 'good taste' prevailed over the specialist scholarship and depth of knowledge that were signal hallmarks of late Victorian and Edwardian England. The trend was partly healthy, but artistic integrity and connoisseurship should embrace both; we have strayed far from a learned approach with traditional grounding in Classical, historical and religious culture and we almost neglect our inherited background and are in danger of severing the cord of continuity that should run into the creation of modern works. But in recent years I have seen 'green shoots' of true creativity and some exciting modern works. Needlework with its practical basis and decorative opportunities will always offer scope for interesting developments and a perfect medium for artistic achievement.

Opposite. 25. 19th century Berlin woolwork, embroidered to a printed squared pattern, with 'modern' chemical dyes and in this case incorporating beadwork for the vase.

Above. 26. Refined craftsmanship and a distinctive love of animals are represented in this 19th century Japanese silk embroidery.

Left. 27. An 18th century Japanese Kosode. Oriental designs had a new influence on patterns in 19th century Europe.

29

The Art of Embroidery

> *There's nothing neere at hand, or farthest sought,*
> *But with the Needle may be shap'd and wrought.*[8]

Restoring, and the conservation of old and valued pieces, was in mediaeval times one of the chief duties of convents and workshops; today this is again one of the most seriously considered tasks of professional needlewomen and men. Artistic judgement and scientific techniques are linked in businesses and charities working to preserve the great heritage that we cherish in Great Britain, Europe, the United States of America and all over the world.

The Royal School of Needlework is one of the leading organisations in both conservation and maintaining the teaching of needlework skills at the highest level. Founded in 1872, it has from that time up till the present played a significant part in encouraging artistic and technical expertise in all forms of embroidery and in training young people to a professional standard. Its history is outlined later in this book (see page 274).[9] The Embroiderers' Guild was founded in 1906 and is also today an important organisation in stimulating good and lively needlework.

> *Yea till the world be quite dissolv'd and past;*
> *So long at least, the Needles use shall last.*[8]

Below. 28. The Royal School of Needlework, now in Hampton Court Palace, has continued to teach fine technical skills since its foundation in 1872.

Opposite. 29. The Robe of Estate made for the coronation of Her Majesty the Queen in 1953, designed and embroidered by the Royal School of Needlework.

CHAPTER ONE

EARLY NEEDLEWORK

First look at the embroideries, delicate and so charming;
You would say they were the robes of the gods.

THE goddess Athene is said to have taught our cultural ancestors, the Greeks, the art of embroidery, but so wondrous is the technique that even its origin was disputed. Edward Topsell in 1608 told us 'Arachne first invented working with the needle, which the mayd of Lydia learned from the spiders, taking her first samples and patterns from them in imitation.' But Athene was displeased with Arachne's pride and after a bitter challenge Arachne was changed into a spider in order to pursue her boastful skill.[1]

The specific origins of the craft are almost entirely lost; the few remaining threads of historical fact are sufficient only for qualified conjecture. Unfortunately, the blessings of a temperate climate here in the West do not provide the phenomenon of perpetual preservation which some cultures have known, and few significant archaeological specimens have been preserved. In South America, Indian embroideries from the fifth century B.C. have been found in considerable quantities in funerary bundles, especially Paracas embroidery from burial sites in southern Peru, of c.300 B.C. to A.D. 200. These show anthropomorphic figures and complex designs of considerable sophistication. A fragment of Greek needlework of the same period has also survived and likewise very early ornamental sewing was discovered in the frozen tombs of Russia. In Mongolia an interesting fragment of embroidery was discovered in 1912, of the early Han period (2nd Century B.C.).[2] The earliest embroidery was indeed probably Chinese and this heritage is discussed later in this book. Silk was cultivated

30. A linen roundel found in Egyptian burial grounds was embroidered with silks in the 7th-8th century and depicts the Annunciation and Visitation.

Early Needlework

The Art of Embroidery

in China over 5,000 years ago and some of the oldest silks known are threads and embroidery in the Summer Palace Museum estimated as being 4,500 years old. This is silk from the cultivated *bombyx mori* silkmoth. In India wild tussah silk was used 5,000 years ago and the cultivated bombyx silk has also been made for at least 2,000 years.

Western textile history cannot be traced back further than the early Middle Ages. Fragments of evidence show that attempts to decorate cloth may have preceded other skills and may have influenced other awakening art forms. Early Egyptians imitated embroidery in paintings and it is thought that their love of colour in enamels, metals and glass was inspired by textiles and dyes. The Phoenicians, whose territory on the maritime border of Palestine became a province of Egypt, were extensive travellers and spread ideas gathered from different parts of the world. In about 1650 B.C. they brought the arts and crafts of Babylon and Assyria across Europe to England in their search for tin. They were highly successful merchants of luxuries and traded above all in Tyre purple, procured from the shell fish *murex* of Mediterranean shores. This brought them great wealth, as it was indispensable to the pomp of sacerdotal and imperial ceremonial. Variations of the colour are still symbolic of the hierarchy of Church and State.

The Romans' continuous conquests in Europe and repeated invasions of Britain brought new aspects of craftsmanship and introduced Christianity. They did not find this island easy to govern, often because of their own injustice. In A.D. 62 they were faced with a colossal rebellion led by Boadicea whose huge number of supporters were brutally crushed. It is said that Boadicea herself was captured wearing a fur-lined mantle of embroidered skins. This garment was probably not unlike ones still made by Eskimos and North American Indians.

Christianity began to spread widely in the early Middle Ages, that is from about the seventh century A.D., and became the chief stimulus of artistic effort and expression. St Augustine, who is credited with conversion of the Britons, carried with him a banner embroidered with the image of Christ and undoubtedly the Irish Christians brought similar artistry to their communities in Scotland and northern England. From earliest times religious iconographical embroidery displayed clearly recognisable symbols and emblems for the propagation of scriptural stories. The embroidery of hangings and vestments took on a didactic nature, as did sculpture on the great churches and illustrations in stained glass windows.

When the power of Rome declined, the far lying island of Britain was left to invasion by Celts, Saxons and Vikings (known here as the Danes), but despite considerable strife and pillaging the country eventually settled down to relative prosperity. Early in the seventh century Aldhelm, Bishop of Sherborne, wrote a poem mentioning tapestry weaving and embroidery, worked by the women of England. From early on until the height of the mediaeval period, when highly organised professional workshops consisted of male needleworkers, embroidery was chiefly the cherished prowess of Anglo-Saxon women. It was done especially by those of noble and privileged position. St Etheldreda, Abbess and patron saint of Ely (died 679) offered St Cuthbert a stole and maniple finely embroidered by herself and worked with gold and precious stones. She was also known by the name of St Audrey, from which the word tawdry, used to describe a cheap kind of lace purchasable at St Audrey's Fair, was derived.[3]

31. Peter the Deacon on part of the early 10th century maniple of St Cuthbert, originally ordered for Frithestan, Bishop of Winchester by Aethelflaed.

Early Needlework

Another early gift was that of Wiklaf, King of Mercia, who presented to the Abbey of Croyland in 833 a cloak embroidered with the battle of Troy.

The earliest surviving pieces of needlework in Western Europe are the much deteriorated but interesting remnants of English needlework at Maaseik in Belgium. Though now only fragments and a glorious ruin, they have been treasured as relics of two female saints, St Harlindis and St Relindis. Of Anglo-Saxon workmanship in the second half of the ninth century, the chasuble must once have been spectacular, with coloured silks, gilt thread and seed pearls depicting birds, animals and monograms in interlacing roundels. The design appears to be related to the illumination of manuscripts. Monks and priests were closely involved with the maintenance and decoration of their magnificent buildings and they participated in the production of manuscripts and vestments. The tenth century Archbishop of Canterbury, St Dunstan, is known to have designed embroideries, as well as being a famous goldsmith and illuminator.

Remarkable and beautiful survivals of about 915 are a stole and maniple discovered in 1827 in the tomb of St Cuthbert at Durham Cathedral. Both have inscriptions indicating that they were made for Aethelflaed, daughter of Alfred the Great, and renowned 'Lady of the Mercians', for Bishop Frithestan of Winchester. They were probably made in that city, then the Saxon capital. Different in style from the Maaseik embroidery, they depict saints with the inscriptions; the stole is embroidered with the *Agnus Dei,* and the maniple with the hand of God issuing from clouds. The figures on both pieces are finely worked but are of a sophisticated hieratic nature, Byzantine in feeling, and showing no signs of the expressiveness that was to be the special characteristic of later English work. These fascinating relics are however certainly indicative of the high standard of embroidery at this early date.

Many saints were made easily recognisable by familiar iconographical emblems, sometimes animals, as the lion with St Mark, or an object as the wheel with St Catherine. St Dunstan is seen on a late fifteenth century chasuble at Stonyhurst College, Lancashire, holding the devil's nose with tongs, a less well known but, for him, conventional image.

Much fine needlework must have been made outside monastic circles for ecclesiastical, semi-ecclesiastical or wholly secular uses. Queen Emma, wife firstly of Ethelred the Unready (died 1016), and secondly of King Canute (died 1036), embroidered many vestments and altar cloths. The latter king's second wife, Queen Aelgiva, gave amongst other gifts an altar hanging with a gold border to the Abbey of Ely; their daughter Aethelswitha also practised gold embroidery.

Of work of a ceremonial nature, we are informed in the writings of William of Malmesbury that King Edward the Confessor's wife Editha, or Aedgytha, embroidered the mantle for his coronation in 1042. Queen Margaret, wife of Malcolm III of Scotland, was also a skilled needlewoman, embroidering various vestments and

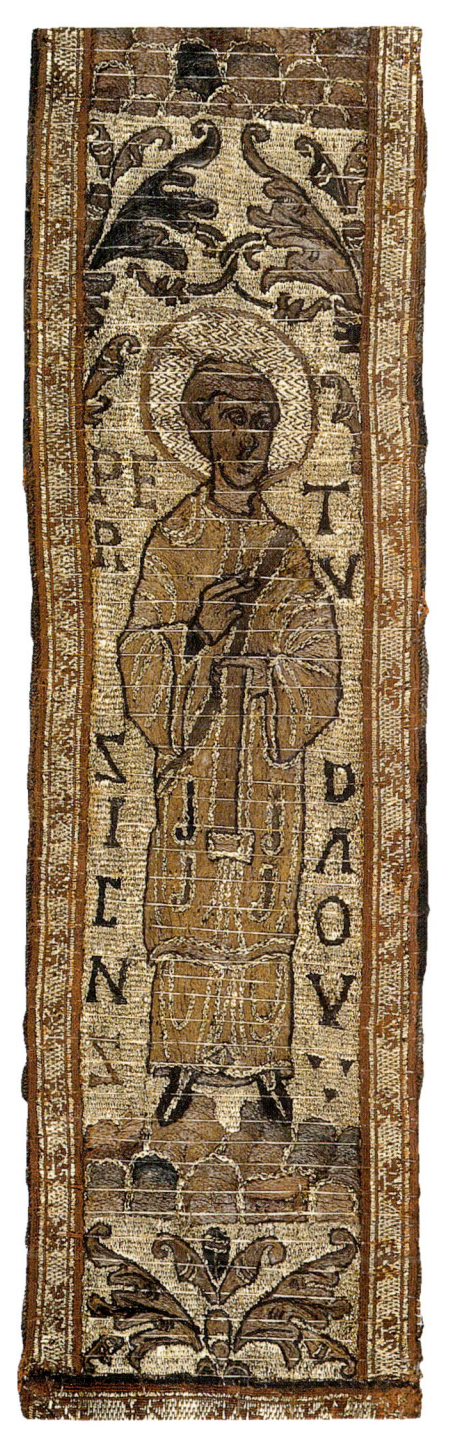

35

hangings. She wrote that her chamber 'was like the workshop of a heavenly artist, there copes for singers, chasubles, stoles, altar cloths and other priestly and church vestments were always to be seen'. This atmosphere of industry is tempered by another more relaxed confession:

> *I do no other work but read my psalter,*
> *Work in gold, silk or cruells, play a tune on*
> *My harp, checkmate someone at chess,*
> *Or feed the hawk on my wrist.*[4]

This romantic mediaeval existence brings to mind the *mille-fleurs* tapestries at the Musée de Cluny where *La Vie Seigneuriale* shows a seated lady doing needlework.

Heraldic needlework too was firmly established; William of Malmesbury again records that King Harold went to the Battle of Hastings with a banner embroidered with a fighting man, worked in gold and enriched with precious stones.

THE BAYEUX TAPESTRY

By far the most remarkable embroidery of the early Middle Ages to have survived is the so-called Bayeux 'Tapestry'. Though not of outstanding technical workmanship, its historical nature and charm make it justly famous. Two hundred and thirty feet (70m) long, by about twenty inches (50cm) high, it consists of a long narrative wall hanging made up of joined parts, probably separately worked by professional teams.

Narrative historical hangings were very much part of the tradition of European needlework but no others have survived. Old texts give us some insight such as the Scandinavian *Volsunga Saga,* which includes a description of Brunhild in her bower: 'overlaying cloth with gold, and sewing therein the great deeds which Sigmund had wrought, the slaying of the Worm, and taking of the wealth of him and the death of Regin withal'.

Early Needlework

The relatively simple needlework of the Bayeux Tapestry is in coloured wools of eight shades; blues, greens, yellow and terracotta red. The hanging is representative of ecclesiastical and non-ecclesiastical decorations of the period and has probably survived due to the fact that no gold was employed but only simple materials. Others of finer workmanship and precious materials are known to have existed. An account by Baudri, Abbot of Bourgueil, described, for example, a much more elaborate 'tapestry' telling the same story, hung around an alcove as bed hangings for Adela, daughter of William the Conqueror:

> *A wonderful tapestry goes around the lady's bed, which joins three things in material and novel skill. For the hand of craftsmen hath done the work so finely that you would scarcely believe that to exist which you know does exist. Threads of gold come first, silver threads come next, the third set of threads were always of silk. Skilful care had made the threads of gold and silver so fine that I believe that nothing could have been thinner… Jewels with red marking were shining amidst the work, and pearls of no small price. In fine so great was the glitter and beauty of the tapestry that you might say it surpassed the rays of Phoebus.*[5]

Almost a hundred years earlier, it was recorded that Aethelflaed embroidered the deeds of her husband Britnoth on a hanging which she gave to the Abbey of Ely, probably shortly after his death in 991.[6]

The Bayeux Tapestry was made between the time of these two others, in about 1070, to commemorate the Norman Conquest of Britain and, specifically, the Battle of Hastings. It was probably commissioned by Odo, Bishop of Bayeux, the powerful half-brother of William the Conqueror, for the new cathedral dedicated in 1077, or for use in a castle. The workmanship appears to be English and the lively design was probably drawn out by an illuminator of manuscripts, perhaps at Canterbury; conventions

32 and 33. The Bayeux 'tapestry', like a Grecian frieze, depicts a long embroidered narrative, the Norman conquest of Britain. These two sections show Harold's visit to Guy and their negotiations, and Duke William boarding a Norman vessel.

The Art of Embroidery

34. Important tents in many cultures were richly decorated. This is a design for a royal tent, probably for the Field of the Cloth of Gold, c.1520.

of manuscript illustration are reflected in border patterns and a diagrammatic portrayal of architecture. Apart from these aspects, there is an extraordinary wealth of detail displaying the genius of an observant and knowledgeable man. A Latin text describes the action, and from a Norman point of view tells the history of the invasion, Harold's defeat, and his death at the Battle of Hastings. The tale lays unexpected emphasis on Harold's visit to Normandy and his swearing allegiance to Duke William as heir to the English throne, though Harold was a natural enemy of the French. Concisely, the story related by the embroidery is as follows.

Edward the Confessor briefs Harold who is then seen setting out for France with falcon and hounds. He prays at a church at Bosham and sails off for France. On arrival he is immediately arrested and taken prisoner. He is taken to Duke William of Normandy and the two are seen together in the latter's palace. They go on an expedition to Brittany where Harold rescues two soldiers from quicksand. They engage in the siege of Dinant and defeat Conan. Harold is honoured by William in a ceremony, ranking between knighthood and enrolment as a supporter of William, and subsequently they go to Bayeux where Harold makes an oath of allegiance to William. Harold returns to England and reports at Westminster to Edward who is on his deathbed. We then see the king's funeral procession. Harold is crowned forthwith as his successor and is told of a comet. In Normandy, William holds a council, prepares to sail for England and sets out in splendid boats. He hurries to Hastings where various domestic arrangements are made, and a feast and council are held. Harold and William prepare for and lead their armies to battle and they attack each other ferociously. Harold's brothers are killed and also many men and horses. Bishop Odo is seen cheering on his troops. Harold is wounded in the eye and finally the English are seen fleeing.

A small part is probably missing at the end but in all an extraordinary cross section of life is portrayed. Some 600 figures are shown and many more animals, birds and

Early Needlework

fish. Members of the two ruling households are depicted with interesting views of buildings including the Palace and Abbey at Westminster. The needlework serves as a document for social historians as it records many kinds of clothing for battle, peacetime, and church use, as well as activities such as farming, hunting, shipbuilding, cooking and the appearance of Halley's comet. The drawing and stitching convey extraordinary liveliness and variety of movement, and, though restored at least twice, the needlework is in very good condition.

Under the influence of the Normans the development of underside couching, whereby laid threads were secured to the surface by a slighter thread pulling them through from the back of the material, meant that designs could be more flexible and free flowing. This led to the special expressiveness of mediaeval needlework.

William the Conqueror's chaplain and chronicler, William de Poitiers, recorded that after the conquest the French took home magnificent English embroidered state robes, far finer than they had seen before. They presented vestments to churches in Normandy and William's wife, Queen Matilda, bequeathed English needlework to the Church of the Holy Trinity at Caen, one piece embroidered at Winchester. She gave her golden mantle to be made into a cope and her girdle for suspending the lamp before the high altar. These gifts are an indication of the great value put on precious textiles.

Shortly after the conquest, William I instigated a colossal survey (1085-87) to assess the nation's worth. This invaluable record, the Domesday Book, mentions fascinating day-to-day facts and arrangements such as the granting of land to a woman referred to as 'Aldwid the maiden' by a sheriff Godric, as a reward for teaching his daughter the art of gold embroidery.

Embroidery had already taken a position of high status; it was held in higher esteem than painting and illumination, both of which were influenced by it. It continued to be the favourite pursuit of Anglo-Norman ladies, as well as being practised professionally in workshops, and in church and secular institutions. Very high standards of design and workmanship were expected and certainly achieved.

35. The Leopards of England, worked in couched gold thread, are on fragments believed to have been part of a horse cover made for Edward III, c.1330-1340.

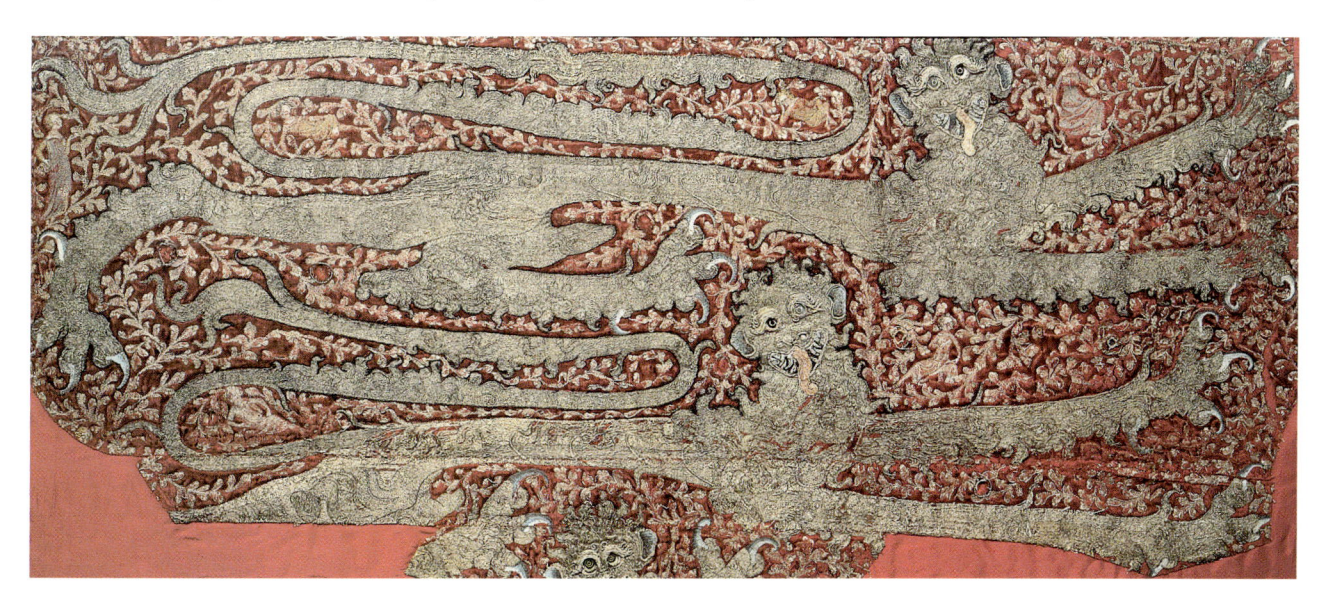

CHAPTER TWO

THE MEDIAEVAL PERIOD

Pen of Steele and Silken incke enroll'd

It is a too little known fact, and certainly no exaggeration, that one of England's greatest cultural achievements and contributions to world art has been her production of superb ecclesiastical vestments, particularly between 1250 and 1350. Known as *opus anglicanum* (English work), the magnificent products of workshops in the City of London and elsewhere were the envy of cathedrals, churches and private chapels all over Europe. Costly items were ordered and exported in surprising quantity. The names and addresses of some embroiderers are now known, for example Alexander le Settère, William Courteray, Thomas Carlton, Stephen Vyne and Robert Ashcombe, in London. The industry must have been prosperous for their work was inevitably expensive; at the beginning of the fourteenth century an embroidered cloth was sold to the Earl of Lincoln for £200, equivalent to the lifetime wages of some lower paid embroiderers. The only signed mediaeval needlework was worked by a nun, Johanna Beverlai, whose late thirteenth century altar frontlet is in the Victoria and Albert Museum. Thought to be non-professional, it consists of a long band with a rust-coloured background. From the 1330s onwards Edward III had an official embroidery workshop in the Tower of London under the direction of the Royal Armourer, John of Cologne, but the work there was presumably principally for ceremonial and military purposes.

All such needlework was of a remarkably high quality in both design and technique and it is not surprising that English pieces became traditionally prized by continental

36. Chasuble from the Convent of Göss, Austria, with choirs of angels under rounded arches, part of a set of vestments probably made by nuns for the donor Abbess Kunigunde II, 1239-69.

The Mediaeval Period

The Art of Embroidery

neighbours. The religious designs were executed in a natural manner and characterised by needlepainting, or *acupictura;* altar frontals and vestments portrayed statuesque figures representing the saints in perfect detail and with delicate paintbrush accuracy. They shared features in common with manuscript illumination, since the ablest artists of the period provided designs for both crafts; it is known indeed that two thirteenth century French embroideresses, Dame Margot and Dame Aalès, were themselves also illuminators. Needlework techniques influenced painting and illumination and may have inspired stained glass. There are also parallels in Limoges enamelwork, bronzework and ivory carving. The horizontal rows of saints in niches, familiar on altar frontals and in vertical columns on vestments, are undoubtedly associated with the architectural tiers of sculptures on the great cathedrals being built around this time.

Tapestry weaving was developed during the twelfth century but it did not displace embroidery, for although it was sometimes used for the decoration of church walls it was not suitable for vestments. In mediaeval woven fabrics there was a certain stiffness of design – heraldic insignia, lattice patterns, rows and circles, confronting animals and birds, but English needlework seems to have liberated this, with softening influences apparently originating from China and Persia and carried throughout Mughal conquests. The great quantity of needlework that was made and treasured is indicated by the fact that over six hundred vestments were listed in the inventory of Lincoln Cathedral, all embroidered, and some encrusted with jewels. There were also mitres, frequently of elaborate needlework, and sometimes bejewelled or decorated with seed pearls, like a later one from the Sainte Chapelle, now in the Musée de Cluny.

37. Detail of a Sicilan coverlet of about 1400, of quilted linen padded with wool, with stories of Tristan.

As artistic decoration passed its zenith in the later Middle Ages, bolder but often less beautiful feats of the embroiderers' skill were displayed. Deep-relief padded work was perfected in Germany in the fifteenth century. The heavier forms of this appear cumbersome, though the intricate backgrounds of couched-down gold thread, sometimes in elaborate geometric patterns, are impressive and are clearly associated with the intricate chasing and engraving of goldsmiths' work. This technique was known as *or de chypre*.

While some representative ecclesiastical needlework has survived relatively well, probably since it was cherished for both its temporal and spiritual values, there was also much secular needlework, which has not survived. I shall refer to aspects of magnificent costume and heraldry later, but domestic rather than ceremonial forms of needlework were relatively simple and plain. The ancient art of quilting had been used in China as a protection from the cold and early on as a form of armour, and later as a lining for armour. It was used extensively in Arabia and Persia where crusaders saw it and adopted it between the eleventh and fifteenth centuries. A similar form was until recently still used for armour in Nigeria, where Fulani warriors wore it and draped it over their horses for protection. An interesting example of early decorative quilting from Sicily, c.1400, depicts scenes from the widely honoured Tristan legend, with inscriptions also in quilting. This hanging, known as the Guicciardini quilt, is divided between the Victoria and Albert Museum and the Museo Nazionale, Florence (Plate 37).

From about the time of the Norman conquest of Britain, the Romanesque style

38. An English mitre of around 1180–1210, said to have been given to Kloster Seligenthal in Germany by the Duchess Ludmilla. Silver gilt embroidery depicts the martydoms of St Thomas and St Stephen.

The Art of Embroidery

was prevalent throughout Europe but did not leave strong surviving traits in needlework. However, an English piece at Sens Cathedral is a good example of the simple interlocking hoop and round-arch patterns that were the essence of decoration within that architectural style. St Thomas of Canterbury, murdered in 1170, was a widely honoured martyr and cult figure; Dean Stanley in 1854 *(Historical Memorials of Canterbury)* refers to the saint's vestments exhibited at Sens Cathedral, with a note 'These vestments are curious in one point of view as confirming the account of his great stature. On the feast of St Thomas they are worn for that day by the officiating priest. The tallest priest is always selected, and even then, they have to be pinned up.' The mitre of St Thomas (Victoria and Albert Museum, on loan from the Archbishop of Westminster) is of lozenge pattern woven silk, with gilt strapwork embroidery and roundels, which together with red silk bands once had enamel or stone ornaments. Another twelfth century mitre in Munich shows the martyrdoms of St Thomas and St Stephen. It is one of four known, each showing St Thomas. They were probably made in Canterbury, part of the St Thomas industry, for a general market rather than as specific commissions (Plate 38). Two other examples of twelfth century European needlework may be noted. Both are altar frontals of about 1150, one German the other Catalan (Victoria and Albert Museum; part of the German one is at Cluny Museum), and they show roundels with Christ in Majesty at the centre of a cross, worked in split stitch on linen.

In the meantime, the tradition of narrative wall hangings, like the Bayeux Tapestry, was continued in several countries. In Norway for example, an interesting hanging from Höylandet of about 1230 depicts the three magi in processional form (Plate 39). Undoubtedly the work of a professional workshop, it shares certain characteristics with the Bayeux Tapestry, one being that it is worked in couched-down wools. The linear forms of the figures and the horses are filled in with interesting patterns giving a shaded effect. A fine secular survival is a wall hanging at Wienhauswen convent in

39. Norwegian wall hanging (detail) worked in coloured wools. Early 13th century.

The Mediaeval Period

40. Part of a German 15th century wool hanging depicting in appliqué the history of Tristan and Isolde.

Lower Saxony of about 1300 depicting narrative scenes of the Tristan legend, interspersed with armorial shields. It recalls mediaeval poetry, especially Chaucer's *Canterbury Tales* and his long narrative poem *Troilus and Criseyde*. Another Tristan hanging from the same region but a hundred years later is of appliqué in woollen cloth in red and blue chequerboard squares (Victoria and Albert Museum) (Plate 40). Wool is the predominant material in late mediaeval German embroidery, from Saxony sheep that were to become popular throughout Europe.

Church needlework, however, remains predominant. We note that from the Norman Conquest there was a development in design from roundels to large scrolling forms, incorporating figures that were less statuesque and showed greater expression. Similarly, scenes were depicted in other linked patterns. An increased fluidity of style and an unsurpassed mastery of techniques combined to make English embroidery the envy of rich patrons throughout Europe. Pope Innocent IV saw certain vestments and orphreys and on being told that they originated in this country exclaimed, 'Surely England must be a garden of delight!'.[1] Popes Alexander IV (reigned 1254-61) and Urban IV (reigned 1261-64) housed at the Vatican an English embroiderer, Gregory of London; he was probably directly employed there by the Prior and convent of Bermondsey who supported him.

OPUS ANGLICANUM

The best English mediaeval needlework has never been equalled and in its own way is as much a wonder and treasured legacy as, for example, its architectural contemporary Chartres Cathedral. As a corpus it contains a seriousness and nobility on a level with the greatest music, perhaps Bach's St Matthew Passion; the two have much in common. Both combine religious narrative with an utter sensitivity of spirit. The

The Art of Embroidery

Above and below. 41. The Pienza Cope made in England in the 13th century is one of a very small number that have not been cut and altered or were not totally destroyed following the Reformation.

embroideries were highly sophisticated, ahead of their time in many respects, and were indeed contemporary with the mere beginnings of musical notation.

The qualities of *opus anglicanum* were essentially twofold; firstly, the technical achievements were exceptional and were carried out with excellent materials: secondly, the designs, layout and religious portraiture were conceived by fine artists and applied with admirable suitability to the embroidery medium. The technique of using underside couching, whereby gold and silk threads were attached to the material by small loops held through the material and secured at the back by another thread, meant that a great degree of flexibility in design was possible. Additionally, this made the finished article less stiff and cumbersome. The greater part of the embroidery worked in coloured silks was of fine split stitch, so minute that extraordinary accuracy could be attained in facial expressions and shading.

Overall designs developed through several basic forms. Flowing circles and geometric patterns in rows, each containing figures and scenes, provided the predominant format. Subsequently these became interlocking and more complex; many are comparable with the divisions of stained glass windows. While a dignified symmetry and iconographical abstraction characterised Romanesque design and representation, the Gothic spirit was full of flowing lines and expressed with a new consciousness the real, natural world and included naturalistic detail. Emotional drama was shown in the depiction of lively themes such as the maternal qualities of the Virgin Mary, legends of the saints and narrative and genre subjects. The finest surviving works of *opus anglicanum* are a group of copes each displaying these combined qualities, each made in London between about 1275 and 1335. Three magnificent examples, a sample from the large number made, must first be noted.

The Ascoli Piceno cope (c.1275-80) was given by Pope Nicholas IV to his birth-

The Mediaeval Period

place Ascoli in 1288. On a linen ground, within scalloped roundels it is covered with scenes from the lives of the Popes from Clement I (90-100) to Clement IV (1265-1268), embroidered in silk thread in split stitch and underside couched gold thread. In 1295 the Vatican treasury boasted 113 embroideries of *opus anglicanum* including this. We do not know, for example, the subject matter of the one which Edward I sent to the Pope in 1291, though the design of the Ascoli cope is probably based on a specific papal order. In about 1295 the king sent another cope to Pope Boniface VIII. A little later Pope John XXII (1316-34) was given several English copes: two of which, along with one embroidered with large pearls, were sent by Edward II and Queen Isabella; a third came from the Archbishop of Canterbury in 1322 and another magnificent one was given by the Bishop of Ely in 1333.

Even more elaborate, and perhaps finer, are two fairly similar copes of 1315-1335, the Pienza cope (Plate 41) and the Bologna cope (Plate 42). The Pienza cope was given to that cathedral in 1462 by Pope Pius II. Its shows, within concentric bands of gothic arcading, scenes from the lives of the Virgin, St Margaret and St Catherine. An orphrey band shows naturalistic birds within a strapwork panel. The Bologna cope is also worked with expressive vignettes, under cinquefoil arches, the upper row showing the Passion and Resurrection and the longer lower row the infancy of Christ and, representing the most celebrated English saint, the martyrdom of St Thomas of Canterbury. Heads of many saints and angels performing music and other duties fill other bands and spandrels.

A glorious English cope of around 1300 at the cathedral of Saint-Betrand-de-Comminges, Haute-Garonne, displays an infinite variety of Passion scenes, the Ascension, the Pentecost and the Coronation of the Virgin in roundels and oval medallions and also many birds and small animals, all against a gold background.[2]

Above and below. 42. The Bologna Cope (1315-35) is a superb example of English mediaeval embroidery, opus anglicanum, with expressive narrative scenes combined in an effective overall design and including much decorative detail.

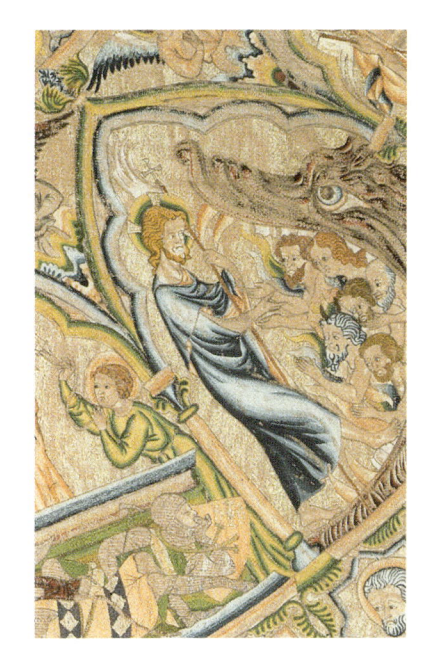

The Art of Embroidery

Above. 43. A fragment from the Steeple Aston cope of c.1320 shows enormous charm and retains part of the lustrous combination of coloured silk with silver and silver-gilt threads.

Right. 44. A panel from the back of a cope of about 1310 shows Christ enthroned, with the sun and moon.

The Victoria and Albert Museum has fine examples of *opus anglicanum*. Though unfortunately every item has been cut and altered, sometimes drastically, each surviving piece is an enthralling and masterly jewel. The Steeple Aston cope fragments (c.1320) have a silver and olive mystery (Plate 43) while the orphrey parts are well preserved and full of the original life. The Clare Chasuble, of a few decades earlier, is characterised by its blue satin ground over which are embroidered neat but languid scrolling tendrils containing animals. The front of this chasuble depicts a group of scenes in the cruciform pattern so frequently employed as an ecclesiastical symbol, and indeed an early Christian architectural form, the shape of a basilica ground plan. A square with apses on each side, this outline form was used at two different angles, diagonal and upright, with effects that seem curiously different, mathematically magical. Church pillars, mouldings, etc have adopted this practical structure.[3]

The Syon cope is entirely covered with embroidery on linen and the design is composed of glorious figures within interlocking cruciform patterns, as above, at both angles (Plate 45). The added orphrey and outer band depict heraldry. Another contemporary plan in design was somewhat freer. This was the tree of life or stem of Jesse pattern, linking saints and vignettes like recitatives and arias within a general narrative framework. This was an age-old device of pictorial representation. The beautiful Jesse cope (c.1300) with embroidery on red silk twill shows elegantly, within a formalised tree-tendril pattern, the sacred ancestor's descendants stemming from his recumbent figure (Plate 6). Another, tighter version of this linking vine pattern can be seen in two thirteenth century fragments of silver-gilt embroidery on velvet at the British Museum. Each tendril contains a half-length figure. These fragments were found in a tomb at Worcester Cathedral. The Daroca cope (Museo Arqueologico, Madrid) has five scenes with birds and includes the creation of fowls and fish. The Melk chasuble (Museum für Angewandte Kunst, Vienna) c.1300 is of an unusual type of *opus anglicanum* having in design two large crucifixion scenes, one on the front, one on the back, representing before and after Christ's

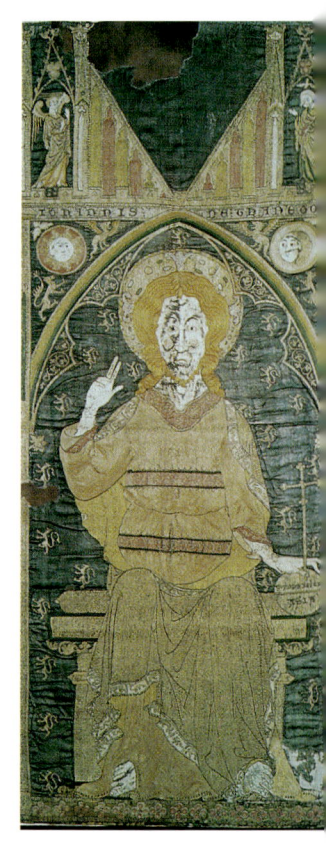

The Mediaeval Period

death. The rest of the chasuble is patterned evenly. The Butler Bowden cope, of the second quarter of the fourteenth century, is an example of later *opus anglicanum*.[4] Of a more complex design, perhaps less ordered, the figures are enclosed by high-Gothic foliate arches while a long orphrey has stiff hieratic figures in jewel-like precision. A chasuble made from a cope of a comparable form is in the Metropolitan Museum, New York (Plate 46).

A panel bearing the name of a patron, John of Thanet, 'a Monk and Chaunter', mathematician and author, of Canterbury cathedral, shows the enthroned Christ in an unusually large format. He is holding the orb of the world which is inscribed EVROPA AFF'CA ASIA. The blue silk background is 'powdered' with lions rampant in silver (Plate 44).

The ultimate method of linking subjects and stories was probably, as already seen, to show them within an orderly framework of pointed arches or niches, as depicted on the facades of gothic buildings. They might be placed in radiating arcs on a cope, in rows on an altar frontal, or in vertical columns on an orphrey. Several magnificent orphreys show elegant and dignified figures against meticulously worked gold backgrounds, usually with variations of interweaving patterns. In contrast to these, but comparable with the Butler Bowden cope, is a fine band of the first half of the fourteenth century depicting scenes from the life of the Virgin worked in coloured silks and metal threads on red velvet. It seems at once full of spontaneous passion and timeless human expression.

By the thirteenth century the making of vestments had become an important and lucrative industry. There were in London, and elsewhere, many workshops of professional male embroiderers with critical standards of workmanship, and these flourished

45. One of the finest English copes is the Syon cope of 1300-1320, a masterpiece of opus anglicanum.

49

The Art of Embroidery

in catering for domestic and foreign orders, and for the requirements of rich city merchants. Some individual craftsmen were well known and sometimes embroiderers went abroad to undertake commissions. The high standard in English workshops was probably founded on a system of standard controls and long apprenticeships as was certainly the case in Paris, but London was slow in forming guilds. Nuns, too, carried out semi-professional work, under the guidance of professionals. Both undertook repairs and restoration work as well as new commissions. In monasteries works were created for the adornment of religious practice and with didactic aims. A monk named Theophilus wrote in the twelfth century:

> *Avoid and subdue sloth of mind and wandering of the spirit by useful occupation of the hands,*

and told his fellow monastic artists to embellish the House of God

> *with such great beauty and variety of workmanship… without which the divine mysteries and the administering of the offices cannot continue.*

Opus anglicanum was exceptionally fine from 1250 to 1350. The best pieces display a wealth of incidental detail but, as in architecture, in a way that never diminishes from the whole layout. Fine vestments were exported to Flanders, France and Italy and are to be found today in many European countries. The Vatican in Rome had more English needlework than any other, as shown in a 1295 inventory of the Holy See. Pope Boniface VIII made gifts of English embroidery to the cathedral of his birthplace,

Opposite. 46. This English chasuble of red velvet is applied with elegant scenes of the Virgin Mary framed within gothic arcading. (Originally a larger vestment). Early 13th century.

Below. 47. Mediaeval needlework made in London is again represented by this burse of the early 14th century, having two cruciform images with dignified expression. 10½in. x 9⅞in. (27cm x 25cm).

The Art of Embroidery

48. Like an Italian panel painting the gold background of this orphrey for a chasuble heightens the poignancy of the expressive figures. English, c.1320.

Anagni, in about 1300. He also gave a very fine altar frontal of an English type, though probably made in Rome, depicting two tiers of arches with saints in the upper, and Gospel scenes in the lower. The piece shows also a revival of Byzantine influences brought about by mosaic artists whose glittering masterpieces were made in and around Venice, and later in Rome.

The Black Death (1348) can roughly be said to mark the end of the flowering of *opus anglicanum*. It caused embroidery workshops, as all other trades, to be horribly decimated. Other deteriorating factors included strains on resources brought about by the Hundred Years War with France and the domestic unrest in England itself. Changes in techniques and materials, some of them quicker and cheaper, altered the especially English appearance of vestments. A greater use was made of fine imported materials from Italy; superb velvets and brocades, replacing plainer silks, were now used for the main body of copes and chasubles – needlework was limited to orphreys or to applied pieces. These consisted of stitching on fine linen which was then attached where necessary over the velvet pile. This new trend, concentrating more on fine fabrics, led to a different aspect of luxury and richness; elegant flowing robes of wonderful textures and colours replaced the jewel-like quality of dense pictorial needlework with its portrayal of scenes of harrowing religious passion. The weavers' art now rose to supremacy. The embroidery itself became more formalised and stiff, unadventurously following continental conventions. The remarkable draughtsmen had moved into other fields; repeated figures were now pricked out and 'pounced'. Quicker and cheaper methods encouraged by excessive demands generally affected the quality of workmanship; long and short, brick and satin stitches often replaced finer varieties and surface couching was substituted for the more laborious underside couching. The characteristic tiny, split stitching of the thirteenth century was replaced by the use of stem stitch.

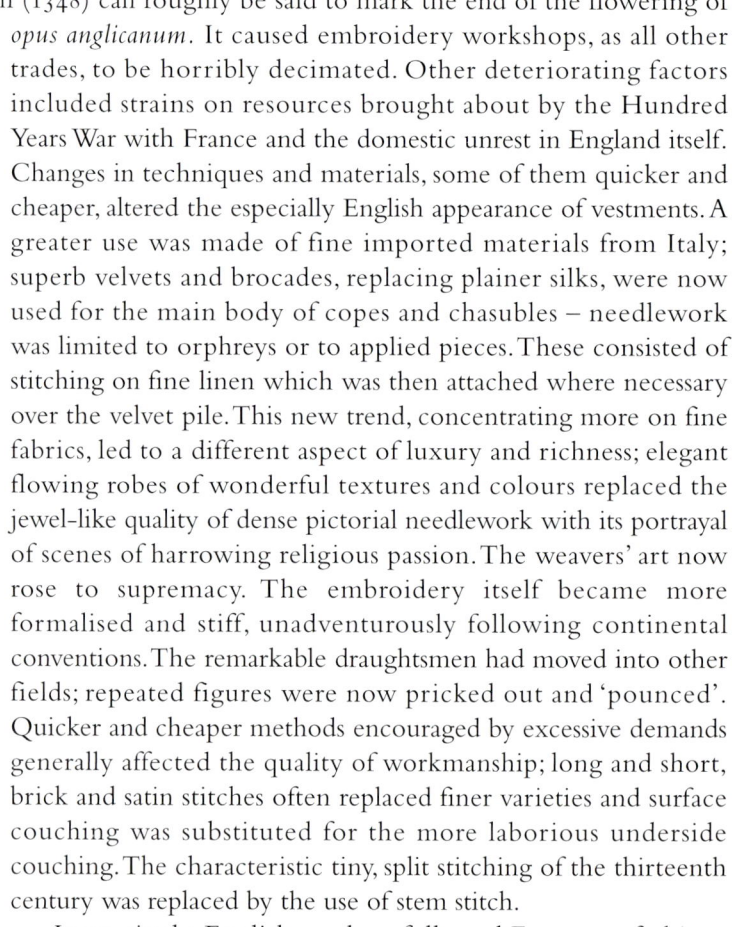

Increasingly, English workers followed European fashions with coarser, padded work and imitations of tapestry weaving. Certain kinds of embroidery, particularly realistic shading in a new form of needlepainting, *or nué,* closer than ever before to the artist's brush, enjoyed supremacy in Flanders but England's past fame was ironically perpetuated in the widespread coarser needlework known as *façon d'Angleterre.*

Or nué or 'shaded gold' was a revolutionary technique. Probably originating in Flanders, but much used in many parts of Europe, it allowed for a new versatility in needle depiction. The principle was a simple one: gold threads were couched-down horizontally by irregularly placed coloured silk threads which gave a shaded effect according to their density, as in

The Mediaeval Period

49. Another piece of English Mediaeval embroidery typifies the colourful and expressive quality of opus anglicanum, *c.1320. (See also Plate 7.)*

painting, against the metallic surface. The strictly horizontal lines of the gold gave an impression of weaving so that the embroidery resembled tapestry; this aspect also eliminated the multiple reflections of light previously caused by threads being laid at different angles. A fine example of the *or nué* technique is a group of twenty-seven pieces in the Museum of Santa Maria del Fiore in Florence. These are after designs made for vestments by Antonio del Pollaiuolo (1431-98) and are well documented. The technique of *or nué* continued in use well into the seventeenth century, and was used by Charles I's embroiderer (see Plate 50).

In France, the ancient method of couching wool, *point couché* (as in the Bayeux Tapestry), continued throughout the Middle Ages and appliqué, or applied work, was also popular. St Louis (1215-1270) of France sent the Tartar King a set of vestments

The Art of Embroidery

and other church furnishings depicting Gospel scenes in applied work. Raised and padded *broderie en relief* was also done.

Flanders was latterly an important centre of European embroidery and weaving. Its long tradition of these is seen in the rich and heavy draperies depicted in Flemish painting. An interesting group of embroideries associated with the story of St Martin, of the early or mid-fifteenth century, is attributed to a Franco-Flemish origin. Formerly part of an altar frontal, a cope, or a set of vestments, the pieces consist chiefly of thirty-three roundels illustrating events in the life of St Martin, though the incident of his dividing his cloak to share it with a beggar is missing. The embroideries have great charm and are shared by the Musée Historique des Tissus at Lyons and the Metropolitan Museum in New York.

Returning now to central and southern Europe, several South German vestments survive from the reign of Henry II (died 1024). They are of fine workmanship, closely associated in design with Regensburg illumination, and show also Byzantine influence. They are largely of gold, couched on to silk, such as the 'star' mantle of St Kunigund (wife of Henry II) decorated with a large number of medallions portraying saints and narrative scenes on dark violet silk twill. An altar frontal c.1300 at Bamburg Cathedral is solidly worked with rows of chain stitch in coloured silks and with gold thread. There was also in Germany a strong tradition from mediaeval times of whitework embroidery, *opus teutonicum*: fine altar frontals, veils and hangings of simple and cheap materials contrasting sharply with the extravagance of the gold embroidery. An altar cloth made by Abbess Gertrude of Altenberg, on the Lahn, second half of the thirteenth century, is of white embroidery on linen with great variety in its design, having figures, animal symbols and pattern (Cleveland Museum of Art, Ohio).

Later German and Austrian needlework was very sculptural. Raised and padded parts appear to imitate features of metalwork and carved wood. Pieces of wood were actually incorporated for relief effects under the needlework. (This was no doubt the origin of the stumpwork that became a short-lived but exuberant passion of seventeenth century English embroiderers.) German and Austrian orphreys in cross form, for example, frequently showed the crucified Christ in deep relief, supported at the extremities of the arms by angels and with

50. This embroidered roundel from an altar frontal after a design by Andrea del Sarto (1486-1530) shows the ability of the or nué technique to depict shading, as in painting.

The Mediaeval Period

God the Father, or saints, or Christ rising from the tomb, above and below, in the same technique (Plate 56). Vestments were often further enriched with pearls and precious stones.

A remarkable, complete set of thirteenth century Austrian vestments is preserved in Vienna. Of late Romanesque style and worked in coloured silks, in slanted gobelin stitch they depict choirs of angels under round arches, animal symbols, geometric key patterns and God enthroned in a starry sky within a circle. This last symbol would seem to be of Byzantine origin. From the former convent of Göss, near Leoben, in Styria, the vestments consist of all five major items: cope, chasuble (Plate 36), dalmatic, tunicle and altar frontal. They were made for the abbess of the convent, probably by the nuns.

Florence was the most important centre of Italian needlework and it was to this city that the French Dukes of Burgundy and of Berry sent patronage for ecclesiastical items. Few of their vestments have survived but inventories shed some light on imports to France. Florentine needlework was especially related to painting, firstly in design and colouring and, secondly, the gold backgrounds adopted a form that imitated the gilt gesso backgrounds of panel pictures. The patterns were achieved by first couching down string and then superimposing gold thread. Superbly executed silkwork figures stood out against these with extreme delicacy and with a statuesque serenity similar to that mastered by Florentine painters. A fine altar frontal, signed and dated by its maker, Jacopo di Cambi, 1336, displays these qualities clearly (Plate 51). It

51. A Florentine altar frontal by Jacopo di Cambi, 1336, shows magnificent embroidery closely related to contemporary painting but with the extra richness of textiles.

The Art of Embroidery

depicts the coronation of the Virgin by Christ surrounded by groups of angel musicians and further flanked by fourteen saints in pointed Gothic niches. A smaller band above depicts in minute and colourful detail scenes from the life of Christ and the Virgin. This and another Florentine altar frontal at Manresa Cathedral, Spain, are well preserved and represent a dignified calmness in contrast to the lively emotion of *opus anglicanum*.

Sicily had a history of sumptuous silk embroidery, especially in the twelfth century. The Royal workshops at Palermo made fine ecclesiastical and court robes including the famous pluvial now in Vienna (Plate 52). In the form of an ecclesiastical cope and considerably inspired by Arab embroiderers, it was made for the new Norman king, Roger II's coronation in 1130 and was later used for the coronation rites of the Holy Roman Emperors. The animal motif (in this case a lion overcoming a camel) in dual symmetrical form is closely related to similar stylised pairs in Middle East art. This heraldic image came to Sicily through Byzantium. The outside border of the cloak is worked in beautiful Arabic script, the colours being limited to the use of gold on red silk in a strikingly bold way.[5] The outlining details on the animals are in double lines of fine pearls, and there are further enrichments with gold ornaments, enamels and jewels.

52. The Pluvial or Coronation Mantle of the Holy Roman Emperors, thought to have been made for Roger II of Sicily, depicts grand animal images within a narrow border of script. c.1133.

56

The Mediaeval Period

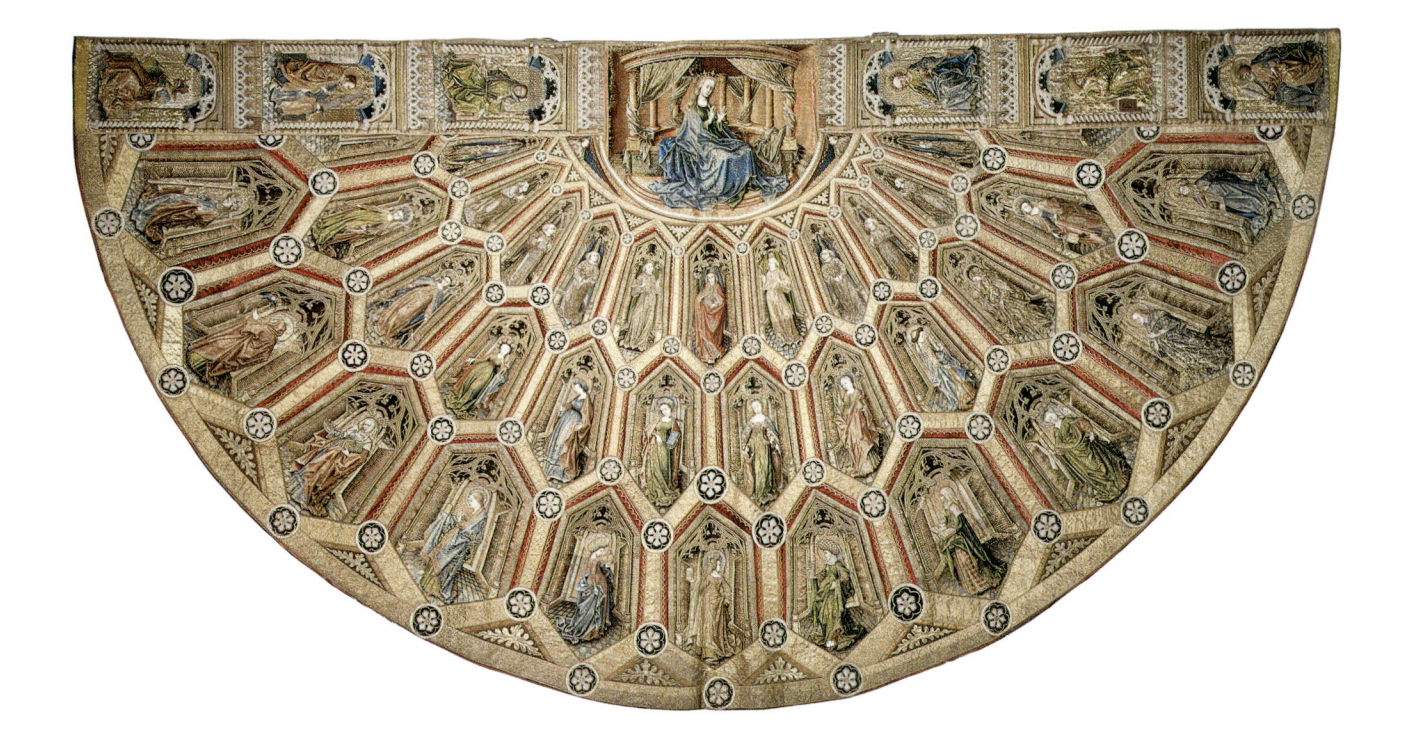

The so-called Mantle of Charlemagne at Metz Cathedral is also probably of Sicilian manufacture. Also based on Mesopotamian-Persian-Byzantine models it is embroidered with an eagle motif. Though both England and Sicily were at this time under Norman rule it is interesting to note how very different were the professional embroideries of these two countries. The cuffs of a purple silk dalmatic (mid-twelfth century) from the vestments of the Holy Roman Empire show Sicilian work to be extraordinarily oriental with couched gold, outlines of small pearls and additional large enamel ornaments. The Eagle dalmatic in the same collection, made in Austria c.1320, also looks curiously like a Chinese robe: of Chinese purple silk damask, it is powdered with eagle medallions and the robe is bordered with embroidered orphreys featuring thirty-nine crowned kings.

Following the French occupation of the island in 1266 and the massacre of them in the Sicilian Vespers in 1282, many craftsmen fled to Italy, thereby boosting the already growing silk industries of Lucca, Pisa and Venice, but virtually ending the long needlework tradition of Palermo.

Another important set of mediaeval vestments of a later period, the mid-fifteenth century, is that of the Order of the Golden Fleece. Probably made in Brussels, they reflect the influence of several painters and consist of three copes, two dalmatics, a chasuble and two altar antependia (a dossal and an altar frontal). They are enriched with jewels and seed pearls and are still in excellent condition.[6] They are remarkable examples of the magnificence of the *or nué* technique and appear close in execution to the works of painters, such as Rogier van der Weyden, who were no doubt the designers. The three-dimensional quality of the designs leans towards an understanding

53. *The Mantle of the Virgin, from the mass vestments of the Order of the Golden Fleece. Probably made in Brussels, mid-15th century.*

The Art of Embroidery

of perspective. They were made for the court of the Duke of Burgundy, as were three other surviving cloaks of mourning black silk decorated with heraldry and the Duke's fire steel symbol, from which emanate glistening waves of sparks (Plates 53 and 54).[7]

In mediaeval Spain the influence of Moorish work is immediately noticeable amongst styles adopted from other parts of Europe. Barcelona was the centre of professional workshops, but other towns, notably Toledo and Seville, produced good work. Gold backgrounds were here again a prominent feature, either worked in lines around the design or interlaced, with a trellis pattern. A highly sculptural effect is created by the padded architectural features of a Spanish dossal and antependium of c.1468, probably from Burgo de Osma (Art Institute of Chicago).

Portugal is especially remembered for a legendary set of robes sent to the Pope by the immensely rich Emanuel, 'lord of the conquest, navigation and commerce of India, Ethiopia, Arabia and Persia', in about 1500. Worked on a gold brocade background, they had a pomegranate design of real gold with rubies and pearls for seeds and flowers, together with other gems. They must have been dazzling in richness, even if somewhat heavy and cumbersome.

Beyond the main courts of Europe interesting local styles developed. It should be recorded that Viking and Celtic settlers in Iceland carried out fine, sophisticated work up to the middle of the sixteenth century. Home made materials rather than silks and velvets were usually the basis for a variety of techniques of couching, appliqué and pattern darning amongst others.

The University of Cambridge, Dunstable Priory and seven of the City of London livery companies[8] have funeral palls of the late fifteenth and early sixteenth centuries (Plate 59). The Saddlers' Company has one of crimson velvet with applied embroidery,

54. A mourning cope of black velvet is applied with heraldic devices of the Duke of Burgundy including fire steels with radiating flames. Southern Netherlands, c.1476.

The Mediaeval Period

first worked on pieces of linen, depicting angels, the sacred monogram IHS and the arms of the Company. The Fishmongers' of the late fifteenth century shows St Peter (he is the patron saint of fishermen) enthroned with angels, and also St Peter receiving the keys from Our Lord. The Vintners' is of Italian velvet and cloth of gold, embroidered with St Martin of Tours. Rows of kneeling figures, with a discrepancy in size usually denoting status, are a familiar feature of palls and a convention also seen on monuments and church brasses. Many churches had funeral palls; St Margaret's Westminster, charged a fee of 8d. for the use of theirs.

An unusual remnant of the sixteenth century is the embroidered badge of the Pilgrimage of Grace, 1536-7. It has an emblematic shield and is preserved at Arundel Castle, Sussex. Another needlework banner can be seen in the National Museums of Scotland, a rare survival in that country which suffered so much iconoclasm. Of about 1520 and known as the Fetternear banner, it may be Scottish or Flemish on account of its symbolism. It depicts Christ, pierced and blood-flecked at the foot of the cross and surrounded by instruments used at the crucifixion, together with the cock perched on a pillar. The banner was not completed and, not having been used, it is in very good condition. It was probably intended for the Confraternity of the Holy Blood of St Giles' Collegiate Kirk, Edinburgh, a religious society whose members included James IV. The border includes the arms of Gavin Douglas, Bishop of Dunkeld (1515-22).

Mediaeval characteristics gradually gave way to Renaissance thinking, discussed in the next chapter. There is no clear dividing line and combined features can be seen, especially in needlework from mainland Europe. The St George altar cloth by Antoni Sadurni of about 1460 preserved at the Chapel of St George in the Palace of the Generalitat, Barcelona, depicts centrally a complex mediaeval rendering of St George with the maiden and the dragon, but this is flanked by symmetrical, stylised panels typical of Renaissance ornament, with Italianate gryphons and shields.

The Reformation prevented a full development of English ecclesiastical needlework in the Renaissance mode. It was the turn of other countries to make the finest vestments. Superb examples of

Left. 55. The central panel of a 15th century altar frontal of the Order of the Golden Fleece depicts the Mystic Marriage of St Catherine in the rich qualities of needle painting.

Below. 56. A late 14th century German orphrey cross is worked in padded relief recalling sculpture and goldsmiths' work.

59

1554 are at Averbode Abbey, Brabant (Plate 9). These have deep orphrey bands decorated with formalised scrolling foliage, grotesque masks, flowers and fruit, around large roundels depicting narrative subjects in superbly worked detail. But even in the Southern Netherlands where these were made, the production of fine needlework soon declined, largely due to religious persecution, which forced many craftsmen to leave the country.

SECULAR EMBROIDERY

Mediaeval secular embroidery was as great in quantity as ecclesiastical. Although perhaps it never reached the artistic intensity of *opus anglicanum,* it was extravagant in the use of materials and extremely rich and colourful. Even the Squire who went on the Canterbury pilgrimage was attired in needlework according to Chaucer:

> *Embrouded was he, as it were a mede*
> *Al ful of freshe floures whyte and rede*

The royal and princely courts of Europe impressed each other and their subjects with luxurious costumes emphasising their power. Hardly any of these have survived, partly because they were not subject to careful veneration, as were church vestments, but continuously used, altered, worn out, taken apart and remade. Another aspect of the secular demand on embroiderers was the making of banners, tunics and horse trappings required for tournaments and ceremonial occasions. But as fashions and customs changed, both costumes and these decorations were allowed to perish. We can build up an impression from illuminations in manuscripts, paintings and written records.

A hint of the tremendously rich and valuable textiles of mediaeval times is gleaned from reports such as the single most expensive item of English furniture recorded, Queen Philippa's bed, which had hangings of green velvet embroidered with sea sirens, and cost the colossal sum of £203. There are many records of embroidered dress also. In 1351, for example, Edward III and Queen Philippa had robes made of red velvet 'embroidered with clouds of silver and eagles of pearl and gold, under each alternate cloud an eagle of pearl, and under each of the other clouds a golden eagle, every eagle having in his beak a garter with the motto "hony soyt qui mal y panse" embroidered thereon'. The King's armourer, John de Cologne, is well recorded for his many duties in providing important embroidered textiles for differing events. The young Flemish Queen Philippa's first embroidered garment was of purple velvet ornamented with golden squirrels and it is also known that it was eventually given to Ely Cathedral where it was turned into three copes. These survived until the Reformation. Another costly commission was the order for three embroidered counterpanes for the churching ceremonies of Queen Philippa in 1330. These required a workforce of 112 people, men and women. Similar counterpanes made to celebrate the birth of the Black Prince were worked with 'beasts, babewyns [monkeys or fantastic animals] and knots'.

The Mediaeval Period

Some early heraldic needlework has survived, however, as on a charter bag of Edward I's reign, at Westminster Abbey. The arms of England, 'three lions passant gardant, or', are embroidered on a red shield against a green cloth background, and with St Paul on the other side. The City of London has two other charter bags from the reign of Edward II, dated 1319.

The great seals of Edward I, Edward II and Edward III show on them the elaborate horse trappings used by mediaeval monarchs. Another illustration is to be seen in a stone carving on the tomb of Edmund Crouchback, Earl of Lancaster, son of Henry III, in Westminster Abbey. He died in 1296. An instance of the conversion of secular needlework to church use are the horse trappings of Edward III which were made into a chasuble (Plate 35) now in the Cluny Museum. Of superb quality, the pieces are of red velvet, richly embroidered with gold and a little silk. The leopards of England are boldly depicted twice, against a background of small foliage and figures. Their sinuous forms are like Chinese dragons in appearance with fierce faces, terrifying claws and overall of couched gold thread. The Black Prince's jupon, a military coat embroidered with his arms, is a fascinating relic preserved by his tomb at Canterbury Cathedral. The quarterings are embroidered on red and blue velvet.[9]

An act of 1364 forbade anybody below a certain income to wear bejewelled costumes and others below another sum to wear any embroidery. But Richard II's court was particularly extravagant with precious garments laden with jewels. As a young man the king himself is said to have had a coat valued at thirty thousand marks. In the Wilton Diptych he is portrayed wearing a rich robe similar to one described in his inventories. When he died in 1399 he left his robes to his servants, after the valuable jewels had been removed. Illustrations of him at the time of his deposing show him dressed in black embroidered with ostrich feathers – his horse trappings and pennon had the same badge. Robes and hangings were frequently decorated in this manner,

57. Part of an altar frontal, c.1540, with Ralph Nevill, 4th Earl of Westmorland, and his family, including twenty children; here his wife Catherine is shown with their daughters.

The Art of Embroidery

'powdered' with symbols, or insignia, with suggested, semi-hidden significance. Animals of an heraldic nature were often used. Richard II's most well-known cognisance was a white hart. Queen Philippa, the Black Prince's mother, Richard's grandmother, had a robe decorated with golden squirrels, as we have noted. Further examples can be cited and the tradition lived on until late Tudor times when these *impressas* carried slightly different emblematic metaphors.

Charming smaller items of costume which have survived in greater numbers are alms purses. These were small bags which hung from the belts of rich men and contained such valuables as jewels, money and even relics. They were sometimes elaborately worked with figures and flowers in silks and metal threads. Caen in France was noted for making them. Articles of this type continued to be made in England well into the seventeenth century.

Other European courts were equally splendid with magnificent needlework. The French dukes of the reigns of Charles V and Charles VI were most lavish and the Dukes of Burgundy and of Orléans were notable patrons of embroidery workshops. There are records of expensive needlework ordered by Philip the Good, Duke of Burgundy, for his duel in 1425 with Henry Duke of Gloucester at Bruges. A Parisian embroiderer, Tierry de Chastel, was called in to supervise the occasion and many others were summoned from France and the southern Netherlands to carry out impressive decorations. The duke's personal embroiderer from Bruges, Simon de Brilles, and an artist, Colart de Voleur, were responsible for his tent, banners, tabards and horse trappings. The tent was of blue and white satin and was decorated with the coats of arms of the duke's various properties, together with his motto and the Burgundian device of the fire steel and flint.

The French, particularly, loved wall hangings *(salles)* that went round a room in series, and these feature in contemporary documents. In an inventory of Charles V, dated 1364, it is recorded that he had several *salles d'Angleterre* including one of red hangings embroidered with lions, eagles and leopards in blue. These secular embroideries must have been beautiful and once again, the motifs had heraldic and symbolic nuances. Scrolls with mottoes on them, monograms and flowers and animals were sometimes included. Again, the records of the Dukes of Burgundy shed light: Philippe le Hardi had hangings of blue satin embroidered with trees by Henriet Goutier of Paris while another duke, Philippe le Bon, had a set of crimson silk hangings with a motif showing a lady bathing a sparrow-hawk. Not all room hangings, horse trappings, banners and streamers were embroidered; some were painted and sealed with wax. Several paintings in manuscripts show walls hung with blue curtains decorated with gold fleur-de-lis. One hastily required order for a large number of embroidered fleur-de-lis motifs in 1352 cited no less than 8,544; they had to be 'broudées jour et nuit en grand haste' and the workers were aided with the provision of candles and wine.

Bed hangings were especially prized, and impressive beds were a symbol of rank and wealth. These are prominently mentioned in records from mediaeval times until the eighteenth century as amongst the most important possessions of their owners. Sir John Cobham in 1394 left a bed embroidered with butterflies, and Joan Beauchamp in 1434 one with swans, leopards and flowers. In 1398 John of Gaunt bequeathed his large bed hangings of cloth of gold, embroidered with gold roses and white ostrich feathers, for use on the high altar of St Paul's Cathedral. A little earlier the Black Prince had bequeathed to Canterbury Cathedral a number of embroideries, including wall hangings, several beds and a green velvet robe embroidered with his arms, another with angels and a third with eagles in blue.

Over a throne or a chair of state there would frequently have been a canopy and this would invariably, as today, have been embroidered with royal arms or ciphers. These called for fine and wonderful heraldic needlework to convey power and status, characteristics that Shakespeare's Henry VI found heavy to bear:

> *Gives not the Hawthorne bush a sweeter shade*
> *To shepheards, looking on their silly Sheepe,*
> *Then doth a rich Imbroider'd canopie*
> *To Kings, that feare their Subjects treacherie?*
> HENRY VI, 3, II

Craft guilds strictly supervised the production of needlework. Apprenticeships lasted seven or eight years and in Ghent it was ruled in 1408 that a would-be master had to prove himself on a figure. He also had to have the recommendation of a priest and to pay a fee. Old materials could not normally be mixed with new ones and the standard and quality of metal threads was regulated. Work considered below standard was destroyed and sometimes craftsmen were fined. However, the scrutiny was relaxed and gradually standards fell. In 1423 the House of Commons petitioned Henry VI to protect the interests of workshops over the self-employed. The Broderers' Company was subsequently formed in 1430.

Following the Reformation there was a fearful spate of iconoclasm and much of the finest English embroidery was destroyed. Vestments were hacked and burned, metal threads were melted down, and other valuables were looted from monasteries, convents and churches. Further terrible destruction was done by the Puritans but happily some good examples have survived these and later outrages. Henry VII commissioned many vestments from Italian weavers and subsequently bequeathed a number to Westminster Abbey but these were burned by the Puritans in 1643. St Paul's Cathedral had a fine collection of vestments, many undoubtedly made in the City of London. 1552 records listed three hundred copes alone; presumably these were also lost to iconoclasm and mercenary salvage. Even in 1688 an over-zealous Protestant mob, celebrating the Glorious Revolution and the crowing of William of Orange and Queen Mary, raided Traquair in Peeblesshire, looting precious ecclesiastical items that had Roman Catholic associations. A description includes, '5 vestments … one of silk curiously embroidered with gold and silver thread… most curiously wrought with a kind of pearl… an embroidered Eucharist box, two embroidered crucifixes…' and ends tersely: 'All solemnly burnt at the Cross at Peebles'.[10]

Many French vestments were lost in the Revolution and were torn, burned and melted down. Perhaps the most sadly missed are a famed set given by René of Anjou to Angers Cathedral. But again, fortunately, there are fine examples to be seen outside France, in Italian and Swedish cathedrals and elsewhere.

CHAPTER THREE

THE POST-MEDIAEVAL PERIOD

*Rayed with golde and ryght well cled
in fyne black sattyn doutremere*

IN sixteenth century Europe there were great changes in religion and culture. The Renaissance, which had been gathering momentum since its origin in Italy, brought an end to the later mediaeval period, now seen as dark ages, and dispelled elements of mystery and superstition that precluded a more human approach to life. A new freedom and liberated spirit of individual thinking led to cultural revival with fresh emphasis on personal human philosophies in the fields of learning, science, the arts, and a study of classical antiquity as a basis for these disciplines.

In the meantime, the Reformation caused the Roman Church a substantial loss of spiritual and temporal power and England, becoming independent from Rome, saw increased secularisation in social life. With the House of Tudor firmly established on the English throne, the unrest of the Wars of the Roses was soon forgotten and the country settled down to a period of stability and rapid cultural growth. Literature flowered in the monumental achievements of William Shakespeare and his contemporaries while the decorative arts also reached new standards of remarkable individuality and quality.

Fine church vestments continued to be made in countries where Roman Catholicism was still paramount, but significant changes of approach can be noted. Pictorial representation became subservient to surface ornament, and realistic narrative scenes were to be confined to roundels and inset panels within a scheme of decorative

58. A detail from The Family of Henry VIII, *artist unknown, c.1545, portrays the richness of embroidered costume, a canopy and cushion at Whitehall Palace.*

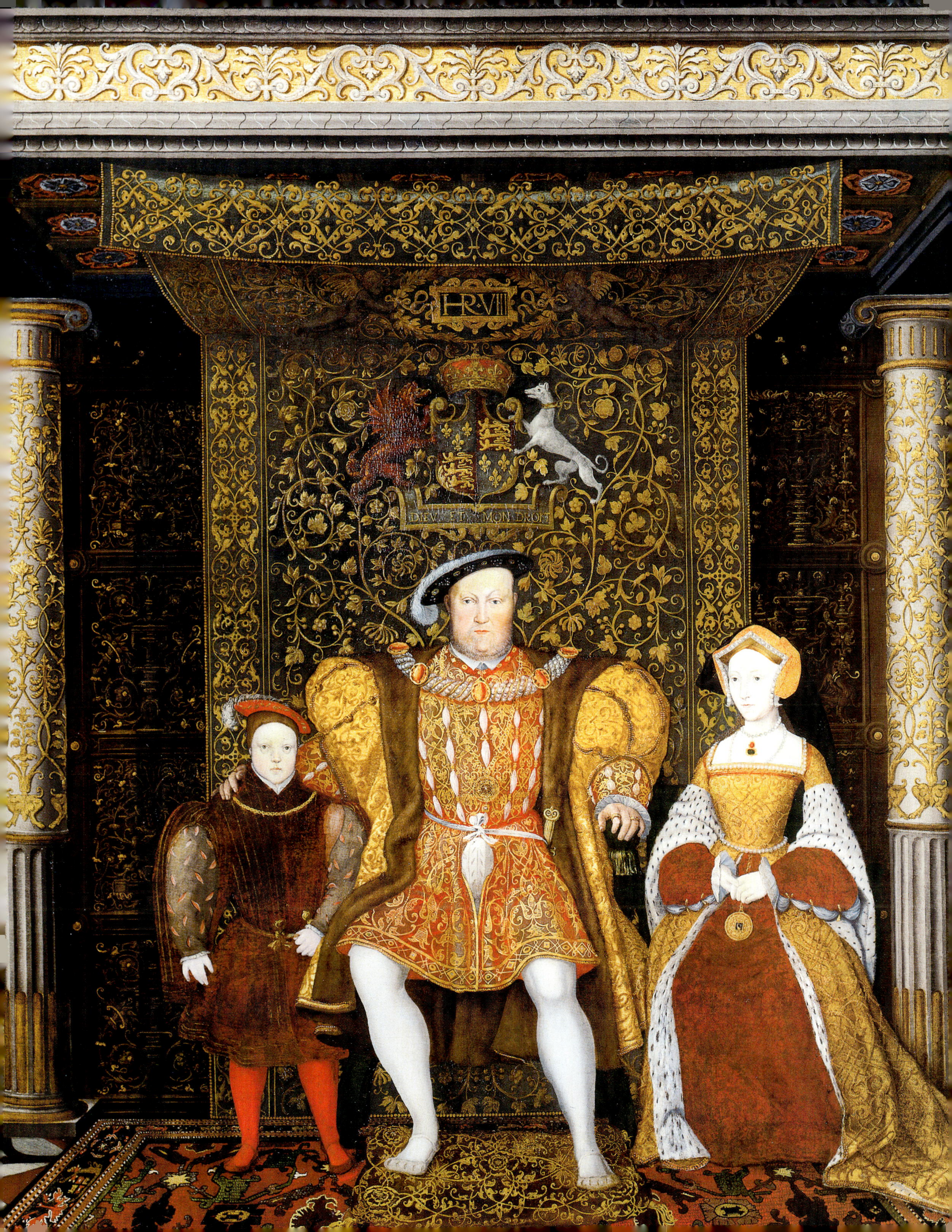
HR·VIII

The Art of Embroidery

panelling, as for example on the fine cope from Brabant (see Plate 9, page 13, and also page 60) This difference marked something of the division of the ways between 'fine art' and 'decorative arts', between paintings and things and ultimately of the different status of artist and craftsman.

Fifteenth century Italian artists were however called upon to draw cartoons for embroiderers of copes and other items; a treatise written by Cerino Cennini in 1437 shows that they were now concerned with such technical problems as perspective. The influence of Giotto is notable, with an introduction of naturalism to religious scenes, transcending the hitherto conventional idealistic conception. Figures began to reflect human nature, more subtle than mere symbols of religious passion.

Antonio del Pollaiuolo (c.1431-98) was a painter and sculptor, especially of works in gold and silver, including some for the baptistery in Florence. In 1466 he designed panels for vestments for the baptistery, twenty-seven of which survive. Like paintings of the period, they show new attempts of perspective and are worked in *or nué*. They tell the story of the life of St John the Baptist and are well documented, with a record of payments made and the names of embroiderers, including two Flemish workers who perhaps introduced the *or nué* technique (Museo di Santa Maria del Fiore, Florence). Another rare documented example of a painter's design and surviving cartoon is one for an altar frontal; the cartoon is by the Turin artist G.C. Procaccini

59. Male and female members of the Fayrey family who donated this pall to a fraternity in Dunstable (c.1500) are shown with St John the Baptist. The top is of Florentine brocade.

(1574-1625) (National Gallery of Canada, Ottawa) and the frontal was made between 1618 and 1623 by Ludovico Pellegrini (Chapel of the Holy Shroud, Turin Cathedral). It is richly padded with gold embroidery and medallions showing the life of the Virgin.

Raised, padded work continued to be a feature in the main part of Europe but this was not done in England, perhaps due to an instinctive suspicion of idolatry. In any case few ecclesiastical pieces were made in this country from the sixteenth century. Those that were produced tend to be of a different nature, having personal, secular connotations, like the fine chalice veil in the Burrell Collection which is embroidered with the royal arms and an inscription in silk and metal threads.

Distinguished artists were also employed for making non-religious garments. In 1493 the Duchess of Milan, Beatrice d'Este Sforza, wrote in a letter that she was having dresses embroidered in silk, designed by Leonardo da Vinci.

English needlework had become more domestic in character and more high quality work was done by amateurs, rather than by professionals exclusively. In fact, most of the best pieces surviving from the post mediaeval period onwards are of a secular nature, largely made at home or for private houses.

Holinshed, in his *Chronicles,* 1577, mentions that needlework was amongst the chief accomplishments of the women of Elizabeth I's court. This had been the case for some time, for it was considered an essential part of a noble lady's education. It was a privileged pastime, not available to all, since the materials were still relatively expensive, especially metal threads; ordinary women were limited to doing utility sewing. Many ladies of high birth did however enjoy needlework. The ladies would carry their embroidery around with them and do it anywhere, in or out of doors. The designs were usually drawn out by a man employed for the purpose, and he would often have an eminent place in the household. Catherine of Aragon is said to have had a skein of embroidery silk around her neck when she faced Cardinal Wolsey and Campeggio to answer Henry VIII's accusations. Frederico di Vinciolo's influential pattern book *Singulaires et Nouveaux Pourtraits pour les Ouvrages de Lingerie* enjoyed great popularity from 1587, with ten editions.

As a result of Renaissance exploration and trade a new class of successful merchants arose. They emulated the nobility, boasting their riches in a display of luxuries, which included exotic imports from distant countries, extravagant clothes and, in their houses, rich textiles, furnishings and needlework. Renaissance textiles, as indeed all design, tended to be formally symmetrical, open and linear, in embroidery, appliqué and cordwork. As in carpets, Islamic in origin, patterns were non-figurative and were 'Mooresque' or 'arabesque'.

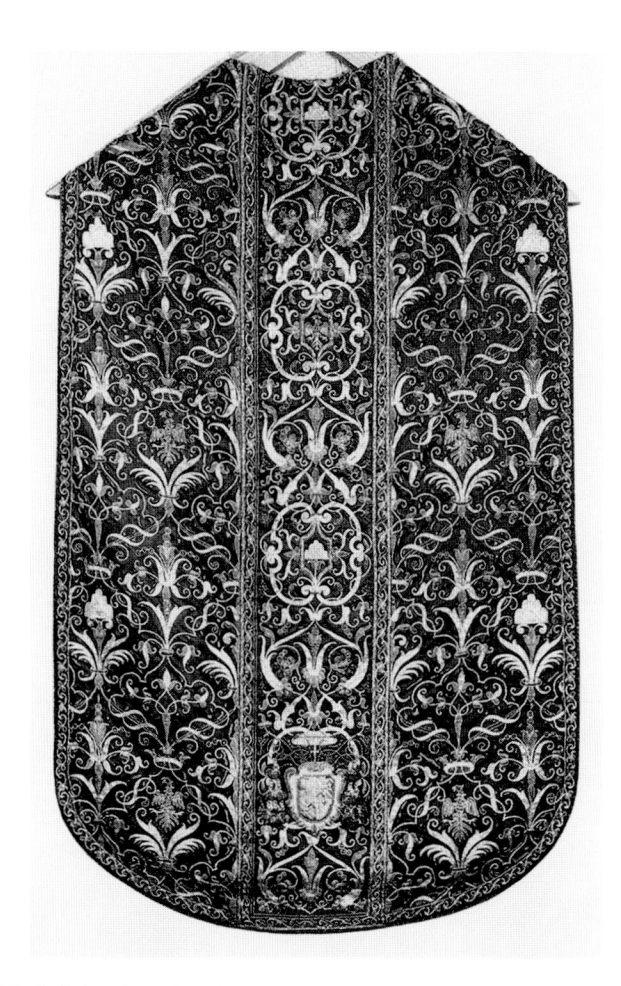

60. An Italian chasuble, of Bishop Madruzzo of Trento, typifies Renaissance formal ornament without obvious religious iconography, c.1600-29.

The Art of Embroidery

61. This detail of a 16th century bed head, probably French, combines curious grotesques and strapwork, both features of Renaissance decoration in Northern Europe.

Early sixteenth century inventories show how secular embroideries and textiles were increasingly fashionable in the greater houses. Hangings for walls and beds, valances, cushions and table carpets are mentioned frequently. One set of silk hangings, for example, were of green say 'embroidered with branches of roses, with wreaths set as pillars, yellow and blue' as listed in the inventory of the Earl of Rutland's house at Holywell in 1529. Such pieces were often worked by amateurs – the ladies of the household. Linen canvas embroidery in tent stitch was by now the most used technique for household furnishings. On some projects the ladies worked together contributing pieces which were joined or applied to form a whole. Many of the most precious Tudor and Elizabethan embroideries have not survived because they have perished, been eaten by moth, been worn out or been raided for their component materials; what has come down to us must be regarded as pitiful remnants, however glorious they seem.

The needlework of Tudor England is curiously divided in its apparent origins of style. In some respects it is clearly related to the Renaissance spirit and is closely associated with Italian, Spanish and Flemish ideas. But in other respects it seems consciously independent of the continent of Europe, maintaining an individual character. Early Tudor portraits, such as those of Henry VIII (Plate 58) show costumes rich with Eastern opulence; the arabesque patterns are similar to those on garments worn at the Sultan of Turkey's court. Renaissance concepts of design partly grew out of interest in oriental culture alongside the classicism and liberal humanism of the times. The prominence of linear forms, often enlivened by remnants of animal motifs, is at the heart of much pattern making. These arabesques were cleverly drawn in symmetrical strapwork, with a combination of flat bas-relief patterns in bands, lines and arcs interlaced over and under each other. Some aspects of the decoration are attributed to the Moors, coming to England through Spain, and others to Damascus as a by-product of the trading which had been established there. 'Moryshe and Damashin' patterns in fabrics and similar forms in other artefacts influenced embroiderers greatly. Geometric shapes had been a feature of mediaeval designs but now more complex forms were developed in all fields including armour, plasterwork, woodwork, pargeting, metalwork, the tooling on leather bookbindings and the lay-out of garden parterres. Strapwork knots in an interlaced link pattern, an ancient and world-wide symbol, having been carved on

The Post-Mediaeval Period

prehistoric stone crosses in Ireland for example, and still engraved on modern African silver and brasswork, appeared in oriental and Tudor arts.[1] Plain examples were carefully recorded in the earliest surviving English sampler made by Jane Bostocke in 1598 (Plate 72). Similar designs are common to pattern and instruction books written for both gardening and needlework. The heavier forms of arabesques, so familiar in late Tudor and Jacobean woodwork, are sometimes aptly referred to as armorial, casque and scrollwork.

Animal head terminals on strapwork were another feature of arabesques, and these were carried to a further dimension in 'grotesques'. Based respectively on Islamic and Roman 'antique' decoration and derived in name from cave-like grottoes because they were found underground and excavated, they have strange combinations of linear and animal forms meticulously composed in a light, whimsical vein. They are crowded with flowers, masks, terms and other semi-human forms, and sometimes with architectural details. Raphael was fascinated by them and inspired others by using them in his decorations of the Vatican.

English versions of these formalised patterns were, however, much less complex than the lavish Renaissance decoration carried out by French nobles in their châteaux. Francis I, Henri II, his queen, Catherine de Medici, and mistress, Diane de Poitiers, all had fabulously picturesque castles. Fontainebleau itself was transformed into a glorious palace. Mary Queen of Scots, who spent most of her childhood at the French court, would have been familiar with these places and must have admired the needlework decorations, supplied mostly by professional workshops. These will have included the arabesque type strapwork (largely of appliqué) that was later developed by Jean Bérain and his son in the seventeenth and eighteenth centuries.

A number of late sixteenth century continental valances and panels are

62. Part of a 16th century Italian valance with silk embroidered arabesques with birds, insects, classical and exotic humans, and cornucopias.

69

embroidered with fantastic ornamental grotesques that include humans, semi-humans, animals, birds, flowers, objects and many decorative elements from architectural motifs to panels of text. Strapwork, sometimes as frames containing vignettes, often has a solid appearance, curling and three dimensional as if of thick leather. Examples of this lively embroidery are now rare, being much more delicate than canvas work, but may be seen at Waddesdon Manor, Buckinghamshire, the Victoria and Albert Museum and the Metropolitan Museum, New York.[2] The last museum also has one from the same set as the example illustrated here, probably Italian, c.1580 (Plate 62).

There were still some professional embroiderers in London but their trade had become more specialised and was centred on ceremonial occasions. They undertook preparations for tournaments and provided horse trappings and barge decorations for important events. Much of their work was heraldic; a number of fine seal bags or purses survive, heavily and impressively decorated with the royal arms and cherubs' heads in raised silver thread work. Other commissions included bed valances, table carpets, livery company crowns, bookbindings, gloves and sweet-bags. The last two items especially were amongst traditional gifts and feature several times in lists of presents given to Elizabeth I at the New Year.

The Broderers' Company, a revered institution formed to protect professionals, became somewhat weakened following the Reformation. It grew back to strength, however, and was incorporated under a Royal Charter in 1561. Sadly, its records were lost in the Great Fire in 1666 but it is known that one of its chief duties was to scrutinise all professional work and destroy unfit pieces. The Company also had its own workshops which carried out official and semi-official commissions for pageants, masques, and livery companies. A number of palls, referred to in the previous chapter, still survive, and also Masters' and Wardens' crowns of the Carpenters', Girdlers', Broderers', and Parish Clerks' Companies. The last has a pair dated 1601 (Plate 59).

In addition to these responsibilities, it should be remembered that professional embroiderers played an important role in teaching, advising and designing for amateurs all over the country, in England and in Scotland. They travelled widely, preparing and drawing out canvases for amateur needleworkers, frequently assisting in matters akin in design but remote in technique from needlework. Their instruction and guidance was invaluable but did not temper the freshness and originality of amateurs' ideas. On the contrary, many pieces are distinctly and often charmingly individualistic.

The favourite subjects worked in Tudor and Elizabethan needlework were flowers, either in sprig form or in continuous scrolling tendril form, country scenes, partly derived from the peasant pictures of Teniers, heraldry, early illustrations of Old Testament stories and tales from Ovid's *Metamorphoses*. Narrative subjects were depicted unashamedly in quaint sixteenth century terms. Pattern books, emblem books, allegories and symbols were also drawn upon and a comprehensive knowledge of idioms was the crux of many designs, as for example in the most famous needlework of the period, the Oxburgh hangings (Plate 84). No great changes occurred in the reign of James I, though there was more use of metal threads, spangles and a new emphasis on subjects worked in deep relief. An altar frontal from The Vyne, Hampshire in the Victoria and Albert Museum shows these bold qualities.

The Post-Mediaeval Period

FLOWERS

Flowers, herbs and plants in general, some of them newly introduced to this country, were of great fascination to sixteenth century ladies. They loved them for their beauty and scent, were curious about their medicinal potency, and were amused and charmed by innuendoes of symbolism. They were frequently portrayed in Tudor and Elizabethan decoration, and in literature are carefully placed in a balance of ornament and couched conceit. But they were beloved by needlewomen especially.

In France, Henry IV's embroiderer Pierre Vallet was an important figure in court circles. He advised on the botanical gardens in Paris and, with Jean Robin, was expected to provide embroiderers with specimen flowers to be used as patterns. These he published in a book of engravings, *Le Jardin du Roi Henri IV* (1608). In England there was also an intense interest in flowers. Women examined specimens in detail and attempted to record plants with scientific accuracy. The flowers they chose to portray were real ones, but they did not slavishly represent three dimensional groups with dull realism. Each flower or sprig was depicted in 'slip' form with a certain treasured formality. Slips were originally derived from gardener's cuttings – ideal as motifs for small tent stitch pieces – to be applied to a ground of velvet. Later they were copied from printed herbals. An alternative was to portray real flowers, joined in continuous scrolling patterns on costumes and pillow covers, sometimes in monochrome 'blackwork'. This age-old classical and oriental device was already familiar in the border decorations of illuminated manuscripts with running tendrils of floral patterns coiling and filling the space evenly.

The love of plants and recording their charms culminated in the seventeenth century Dutch floral paintings which gave needleworkers new compositional ideas, but the plain elegant woodcuts that began the floral tradition were particularly appropriate for transposition into needlework. Subject and medium were perfectly suited.

Printing had been invented in the mid-fifteenth century in Gutenberg and soon affected amateur needlework through a greatly increased circulation of designs. By 1550 several pattern books for needlework were available throughout Europe – published in Augsburg, Cologne and Antwerp. Schonsperger's *Ein Neu Modelbuch*, 1524, was the earliest. Others followed from France and Italy. In London in 1548 Thomas Geminus published *Morysse and Damashin renewed and increased Very profitable for Goldsmythes and Embroderers*. A sole copy

63. A red satin cushion of about 1600 is decorated with naturalistic flowers and fruit within heart-shaped tendrils, all in metal threads. 20¼in. x 19in. (51.5cm x 48.5cm).

72

of this is preserved in Munster. But books of less direct relevance such as herbals and bestiaries also provided considerable inspiration for embroiderers. Lace pattern books suggested certain patterns and woodcut block illustrations in various works instigated others. The chief sources, however, began with German woodcuts in *Furm und Modelbuchlein* (1523), while a later book, Johann Sibmacher's *Schön neues Modelbuch*, published in Nuremberg in 1597 had a wide influence for at least a hundred years. In England, Conrad Gesner's *Catalogues Plantarum*, the first principal herbal, was published in 1524 and was the basis of such works as John Gerard's very popular *Herbal and General History of Plants*, originally printed in 1597 and continuously produced up to 1636. Thomas Johnson's expanded edition of this book (1633) had 2,677 woodcuts. William Morris knew it well and was influenced by it. Gardening and embroidery were always acknowledged to be closely associated in spirit, and they have remained so.

Amongst other early flower studies was *La Clef des Champs* by a Huguenot, Jacques Le Moyne de Morgues (London 1586). The dedication indicated that it was intended for all sorts of craftsmen, including embroiderers and tapestry weavers. Some of the illustrations in surviving copies indicate that they were pricked out with pins, for pouncing, a method of tracing a pattern. Wild and garden flowers were included as well as animals, birds and fruit. Like many illustrated books, it showed a complete disregard for relationships of scale between plants, animals and insects; woodblocks from different sources were juxtaposed with childlike abandon. This scrap book feature was copied in needlework renderings. Crispin de Passe's *A Garden of Flowers* (1615) was especially useful as a pattern book, the engravings having bold outlines and a formal elegance suited to embroidery, instead of being entirely naturalistic. Flowers and fruits are shown in little clumps, often on a hillock, and with small animals around the bases. Volumes such as *Icones Stirpium* by Matthias de l'Obel, Antwerp 1591, would have inspired designs. De l'Obel was born in Lille and died in Highgate having superintended Lord Zouche's botanical garden in Hackney and having been King's Botanist to James I.[3]

Costume offered wonderful opportunities for fine needlework and was well suited to floral patterns and combinations of small flower portraits. In some respects laborious and magnificent embroidery of this kind replaced the efforts that would earlier have been directed towards church vestments and the method of applying motifs was carried on in a secular context. Such decoration was highly fashionable until the middle of the seventeenth century when Caroline ladies turned to the colours, sheen, textures and rustle of plain silks. Queen Elizabeth's wardrobe inventory of 1600 listed, for example, a gown of: 'black satten, embroidered all over with roses and pauncies, and a border of oaken leaves, roses and pauncies, of Venice golde, silver and silke'. Others were decorated with: 'pomegranatts, roses, honisocles, and acornes'.

Roses were especial favourites, as in every period since. Their intriguing origin in Persia, their relationship with the common briar, their combination of sweet scents and difficult thorny stems, are each aspects of their alluring charm. For Tudor ladies, white and red roses were also badges of the now united houses of York and Lancaster. The white musk rose with its rambling tendrils was particularly adaptable to pattern making. Carnations, known as gilliflowers, were another favourite and continued to be used in more or less stylised forms well into the eighteenth century, when all flowers were again treated naturalistically. Pansies, referred to by Chaucer and Shakespeare as 'love in

64. A number of motifs, clearly derived from woodcut illustrations, are shown together on a panel of c.1600 at Traquair House.

The Art of Embroidery

idleness', were very much a hallmark of the sixteenth century, and frequently carried innuendoes of love. Irises, or fleurs-de-lis, peonies, of Chinese origin, and foxgloves, created by Juno when Jupiter threw down her thimble, were amongst other favourites. Also seen were primroses, daffodils, cornflowers, lilies, snowdrops, violets, bluebells, daisies, peascods and marigolds. Honeysuckle is particularly decorative for its unusually shaped flower (the classical palmette) and the crawling nature of its growth led to pattern-making and formalised borders. Trees and ferns were depicted but not as often as herbs and fruit. Borage, rue, rosemary, lavender, thyme and germander were delineated in Thomas Tusser's *A Hundreth good points of Husbandrie* first printed in 1561, and these became part of the grammar of sewing, having long been important domestic herbs. A less frequently portrayed newcomer to England was the potato plant, brought from Peru. Raspberries were occasionally embroidered, and strawberries often. Desdemona's problematical handkerchief in Othello was 'spotted with strawberries'[4] – these were the wild variety, a symbol of purity. They were brought from the woods, unspoiled by less natural and coarser vegetables grown in the garden. Grapes, in bunches, sometimes alternating with flowers, formed an ancient bacchanalian pattern and with their vines were another favourite. The Madonna lily is linked with purity and is a symbol of the Annunciation while the columbine (aquilegia), having the white wings of a dove, represented the Holy Spirit. The pomegranate is an example of a Christian adaptation from classical mythology with pagan associations of fertility. On ecclesiastical vestments it conveyed the idea of the universal church with many seeds in one fruit but it was also the Greek symbol of Persephone, daughter of Demeter, goddess of agriculture. Adopted through Ottoman textiles, it is seen more widely in French needlework than in English. Another universal plant is the lotus flower, the Buddhist symbol of purity, taken to China from India. More parochial however, is the thistle, which like the rose was emblematic, being used in reference to Scotland or Mary Queen of Scots. It is seen in two pieces at Hardwick Hall, probably cushion covers, worked by Mary, that depict thistles, roses and lilies (for Scotland, England and France) within a net of vine stalks, on a yellow background.

Insects and wild animals also occur frequently, either in tent stitch appliqué pieces 'powdered' over curtains and upholstery, or incorporated in the continuous designs typical of costume. Creatures were derived from natural history books and pattern books such as Conrad Gesner's *Historia Animalium*, 1560. There was also a great fascination for emblems and personal *impressas*, symbols adopted as semi-emblematic badges. Both allusive and illusive, they were part of the colourful language of allegory that was enjoyed for veiled meanings. The spirit of this acrobatic imagery culminated in the metaphysical poems of John Donne, in which he contrived 'conceits' and 'wit' in much the same manner as was sensed by ingenious amateur needleworkers. The best embroideresses combined narrative elements, such as Aesop's *Fables,* with devices, mottoes, proverbs, emblems and symbols; indeed the language of Shakespeare, Spenser and Donne is felt throughout their work. Emblem books that were widely influential were Claude Paradin's *Devises Heroiques* (1577, English edition 1591) and Geoffrey Whitney's *A Choice of Emblemes* (1586). These are just two of some thousand emblem books of the sixteenth and seventeenth centuries produced by six hundred authors, delineating many thousands of individual emblems.

COSTUME EMBROIDERY

Portraits of Queen Elizabeth I in the National Portrait Gallery, at Hardwick Hall and Hatfield House show her dressed in magnificently embroidered costumes. Each was a kind of political poster, designed to impress and convey qualities of the Queen's official character. It is possible that some of these semi-political outfits were painted and furthermore it is probable that others shown in pictures never actually existed in any form. Some, however, were certainly embroidered. The Queen's dresses are respectively decorated with foliate arabesques in gold thread, flower slips, a combination of flowers, sea creatures and birds, and a collection of emblems. The last

65. *Queen Elizabeth I, c.1585-90, a panel painting attributed to John Bettes the Younger.*

of these dresses, in the 'rainbow' portrait at Hatfield, was probably conceived as an idealised, symbolic costume which never existed, but the eyes, ears, serpent and rainbow represented vigilance and sympathy, and these emblems are typical, though extreme examples, of the thinking behind embroidered messages. Symbols such as a rainbow for peace, a compass for constancy and a garland or olive branch for victory were immediately recognisable, while others were tentatively suggestive of equivocal characteristics. Another portrait of the Queen, in the garden of Wanstead, 1578 (Wellbeck), attributed to Marcus Gheeraerdts the younger, shows a dress with sprigs of roses and a great cloak. Elizabeth's portrait painters were required to paint her in flattering terms for propaganda purposes, but on other occasions artists portrayed the wonder of their sitter's costumes with great accuracy. A portrait of Margaret Laton displayed alongside her bodice in the Victoria and Albert Museum is stunning testimony to the true representation that was customary (see page 112, Plates 97 and 98). Fine coifs were made to similar designs but are seldom shown in the paintings, unlike bodices. The decoration consists of stems in plaited braid stitch with flowers and leaves in a variety of detached buttonhole fillings in which the needle only enters the fabric at the beginning and the end of each row. This was an English speciality derived from needlepoint lace and subsequently also used in later seventeenth century stumpwork and embroidered panels where leaves could be worked in free relief.

Tudor and Elizabethan portraits show magnificent stitchery which has never since been equalled on costume. Precision work, akin to the remarkable miniature painting of the period, and attention to detail contributed to a jewel-like style, displaying a superb, shimmering richness. Intricate mixtures of patterns were embroidered on every available space, frequently highlighted with jewels. Even underwear was finely embroidered and the overall costume effect was augmented by accessories, including lace ruffs, feathers in hats, rosettes on shoes, and often a fine lawn or gauze veil worn over embroidered garments. Monarchs naturally had to outshine their courtiers. In 1517 it was recorded that almost 450 ounces of fine gold and 850 pearls were removed from the robes of Henry VIII for re-use. When Elizabeth I died at the age of seventy she left over a thousand dresses heavy with bullion, jewels and gimps.[5] Mary Queen of Scots' inventories are full of interesting detailed lists of her embroidered clothing such as: *Une robbe de satin bleu faicte a borletz tout couverte de broderye en fason de rosse et feullages faictz dargent, et le rest cordonne dor bordee dung passement dor.*[6] This was almost certainly professional work. Most amateur embroidery was done on smaller articles of which there was a great variety. This included jackets, waistcoats, coifs, bonnets, men's (undress) caps, hoods, sleeves, stomachers, partlets, gloves, scarves and handkerchiefs as well as smaller carried items like sweet-bags and bookbindings. Reticella and needlepoint lace collars, cuffs and fringes provided a contrast to colour, though no less elaborate.

BLACKWORK

Lighter garments were embroidered neatly with blackwork, otherwise known as Spanish work. This monochrome needlework, often but not always done in black, was once thought to have been introduced to England by Catherine of Aragon but, in

66. Mary Cornwallis, Countess of Bath, by George Gower, c.1575. The bold flower and leaf design on her sleeve and the strapwork on her skirt represent contrasting types of blackwork.

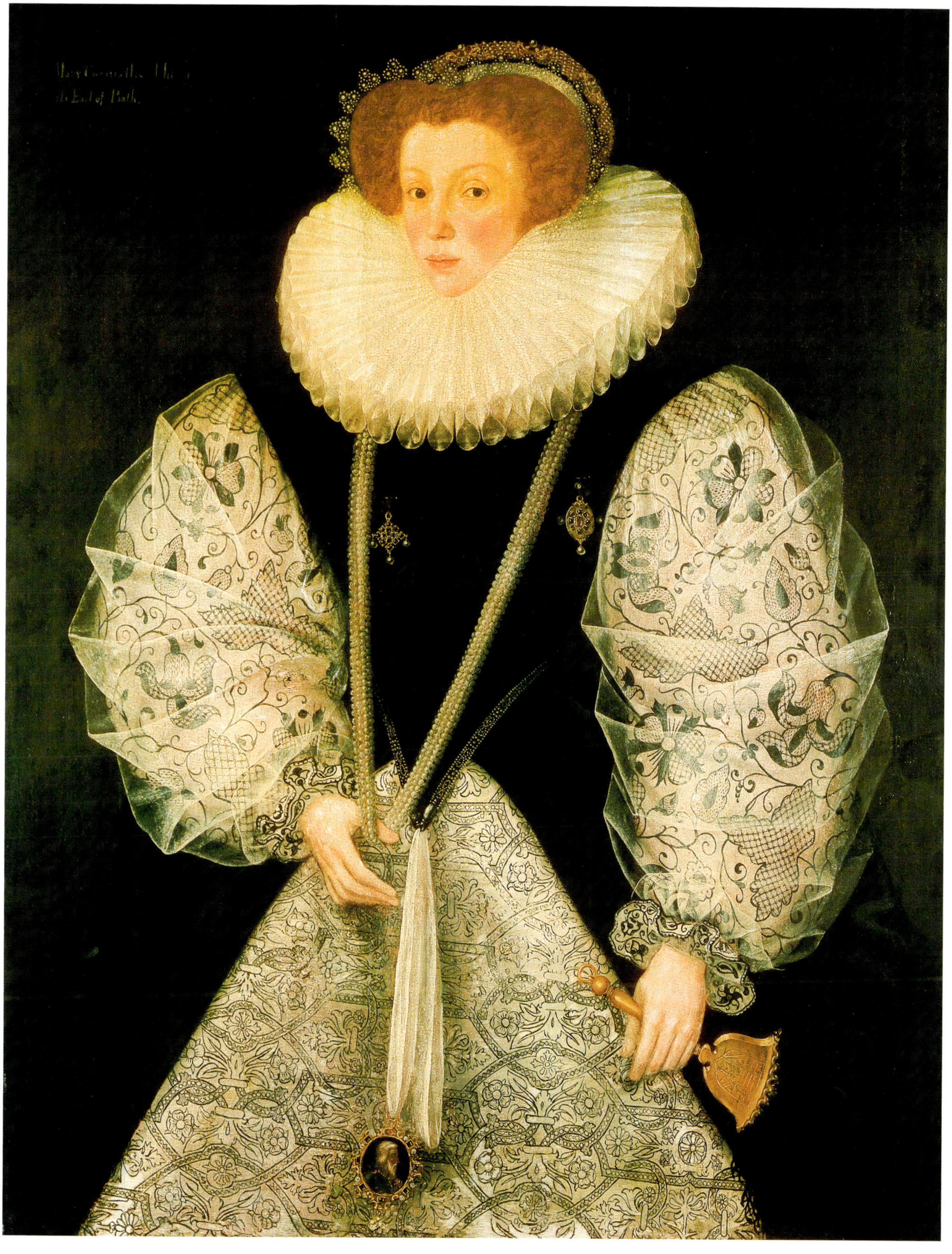

The Art of Embroidery

67. Thomas Nevile, Master of Trinity College, Cambridge wore a silk embroidered cap for his portrait.

fact, the technique was known here before her arrival.[7] Its Moorish qualities, ultimately Persian in origin, are clear in its strapwork designs but these are also contrasted with curvilinear vine tendrils on both costume and household furnishings, such as pillow covers. A portrait by Gower of Mary Cornwallis (Plate 66) shows magnificent blackwork of both forms[8] and one of Elizabeth I at Hever Castle, Kent, shows that even this light work was sometimes enriched with jewels.

Blackwork is equally associated with Henry VIII and his children. Holbein's portraits of them have led to the characteristic double-running stitch technique being termed Holbein stitch. Ruffs and cuffs called for very tidy workmanship with equal neatness on both sides of the material since both sides of the wavy frills showed. Simpler designs were worked on less prominent garments. An example is Dorothy Wadham's shirt which is at the Oxford college founded in her name. In this case narrow diagonal strips are embroidered with vine leaves in purple thread, an unusual colour. Red was sometimes used (as on a woman's coif and a jacket, both in the Victoria and Albert Museum), also blue, but black was the most frequent, perhaps reflecting the printer's ink of woodcut illustrations. A sense of shading was achieved by the use of delicate speckling stitches, sometimes very minute and imitating engraving. Patterns were occasionally geometric, even with such motifs as a repeated starfish, and often the embroidery was highlighted with gold or silver thread and interspersed with metal spangles (sequins). Always incorporating real flowers and fruit, scrolling patterns were worked on caps, purses and pillow covers (known then as pillow beres).

Caps or 'coifs' had been worn throughout the Middle Ages but were elaborately embroidered in the sixteenth and early seventeenth centuries (Plate 68). Elizabethan ones had a turned up brim around them, others were close-fitting and simple in shape. They were not for night wear, but were used on semi-formal occasions when a wig was not worn and were sometimes proudly worn by distinguished men in their portraits. At Audley End, Essex and Trinity College, Cambridge there are portraits of Thomas Nevile wearing a splendid cap. Sir Walter Raleigh purportedly wore one under his hat on going to the scaffold and another, said to have been worn by Charles I at his execution (supported by a print in the British Museum), was sold at Christie's in 1983. Women's coifs were hood-shaped and were sometimes accompanied by a 'forehead cloth', similarly embroidered, and occasionally worn at the same time. These were also worn on domestic occasions such as bed receptions and might be of blackwork, perhaps enriched with silver or gold thread, or alternatively of colourful silks. They were sometimes scented with the perfumes of various flowers, particularly lavender, which was believed to have medicinal qualities. William Turner wrote in his *Newe Herball* (1551) of spikes of lavender: 'quilted in a cap and dayly worne they are

The Post-Mediaeval Period

good for all diseases of the head that do come of a cold cause and they comfort the braine very well'.

A further curiosity of blackwork embroidery is a reported linen cloth edged with silver lace which was used as a toothbrush: 'From Mistress Twist, the Court Laundress; Four tooth cloths of Holland, wrought with black work and edged with bone lace of silver and black silk…'.

On larger blackwork pieces the infilling patterns, on vine leaves for example, were often highly varied, with contrasting textures reminiscent of, and probably influenced by, needlepoint lace. This feature and the flowing tendril forms of blackwork developed in the seventeenth century into the great expanded crewelwork designs that became so fashionable and were so uniquely English. Simultaneous with the fashion for blackwork and outliving it was the practice of working similar designs much more richly with brighter materials, of the type already referred to in connec-

68. This gentleman's cap of about 1620 would have been worn in smart informal circumstances and was probably the work of his wife or a daughter.

The Art of Embroidery

69. A blackwork coif or headdress (opened out) with a leaf and berry design and enriched with gilt spangles. Late 16th century.

tion with Margaret Laton's bodice. Coiling stems might be worked in gold, linking and enclosing flowers, insects and creatures, in brightly coloured silks, while backgrounds were 'powdered' with jewels, pearls and spangles. Gloves of this nature were a status symbol, and were often official gifts. They were usually made professionally and provided a regular trade for a number of craftsmen, culminating in 1638 in the formation of the Glovers' Company under Royal Charter. Elizabethan gloves were of thin tight-fitting leather, doeskin or kid, with gauntlets of embroidered silk and scallop-shaped edges fringed with gold lace. They were often scented. In earlier times a symbol of combat challenge, they were now given formally in presentation ceremonies as a mark of honour, or simply as presents. Sir Thomas More, Chancellor to Henry VIII, was given a pair filled with angels (coins) as a New Year's gift by an admiring and grateful plaintiff, and Queen Elizabeth I was often the recipient of gloves, as on the occasion of her visit to Cambridge University in 1578:

> *Also with the book the said Vice-chancellor presented a paire of gloves, perfumed and garnished with embroiderie and goldsmithe's wourke, price 60s…In taking the book and gloves, it fortuned that the paper in which the gloves were folded to open; and hir Majestie behoulding the beautie of the said gloves, as in great admiration, and in token of hir thankfull acceptation of the same, held up one in hir hands. And when the Oracon was ended, she rendryed, and gave most heartie thanks, promiseing to be mindful of the Universitie.*

A pair of gloves in the Ashmolean Museum, Oxford were reputedly left behind to mark the Queen's visit to that University in 1566.

The Post–Mediaeval Period

The Elizabethan custom of giving New Year's gifts, especially to the sovereign, must have stimulated much needlework. It was known that the Queen was fond of it and many embroidered items were amongst the presents that were traditional from all of position and rank, in church and state. Many of the gifts were subsequently given away as return presents; in other cases pieces of silver gilt were given. Gifts to Elizabeth included money, jewels and clothes. Frequently small purses otherwise known as sweet-bags were given. Measuring about 4in. x 3in. (10cm x 7.6cm), they were finely embroidered with metal and silk threads, having drawstrings and tassels of silk. In 1561, the Earl of Derby gave the Queen a New Year gift of twenty pounds 'in a purse of cypresse satten, embrawdered with gold, in demy sovereynys'. Books in embroidered bindings and scarves were among other gifts that Elizabeth I received. She herself embroidered a scarf which she sent to Henry IV of France. A little later, pairs of knives appear to have been gifts, in needlework sheathes. Some in the Victoria and Albert Museum include a set with cord and tassels containing two amber, steel and damascened knives, c.1610.

Below. 70. Princess Elizabeth, later Queen Elizabeth I, worked this bookbinding for her stepmother Catherine Parr in 1554, with a silver knot pattern and pansies.

71. A late 16th century sampler by Susan Nebabri includes the royal arms, bands in metal thread and many Italianate whitework patterns.

BOOKBINDINGS

Tudor and Stuart bookbindings were a fascinating though short-lived phenomenon. A good many have survived so they must have been numerous. They are mostly small, formal in design, often the work of professionals and with one exception the embroidery bears no reference to the actual book inside. Most were worked on crimson velvet though numerous cases of other colours and materials are known. The royal monograms H, JR and ER with insignia such as Tudor roses and coats of arms are a frequent form of decoration, beautifully laid out and executed, sometimes with seed pearls in addition to metal threads. A very beautiful example in this category, in the Bodleian Library, Oxford, is a Bible which the printer Christopher Barker had bound in an embroidered binding in 1583 for presentation to Elizabeth I. Metal threads and seed pearls form a delightful composition of Tudor roses linked by stylised stems, leaves and birds. Another binding in the same library containing the epistles of St Paul is said to have been worked by the Queen herself, when princess, and been given by her to her stepmother Catherine Parr, in 1544. Silver threads are worked in this case on a blue silk

The Art of Embroidery

background. A book printed in the same year, Petrarch's *Opere Volgari,* was given an embroidered binding by Catherine Parr herself. She worked her own complex coat of arms on linen and applied this to purple velvet. It was no doubt a rare work for her since she is alleged to have stated: 'My hands are ordained to touch crowns and sceptres, not needles and spindles'. A Psalter presented to Queen Mary in 1553, the year in which she became Queen, and now in the British Museum, is decorated with a large flower on each side, reminiscent of ecclesiastical needlework.

Archbishop Parker's *De Antiquitate Britannicae Ecclesiae* (1572) was the first privately printed book in England and a presentation copy was given to Elizabeth I, with an embroidered binding. This has the exceptional feature of alluding in punning fashion to the author in that it depicts a park fence with trees and deer within, on green velvet. Heraldic devices were often used to decorate books: the embroidered binding of a small volume in the Victoria and Albert Museum of c.1598 was made for Lord Henry Norreys and his wife Margaret. While the spine is decorated with flowers in tent stitch the front and back have the arms of husband and wife on a gold thread ground, with flowers.

Bookbindings too, were often scented, perhaps partly to disguise a smell of glue. But when Elizabeth visited Cambridge the Vice-Chancellor was particularly warned that the New Testament bound in red velvet embroidered with the Queen's arms should have no 'savour or spike' (i.e. lavender). The records have not disclosed why.

SAMPLERS

There is evidence in records and inventories to show that samplers were worked extensively in the sixteenth century. They were apparently collected for reference purposes: an inventory of Joan the Mad, Queen of Spain, dated 1509, lists as many as fifty, worked in silk and gold thread.

The sampler takes its name from the French *essamplaire* and Latin *exemplarium* meaning example, and consisted of a small length of cloth on which were recorded examples of stitches, border patterns and motifs (see Plate 110, page 125). Originally samplers were limited to the specific function of being a kind of notebook which was always at hand, embroidered with snippets of model techniques and designs for adapting to costume decoration. These were jotted down at random, usually by adults, but by the seventeenth century they began to be regarded as exercises in mastering techniques and designs for young children, in addition to being private collections for continuous reference. In the eighteenth century they were looked upon as achievements in themselves to be admired as diminutive works of art. Instead of being kept rolled up in the sewing box, they were framed and hung on parlour walls.

Samplers are mentioned several times in Elizabethan literature, notably by Skelton and Sir Philip Sidney, while Shakespeare indicates how girls were so involved in sewing them that they became useless in conversation:

Fair Philomel, she but lost her tongue,
And in a tedious Sampler sewed her mind[9]

ABCDEFGHIKLMNOPQRSTVWXY JANE ROSNICKI 1598
ALICE LEE WAS BORNE THE 23 OF NOVEMBER BE
ING TUESDAY IN THE AFTER NOONE 1596

The Art of Embroidery

72. Jane Bostocke's sampler of 1598 has a random collection of 'sample' patterns and lettering.

73. Penelope, flanked by Perseverance and Patience is shown in a large 16th century hanging at Hardwick Hall, made of appliqué using older fabrics, probably from vestments.

Barnaby Riche, in his story of *Of Phylotus and Emilia* (1581), relates how Emilia will live in comfortably rich circumstances when married and will go about various activities including the use of her samplers in the way they were originally intended:

> *Now, when she had dined, then she might seke out her examplers, and to persue which worke would doe beste in a ruffe, whiche in a gorget, whiche in a sleeve, which in a quaife, which in a caule, whiche in a handkercheef; what lace would doe beste to edge it, what seame, what stitche, what cutte, what garde: and to sitte her doune and take it for the little by little, and thus with her nedle to passe the after noone with devising of things for her owne wearynge.*

The earliest reference to an actual sampler in England is in an account book of Queen Elizabeth of York[10] of 1502 where there is an entry: 'an elne of linnyn cloth for a

The Post-Mediaeval Period

sampler for the Queene, viijd.' There are other references to samplers of both coloured threads and plain white cut and drawn work, but the first indicating the purpose of a sampler is in Edward VI's inventory of 1552 where there is a record of 'a sampler or set of patterns worked on Normandy canvas with green and black silks'.

A fine whitework Tudor sampler in the London Museum is in the traditional form of a long thin band worked with many rows of embroidery and lace patterns across the narrow width, including the royal arms. One row is worked in gold thread and another in silver; the use of coloured silks incorporated in such pieces is very rare (Plate 71).

Though no early ones have survived there must have been a practice too of making polychrome samplers in non-whitework techniques. These were, as already indicated, made in preparation for the embroidery of dresses; designs gradually grew to include arabesques, natural history motifs and emblems, in addition to a variety of border patterns and other motifs, as we shall see in the next chapter.

DOMESTIC FURNISHINGS

Renaissance liberalism and increased trading brought to the sixteenth century nobility a desire and taste for greater comfort and luxury. Fine materials had become more accessible and the emphasis of workmanship that had been directed to church use was now available for secular patronage. Professional embroiderers were employed to a considerable extent on the provision of furnishings for important houses. In England a great part, perhaps the larger part of the needlework done for domestic use, was

74. Actaeon was turned into a stag by Diana when he spied her bathing, the subject of a large 16th century cushion cover at Hardwick Hall.

The Art of Embroidery

carried out by the enthusiastic amateurs of the household. Bess of Hardwick's great new mansion, Hardwick Hall, for instance, was remarkable for its needlework furnishings, and remains so today; many of these appear to have been worked by Bess herself, her friends, companions and staff. She was undoubtedly guided by professional draughtsmen, but the actual sewing was also the much enjoyed and envied pursuit of the privileged ladies who had the time to do it. The Duchess of Beaufort, for example, in *Lives of the Norths,* says that she had 'divers gentlewomen commonly at work embroidering and fringe making, for all the beds of state were made and finished in the house'.

Amongst the quantities of textiles that became a feature of the greater houses and made them less draughty and more comfortable were, in addition to imported tapestries and oriental carpets, needlework and appliqué hangings for walls and for large four poster beds, and also table carpets, cushions, pillow covers and smaller items. Archetypal pictorial themes, already familiar in woven tapestries, were finely worked, often on a large scale. Margaret Swain has identified a number of engraved sources. Of both a decorative and also a moralistic nature, subjects included Bible stories, some derived from a book first published in Lyons in 1553, *Quadrins de la Bible* with verses by Claude Paradin and woodcuts by Bernard Salomon and published by Jean de Tournes. There was an English edition in the same year, *The true and lyvely historyke purtreatures of the Woll Bible,* and this was much copied for at least one hundred years. It was followed by Gerard de Jode's *Thesaurus Sacrarum Historiarum Veteris Testamenti* (1585), the fine engravings for which were sold both loose and bound together and

75. The border of the Bradford table carpet has a continuous landscape filled with lively scenes while the centre is of a formalised vine pattern. Early 17th century. Border 17in. (43cm) deep.

The Post–Mediaeval Period

76. Chatsworth, as it was in the late 16th century, with impressive glass windows, and bordered with Cavendish snakes, is depicted on a large cushion cover of the period.

were used as a source for many needlework designs. Of classical themes, Ovid's *Metamorphoses* with woodcuts by Bernard Salomon (1557) was also a popular source, with subjects such as Orpheus charming the animals with music, Mercury and Herse, Europa, Ganymede, Pyramus and Thisbe, Apollo and Marsyas, Narcissus, Apollo and Daphne, Atlanta, Leda and the Swan and the Rape of Helen. Versions of the Rape of Europa and the Death of Actaeon can be seen on large cushion covers at Hardwick Hall (Plate 74).

Two large petit point hangings at Scone Palace, Perth, are in a form more familiar in tapestry weaving, and must have been made by professionals. The larger one depicts Justice and Mercury embracing, within a complex border of symbolic figures, animals and putti. The gods are supported and crowned by putti and the landscape background incorporates religious and pastoral scenes. This subject is closely based on an engraving for Psalm 85 by Jean Wievix of Antwerp, of c. 1574.[11]

Needlework carpets were made in both England and in continental Europe with designs closely imitating Turkish knotted ones. Interlocking geometric strapwork formed the basis of the patterns and included a modification of the Eastern Cufic pattern.[12] These should not be confused with 'turkeywork' imitations of oriental carpets made by knotting, which enjoyed great popularity and were also used for upholstering furniture. A set of twelve cushions of this technique, ten of which are now in Norwich Cathedral, were made for the use of aldermen when using Blackfriars Hall in Norwich. Carpets of this type and needlework ones in an oriental style, and true oriental rugs were used simultaneously; indeed the 1601 inventory of Hardwick Hall shows that these, needlework carpets and more conventional European forms were interchangeable: 'a long table of white wood, a fayre Turkie carpet for the same table, an other fayre long carpet for it of silk needlework with gold frenge lyned with crimson taffetie sarcenet…'.

English needlework carpets were often elaborate and usually more Renaissance than Middle Eastern in design. They are so perfect in execution and design that it is

The Art of Embroidery

likely that many were made professionally. A good number of surviving examples have complex overall patterns lacking the naïvety which one would expect to see in amateur work. Two carpets in the Victoria and Albert Museum illustrative of this are the Gifford table carpet of about 1550, and the Bradford table carpet of a few decades later (Plate 75). Both are worked in silk tent stitch on canvas. The first has small geometric patterns overall with three large medallions, one containing the Gifford arms, while the others have vignettes showing a stag sitting under an oak tree. Each medallion is framed by a wreath of flowers. The Bradford carpet has a large main panel of trellis over which are tightly wound tendrils of vine, heavily laden with grapes, arranged in a stiff formalised pattern, in the Renaissance tradition. Around this there is a border depicting, in superb detail, scenes of rural life on hillocky ground. Hunters, shepherds, fishermen and gentry with many domestic and wild animals are seen with a variety of castles, farmsteads, mills and bridges. The whole piece is full of life and portrayed with wonderful workmanship. Since there are no signs of naïvety and as the pattern is repeated on both sides of the carpet, it seems the more certain that it was made by professional embroiderers. The repeat pattern parts of both carpets would have been exceedingly tedious for an amateur to have sewn.

Another entry in the Hardwick inventory notes a carpet: 'of nedleworke of the story of David & Saul with a golde frenge and trymmed with blew taffetie sarcenet…'. This may have been of the densely crowded courtly style supposedly introduced from France by Mary Queen of Scots. Close to tapestry in design, this type of needlework is seen on bed valances, table carpets and cushions. Large figures in classical and religious scenes are portrayed either in archaic dress or in the full courtly costume of sixteenth century France. Another carpet in the Victoria and Albert Museum, of this style, shows an extraordinary group of courtiers playing out the story of Lucretia's Banquet (Plate 83). Around them are small sections containing fruit trees, a unicorn, birds, dogs and other animals, within broad strapwork divisions. Curious Tudor heads in the four corners support plumes of feathers, an 'Indian' device, derived from Bérain. Several other similar versions exist; some may have been made in France. Another

77. This pair of bed valances has pictorial panels bordered with delicate appliqué edged with cordwork. French, c.1580.

The Post-Mediaeval Period

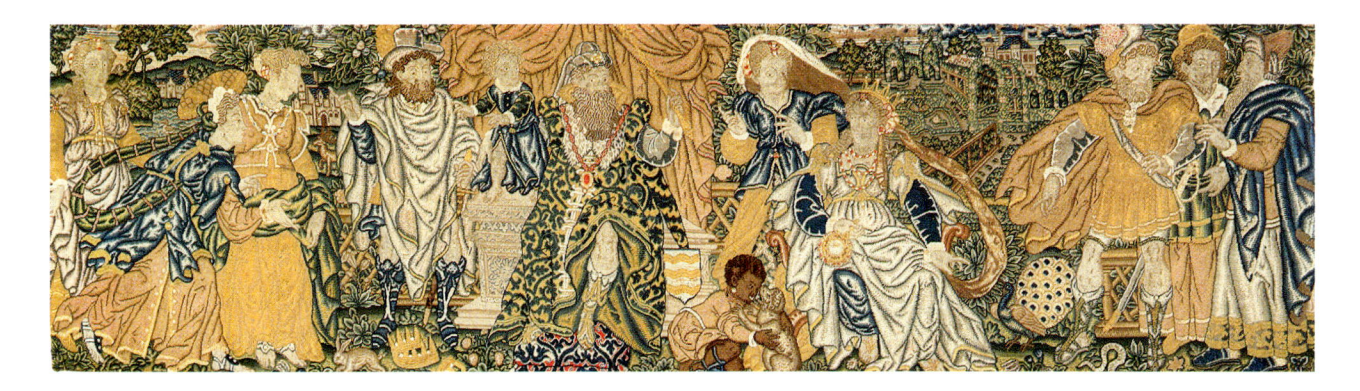

Elizabethan table carpet at the Bowes Museum is decorated with religious scenes, but apparently some carpets were purely of an ornamental design: Kenilworth Castle Inventory of 1588 lists: 'A carpet of needle worke of sundrye coloured silks, the ground sad green, with a border of roses, and sundrie posies about it, the ground of the borders orange tawnie, six yards long, 1¾ wide.'

Cushions were another symbol of prosperity and luxury. Listed as 'cushyns', 'cosshens', 'quitions, 'kussons' etc., they occur frequently in inventories and records. Though quite large in size, they were less ambitious exercises in needlework and more manageable. The underside was never worked but was 'lined' with plain material. They softened hard furniture and were scattered about the best rooms. It was a status symbol to have them; even 'a fair large cushion made of a cope or altar cloth'[13] was worth re-marking on. The Queen herself liked sitting on the floor and cushions were warmly welcomed as New Year's gifts. Mr Fynes gave her a long one of purple satin embroidered all over with gold and seed pearls, trimmed with matching fringing and huge tassels.

Professional embroiderers were commissioned to make for the Ironmongers' Company, in 1563, twelve cushions 'with the company's arms wrought in every of them' but, on the whole, surviving examples appear to be of amateur workmanship. They can be divided into roughly seven varieties. Firstly, there were large oblong tent stitch cushions depicting allegorical or mythological subjects, others with courtly-costumed figures, and others with armorial devices sometimes surrounded by stylised foliage. There are good examples of each kind at Hardwick Hall. There are also

Above. 78. Late 16th century bed valances of the French type often portrayed stories in contemporary dress, in this case courtly figures with gardens behind.

Below. 79. Another fine valance, perhaps Flemish, showing a moral tale with symbolic figures in a rich setting.

The Art of Embroidery

80. In the State Bedroom at Clandon the 17th century bed, large armchair and side chairs are all upholstered with colourful needlework in the French manner with a background of diaper stitches in white.

cushions of velvet decorated with applied embroidered slips, and cushions with raised embroidery including metal threads, depicting insects, animals and flowers. Finally, there were mourning cushions, as listed amongst the possessions of the Earl of Shrewsbury at Sheffield Castle, and a humbler sort of woollen cushion, examples of which are at Chastleton House, Oxfordshire. Occasionally topical events were embroidered. A panel, probably for a cushion, in the Lady Lever Art Gallery commemorates a safe deliverance following the Armada and the Gunpowder Plot. As a young girl, Elizabeth I made a cushion for her governess in silk and wool, in tent and cross stitches and in 1598 Paul Hentzner, a splendid recorder of his travels, noted seeing at Windsor Castle a cushion 'most curiously wrought by Elizabeth's own hand'.[14] A charming cushion in Cogenhoe Church, Northamptonshire, of about 1600, depicts flower slips within an interlacing knot pattern, with a red scale pattern border.

BEDS

Hentzner also mentions the magnificent state beds of Edward VI, Henry VII and Henry VIII at Windsor which he says were each 11ft. (3.35m) square and had brilliant gold and silver quilts. Mediaeval manuscripts and early paintings show how important fine beds were and what efforts were made to make them splendid; their frequent inclusion in illustrations indicates how much they were treasured. In the sixteenth century new energies were directed towards fine bed hangings, bed coverlets and pillow covers (then known as pillow beres).

There were three principal types of needlework bed hangings. No complete sets have survived since they were exposed to dirt and heavy use. Of the first, and principal kind, the valances, rather than curtains, have tended to last better due to the fact that they were non-moving parts and were not subjected to continual handling. These were of a type, similar in style to the carpets and cushions mentioned above, that display narrative scenes with courtly figures (Plates 78 and 79).

Originally thought to be French, and sometimes Flemish, some are equally likely to be professional work made in Scotland, in Perth or in Edinburgh. Of complex design and workmanship in tent stitch, they are visually busy, showing elaborately costumed peopled packed closely together. The costumes were believed to be French, so the tradition grew that the

The Post-Mediaeval Period

hangings were brought from France by Mary Queen of Scots. But since the styles appear to post-date Mary's arrival in Scotland, it is more likely that they were of Scottish manufacture of the 1580s and 1590s, perhaps in a French tradition. Three small French valances, in the Victoria and Albert Museum, of fine tent stitch, depict typically King Solomon and the Queen of Sheba while another set of about 1600 at Muncaster Castle, Cumbria show the story of Lot and the destruction of Sodom, in brightly preserved colours. The first of these valances shows couples merrymaking outside the gates of Sodom, Abraham and the Strangers with Abraham interceding for the righteous in the city and Lot bowing before two angels outside the city gate. In the second the angels pull Lot back inside his house; Lot remonstrates with the men of Sodom and offers them his daughters in marriage and the safety of his house. The third depicts the salvation of Lot and his family; Lot's wife turned to salt; the destruction of Sodom and the thanksgiving of Abraham. This is typical of hangings with stories. There are several valances in the Untermyer collection in the Metropolitan Museum, New York including a pair showing the story of Philomela, patron saint of needlework. She is shown working at her embroidery frame, depicting her tribulations. In the same collection are three valances from the Duke of Somerset based on engravings by Philip Galle after Hans Bol, Amsterdam, 1582. The same engravings were also used for silver plates, beakers and hunting knives.

A variant form, also in tent stitch, shows a number of framed scenes in strip cartoon form (Plate 77). One example is dated 1594. These valances were ideal for a narrative sequence of events often being based on engravings of classical stories or Bible illustrations, especially ones by Bernard Salomon and from *Antiquitates Judaicae* (Frankfurt 1580) and *Thesaurus Sacrarum* (Antwerp, 1585). These were curiously transposed into elaborate modern dress, depicted in detail. Additional incorporated scenes show interesting views of gardens or domestic furnishings. A well-preserved valance in the Art Institute of Chicago has biblical scenes divided by bright orange mannerist motifs. Sometimes the needlework shows personal insignia. A set of valances in the Burrell Collection has the arms and initials of Sir Colin Campbell of Glenorchy and his second wife Katherine Ruthven with scenes depicting the Temptation of Adam and the Expulsion from Paradise.

The second type of bed hanging is represented by a curtain in the Royal Scottish

81. A bed at Parham Park combines late 16th century French silk embroidery with later curtains and valances of flame stitch, also known as Florentine work.

The Art of Embroidery

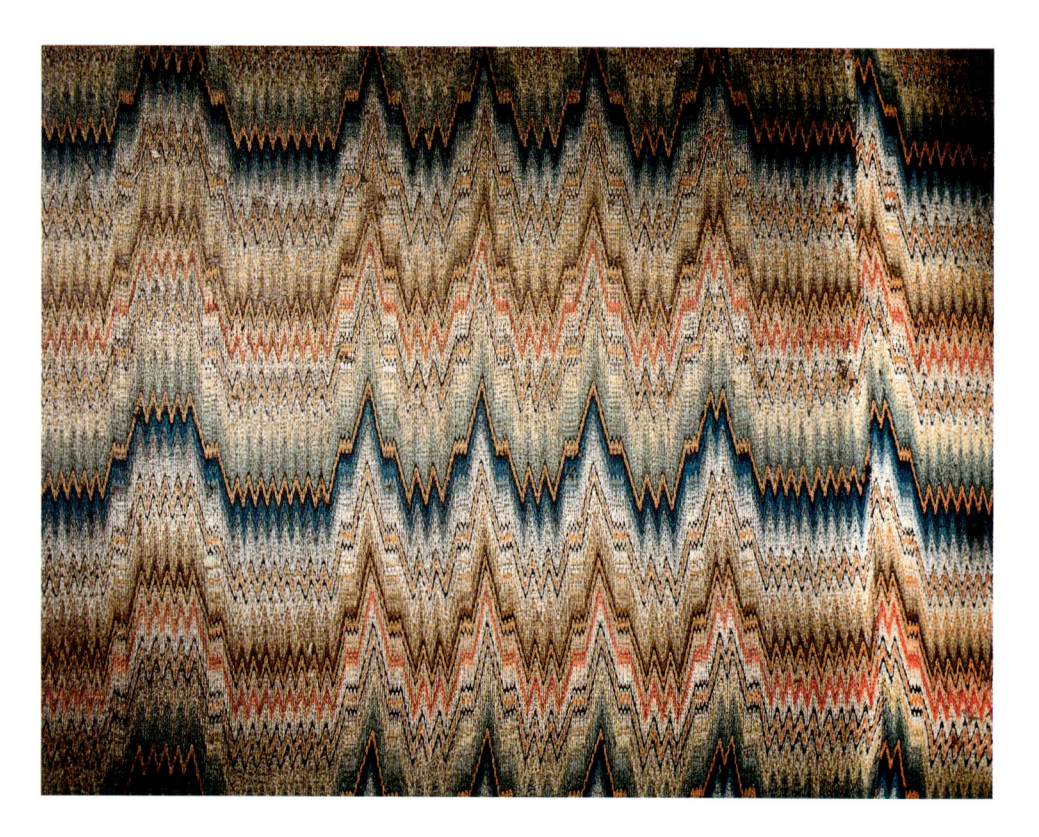

82. A 17th century wool wall-hanging at Chastleton House, worked in flame stitch.

Museum, Edinburgh, from Linlithgow Palace. This is of a red woollen material with appliqué large formalised plants, small heraldic lions and borders, each worked in yellow silks on black velvet. Such hangings are very striking, and survivals of the kind are rare.[15] There are similar fragments in the Victoria and Albert Museum.

The third type was more numerous. These were of amateur workmanship, closely related to the floral needlework discussed earlier. Based on woodcuts, the motifs applied on them included flowers especially, but also animals, heraldry and biblical subjects, each with naïve charm and spontaneity. Sometimes many hundreds of small pieces were attached to velvet curtains and to provide the motifs as many sewers as possible were gathered together. Bess of Hardwick wrote in 1585 that she had called upon all sorts of her staff to assist: 'grooms, women and some boys she kept wrought the most part of them'. A number of embroidered flower pieces and insects made by the Fitzwilliam family have survived at Milton, near Peterborough, being preserved in folios dated 1587-93, while at Glamis Castle, Angus, there are magnificent blue linen hangings applied in the late seventeenth century with slips worked about one hundred years earlier. Mary Queen of Scots is said to have been associated with the bed hangings of Scone Palace and Florentine ones at Parham Park, Sussex (Plate 81); more certain is that she worked with Bess at Hardwick on the magnificent needlework hangings of a slightly different nature now at Oxburgh Hall, Norfolk, to be discussed shortly.

Other beds had 'paned' hangings, that is curtains of joined panels of material, with contrasting colours or textures. They might be of plain silk, damask, velvet or needlework.

The Post-Mediaeval Period

Pillow covers were extensively made for use in bedrooms. They were often embroidered with blackwork vine or floral patterns on linen. Roy Strong tells us that at night-time Elizabeth I was undressed by her ladies and helped to bed

> *in her nightdress of cambric wrought with black silk. When at last she placed herself between the sheets 'worked all over with sundry fowls, beasts, and worms in silks of diverse colours' she then laid her head on her pillow 'of fine cambricke, wrought all over with Venice gold and silk.'*

A further form of hanging was made of applied materials. These were used more for wall decoration than for beds, and perhaps for screening. They are well represented by a fascinating set of five at Hardwick, one of which is dated 1573. They were probably made by professionals on account of their large scale, these being 12ft. (3.66m) high. A wide variety of rich fabrics was used, including pieces of velvet damask and cloth of gold taken from old vestments. The hangings depict the Virtues and figures representing qualities and their opposite 'vices' such as Hope and Judas, Faith and Muhammed. The Virtues – Magnanimity and Prudence, Constancy and Piety, Fortitude and Justice, Chastity and Liberality – are depicted with the characters of Zenobia, Penelope, Cleopatra and Lucretia illustrating them. Personified sciences are

83. The central part of a late 16th century French hanging portrays Lucretia's Banquet in 'modern dress'.

93

94

also shown, under arches – Grammatica, Rhetorica, Arithmetique, Architecture, Perspective and Astrology (Plate 73).

MARY QUEEN OF SCOTS

Repeatedly buffeted during most of her life by political and religious dispute, and always weighed on a curious balance of admiration and threat in the eyes of her cousin Queen Elizabeth, Mary Stuart, Queen of Scots, was also a remarkable figure in the history of needlework. She became devoted to it in childhood and practised it up to the day of her execution, at the age of forty-four.

The daughter of James V of Scotland and Marie de Guise (also known as Mary of Lorraine), Mary was born in 1542 and on the death of her father only six days later became Queen of Scots. At the age of six years, she was sent to France where she was brought up in the court of the French King, Henry II, and was pronounced Queen of England by the Catholic world which considered Elizabeth illegitimate. At sixteen she was married to the Dauphin Francis, and in the following year they became King and Queen of France. Following Francis' death eighteen months later, Mary returned to Scotland in 1561 and from that moment was at the centre of controversy, loved by many but suspected by others. Political plots and stormy relationships tried the loyalty of her nobles and caused her to be subjected to miserable periods of doubt and anti-Catholic feeling. Only six years after her return to Scotland she was taken prisoner and subsequently spent the last twenty years of her life in custody in Scotland and in England. But throughout her troubled reign, Mary took solace in her embroideries. Roy Strong was not exaggerating when he wrote charmingly of them as: 'silent letters to posterity in handwriting of rainbow silks and metallic thread telling of the misfortunes of a martyred Queen'.[16] They demonstrate her sadness in terms of allegory and symbol. It would have been too dangerous to express her thoughts in words. Needlework of this nature was on a bed that the Queen left to her son James VI of Scotland and James I of England, and in the Oxburgh hangings (Plate 84). The bed was decorated with *impressas,* heraldic and proverbial, and with Latin and Italian tags in similar vein, or anagrammatic. Many were sad, as recorded in detail by William Drummond of Hawthornden in a letter to Ben Jonson: '…An emblem of a Lyon taken in a Net, and Hares wantonly passing over him…' and '…a vine tree watered with Wine, which instead to make it spring and grow, maketh it fade…'.

The young Mary Stuart had the benefit of a sound training in needlework at the French court and was no doubt taught with the other princesses by their mother, Catherine de Medici. Queen Catherine was herself an expert, having learned the art at a convent in Florence. She was an especially able worker of lacis (darned net whitework) and when she died in 1589 left nearly a thousand pieces of this work. Wool was bought for Mary Stuart when she was nine for her to 'learn to make works' and no doubt she quickly graduated to silks.

When she returned to Scotland she brought certain French servants with her including an embroiderer, Pierre Oudry, but life was made difficult for them as it was for the Queen. Pierre Oudry was a portrait painter (his subjects included the Queen)

84. The central panels on one of the Oxburgh hangings, these worked by Mary Queen of Scots with her name and an emblematic picture allusive of her troubles. 1570.

but he also prepared needlework, drawing the designs and doing preparatory outlining in black silk. Mary also employed, at various times Ninian Miller, of Edinburgh, and another Frenchman, Charles Plouvart. In 1567 Mary was imprisoned in Lochleven Castle for ten and a half months. It was during this period that she is supposed to have worked the many large pieces which are probably wrongly attributed to her. Certainly she could not have achieved them all; it is unlikely that she had such a calm time, the necessary assistance or the right materials. She had to plead in a letter to the Lords of the Council for an apothecary, a page and 'an imbroiderer to drawe forth such worke as she would be occupied about'. During this unhappy period Mary worked in silks 'little flowers painted in canvas'. These were the sort that were later applied to velvet bed curtains such as the examples at Scone Palace.

After escaping from Lochleven, Mary fled to England and in the following year, 1569, she was placed in the custodianship of the Earl of Shrewsbury at Tutbury Castle. This semi-imprisonment satisfied Elizabeth I that the threat of a political uprising was limited but by fortunate chance it led to a great needleworking partnership between Mary and her custodian's wife, Elizabeth Shrewsbury, otherwise known as Bess of Hardwick. Both were passionate embroiderers and stimulated each other, and Mary turned to this as relief from her political fate.

'This Queen continueth daily to resort to my wife's chamber where…she useth to sit working with the needle in which she much delighteth and in devising works.'[17] So wrote Lord Shrewsbury to Sir William Cecil, Elizabeth's Secretary of State. At the same time Nicholas White, an envoy, wrote to him reporting a meeting under a canopy of estate, embroidered with Marie de Guise's motto and *impressa,* a phoenix in flames. He, too, described how Mary occupied herself:

> *I asked her Grace, since the wether did cutt off all exercises abrode, howe she passed the thyme within. She sayd that all that day she wrought with her nydill, and that the diversitie of the colors made the work seme lesse tedious and contynued so long at it till veray payn made her to give over…*

Bess of Hardwick was twenty-two years older than Mary Queen of Scots but the two women undoubtedly enjoyed each other's company. Bess was ever eager to build new houses and furnish and decorate them magnificently. Certainly she must have learned a great deal from the exiled Queen who had known considerable splendour at the French court and to a degree in Scotland. They did much needlework together including, especially, a remarkable memorial to both of them, the Oxburgh hangings.

There were four of these hangings in all, but one has since been cut up. Two of the surviving ones are associated with Bess, the third with Mary. These three are at Oxburgh Hall, Norfolk and other similar or related parts are in the Victoria and Albert Museum, at Hardwick Hall and at the Palace of Holyrood, Edinburgh. One hanging is dated 1570.

Not necessarily intended for use on a bed, they consist of green velvet curtains with over a hundred variously shaped appliqué panels of tent stitch needlework,

The Post-Mediaeval Period

linked by a light pattern of red and silver threads. Each hanging has a central symbolic picture surrounded by eight octagonal pieces and up to twenty-eight others in cruciform shape. About thirty pieces are signed with royal or personal monograms of the Queen, and fifteen with Bess's initials, E.S. The designs are derived from several natural history and emblem books, many from Conrad Gesner's *Historia Animalium* (c.1560) and others from sources such as Claude Paradin's *Devises Heroiques* (1557), Whitney's *A choice of Emblems* (1586) and Gabriel Faerno's *Fables* (1563). But they also include many personal emblematic pictures and devices. Mary's embroiderer, Pierre Oudry, may have drawn the outlines on canvas following and adapting woodcut illustrations. The three central panels are especially allusive: the one on Mary's hanging depicts a hand reaching from the sky with a sickle pruning a vine, between two other fruit trees. A motto, a cipher and the Scottish Royal Arms are also shown. Bess's two main panels show tears falling on quicklime, and a jackdaw drinking from a large vase, alluding respectively to her late husband Sir William Cavendish and the Earl of Shrewsbury. Bess was married four times and her needlework refers repeatedly to her husbands.

The Marian hanging also includes, in octagonal panels, monograms, a crowned palm tree with a tortoise climbing it, and a marigold reaching for the sun, each alluding to Mary's repressed status. Cruciform panels show a phoenix (her mother's *impresa*), a dolphin, a lion, a unicorn and exotics such as 'A Sea Moonke'. This curious fish resembling a tonsured monk with a scaly body, fins and flippers, was supposed to have been washed up on the Dutch coast and to have lived and worked with the local women for some time.

The Oxburgh hangings are delightful for their great charm as well as being unusual needlework and historically important. This is the only needlework certainly ascribed to Mary Queen of Scots, apart from the two cushions at Hardwick, already referred to. The green velvet backing is probably a later replacement but in essence the hangings convey much of the feeling and mood of the period.

An inventory of the Queen's possessions made at Chartley Hall in 1586, shortly before her execution, lists large quantities of needlework including flower slips, 'birds of different kinds', fish, and 'four footed beasts'. This could well refer to parts of the Oxburgh hangings or may be additional work carried out by, or under, the supervision

85. Probably Spanish, this early 17th century cover is of squares of lacis and needle lace bordered by bands of embroidered linen with cutwork.

of Charles Plouvart who was Mary's last embroiderer. He, with her other servants, was eventually dismissed by her captors as unnecessary. Even when the Queen was charged at Chartley and committed for trial she was robbed, not only of her papers and jewels, but also of her embroidered doublets, scarves and silk stockings.

Though her son James was under the guardianship of lords hostile to Mary's cause and was subject to their influence, he received from her many letters and gifts. She wrote for him 'all with her own hand' a book of French verses and nearly twenty years later the Bishop of Winchester reported that Mary 'wrought a cover of it with a needle and is now of his Majestie esteemed as a precious jewel'. Unfortunately this has not survived, but at Arundel Castle, Sussex, there are some child's reins with a breastplate said to have been worked by the Queen of Scots for her son. They are decorated with likely symbols – sceptres, a lion, an infant and a heart, each crowned on red silk in gold and silver threads.

A remarkable number of interesting records of the Queen's possessions and accounts survive; for these we must thank her splendid and loyal servants. Her devoted French chamberlain, Servais de Condé, must be specially remembered for his meticulous lists of furnishings and textiles. Mary's will clearly indicates items to be distributed to friends and servants. Amongst them was: 'furniture for a bed wrought with needlework, of silk, silver and gold, with divers devices and arms, not thoroughly finished…to be delivered to the King of Scottes'. This is the bed referred to earlier and described in a letter to Ben Jonson in 1619. Unfortunately it has not survived. A caged bird watched over by a menacing hawk was another emblem on it, typical of the ironic embroidered decoration. Mary also left a set of lacis bed hangings, only partially completed. These were to go to Jane Kennedy, one of the two women who accompanied her to the execution block. At Conway Castle there is a contemporary example of this darned net work.

St Paul's and Exeter Cathedrals have records of early pieces of lacis, but on the whole it was more popular on the European continent than in England (Plate 85). Perhaps the earliest survival of whitework in England is the drawn-thread linen pyx-veil of the early sixteenth century, in the British Museum. Fashion led to ornate collars and cuffs and openwork effects were developed throughout the sixteenth century culminating in grand starched standing ruffs, around 1600, with drawn thread, cut-out pieces and complex in-fillings. This was followed by work achieved without an original background fabric, over a grid of threads laid on parchment. This was the first true needlelace. Bobbin lace had emerged a little earlier, as an offshoot of plaiting and the weaving of braids. Both forms of lace had geometric designs but bobbin lace became more fluid while needlelace was tied to the geometric forms of its ground threads. The latter was abandoned for costume but was still used for domestic linen and was carried forward into the seventeenth century in samplers and other occasional usage.

Before leaving this period, it is interesting to note how contemporary embroidery in other parts of the world was mostly of a very different nature but nevertheless was destined to have an influence on English embroidery to a greater or lesser extent. By the sixteenth century, this country had developed an individual and unique style, related in some respects to oriental and European patterns and imagery, but significantly idiosyncratic in relation to embroideries worked outside Britain. Spain had strong links with North Africa and Latin America. Portugal had a similar link with India, as a result of opening up the sea route to Asia in the previous century. Considerable exchanges of trade were already in operation. For example, fine yellow silk embroidery on white cotton was being imported for the European market from Bengal; large coverlets were densely covered with chain stitch in natural yellow wild silk (often faded to buff) and in pictorial form incorporating a large range of oriental and European subjects (see also page 316).[18] This was followed by red and blue work from Gujarat and Goa, which reached a height of popularity and then died away soon after the eighteenth century. Nothing could have differed more from English emblematic needlework.

Meanwhile, far afield in another direction, in Russia a strong tradition of embroidery produced remarkable ecclesiastical work in the Byzantine tradition which was fully established by the sixteenth century. In the fifteenth century, for example, full length embroidered shrouds were made representing saints, and processional hangings and religious furnishings. Coloured silks were heavily embroidered with couched silver, silver-gilt and gold threads, also with vast quantities of pearls and jewels, especially rubies and emeralds. A chalice cover made in 1598 in the Tsarine's workshop demonstrates these lustrous features.[19] A bold inscription worked in gold threads is designed so as to form a border; within this saints, with flesh parts minutely worked, are of the mediaeval tradition, with infinite expression. In Russia great expense and effort was directed to needlework ostensibly for church use and this was unaffected by the new thinking in Western countries following the Reformation and Renaissance.

In France, England and other neighbouring countries, the focus of riches was placed on the secular and personal, and worldly luxury. Where expensive items were made for church use they were decorated with secular, even conventional, decorative motifs, though the flowers and symbols had religious overtones. A chalice cloth at Ripley Castle, Yorkshire, for example, was embroidered with the columbine whose white dove-like flowers represented the Holy Ghost and with pansies (heart's-ease) for the Peace of God. This also has strawberries for the fruits of the earth, the vine for wine, and for prayer the 'Mary' rose of which the petals are each wired so as to stand out, and white caterpillars are made of feathers sewn down. These were safely non-idolatrous symbols but they also reflect the new secular nature of ornament in general. Furthermore, it was known that a great display of magnificent costume, houses and furnishings won political and personal sway, almost coveted as much as salvation of the soul. It is not surprising that complaints were sometimes audible, such as those made concerning Catherine de Medici in 1586: 'all the revenues are wasted on embroideries, insertions, trimmings, tassels, fringes, hangings, gimps, needleworks, small chain stitchings, etc., new diversities of which are invented daily'. The formal nature of French needlework would have appeared opulent if compared with the more domestic work of English amateurs, but perhaps lacked something in idiosyncratic charm. Trimmings, tassels, fringes and gimps, however, were soon to be amongst the novel luxuries perfected in all the palaces and great houses of England and Europe in the seventeenth century.[20]

CHAPTER FOUR

A Note
on Heraldry

...with crowned insignia IRCR, 1719

In mediaeval times, and to a lesser extent ever since then, heraldry was an essential language of society, a means of identification, and textiles provided one of the chief methods of depicting it. The basic badges of family and clan, nation or cause were shown in colourful representation through forms of needlework. In wartime battles and peacetime tournaments horses, riders and banners carried clearly and boldly the distinguishing blazon of noblemen and gentry. The display of their arms was as large and impressive as possible to emphasise the power of the bearer; mediaeval documents show how spectacular such occasions were. The designs were usually of appliqué in bright, basic colours with much use of the metals gold and silver. Smaller pieces were often of raised (padded) work, and the majority were produced in workshops by professional craftsmen.

The identification of heraldry today is a complex science but it is logical and even a slight reading knowledge greatly increases an appreciation and understanding of historical contexts and gives better meaning to all artefacts, including needlework. The great seals of mediaeval monarchs, such as those of Edward I, II and III, show their chargers clad in fine heraldic trappings; effigies on tombs depict a wealth of heraldic embroidery of a formal and official nature but are also magnificently decorative. The Luttrell Psalter (c.1340) shows, in splendid illumination, Sir Geoffrey Luttrell receiving his helmet, lance and shield from two ladies. Horse, knight, donors and all the elaborate equipment are decorated with heraldic martlets on a patterned blue background.

*86. This magnificent velvet backcloth displays the arms of
Cavendish and Bruce, 16th century embroidery made for Christian Bruce,
wife of the 2nd Earl of Devonshire.*

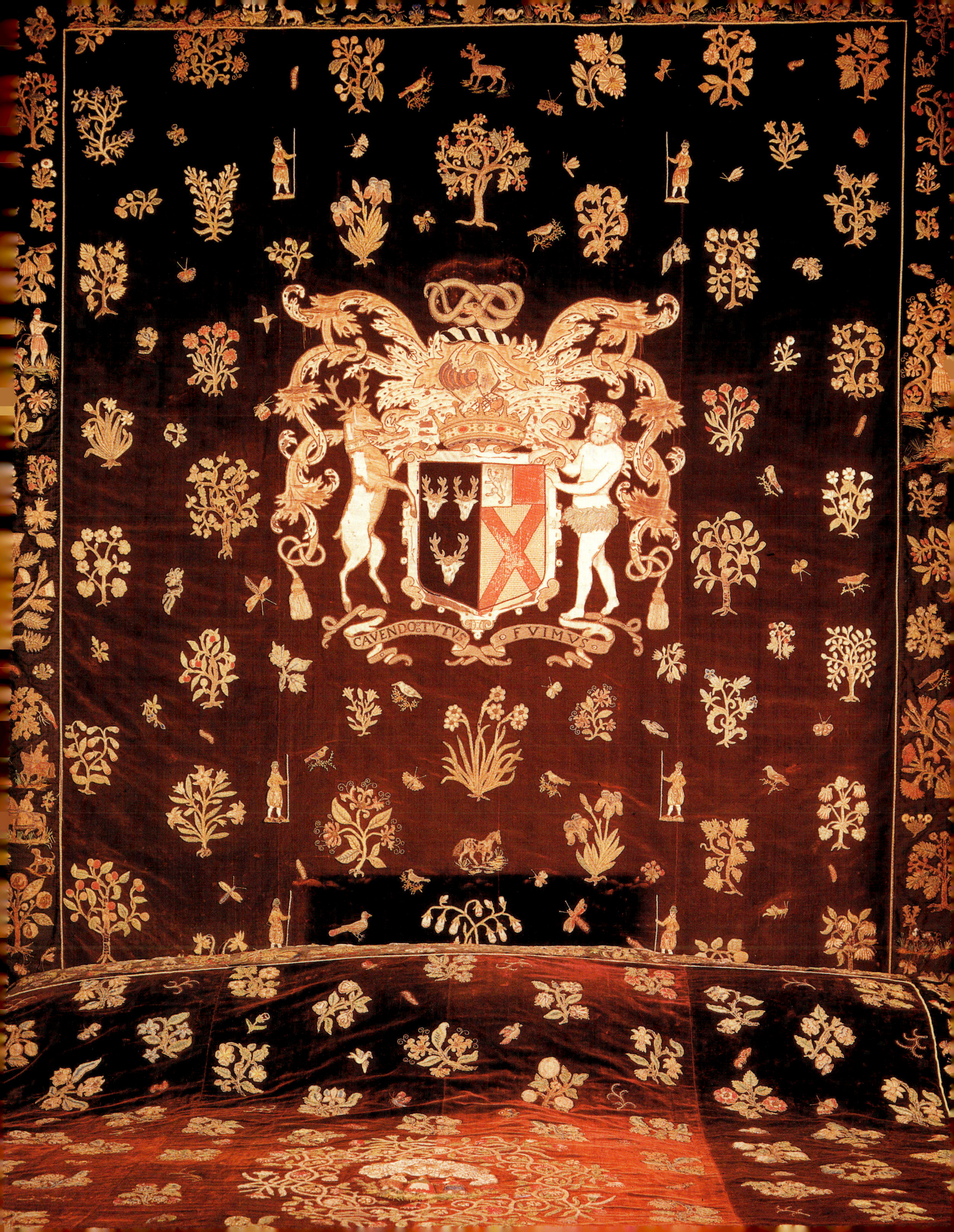
CAVENDO TVTVS
FVIMVS

The Art of Embroidery

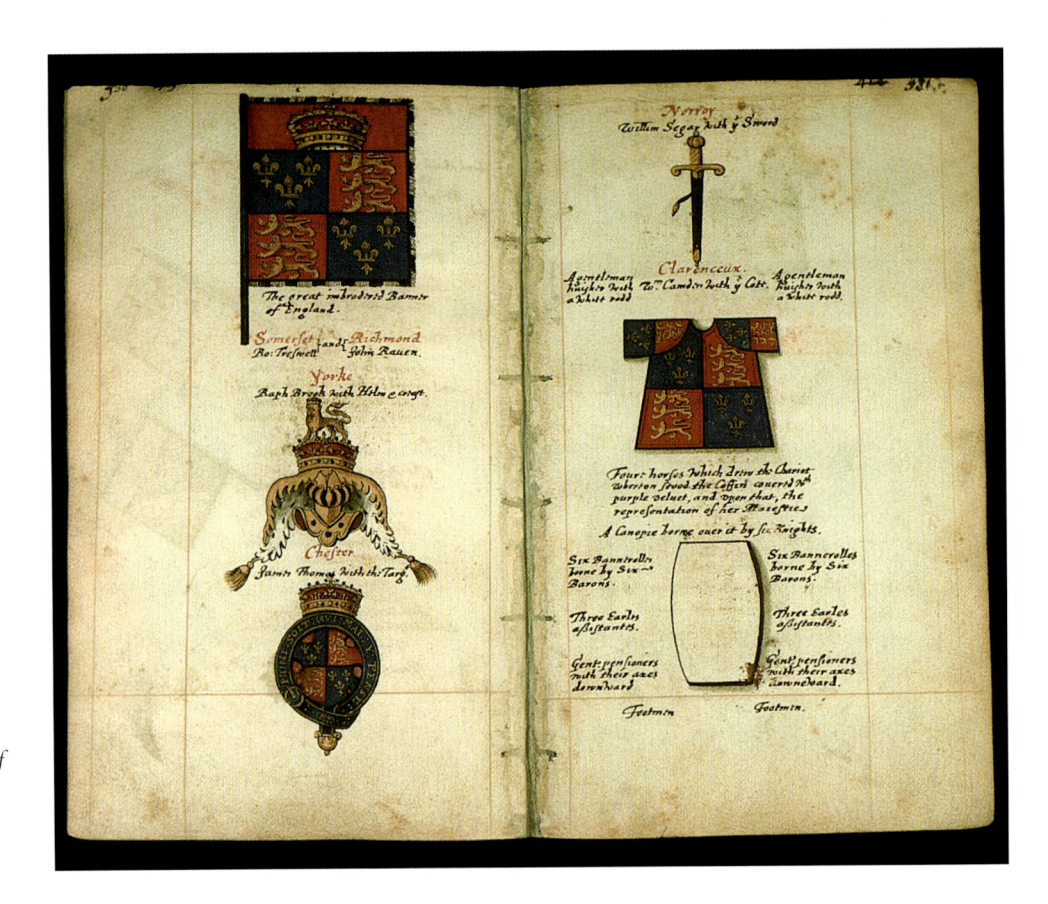

87. A document of 1603 in preparation for the funeral of Elizabeth I, illustrates 'the great imbrodered banner of England'.

Reference has already been made to the Black Prince's jupon of quilted embroidery with the royal arms on velvet, which was suspended over his tomb in Canterbury Cathedral. This is a rare and fascinating relic. Old and modern heralds' tabards, as for example the series in the Victoria and Albert Museum that belonged to two generations of the Anstis family, both Garter Kings of Arms, have similarities of form being heavily embroidered with a clear display of the royal arms on back, front and sides for easy recognition. Other tabards are at Kensington Palace, London.

Mediaeval banners, from which modern flags are derived, were strictly heraldic and were carried in battle and flown on tents and castles. They were symbols of their bearers' presence or of allegiance, a recognisable mark of authority, and used in the same way as the Royal Standard and Arms are today, that is, personal, official or bound by official recognition. The length of mediaeval banners was gauged according to rank. The king's standard was eight to nine yards long, a duke's seven, an earl's six, a baron's five, a baronet's four and a half and a knight's four yards long. Pennants, badges, shields and streamers all glittered at tournaments especially, but battlefields were colourful too. Beauchamp, Earl of Warwick under Henry VI, took to France with his army 'sixteen standards of worsted entailed with the bear and a chain' which was his heraldic symbol. He also took a colossal streamer, forty yards long and eight yards wide, similarly embroidered with heraldic creatures. Other banners bearing religious symbols in heraldic fashion were taken to battle representing the Trinity, Our Lady, St

A Note on Heraldry

George and other saints. Henry V took several such banners to Agincourt as well as ones with his arms. Banners were of course finished on both sides, the embroidery being *à deux endroits*. When Henry VIII met François I at the Field of the Cloth of Gold, he took banners embroidered with the red dragon representing his Welsh ancestry as well as others with symbols of Our Lady, of the Trinity, and the arms of England. Heraldic costumes were very elaborate. Froissart records that the French lords setting off against the Turks in 1396 were so richly dressed in emblazoned surcoats that they looked like little kings.

Heraldry was also prominent in non-military circumstances and was worn by servants and supporters in extended retinues of rank and splendour. Likewise its use reflected recognition of patronage even used in combination with the religious iconography of ecclesiastical vestments. The early fourteenth century Syon cope (Victoria and Albert Museum) has a complete border of arms in lozenges and roundels, albeit probably a later addition. In other instances heraldry alone formed the decoration, as on the Duke of Burgundy's vestments already described (page 58). These were mourning cloaks. Funeral palls also displayed heraldry. An early sixteenth century one in Cambridge is of Florentine, black, cut velvet on a gold ground, with the royal arms

88. A 19th century herald's tabard richly embroidered by professionals for ceremonial use.

103

The Art of Embroidery

of Henry VII and a crowned Tudor rose and crowned portcullis embroidered in silk and gold threads on linen, applied to cross bands of wine-coloured velvet.

City livery companies and parish churches had fine palls, often with heraldic needlework. The Pewterers' Company has a pall dated 1662 of cloth of gold with its arms on it. The Company also had a banner made with its arms for use at pageants. Funeral decorations for mourning ceremonies often included an elaborate use of heraldry, as for example described in connection with the lying in state of the 1st Duke of Albemarle in 1670, by Francis Sandford.[1]

Heraldic embroidery of an official type is represented by such items as the charter bags of Edward I's and Edward II's reigns preserved at Westminster Abbey and also in the possession of the City of London. The former is of green cloth, with a red shield embroidered with the arms of England, 'three lions passant gardant, or'. The royal arms were often displayed on throne canopies and usually in raised form. Two interesting survivals of 1617 and 1660 are preserved in the National Museums of Scotland, Edinburgh, while others can be seen at Hampton Court Palace. These were on a large scale; see for example the one over Henry VIII shown on page 65. Often depicted on seals and the illumination at the head of charters, canopies of state followed a traditional form changing little since the Middle Ages up to the present time. In the Presence Chamber at Hampton Court, a canopy of state made for William III in 1700

89. Official embroidery is often heavy with rich metal thread, as this Elizabeth I burse, which displays the royal arms and insignia on red velvet.

104

A Note on Heraldry

is 'trim'd with crimson silk fringe… the canopy embroidered with his Mats arms and badges round ye vallances…'. The badges depict the royal cipher of William and the national emblems – a rose, a thistle, a harp, a fleur-de-lis. The backcloth displays the royal arms.

Many surviving examples of embroidered arms, insignia and ciphers outlasted the silk hangings on which they were mounted and have been re-used in unofficial circumstances. An example is the state bed of red damask at Blickling Hall, Norfolk, which has the insignia and arms of George II and the arms of Queen Anne on the bed cover. Hugh Roberts has drawn attention to other cases where arms are adapted to new uses at Grimsthorpe Castle, including a velvet backcloth from the House of Lords throne canopy, embroidered by Richard Harrison, 1761, and re-made as a bed canopy. Similarly there is a velvet backcloth from the Prince's Chamber throne canopy embroidered by Sarah Greene, in the same year, mounted as a screen, and also now as a bed, a giltwood and papier mâché throne canopy from the House of Lords, made by

90. *A red damask trumpet banner bears the arms of Charles II, partly padded, and worked in silver, gold and coloured threads. c.1670.*

The Art of Embroidery

91. An 18th century panel depicting Yate family arms (with gates), in black, brown and cream silks on a green background, probably for a firescreen.

Bielefeld in 1835 with an embroidered valance of c.1820 and a late eighteenth century backcloth with a crowned monogram.[2]

The royal arms on a smaller scale are seen on many associated articles varying from beds to books, and chairs to costume. Charles II's nightdress case, dated 1664, and a dispatch bag of Lord Privy Seal William Fiennes, 8th baron and 1st Viscount Saye and Sele are just two examples to be seen at Euston Hall and Broughton Castle.

Heraldic devices were also embroidered in a less formal, more decorative manner on costume and furnishings. Illustrations of Richard II at the time of his deposing show him dressed in black, powdered with ostrich feathers; his horse trappings and pennon bore the same badge. Similarly, furniture was decorated with individual insignia, *impressas*, and emblems of varying degrees of heraldry or metaphor. The Black Prince bequeathed in 1376 'our bed of camora (camel hair and silk) powdered with blue eagles'. His widow bequeathed in 1385 'my new bed of red velvet embroidered with ostrich feathers of silver and heads of leopards of gold with boughs and leaves issuing out of their mouths'.

In the Tudor period heraldry took on an important decorative role but it also maintained full political and social significance. Chairs of state and beds proudly displayed their occupants' insignia. Henry VIII had a bed with 'The Kinges Armes holden upp withe great Anteloppes upon the Testor…the said Testor beinge…fringed on bothe sides with a narrowe fringe of Venyce golde read and purple silke and lyned with red bokeram.' The royal arms, crests and monograms continued to be embroidered (professionally) on beds, especially valances, well into the eighteenth century. They were also, of course, prominent on symbols of high office: a portrait, dated 1579, of Sir Nicholas Bacon, Lord Keeper of the Great Seal of England, shows him with an embroidered bag which contained the seal. Other officials of State had similar bags, burses, or purses, magnificently embroidered with the royal arms. Lord Eldon, who held high office for a long period, 1799-1827, had so many that his wife had them made into bed hangings.[3] Documents describe sumptuous heraldry of the past: 'the great imbrodered Banner of England' is described and illustrated in a heraldic document concerning the funeral of Elizabeth I and likewise another for the funeral of James I (College of Arms, Plate 87).

From the late sixteenth century heraldic shields became a principal motif in domestic needlework – on embroidered cushions, table carpets and similar household furnishings. Mary Hulton's cushion and the Gifford table carpet, both in the Victoria and Albert Museum, depict arms prominently and charmingly. Armorial cushions were popular for a long time, partly in imitation of, or as alternatives to, Dutch tapestry ones. They provided a formal though decorative display of status and were worked in wools in long and short stitches more often than tent-stitch on canvas.

A Note on Heraldry

The orders of chivalry called for needlework. An early garter (c.1489) of the Order of the Garter is at Anglesey Abbey, where other heraldic embroidery is also to be seen. A mantle of the Order of the Thistle in a private collection was worn by the Earl of Perth when the order was revived by James II in 1687. Of green velvet embroidered with more than 250 gold thistles, it has a shoulder badge depicting St Andrew.[4] Queen Anne re-formed the order in 1703, instituting a plain green velvet mantle.

A large amount of elaborate regimental needlework was carried out from the seventeenth century; examples may be seen in the Army Museum and other collections. Regimental colours, trumpet and kettle-drum banners display splendid, professional heraldic needlework. The styling has changed little over two hundred years. Examples are preserved in country houses, churches and museums all over the country. A purse of the Honourable Artillery Company dated 1693, on red silk decorated with the arms of the City of London, trophies and the initials 'WM' is in the British Museum.

Crowned and plain monograms were often embroidered on household furnishings, hangings, book covers and boxes. An example in gold appliqué of c.1690 is to be seen on a walnut settee at the Palace of Holyrood, Edinburgh,[5] and at Althorp there are crowned Ss on a blue bed of c.1656 (re-applied), as also at Hardwick Hall. Samplers show how girls learned to mark linen with neat initials and various forms of crowns and coronets, as well as dates and alphabets.

From the early eighteenth century, heraldry was increasingly depicted as decoration on carpets, on banners and screens, especially small pole screens. A successive tradition of similar work continued throughout the nineteenth century to the present day. The designs were often provided by professionals. In 1738 'David Mason, Japanner' advertised services, offering 'Coats of arms, Drawings on Sattin or Canvis for Embroidering'. In New England memorial hatchments were made in needlework, a practice not attempted in Great Britain. Several examples may be seen at Winterthur Museum, Delaware.

Above. 92. The Garter of Maximilian I, King of the Romans, c.1489, the earliest surviving one of this ancient order.

Left. 93. Superbly fine European whitework heraldic embroidery on fine muslin, probably German, c.1790.

The Art of Embroidery

94. This firescreen commemorating the coronation of George IV depicts the full arms of Dering with a great number of quarterings. c.1830.

Though much associated with earlier beds, heraldry is not often seen on eighteenth century beds or in crewelwork, except in reusing official canopies (page 105). The embroidered bed at Houghton Hall, exceptional in any case, has finely worked arms, however. A more woolly example of crewelwork heraldry is the horse trappings, saddle cloths, etc., at Traquair, embroidered on a royal blue fabric.

Eighteenth and nineteenth century furniture, particularly chairs and firescreens, was often upholstered with tent or cross-stitch needlework showing heraldic devices. A fine set of mid-eighteenth century sofas and stools at Squerryes Court, Kent, have twelve drop-in seats displaying family arms while a pair of walnut armchairs sold at Christie's (29 March 1984) have the arms of the Suckling family in marquetry on the backs as well as in needlework on the seats, within a framework of flowers, and dated 1732. Cushions offered another opportunity for heraldic decoration, a use continued to modern times. Sir Hardy Amies has made two pairs of cushions, one with heraldry associated with Elizabeth Stuart, the Winter Queen, the other showing the arms of the city of New York, under Dutch and British rule.

George IV had a passion for what was almost theatrical decoration. The military uniforms and heraldic emblems of his time are lavish and a number of sabretaches and pouches with finely worked badges of 1800-1826 are in the Royal Collection. His coronation robe (see also page 249) is to be seen at Kensington Palace. Domestic heraldic embroidery has more recently included the arms, crests or badges of institutions, colleges and regiments, worked as pictures, chair seats, cushions and kneelers for churches. These call for skill and accuracy without great artistic demands, but the designs and métiers are timelessly appropriate, effective and very decorative.

Flags also of course continued to be by definition heraldic textiles on national, official and personal levels. Many from the last two hundred years show superb professional embroidery, especially regimental colours and banners. These can be seen laid up in churches, in museums and in country house collections such at Belvoir Castle and at Dunrobin. At Charleton, Fife, a bookcase is lined impressively with a large number of trumpet banners.

Late nineteenth and early twentieth century picture panels were made with national, naval and regimental emblems in bright wools or floss silks, often couched down. Visitors to China, including the Navy especially, could buy these with personal colours, photographs and inscriptions as well as embroidered pictures of their ships. These souvenirs followed much trade of Chinese exports to Europe – porcelain and embroidered silks decorated with family coats of arms, crests, and mottoes. In the Victoria and Albert Museum there is part of a bedcover embroidered in coloured silks on a yellow ground, blazoned with the arms of the Duke of Chandos, impaling those of his second wife, and thereby dating the piece to 1719-1735.

A Note on Heraldry

Meanwhile in Ghana a Fante tradition of flag making became established using appliqué in cotton, silk and any other available material and creating flags that combined the Union Flag (Jack) with animal, human, and unlikely objects as additional motifs. These have a national and modernist quality very different from, but in essence related to, the earliest heraldic embroidery, especially that of mediaeval pageants.

95. *The royal arms of King Edward VII, crowned in 1901, embroidered by the Royal School of Needlework. Gold and silver thread on a red background of long and short stitches.*

109

CHAPTER FIVE

THE SEVENTEENTH CENTURY

*Home to my poor wife, who works all day like a
horse, at the making of her hangings
for our chamber and bed.*

TUDOR showmanship and ever growing opportunities for luxurious living saw the seventeenth century begin with the full flowering of Elizabethan needlework; it became increasingly rich, with more use of coloured silks and more silver and gold thread. The characteristic lightness of silk blackwork was less favoured, though its monochrome form was adapted to similar embroidery in wool, leading to crewelwork designs for bed curtains. A jacket decorated with scrolling tendrils of flowers in red at the Victoria and Albert Museum is representative of an intermediary stage in this development.

Late Elizabethan embroideries, in the meantime, quickly reached a crescendo in bejewelled colour, and with fanfares of metallic threads heralded the grander raised and padded needlework that predominated during James I's reign. Good examples of this latter type, though perhaps not English, are a panel at Compton Wynyates, Warwickshire, showing Orpheus charming the wild animals,[1] and a gilt bullion casket at Drayton House, Northamptonshire, with raised flowers and animals worked entirely in seed pearls. Formal mannerist strapwork, linear and angular and with curling scrolls, is especially a feature of all English design in this period and these forms in embroidery were overlaid with silver or gilt metal threads linking cartouches or framed panels. Such formal designs of precise professional workmanship subsequently gave way to more personal, and usually amateur, needlework throughout the rest of the century, and this in turn led to various fashionable forms. These included sampler

*96. Part of one of a set of Elizabethan pillow covers in
pristine condition. A variety of flowers are embroidered in silk and
the background is of gold thread.*

III

The Art of Embroidery

97. *Above and opposite. The rare survival of Margaret Laton's portrait and her embroidered jacket, of about 1620, is fascinating for a number of reasons, not least as a demonstration of the accuracy of depiction of 17th century costume.*

making, stumpwork and crewelwork, each highly individual and hardly related. The century ended with embroideries reflecting Protestant confidence, ensuing Dutch influence and once again an emulation of French grandeur, yet blended and tempered by English taste and craftsmanship.

Throughout the century there was a preponderance of flower ornament, in more complex and varied uses and, by the reign of William and Mary, a noticeably greater quantity of colour. Real flowers gave way at times to stylised forms or exotic oriental varieties.

Fashions did not change dramatically after the accession of James I in 1603. Margaret Laton's bodice of about 1610, as already mentioned, with her portrait in which she wears it (Plates 97 and 98) shows this period's embroidery at its best. Curling gold tendrils support numerous flowers, birds and butterflies, with madrigal-like rhythm and variation. Caps, bags and many other articles were similarly embroidered, frequently with backgrounds of gold or silver threads (Plate 96).

The precision of the designs and the quality of the stitchery suggest that a good deal of this needlework was made professionally. Like the many formal New Year gifts given to Elizabeth I, it is probable that some articles were made in workshops for presentation purposes. Sweet bags were frequently given; an inventory of Henry Howard, Earl of Northampton, of 1614 describes no less than seventeen. One was 'embroidered with highe embosted mosse worke having two sea nymphes upon dolphins and other figures of fowles, edged about with lace of silver and gold, lined with carnation'.[2] Others are described as having 'knottes of silver Oes with burning hartes'. These small bags were sometimes accompanied by a tiny tasselled pincushion or heart-shaped purse. The most usual decoration was formalised Tudor roses, and other flowers within curling tendrils, on a metal thread background.

Richard Boyle, Earl of Cork, never forgot a religious holiday, a birthday or even a Valentine's day which offered an excuse for giving a present:

> *I gave my Valentine, Mrs Mary Jones a sweet bag of carnacon spangled and embroidered with gold twist, a Spanish pocket and a pair of Spanish gloves, all richly perfumed that were my wives.*
> (He had two wives.)

The Seventeenth Century

Gloves were a popular gift. Stuart ones were larger than the Elizabethan, with more stylised embroidery that extended on to the glove itself from the gauntlet, which was often zigzag shaped at the opening and trimmed with gold lace. Deep fringes of white linen lace later became *de rigueur*.

Another unusual survival is a set of early seventeenth century falconer's accoutrements embroidered with musk roses and mistletoe. Consisting of bag, lure, gauntlet glove and three hoods, they were purportedly left by James I at Wroxton Abbey as a souvenir of his visit to Lord Dudley North, and are now in the Burrell Collection. Another fascinating relic, at Parham Park, Sussex, is a state saddle used by James II on a visit to Bristol in 1686. At Rosenborg Castle in Denmark there is a fine saddle made for the wedding of the Prince Elect of Denmark, supplied by Gert Osserijn 1633-34, of velvet with gold thread, pearls and gems.[3] In the Swedish Royal Collection there is a remarkable group of twelve horseblankets, seven saddles and eight caparisons, part of a state gift from Louis XIV to Charles XI of Sweden in 1673.

All the foregoing were made in professional workshops, but much was also done by amateurs. Women made sure that their daughters were studious in embroidery discipline and training, to inherit from them as many skills and stitches as they knew. Girls were increasingly expected to work samplers to record and practise borders and motifs. From this they graduated to doing test pieces in pictures, stumpwork, bead-work or crewelwork. Samplers gradually became removed from practicality with more elaborate patterns than were useful for costume, and the other exercises were each looked upon as separate crafts, combining a training in discipline, practice in sewing and entertainment. Seventeenth century stitches were numerous and have evocative names such as plaited braid, guilloche, Russian overcast, Algerian eye, Montenegrin cross, Romanian and double running, to name just a few. They could be worked with rich materials, which were now easier to obtain. Silks and velvets, even when cut or figured, did not necessarily wholly displace embroidery but were combined or contrasted with it. A magnificent French

99. A 17th century purse embroidered with a leopard under a tree on one side and hunting animals on the other.

The Art of Embroidery

100. Part of a 17th century Spanish chasuble shows floss silks couched down to make bold motifs in colourful shades.

bed in the Louvre from Château d'Effiat is of figured red velvet with elaborate embroidery. A combination of fine textiles was a feature of both private work and professional workshops and, especially, in the making of church vestments.

Archbishop Laud took office in 1633 and advocated the reintroduction of High Church traditions. He took steps to re-establish fine needlework, and some good pieces were made. Two have survived from a set of pulpit and altar hangings commissioned for the Chapel of the Holy Ghost, Basingstoke, by the Sandys family of The Vyne. They are of purple velvet with, respectively, embroidered cherubs' heads with scroll ornaments, and the Last Supper. Other ecclesiastical needlework was imported from continental Europe where, following the Counter Reformation, notable work was carried out. In Austria, for example, gold monochrome embroidery was done on bright satin, often red. A shimmering effect was produced with a variety of metal techniques in dramatic stylised patterns. Other good vestments were made in Augsburg where workshops had been influenced largely by Bohemian art, and a fair number of Italian and French ecclesiastic items have survived from the seventeenth century. A fine set of French vestments, including a cope, a chasuble and two dalmatics, in bright silk chenilles couched on cream damask, from the Carmelite Convent in Darlington, are to be seen at the Bowes Museum, Yorkshire, while a set of Spanish vestments at the Whitworth Art Gallery, Manchester, also represent secular designs for use in churches. An interesting curiosity is the Bedingfeld chasuble from Oxburgh Hall, Norfolk, made for Requiem Mass with white beadwork on black velvet and dated boldly '24 FEB 1684'.

Some of Russia's finest ecclesiastical needlework was made in the seventeenth century. Of outstanding richness in design, as well as in materials and workmanship, it continued in the Byzantine tradition but also adopted Islamic elements of Mughal origin. Especially from the thirteenth century onwards sacred textiles were made for ceremonial use, some derived originally from cloths that covered the holy vessels but were later on a larger scale as didactic objects for veneration purposes. An example in the Victoria and Albert Museum is dated 1407 and has a background of curling tendrils enclosing leaves, an age-old and almost universal pattern. The sixteenth and seventeenth century embroideries are notably luxurious with much use of metal threads, pearls and semi-precious stones. A cope in the Kremlin is of cut red and green velvet pile of cloth of gold with a border of silver and gold lace on yellow silk. It has a deep collar of emerald green, densely embroidered with pearls and sequins, with a border bearing a long inscription worked in pearls, the lettering being about an inch (2.5cm) deep. While this cope shows designs of Islamic influence, a superb coffin cover of 1678, also in the Kremlin museum, displays Russian Orthodox figure embroidery in some respects comparable with *opus anglicanum* of 1350 (Plate 101). It is in the traditional form of a Greek Orthodox *epitaphios*. The main panel depicts Christ's

The Seventeenth Century

prostrate figure, adored by saints and angels, in gloriously varied textures and colours. Our Lord's body and the Virgin's head are outlined in pearls, and the gold thread parts are worked in geometric patterns. A deep border shows half-length figures of saints in interlocked roundels on a green silk background. Again, inscriptions are worked into the embroidery as an integral part of the decoration.[4]

Tapestries were now widely produced in many European countries for palaces and great houses. James I founded the Mortlake factory near London in 1613 and encouraged the planting of mulberry trees to stimulate the silk industry. The factory had a short but positive influence on other English textiles, especially since both the designs and the workers were introduced from abroad. Charles I also patronised tapestry weaving and commissioned the immigrant Rubens to design a series depicting the History of Achilles. Francis (Frantz) Cleyn was also brought to England and employed on tapestry design; he was later a celebrated illustrator of Virgil etc., and his work was much adapted to chair seats, pictures and other pictorial mediums.

In France, Louis XIV set out to create a unique palace at Versailles and encouraged artists in every field, including tapestry weaving. His financial wizard Colbert founded

101. A Russian coffin cover made in Moscow, 1678. Gold, pearls, jewels and bright silks are combined with superb craftsmanship to create an intense depiction of Christ's entombment and portraits of saints.

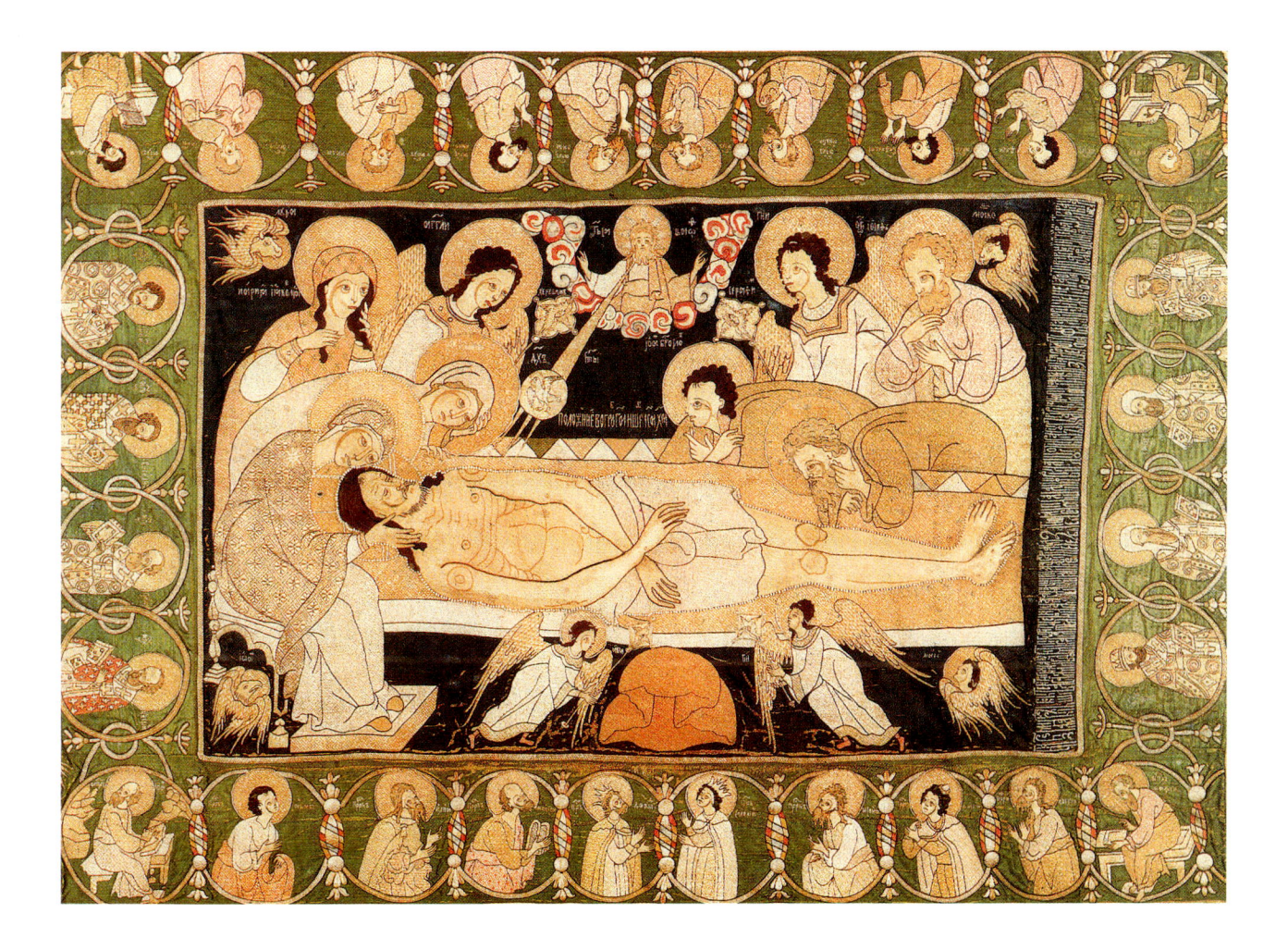

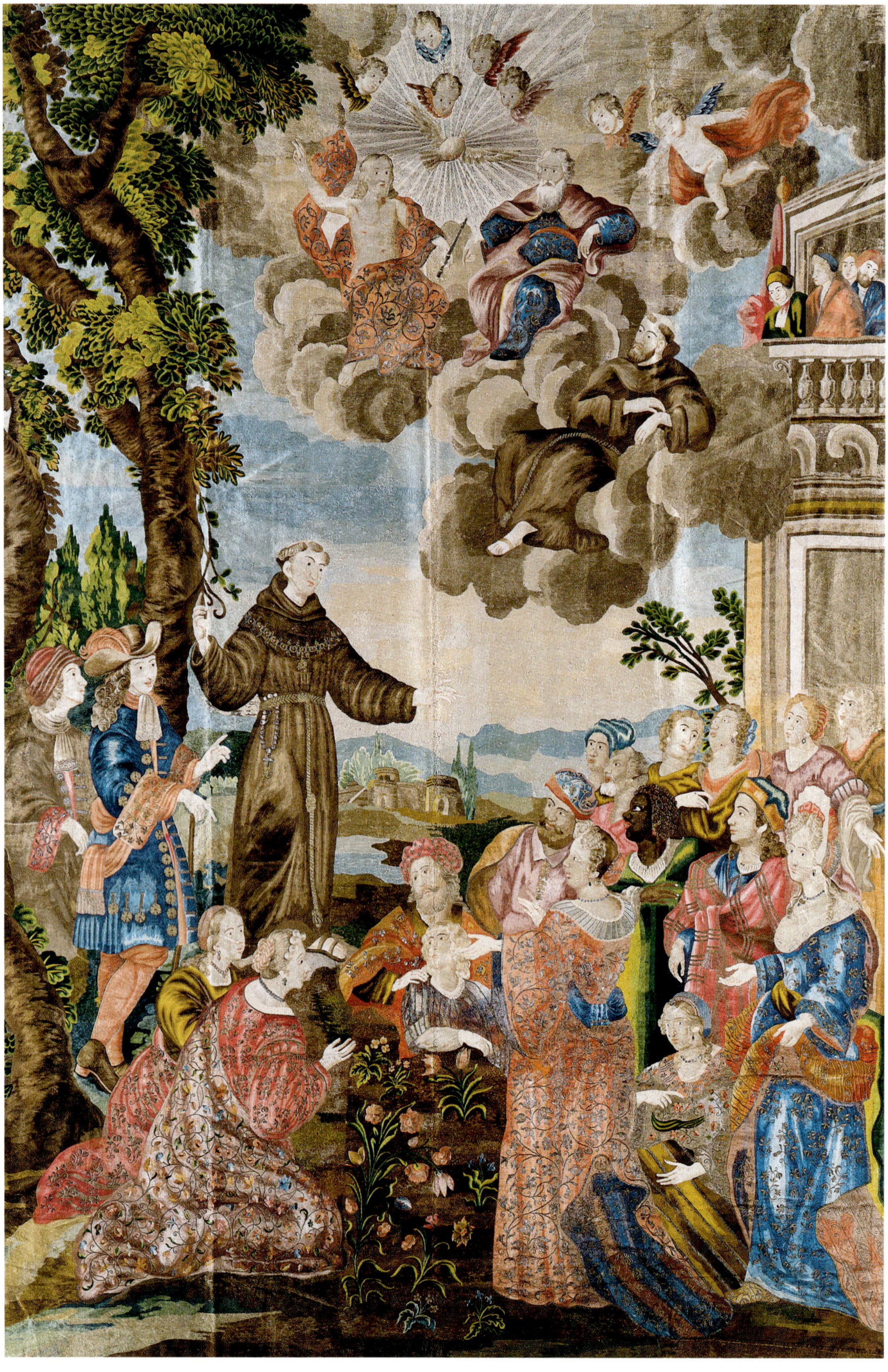

The Seventeenth Century

factories at Gobelins in 1662 and Beauvais in 1664. In London, in 1689, another factory was set up, this time in Soho. Tapestries were sometimes enriched with embroidery, especially with silver and silver gilt threads. The mid-sixteenth century Flemish *Bridal Chamber of Herse,* for example, made by Willem van Pannemaker and his workshops, shows such enrichments, depicting a grand bedroom with bed hangings, wall hanging and costumes all ornamented with silver and gilt metal embroidery (Metropolitan Museum of New York).

Large needlework hangings were also made in imitation of, or to rival, weaving. A fine early series of Spanish tent stitch hangings of c.1600 depicts the History of Galcerán de Pinós. A later French example in the Musée Nissim de Camondo in Paris depicts a characteristic Louis XIV trophy – a huge group of weapons, armour and banners. Another of similar form at Versailles, after a design by Le Brun and worked in a convent, is even more elaborate and there is a remarkable set of four at the Metropolitan Museum (Plate 105). In Italy likewise, large pictorial hangings embroidered in silk were made, imitating tapestries. A set of five in the Royal Collection depict New Testament scenes, after Tintoretto and others, within a border of arabesques, baskets of flowers and at the corners biblical vignettes contained in roundels.[5] Other Italian needlework did not so much imitate as provide an alternative to tapestries. These sometimes showed religious events such as scenes from the lives of saints.

Three spectacular silk embroidered friezes, probably Roman or North Italian, were seen at Sotheby's (13 December 1991). They depicted equestrian battle scenes in landscapes with a castle, trees and with raised metal thread embroidery on armour and harness. A huge banner with lambrequins at the base, in Milan cathedral, shows a Murillo-style crowned Virgin Mary supported by cherubs, on a cloud and with New Testament scenes in smaller medallions in the wide border where there is also raised metal thread decoration. The Virgin's dress is also delicately embroidered with silver and gold floral decoration.

Above. 103. Italian silk embroidery was worked with an accuracy of detail resembling painting as in this frieze depicting equestrian figures galloping together in confrontation. Roman or North Italian, 17th century, 2ft.11in. x 7ft. (89cm x 213cm).

Opposite. 102. Large Italian silk needlework hanging, partly enriched with silver thread, depicting St Anthony of Padua preaching and St Francis with the Trinity above. 17ft. x 11ft.1in. (518cm x 338cm)

The Art of Embroidery

104. Two hangings of satin-stitch embroidery made to designs by Daniel Marot for Hampton Court Palace in the 1690s.

Louis XIV clearly liked needlework; he had a considerable amount made for Versailles, including furnishings for two of the most important rooms, the Throne Room and the King's Bedchamber. Most was ornamental rather than pictorial and consisted of formalised patterns ranging from complex arabesques to massive trophies. The Throne Room was hung with gold and silver hangings with architectural perspectives worked in high relief and 'after the fashion of marble'. Caryatid figures in gold embroidery, as much as 15ft. (4.5m) high, were recorded amongst the extraordinary decorations at Versailles and payments were made to several individuals for 'embroidered landscapes', 'embroideries representing the capturing of birds in flight' and 'patterns for embroideries on furniture in the gallery at Versailles'. The King's embroiderer Simon Delobel and others were employed for twelve years on furnishings for the King's Bedchamber. Sadly, nothing of this now survives; the needlework was exposed and prone to natural deterioration as well as to later violent destruction. One contemporary described the King's bed as 'hung with crimson velvet so richly covered with gold embroidery that the background can hardly be made out'. Some tent stitch hangings of the period do survive such as those mentioned above. One shows the King as Jupiter and Air, part of a set of the Elements. It has a wide border of flowers, game birds, musical instruments, insects, cornucopias, a sun-burst motif and around this an embroidered gilt frame moulding. Other panels in the Metropolitan Museum show in equally baroque surroundings allegorical images of two of Louis XIV's illegitimate children, Mademoiselle de Nantes as Summer and Mademoiselle de Blois as Spring, in rich silks on silver backgrounds (Plate 105). These were probably embroidered in about 1683 at the Maison des Filles de la Providence, Paris. A needlework state bed canopy shown in the same room also reflects the massive grandeur and solemnity of Le Brun's designs which were soon to be challenged by the more delicate whimsy of Jean Bérain. It is said that the embroideries at Versailles had chased silver plaques for the human parts. The professionals involved in such works and in costume embroidery belonged to various guilds, but court workers were exempt from most regulations. Jean Bérain (1640-1711), who graduated from being a theatre designer to the King's chief interior decorator in 1674, magically transformed the great and grand formality with new ornamental designs including sober and stately strapwork and whimsical grotesques full of life and humour. Bérain and others developed these forms that ultimately had their origin in Raphael's adaptations of the antique, but adding chinoiseries, *Commedia dell'Arte* performers, architectural fantasies and singeries.[6]

The Seventeenth Century

105. One of Louis XIV's daughters is represented as Spring in this canvas work hanging of about 1685, part of a set of four. 13ft.6in. x 9ft.2in. (419cm x 279cm).

In England there was not as great a demand for grandiose palatial decoration; displays of riches were certainly made but in more domestic and less formal circumstances. In design, the influence of Daniel Marot created a smart grandeur, however, and beds and curtains with bold mannerist pelmets presented a dignified formality. A set of chairs, daybed and hangings at Penshurst Place, Kent, have rose damask with an appliqué design in velvet and coloured silks in the manner of Marot. It is likely that these were a perquisite from a royal house. Henry Sidney, Earl of Romney, was Groom of the Stole at the time of William III's death in 1702. The hangings and furniture en suite are attributed to Philip Guibert, an upholsterer with premises in Jermyn Street, London; he supplied similar furniture to the Royal Household in 1697-98. Directly corresponding to a drawing by Daniel Marot, however, is a set of eight embroidered woollen hangings at Hampton Court Palace. Of tall and narrow proportions, they are richly decorated with grotesque ornament, scrolling foliage, classical figures, cornucopias, flowers, birds and medallions. While it is not known for which apartment at Hampton Court the hangings were made, it is worth remembering a set described in 'Queen Mary's Closet' in George Bickham's *Deliciae Britannicae,* or the *Curiosities of Hampton Court and Windsor Delineated...* published in 1742; 'the Hangings are all Needlework wrought by the Queen's own hand: Here are likewise an Easy-Chair, four others, and a Screen, all said to be the work likewise of that pious Queen... The work we are now speaking of must be allow'd to be extremely neat; and in particular the Figures, which are chiefly Flowers, are all well shadow'd, perhaps equal to the best Tapestry, and show great Judgement in the drawing' (Plate 104).[7]

Costume was flamboyant and lavish but there was a conscious attempt to prevent extravagance becoming a general fashion, spreading through the gentry and lower orders. James I forbade a servant girl to wear 'tiffany, velvet; lawns of white wires on the head, or about the kerchief, koyfe, crest cloth, but only linen; no farthingale, the ruff restricted to four yards in length before the gathering or setting of it'.

By the middle of the century, noblemen's costumes were often more elaborate and ornate with embroidery than their ladies'. Full length portraits show them in complicated, sumptuous garments, trimmed with rich lace ruffs and cuffs, and with rosettes on their shoes. With military costume they wore needlework scarves, as seen for example in a portrait of an armoured man at Hardwick Hall. A splendid surviving example in the Victoria and Albert Museum is said to have been worn by Charles I at the Battle of Edgehill. In contrast, Caroline ladies developed a taste for plain silks, costly and beautiful, decorated only with lace. The lustrous colours and sheens of these have been captured in the portraits of Van Dyck and Dobson.

This change in fashion caused needlework to become more specifically a pastime and hobby; girls devoted their energies towards making samplers, pictures and caskets for the dual purpose of general practice in sewing and for fun. Many new pattern books were now available to inspire them, and artists were called upon to transcribe designs. In the accounts of Lady Shuttleworth of Gawthorpe (1619) it is recorded that the steward paid 2s.4d. to Mr Bradell 'for drowing a waste coate and a night cappe'. Curiously, Mr Bradell was a distinguished and rich neighbour, and Receiver General to the King for the Duchy of Lancaster. He must have been accomplished in drawing as well, and have been keen to help embroiderers. In general, most motifs were collated in pattern books,

The Seventeenth Century

with wide circulation and not much variation. Designs were adapted from these to linen, canvas, satin and other materials for working. Apart from their arrangement they had little originality, but great charm. A delightful set of panels at Traquair, Peeblesshire, shows a variety of fruit, flowers and creatures clearly derived from woodcuts and presumably intended for cutting out and applying to hangings (Plate 64).

PATTERN BOOKS

Books were still scarce in most country houses and were not a feature of them despite other shows of wealth and culture. Pattern books and similar sources must have been shared around. Even Bess of Hardwick, in spite of her wealth and connections, had

106. A detail of a pair of blue wool curtains applied with floral slips and with floss silk embroidery. French, c.1635. 6ft.6¾in. x 3ft. (200cm x 91cm).

The Art of Embroidery

107. A page from Richard Shorleyker's pattern book A Schole House for the Needle, *1632. The darkened area is caused by pouncing, chalk having been rubbed through pin holes to transfer the pattern.*

only six books at Hardwick, kept in her bedchamber.

Seventeenth century pattern books essentially carried on the tradition established by those of the late sixteenth century, with sources such as Gerard de Jode's *Thesaurus Sacrarum Historiarum Veteris Testamenti* (Antwerp 1585). Their charming titles and illustrations conjure up a magical atmosphere that must have made fingers itchy for sewing: *A Book of Beast, Birds, Flowers, Fruits, Flies and Wormes, exactly drawne with their Lively Colours truly Described* was published by Thomas Johnson in 1630. It consisted of engravings borrowed from English, Dutch and German sources, printed in unrelated scales, the cause of similar discrepancies in needlework renderings. Richard Shorleyker's *A Schole House for the Needle* (1624) was very popular. The second edition indicates how adaptable the patterns were intended to be: 'sundry sorts of spots as Flowers, Birds, and Fishes, etc., and will fitly serve to be wrought, some with Gould, some with Silke, and some with Crewell, or otherwise at your pleasure'. James Boler's *The Needle's Excellency* (1631) was printed in many editions and was prefaced by 'the water poet', John Taylor's poem *The Prayse of the Needle,* which is full of information on contemporary needlework.[8] Another delightful title was *The History of four-footed beasts and serpents. Whereunto is now added the Theatre of Insects,* the first part produced by Edward Topsell (1607) and the second by Thomas Monffet (1658), and re-circulating designs from Sibmacher's *Modelbuch* of 1597. Robert Walton in St Paul's Churchyard advertised in 1677 a book, *The Whole View of Creation in Eight Parts; being a book of Beasts, Birds, Flowers, Fish, Fruit, Flyes, Insects, containing a hundred and thirty half sheets of paper neatly cut in Copper.* Peter Stent published a *Booke of Flowers Fruits Beastes Birds and Flies* in 1650. Twelve years later he was advertising, in addition, over 500 engraved prints in sheet form ranging from portraits of kings and queens to the seasons, senses and continents, as well as natural history subjects. Picture books of Bible stories and emblems were also available. Lions, leopards, elephants, unicorns, stags and camels often found their way into needlework, usually as curiosities, but occasionally with symbolic significance. The Cutlers' Company had twelve cushions 'with oliphants', clearly in this case a heraldic reference to their arms which displayed an Elephant and Castle crest and two elephants as supporters. There has always been great delight in animals, birds and sea creatures, real and mythological. Dotted over a canvas, they are sometimes marshalled by Noah or charmed en masse by Orpheus, as in a picture in the Untermyer Collection, Metropolitan Museum, showing every creature from bear to cat. The Garden of Eden (with Adam and Eve) offered a similar opportunity for a display of creatures, as adapted, for instance, from the frontispiece of the *Bishop's Bible* printed by Robert Barker, London, 1583. The Untermyer Collection has also a wonderful panel showing the Garden of Eden, derived from various sources.

The Seventeenth Century

    Certain flowers and fruit were particularly favoured and often represented; some had emblematic overtones. Nuances of virtue were derived from such books as Henry Peacham's *Minerva Britannica of a Garden of heroical devices*.... Peacham explained the fashionable cult (much loved by James I) as the wish 'to seede at once both the mind and eie by expressing mystically and doubtfully our disposition'. A Dutch carol sings of floral imagery:

> *King Jesus hath a garden, full of divers flowers…*
> *…The Lily, white in blossom there, is Chastity;*
> *The Violet, with sweet perfume, Humility.*
> *The bonny Damask-rose is known as Patience;*
> *The blithe and thrifty Marygold, Obedience.*
> *The Crown Imperial bloometh too in yonder place,*
> *'Tis chastity, of stock divine, the flower of grace.*
> *Yet mid the brave, the bravest prize of all may claim*
> *The Star of Bethlehem – Jesus – blessed be his Name!…*

108. *A partly worked silk picture with scenes from David and Bathsheba demonstrates both the fine outline pattern drawn on a satin ground and unfaded silk embroidery. c.1660.*

123

The Art of Embroidery

Below. 109. This detail of a 17th century band sampler shows 'boxers', figures derived from an image of couples exchanging flowers and cupids.

Opposite. 110. This early 17th century spot motif sampler includes both elements of pattern and fascinating pictorial motifs including a falconer. 21½in. x 17in. (55cm x 43cm).

Strawberries suggested purity and righteousness, pansies meditation, and carnations (or pinks) love. The last were derived from Persian ornament and appear even more frequently than roses, the old badge of state. In the insect world, moths hinted at the transitoriness of human life, snails at laziness, silk worms at industry, and bees at diligence and orderliness. Huish suggested that the caterpillar was a badge of Charles I.[9]

The oak and acorn were certainly associated with this king and also with Charles II, who hid in an oak tree after the battle of Worcester; these are frequently seen, as are oak leaves and oak apples. Figs and pineapples, tulips and thistles are also found on seventeenth century samplers. In the bird world, pelicans represented Christian sacrifice, pecking their breasts to release blood to succour their young. Ostriches were supposed to be able to eat iron; one is depicted in the Oxburgh hangings with a horseshoe in its mouth. The oriental peacock was adopted as a symbol of Christ as eternal life and resurrection. It was thought that its flesh never decayed. Pairs of peacocks are often shown flanking a fountain and standing in vines. A related device is seen in many samplers and the origin, though obscure, is probably ancient. None of these motifs should, however, be too strongly emphasised as symbolic since it is likely that they were often chosen at random or by convention, irrespective of earlier meanings and nuances.

SAMPLERS

Though sampler making had earlier become a fully developed aspect of sewing, few survive from before 1650. There were references in inventories and literature as mentioned before, but it was in the seventeenth century that samplers reached a peak of excellence before developing into decorative conventional forms in the eighteenth and nineteenth centuries. A good number have survived from the second half of the seventeenth century, regarded as heirlooms and sentimental mementoes of a previous generation. Many were signed and dated; the age of the embroiderer is not usually indicated. Most were kept safely rolled up in workboxes, and some were protected by being framed and glazed.

They were sometimes worked by women but more often by teenagers, occasionally by children as young as six and a half (Plate 112), at home and in schools, as part of their basic education and as a training for marking linen and doing other domestic sewing. Samplers were especially necessary for recording patterns as there was still a shortage of printed design books and they were certainly too expensive for most English house-

125

The Art of Embroidery

111. Early samplers, as this one of about 1620, were for recording and practising samples of pattern for later use.

holds. Samplers were always neat, of precise workmanship, and showed experiments and records of colour combinations, in addition to patterns with exquisite detailing. They were not usually first efforts but followed practice elsewhere, though some have random characteristics, mistakes and re-working that indicates experimentation. Religious texts appear from the middle of the century, a moral aspect that shows a change in attitude to sampler making from purely practical exercises to objects in themselves. Puritan ethics no doubt saw them as a prevention from idleness and thereby laid the foundations of the misery that was to be borne by some children in struggling with tedious set works with pious texts.

Seventeenth century samplers Plates 111 and 112 were usually worked on long narrow lengths of bleached, or unbleached, linen about 6-8in. (15-20cm) wide and of various lengths, in rare cases even up to about 3ft. (1m) or more. Length allowed for many strips or bands of border patterns; width was unnecessary as these were repetitive. They were embroidered with white and coloured silks and metal threads. The border patterns, texts and motifs were worked in parallel bands, and as a result the term 'band sampler' is often used. The linen was imported and fairly expensive, so the bands were packed closely together; each was short, concise and compact.

Mostly of sixteenth century Italian origin, the band borders were collected as an anthology and contrasted to make an impressive carpet of patterns. The Italian element reflects Renaissance arabesques, grotesques, vines and acanthus turned into angular stems with naturalistic flowers. Turkish, Anatolian and Caucasian carpet motifs contributed linked S and swastika patterns while the Roman excavations at the end of the fifteenth century gave rise to Raphaelite grotesques, here simplified to band form. Seventeenth century whitework samplers, especially, show Italian origins with patterns of the previous century. A sampler in the Goodhart Collection (Montacute House, Somerset) shows, for example, a band with birds and flowers derived from a pattern published by the Venetian, Frederico di Vinciolo in 1587. Certain patterns were repeated relatively often, such as a courtly couple from Johann Sibmacher's *Neues Modelbuch* (Nüremberg 1597) seen on another whitework sampler in the Goodhart Collection, a whitework sampler of 1667 in the Royal Scottish Museum and a sampler by Mary Smith of 1729 in the Victoria and Albert Museum.

Cut and drawn work was usually in white. Referred to in Taylor's poem as 'Italian cutworke' and 'Frost-worke', it was increasingly popular, and culminated in contemporary needlepoint lace. It was particularly used on ruffs and cuffs as well as other items of costume, chiefly in geometric patterns. Whitework figures and animals

The Seventeenth Century

are occasionally seen in samplers and sometimes pieces of needlepoint lace are incorporated. Samplers entirely of whitework are seldom dated, but a long whitework band sampler with needlepoint lace seen at Mallett, London, was dated 1655; it included a depiction of Adam and Eve. Another interesting example worked in fine wool on linen, with needlepoint lace, from Co. Wexford, Ireland, and signed MR 1662, is in the National Museum, Dublin.

Italianate borders were sometimes interspersed with other motifs, smaller floral and geometrical patterns. Flowers depicted included some of those already mentioned – roses, pansies, carnations, honeysuckle with strawberries, acorns, etc. Pea flowers and an open pod motif are often seen. Any animals were of a stylised nature unless they were of the 'spot motif' type in which case they were realistically shaded.

Samplers with motifs shown in outline only, like drawings, were similarly no doubt derived from Italian sixteenth century needlework, with the background worked in a single colour and the subjects left as plain linen with a few line details. Outline forms, in single colours, are a feature of English samplers but are also seen on a large sampler dated 1661, said to be German (Victoria and Albert Museum).

Towards the end of the century, samplers taught not only sewing but alphabets, counting and religious texts. These features grew rapidly in popularity to become an essential part of sampler making. The earliest examples are not often signed, but some have initials, others a date; some later ones have both a signature and date. Occasionally, the age of the sewer is included and even worked into a little sentence. Huish cited an example: 'Mary Hall is my name and when I was thirteen years of age I ended this in 1662'. In the course of the next two centuries it became unusual not to have either a name or date. Sometimes these details on seventeenth century ones are upside down in relation to the rest of the sampler. 'Boxers' were a curious feature and appeared usually in pairs. Possibly derived from a European motif of lovers exchanging gifts, they are small figures, either naked, or in shorts, or with contemporary costume, and apparently have wings, which prompts some to suggest that they are an adaptation of cherubs or putti, as in sixteenth century Italian work. They always face out and have either straight hair or curly, like a wig. With one foot forward, they hold up in an enlarged hand an apparently strange object, possibly flowers. They are usually depicted between highly stylised tree motifs, thought to be a corruption of

112. This well laid out sampler was made by a six and a half year old, Elizabeth Hearne, 1698.

128

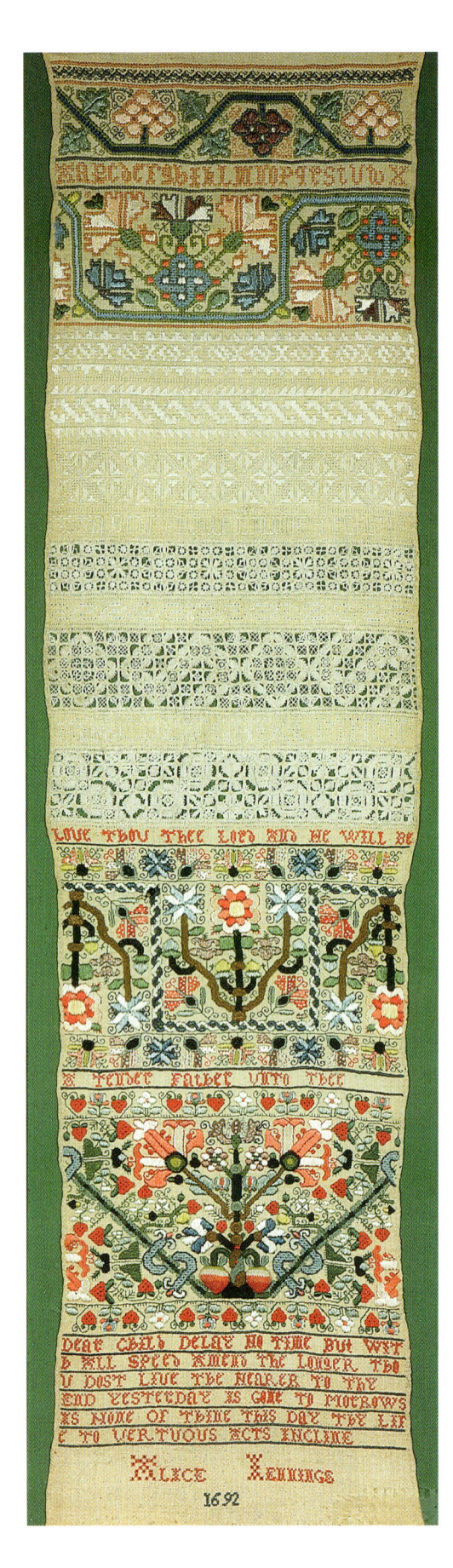

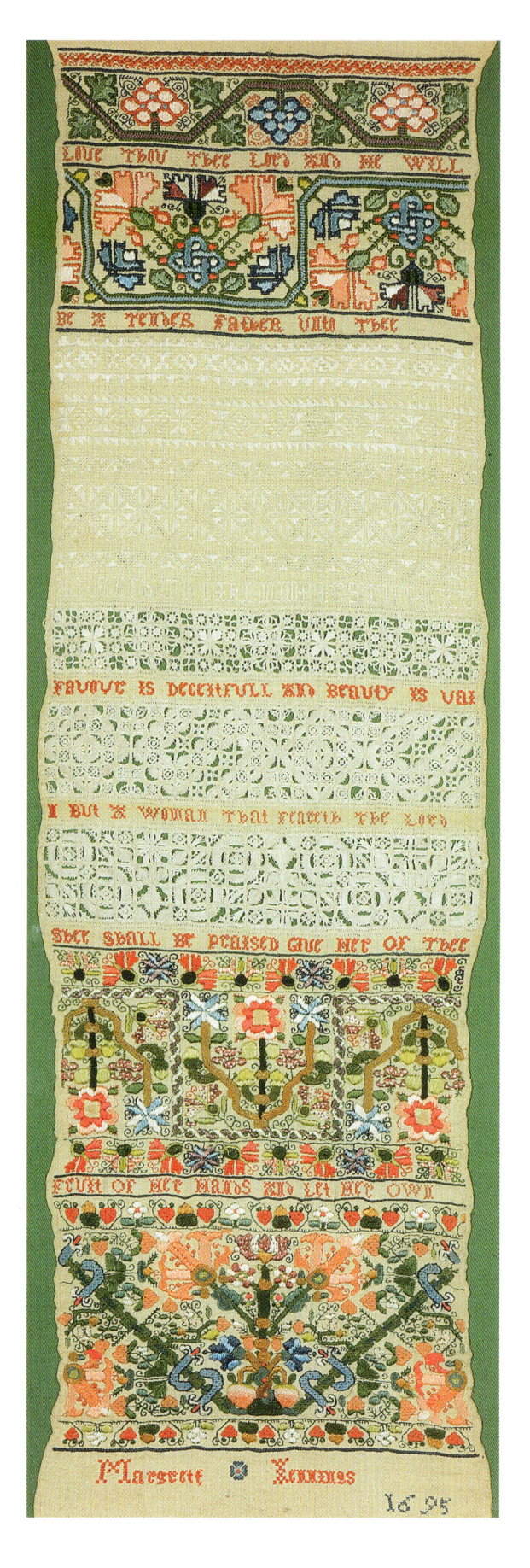

The Seventeenth Century

corresponding female figures (Plate 109). An Italian border fragment of the sixteenth or seventeenth century in the Victoria and Albert Museum has this motif precisely.

Sometimes portions of overall pattern were included, in colourful flame stitch, or in scale or diaper patterns for example. Geometric patches of such type are found on random or 'spot' motif samplers where a number of animal, flower or pattern motifs are spotted irregularly over a piece of linen. These motifs are at times included at one end of a band sampler, as for example one with animals and fish at the top, but more often spot motif samplers were limited to a combination of small pictures only. Animals, birds and insects already mentioned are typical of this genre, shown at random and unrelated in scale. Lions, kingfishers, caterpillars, human figures and plants were also depicted and all were in realistic, shaded colours, interspersed with beautifully stitched fragments of darning or border patterns. Heraldic devices, embossed metal thread work, and occasionally padded stumpwork are found too, and sometimes sequins, beads and pearls.

Samplers with figures embroidered in them are sometimes seen. One sold at Christie's, London (10 May 1983) was dated 1659 and had a crowned Tudor rose, lions, the initials ER and two girls wearing pink and blue robes which open to reveal pink petticoats of eye stitch.

Crowns were another popular motif, a feature probably introduced from Europe. Sometimes they are drawn and labelled in series of status with initials K (King), D (Duke), M (Marquis), E (Earl), V (Viscount), but often a repeated one was used simply to fill up lines of lettering or numerals.

A few interesting samplers recorded historic events. Huish describes three, commemorating William of Orange's arrival in England, his defeat of the French in 1692, and an earthquake in the same year. In this last, Mary Minshall sewed: 'There was an earthquake on the 8 of September 1692 in the City of London but no hurt tho it caused most part of England to tremble'.

It is an indication of how American needlework in an English tradition was well established early in the seventeenth century that the first recorded American sampler was made in about 1635. By Loara Standish, it is in much the same form as English ones of the period, but interestingly has a verse recording her name and showing a dutiful approach to her task as one leading to virtue and religious piety.

There were many common features in the samplers of Great Britain and other European countries. German, Dutch, Italian and French ones each have similarities. German samplers, often square in shape, were usually of fine cross-stitch and were neatly finished on both sides of the material. An early one, dated 1618, has columns of

Opposite. 113. Sisters worked these fine samplers with minor variations. They included whitework techniques, alphabets and texts.
Above. 114. This sampler is made up of 'bands' of Italianate ornament including one resembling blackwork with coloured in-fillings, above a collection of heraldic animals. c.1630.

stitching in red and green silks, and other parts show cut and drawn work with needlepoint lace stitches.

Dutch samplers were originally about 25in. (64cm) x 12in. (30cm), or were long and thin, depending on loom sizes. Later they became a more standard 18in. (46cm) square. They were often characterised by a border surround, with spot motifs in the centre. Tulips, as an exotic novelty, were depicted together with flowers, windmills, animals, biblical motifs and a variety of lettering, though this was sometimes omitted.

The Italians were especially known for whitework, and their samplers in this form were worked with beautiful, elaborate designs which were considerably more complex and finer than similar techniques subsequently developed in other countries.

Early French samplers are not often found and they were probably less frequently made. They were usually signed at the bottom, but were otherwise similar to English ones.

Embroidered Pictures and Stumpwork

Girls made at least one sampler, often progressing to other works such as needlework pictures, small cabinets or caskets covered with needlework, and panels of beadwork. A remarkable series of pieces worked by Martha Edlin has survived. Firstly, at the age of eight, in 1668, she completed a coloured sampler. In the following year she did one in whitework. In 1671 she finished a casket depicting the Seven Virtues, with Justice and the Elements, and in 1673 a beadwork jewel box of which the lid only has survived.

Pictorial embroidery was popular in the Elizabethan period for cushions but by the middle of the seventeenth century much larger numbers of small panels were made in fine tent stitch and in raised padded work, which was given the name stumpwork in the nineteenth century. There was a small amount of raised work in Elizabethan embroidery, and more in Jacobean. But the fashion for padded embroidery was partly derived from the more serious sculptural use of the technique in European ecclesiastical vestments following the late Middle Ages. German baroque and Hungarian vestments were also highly embossed, with a resemblance to metalwork or carved wood; they were frequently encrusted with seed pearls, another feature adopted by English stumpwork, though in much smaller quantities.

These small pictures enjoyed a tremendous vogue. Many beautifully worked ones have been preserved, partly because they were framed and behind glass. They were invariably of amateur workmanship; the standardised subjects have a childish naïvety and sameness but if the condition is good they can be very charming. The various kinds of embroidered picture show great patience and technical skill. The designs were similar, though tent stitch versions are apt to be more orderly with fairly coherent compositions and related vignettes. Stumpwork pictures display a collection of motifs, haphazardly associated, with little or no unity. Both were made up of conventional 'spots'.

Mirror frames and caskets (small cabinets with drawers and lids), as well as pictures, were made up with a collection of smaller panels of the same style. Even large cabinets, on stands, were decorated with needlework panels enclosed behind doors,

The Seventeenth Century

such as a magnificent inlaid walnut one from Groombridge Place, Kent, which contains portraits of Charles II and Queen Catherine. All such embroideries were of three basic varieties: finely worked tent stitch, flat floss silk embroidery (laid and couched), and raised stumpwork. The last two were done on cream satin, though the flat silk stitching often covered the whole surface. In pictures, the satin background was sometimes dotted with sequins or tiny tendrils of embroidery. Similar pictures were also worked in coloured glass beads; panels, caskets, mirror frames, glove trays or baskets and other items in this form give us an idea of the original colouring of their embroidered contemporaries, most of which have inevitably faded somewhat (Plates 125 and 129). The glass beads are, of course, of vivid colours, interesting and lovely in their own way, but having a hardness which contrasts with the subtler shades that the embroideries have. Some caskets have been remarkably well preserved and some still have their original oak boxes in which they were protected. These were made by a professional cabinetmaker, or upholsterer, who was employed to make up the caskets from the needlework panels supplied by their maker. A note inside Hannah Smith's box (Whitworth Art Gallery, Manchester), written by her, records how her needlework was sent up to London from Oxford for this purpose: '…I was almost 12 years of age; when I went I made an end of my cabbinette, at Oxford… and my cabinet, was made up, in the year of 1656 at London'. This casket is also interesting for the representative variety of techniques employed in its workmanship. The doors are of fine tent stitch and a stumpwork lion and leopard are on the canted angles of the lid. The top surface

Opposite. 115. Another sampler shows highly disciplined infilling patterns, familiar in blackwork.

Below. 116. A large cushion cover is decorated with a number of spot motifs around two muses holding up a mappa mundi. Other figures include Turks, a representation of Charity, crowned angels and the sun, all embellished with silver and gold threads and with comets in the spangled background. 3ft.10½in. x 2ft.6in. (118cm x 66cm).

The Art of Embroidery

117. A small mirror, so precious that it was framed and enclosed within needlework. Back and front views. c.1670

itself is of flat stitches with metal thread; seed pearls are used for a necklace and crown. Another charming box, by Hannah Trapham, with her name and the date 1671 engraved on a silver catch, is at Sudbury Hall, Derbyshire. Later, caskets, mirror frames and pictures were often trimmed with tortoiseshell mouldings (Plates 120 and 121).

A variant to these forms of needlework was decoration in filigree paper, in neat rolls or tiny cut pieces built up in formation to frame pictorial, and make heraldic devices, or floral decoration with colours and gilding. Cora Ginsberg recently showed a casket decorated with coloured paper fronds while Malletts had a William and Mary mirror with rolled paper panels showing houses, set into the cream japanned frame.

The main themes depicted in tent stitch pictures were sometimes adapted, like tapestries and bed valances, from Flemish and Dutch engravings, but the great tapestry themes are not seen in amateur embroideries as much as might be expected. The Raphael cartoons, for instance, were not worked in needlework. Subjects were usually classical or religious but, despite this, a sense of humour is suggested in curious combinations, with homely rabbits and insects cavorting alongside the solemn protagonists of Old Testament stories, or Ovid. An ambitious portrayal of Pharaoh's crossing of the Red Sea (at the Lady Lever Art Gallery, Port Sunlight) in the clumsy terms of stumpwork is full of amusing drama.

New Testament subjects were not yet fashionable, though seen occasionally; they were too 'religious' for Protestantism whereas the stories of the prophets were accepted

The Seventeenth Century

Above. 118. Like a sampler this panel shows practice in numerous forms and varied techniques, especially in different workings of the fruits for example. c.1630.

Below. 119. With a silver background this picture portrays the Judgement of Solomon and a great variety of motifs including exotic birds and a snail, all charmingly out of scale. c.1650.

The Art of Embroidery

The Seventeenth Century

as quaint and 'historical'. Bible stories represented particularly frequently include the following:

Adam and Eve	Genesis I
Abraham and the Angels	Genesis XVIII
Abraham and Hagar with Ishmael	Genesis XXI
The Sacrifice of Isaac	Genesis XXII
Rebekah	Genesis XXIV
Jacob's Dream	Genesis XXVIII
Jacob wrestling with the Angel	Genesis XXXII
Joseph and his Brethren	Genesis XXXVII
Joseph and Potiphar	Genesis XXXIX
Moses in the Bulrushes	Exodus II
Jael and Sisera	Judges IV
David and Goliath	1 Samuel XVII
David and Abigail	1 Samuel XXV
David and Bathsheba	2 Samuel XI
The Judgement of Solomon	1 Kings III
Elijah and the Ravens	1 Kings XVII
Jehu and Jezebel	2 Kings IX
Solomon and the Queen of Sheba	2 Chronicles IX
Esther and King Ahasuerus	Esther II
Judith and Holofernes	Apocrypha
Susannah and the Elders	Apocrypha
Tobias and the Angel	Apocrypha

Opposite. 120. A 17th century dome-topped casket with many exterior and interior three dimensional 'stumpwork' panels that include classical, biblical and everyday domestic themes, all on satin. Dated in seed pearls 1660. 11⅔in. x 11in. x 8⅝in. (30cm x 28cm x 22cm).

Below. 121. Two views of a casket with panels on all sides depicting the story of Joseph, retaining remarkably fresh colours. c.1660.

The Art of Embroidery

As more Bible illustrations were generally available the themes were more exactly portrayed, especially on eighteenth century seat furniture. Other works showed the seasons, the senses, the elements, the continents and portraits. As in sixteenth century valances, figures were depicted in 'modern dress' and the chief prophets, kings and queens were regularly depicted in the forms of Charles I and Henrietta Maria. Charles I had become a cult figure, king and martyr, and it is interesting to notice that though he and his queen were repeatedly shown in allegorical terms, Charles II and James II were not.

Extraordinary trouble was taken in perfecting minutely worked pictures. In the Victoria and Albert Museum a version of King Solomon receiving the Queen of Sheba shows the use of real hair and crowns of gold set with pearls. The silk and gold thread canopy has loosely hanging movable curtains of embroidered old brocade; the figures are adorned with strings of real pearls and lace. The three-dimensional effects of stumpwork were achieved by stuffing individual embroidered pieces with wool, hair, cloth or pieces of wood, while hands and faces might be of wax, wood, bone (or ivory), painted satin or, in the finest examples, of split stitch with the tiny features in stem stitch. Windows in buildings and the water in ponds and fountains were represented by pieces of mica (talc). Some caskets contain, or have on the top, a garden of free-standing flowers and ornaments; one of this type has a garden or meadow with figures, a

Below. 122. The padded stumpwork of this picture is especially bold and uses a large proportion of silver thread.

Opposite. 123. A 17th century picture of a king receiving a queen in a landscape filled with lively creatures.

137

The Art of Embroidery

124. Finely worked in tent stitch and signed F.W., this picture shows King Solomon receiving the Queen of Sheba, in 'modern' dress and honouring the dead King Charles I and Queen Henrietta Maria. c.1660.

shepherdess under a tree, sheep, other trees and a wild rose. Many have flapping leaves with shadows behind them worked in flat stitching. Three-dimensional effects, flowers, leaves, animals and tents, developed out of techniques of detached buttonhole stitches as already used in semi-raised Elizabethan and Jacobean embroidery. Later, Charles II stumpwork was less padded, giving way increasingly to flat and laid stitch work.

Both stumpwork and tent stitch pictures could depict a story, albeit often in a fragmentary sequence of vignettes, like a comic strip. Some, more clearly based on actual engravings are more orderly and coherent. While stumpwork pictures usually have a white satin background with the motifs applied, a few fine examples have tent stitch backgrounds, such as *The Return of Jepthah* based on a print by Martin De Vos (Untermyer Collection).

The variety of motifs was almost infinite, though the range of subjects was limited. The curiously disassociated juxtaposition of 'curiousities', mythological, religious, natural, historical and even heraldic, in unrelated scales, combined in creating an atmosphere of magic or fantasy (Plate 122).

The Seventeenth Century

Tent-stitch pictures were rather more orderly, as I have intimated (Plate 124). The designs were drawn out by professionals with various elements derived from engravings.[10] A small, finely worked panel at Alnwick Castle, Northumberland, depicting galleons engaged in battle at sea, with Neptune and nymphs in the foreground, must have been copied or adapted from an old print, the subject already being considered quaint and historic. Some pictures of the 1660s onwards were embroidered in wool only, in long flat stitches, colourful and charming but of distinctly less intricate workmanship. A good example in the Metropolitan Museum depicts familiar motifs including a king and a huge butterfly against a vivid background of red, green and blue. Two others, dated 1681, are at Glamis Castle.

Amongst unusual pictures of the earlier part of this period is a large panel at Dorney Court, Buckinghamshire, with the Palmer family arms, crests and full length portraits of eight distinguished sixteenth century Palmer Knights, on satin, closely speckled with applied pieces of purl. It was probably a wedding present to Thomas Palmer, married in 1624, from his widowed mother or grandmother. Another

125. A 17th century beadwork basket partly sewn and partly threaded on a wire framework. c.1650.

139

The Art of Embroidery

126. A charming small cushion filled with incident around the musicians. c.1670. 7¾in. x 12½in. (20 x 32cm).

unusual picture at the Lady Lever Art Gallery commemorates the defeat of the Spanish Armada and the Gunpowder Plot, with an inscription: 'to God in memory of his double deliverance from the invincible navie and the unmatchable powder treason'. This was a rendering by Dame Dorothy Selby from a popular print published in Amsterdam in 1621. Dame Dorothy was a notable needlewoman who died in 1641 of an infected needle-prick it is said. Her monument in Ightham church is inscribed:

> *She was a Dorcas,*
> *Whose curious needle turn'd the abused stage*
> *Of this lewd world into the golden Age…*
> *Prudently simple, providently wary*
> *To the world a Martha, to Heaven a Mary.*

Half worked examples are beautiful in themselves. One, depicting the story of Diana and Actaeon, shows precise drawing with no errors that could lead to confusion for the sewer, with motifs carefully and evenly spaced out. It would seem likely that the needleworker herself chose the subjects and incidental vignettes that the draughtsman

The Seventeenth Century

laid out for her. Had this not been the case, artists would have developed more obvious, perhaps duller, compositions.

Graceful needlework portraits of ladies were popular, usually in an oval format surrounded by bands of metal purl (coiled silver wire), with additional features shown in the background and in spandrels. Small portraits were sometimes placed within a larger picture, or in the border of a mirror frame, such as a lady holding a lute. Even a minutely worked landscape, perhaps bought as professional work, might be included within a larger panel, reminiscent of seventeenth century engravings on silver contained within ovals in a broader design. Either might be framed by flowers or a raised wreath.

Miniature oval portraits of Charles I were made after engravings by Sir Anthony van Dyke (1599-1641). Some may have been made by professionals and some are even said to be partly worked with the King's own hair (fanciful), thereby to be regarded as relics of Charles the Martyr. A version in the Victoria and Albert Museum has hair worked in with silks. The King was commemorated in tent stitch pictures (see pages 176 and 177), almost always seated as in his official portraits, thereby concealing his short stature. A splendid bust portrait of Charles II in the Metropolitan Museum,

127. Signed and dated 'A.M. 1653', embroidered motifs are here applied to an unusual blue satin.

The Art of Embroidery

boldly labelled as in a print 'Carolus II', depicts his lusty features and a magnificent dark wig.

Court art and decoration in Britain was considerably influenced by European workshops, though neither techniques nor styles deflected English girls from their passion for domestic pictures. In Holland landscapes, seascapes and still life flower groups were worked with the needle in reflection of Dutch painting. A 'Landskipp peace done in Holland-with a needle in Silke' was presented to Charles I, together with other pictures, in 1635.

Edmund Harrison (1589-1666) who was embroiderer to James I, Charles I and Charles II, worked in a manner more typical of Flanders than England. He may well have been trained there as he used especially the technique of *or nué*, or shaded gold. He undertook and supervised various work for court functions including masques, plays and heraldic banners. We now have only some of his religious pictures, worked in silk on canvas, in the form of needlepainting. His figures were done separately, then applied to another fabric, as stumpwork, but they were not padded. They have a sculptural quality as a result of the combination of 'old master' subjects with the

128. The lady in this minutely worked silk picture may represent one of the Senses, Hearing. c.1660.

The Seventeenth Century

metallic nature of the *or nué* technique. *The Visitation*, *The Betrothal* and *The Adoration*[11] were made for William Howard, Lord Stafford; all are dated 1637.

Much seventeenth century needlework included the use of metal threads, silver and silver gilt, often raised with padding behind. This is featured especially in professional work such as for church fittings or ceremonial furnishings including splendid saddles and saddle cloths. Metal threads, purl and sequins are also a feature of the much smaller amateur works, the panels made by young girls which we have considered here (Plate 129). To some extent bookbindings were decorated with metal threads. In all these cases they were usually combined with coloured silks. Following a few words on bookbindings we will examine contemporary but contrasting forms of embroidery that were done in wool alone, never highlighted with metal thread, but every bit as spectacular on a large, colourful and exuberant scale.

129. This splendid small beadwork picture portrays a courtly couple by a fountain, the background filled in with spangles. c.1660.

The Art of Embroidery

BOOKBINDINGS

Seventeenth century embroidered bookbindings for precious volumes were sometimes of velvet or were decorated with images like pictures and were made by both professionals and amateurs. Professionally made ones were usually for presentation. A purple velvet binding in the British Museum, of c.1615, was made in Paris for Mary de Medici, wife of Henry IV of France. It has a crowned shield, crowned Ms and fleurs-de-lis, all in metal threads and with colours on the shield. At Windsor Castle there is a *Book of Common Prayer* of 1638 bound in blue velvet and embroidered on it the Prince of Wales' badge of three feathers enclosed by the Garter, surmounted by a crown, with the monogram CP worked in gold and silver thread. Charles II had an embroiderer, John Morris, who undertook bindings, probably of a formal nature.

Bookbindings generally fall into four categories. Firstly, there were those of tent stitch, depicting religious and allegorical subjects, sometimes with a silver background. A largish book in the Victoria and Albert Museum has a binding of this kind depicting Jonah and the Sacrifice of Isaac and dated 1613. Secondly, there were ones with raised work in a mixture of silks and metal threads on a velvet ground. Thirdly, there was silk embroidery on white satin, either in floral patterns or with oval portraits within flower borders, perhaps with metal threads, sequins and pearls. The spines of these would be decorated with heraldry, monograms and other formal patterns. Francis Bacon gave a copy of his *Essays* to the Duke of Buckingham with an embroidered portrait of the recipient in the centre of the dark green velvet cover (Bodleian Library).[12] Some bindings were partly inspired by the tooling of leather, with strapwork, cherubs' heads, initials and a variety of spandrels. There are a number of fine embroidered bindings in the British Museum including some made by the Little Gidding Community, Cambridgeshire, for Charles I and his two princes. The community made embroidered book bindings, especially for their *Harmonies,* selections from the gospels.

Books were held closed either with silk ties or silver clasps. Many had bags to protect them, large enough to hold them loosely; these were also finely worked, but not in relief, and with the same design on both sides. Silk and metal thread book markers, with coloured ribbons, plaited cords or tassels, were also made.

Small, tightly stuffed pillows or cushions were frequently made to hold prayer books and Bibles, or for other uses. They too were similarly decorated with pictorial or patterned motifs on one side only, sometimes with tassels and a fringe of gold or silver lace (Plate 126).

130. The cover of a prayer book presented to William Murray by Charles I displays the King's arms and insignia rather than religious emblems.

144

The Seventeenth Century

Crewelwork and Oriental Influences

Of all seventeenth century needlework, the densely rich wool embroidered curtains, known as crewelwork, with bold and colourful trees, bulbous exotic flowers and fat curling foliage, epitomise the English Baroque. Though less rich than continental materials of the time, these convey the weighty grandeur of the period. In general the elaborate style expressed release from the devastation of the Thirty Years War and a counteraction to the austerities of Reformed church movements, with magnificence. Bold commitment dominated sculpture, painting and the lives of the ruling classes. Art, architecture and decoration flourished on a grand scale. Crewelwork was domestic but may be seen against this background.

Large scale wool embroideries, like the Bayeux Tapestry, had not been worked for over five hundred years when there was at last a new development of the technique in the early seventeenth century. It appeared to happen inevitably that the coiling, mono-

131. *Part of a crewelwork bed curtain, one of a set, this one signed and dated B. H. 1689, the monochrome tree of life pattern with baroque curling leaves of oriental origin.*

The Art of Embroidery

132. A crewelwork curtain of red wool with repeated flower sprigs, squirrels, birds, butterflies and caterpillars. Signed and dated 'LHE, 1646'. 4ft. x 4ft.11in. (121.92cm x 149.86cm).

chrome flower patterns of Elizabethan costumes were enlarged and embroidered in great expanses for bed hangings. A skirt in the London Museum of a large blackwork pattern is almost identical in design to curtains, especially like ones on a bed at Cothele House, Cornwall. In both cases the embroidery is of wool on linen twill, with circular tendrils containing real flowers. The wool was known as crewel ('crule', 'crewle' or 'croyl'), an inexpensive worsted yarn, closely twisted, of long staple wool with the fibres lying parallel. Its use was very ancient. The word crewel was originally pronounced as a monosyllable but in two syllables by the mid sixteenth century when it was also known as 'caddis', 'caddas'. 'caddiz', 'caddice', etc. The linen twill was often homespun, with linen warps on cotton wefts, being strong and less costly than imported materials.

Though much crewelwork of the seventeenth and eighteenth centuries must have been made in workshops, an equally large quantity was entirely made by amateurs, middle class people, in Defoe's words 'the middle sort who live well'. The cloth, spinning and dyeing could all be home produced and, indeed, the fashion for doing crewel embroidery soon became an absorbing passion amongst women, just as stumpwork was with their children. Pepys, the diarist, tells us that every woman, including his wife, was involved in extensive projects making new 'furniture' for beds (see his diary entry in the epigram heading this chapter, page 110). It was laborious work but they covered ground relatively fast and had no background to fill in with the tedious tent stitch of canvas work. The finished effect was baroque, bold, and colourful.

The patterns, as stated, originated from Elizabethan blackwork (monochrome, but not always black), but they were also considerably influenced by Flemish ('choufleur') verdure tapestries with stylised curling leaves, and also Venetian needlepoint lace which had similar leaves with characteristic infilling patterns that seem to have been adapted to wool stitches. These had already influenced blackwork. The curling leaves in earlier crewelwork patterns had coral-like veins and dots like speckling in woodcuts. There were, increasingly, heavier leaf designs as in French and Italian baroque silks, which were bold, formalised and no longer naturalistic, and themselves partly derived from Ottoman patterns. But perhaps the greatest source of inspiration came from the Far East and this developed throughout the century. Oriental exchanges of taste and technique gave our entire culture inestimable new stimulus in quality, design, colour and charm. Fantastic flowers and leaves were to some extent a transmutation from lotus leaves and flowers familiar on Chinese porcelain and the winding and scrolling plant forms have distinct parallels, though the original Buddhist significance was not relevant to the Mughal Islamic world where these new designs were developed.

Venice and Portugal had carried on trade with the East since the Renaissance and England savoured a few magical imports. In 1600 the East India Company was incorporated by Elizabeth I's charter and this was endorsed by James I. Trading at Surat was agreed to by the consent of the Mughal rulers of the State of Gujarat on the Coromandel coast of India in 1612 and a lively business exchange flourished for seventy-five years. In 1687 the Company transferred its headquarters to Bombay which had been ceded to England by Portugal as part of the dowry of Catherine of Braganza on her marriage to Charles II. Even the Lord Chancellor, Thomas Cromwell, little knew what far reaching results the deal would have, and when asked where the new territory was, merely replied: 'It is a paltry island a little distance off the coast of Brazil'. Extraordinary vagueness and an air of glamorous mystery surrounded the fabulous riches of the Orient. The 'Indian' provinces from which the superb luxuries of silks, embroideries, pearls, jewels, spices, perfumes, porcelain and lacquer were brought were regarded with the greatest fascination. Goods came from China and India, and many other places linked to the merchant routes. But all these countries were thought of as a single land bordered on the far side by a range of mountains which the Flood had not covered. Beyond this was Cathay, a Paradise land. The precious merchandise was therefore valued as the magical elixir of a land bordering heaven, redolent with the romance of the beautiful and remote Garden of Eden.

Indian textiles were already ancient and highly sophisticated before Mughal rule introduced Persian characteristics. Woven textiles had been admired throughout the ancient world and were referred to by the Greeks and Romans. Workshops were

The Art of Embroidery

Below. 133. French 17th century crewelwork curtains were formal in design, the pattern here derived from Jean Bérain.

Opposite. 134. The densely rich crewelwork embroidery on this large bed hanging depicts birds, animals, flowers and fruit in a tree of life stemming from a hillocky ground. English c.1690.

established in many places. Mughal tent hangings form a large and impressive corpus of professionally designed and made embroideries spanning at least two centuries. They formed the palace decorations of the essentially nomadic court and imperial city. The Maharajah of Jodhpur's red velvet tents with rich gold embroidery of the early eighteenth century are notable. The Mughal princes dressed in fine embroidery, partly inspired by European fashion and pattern books. A falconer's hunting 'jauva' in a gouache painting of c.1600 is apparently embroidered with fowls and animals like the magnificent early seventeenth century riding coat decorated with minute silk figures in the Victoria and Albert Museum (Plate 303). Indian embroidery of extraordinary fineness and sophistication continued to be made for Mughal rulers and for export throughout the century and well into the next. Hangings, huge floor carpets, and coverlets, mostly in fine chain stitch and in bright lustrous silks on cotton grounds displayed oriental and western floral features within conventional patterns of Persian and Chinese origin. Hangings and bed covers (or carpets) in the Victoria and Albert Museum and at Colonial Williamsburg show these bright works, the earlier ones principally in red and blue, but otherwise more colourful, while the large yellow silk floor spreads already referred to from Bengal were equally remarkable. (See also page 316.)

Textiles imported to Europe from the Orient were very popular and gave new inspiration to English manufacturers. The earlier crewelwork curtains embroidered in the tradition of blackwork had a single overall pattern, usually of leaves, endlessly repeated over the fabric with just a narrow border of the same pattern in a smaller form around the edges. The colours were originally monochrome, most often a deep blue-green, but subsequently of two shades such as blue-green with brown, combinations of blues and greens, red and black, and flame colours as seen on a bed at Doddington Hall, Lincolnshire.[13] (See also Plate 159.) At the same time a wide variety of stitches was used.

It is in the next stage that signs of direct Asian influence are noted, namely the concept of varied designs for each curtain instead of a repeated pattern. These were based on the ancient tree of life motif, in the form of a semi-natural, semi-stylised tree winding from the base all over the hanging to its extremities. The idea was adopted from the first imports of Indian *pintadoes* and *palampores*. At first they were of white designs on a coloured ground, usually a deep red and painted or printed by a wax process, but as these were not particularly well received in England, the East India company requested a reversal of the colour scheme, and suggested the introduction of other colours. They even went so far as to send out models 'in the Chinese taste' for copying in paint, print and needlework. The mutually developed products enjoyed a colossal success and European demand clearly helped shape the delightful oriental 'export'

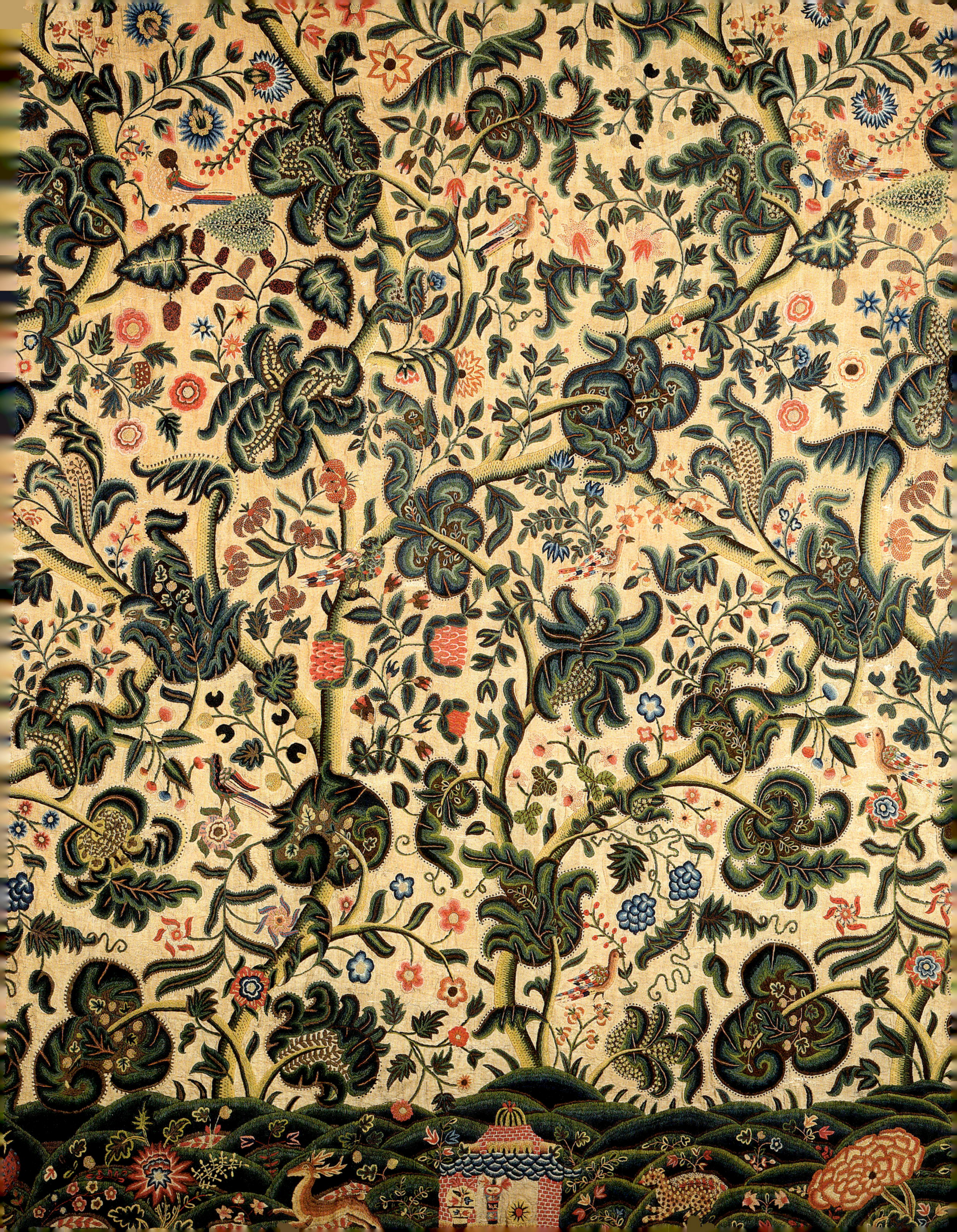

The Art of Embroidery

135. A detail of an English bed hanging of about 1700 shows chinoiserie and Indian influence and is worked in twisted wools.

items. In 1683 the directors of the East India Company wrote to their suppliers in Surat saying that imported chintzes were exceedingly popular and ordered a hundred sets of painted curtains for immediate delivery. They reported that all but the very poorest in England now had curtains and valances for their beds. They also ordered large numbers of cushions: 'each bed to have 12 cushions for chairs of the same work'. At first there was a market in India for English needlework but the Orientals quickly learned to imitate it, and made their own competitive varieties.

Crewelwork patterns developed in exotic forms with luscious tropical leaves, heavily curling on upward winding branches from a rooted base and growing out of undulating or hillocky ground. This last feature of Indian hangings may have originated from the stylised mountains and wave-like patterns around the base of Chinese robes; it certainly developed into the hillocky groundwork in later English tent stitch pictures. Much of the woolwork was dense and heavy in appearance but lighter designs were also carried out. A magnificent bed at Houghton Hall, Norfolk is hung with finely worked polychrome embroidery, chiefly in chain-stitch on a quilted ground that was made in India to English specifications. This imported needlework no doubt influenced the more refined English crewelwork of the 1730s. Also with Sir Robert Walpole's heraldic devices, this bed and another similar set of hangings (Plate 17) show a wide variety of European and oriental flowering shrubs with magnificent birds, closely related to Chinese coromandel lacquer and painted wallpapers. The beautiful Chinese papers, made solely for the European market, were originally a cheaper decorative version of the fine silk and embroidered hangings seen in China.

Transposed Chinese and Indian patterns such as these should be distinguished from a more playful and decorative aping of Chinese styles, known as chinoiserie. It was in a different spirit that Europeans began imitating oriental art, reasonably closely, but actually somewhat superficially. It became the height of fashion and entertainment to embroider, paint and even do lacquerwork 'in the Indian manner' or 'in the Chinese taste', these terms being synonymous. English imitations of lacquer were known as 'japanning' and instructions for amateurs were laid out in Stalker and Parker's *Treatise of Japanning and Varnishing* (1688), which included a number of 'quaint' motifs. The desire for chinoiserie gathered momentum in furniture, tapestries, porcelain and crewelwork and by the eighteenth century it had become widely popular. An English silk bedcover, in the Victoria and Albert Museum, one of two similar ones, has chinoiserie motifs including rocks, trees, pavilions, pagodas and bridges. It is signed 'Sarah Thurstone' with the date 1694. Many other embroideries included chinoiserie motifs.

It is hard to assess which crewelwork was domestic and which was made by professionals, but some examples are clearly homely. Abigail Pett's hangings in the Victoria and Albert Museum are signed by her. They consist of plant and animal motifs, drawn and spaced out over the fabric like stumpwork, but the plants are unreal, tropical and exotic, each growing from a characteristic Chinese rock formation. These craggy rocks, full of holes, like caves, are a principal feature of Chinese lacquer and textiles, and were incorporated in Indian *palampores*. They became an important motif in chinoiserie and were imitated in Italian and English garden grottoes. John Nieuhof in *The Embassy to the Grand Tartar,* translated from Dutch in 1669, illustrates 'cliffs made

The Art of Embroidery

136. One of a pair of red wool embroidered panels each representing stories of King Solomon and worked with shading suggestive of woodcut origins. c.1650.

by art'. A polychrome crewelwork fragment in Boston Museum of Fine Arts and the Ashburnham Indian hanging in the Victoria and Albert Museum are closely related in design. Both have the craggy rock formation, similar stylised animals, oriental figures and European flowers. They show clearly the interrelationship of style in the two countries and their common derivation from Chinese sources.

Abigail Pett's needlework also shows birds and animals, a curious mixture of stumpwork-type lions and stags, and Chinese cranes and phoenixes. Her hangings are interesting also in being a complete set for a domestic bed, of a non-stately type. It was part of the rich decorative quality of crewelwork that it adapted and combined successfully such diverse emblems. On occasions when flowers were less stylised, one can see a mixture of European and oriental varieties, including some of the Taoist and

Buddhist symbols associated with the seasons. Spring is represented by magnolias and peonies, Summer by lotus flowers, Autumn by chrysanthemums and vines, and Winter by roses and prunus blossom. An ebony bed, associated with Catherine of Braganza, at Boughton House, Northamptonshire, is hung with interesting crewelwork of a vine pattern. Profuse bunches of grapes are worked in a kind of stumpwork.

The passion for crewelwork reached even the remotest parts of the country, as testified by a list made in the Orkneys in 1650 after the death of Lady Morton. This includes many fascinating items and reads like poetry, with delightful descriptions of fine quality pieces, and gives an indication of how much they were treasured. Items such as '1 Gryt Sweet Bagg soad with pitty point' and '2 Dosson fox skinns' are recorded but of crewelwork there was: '1 Whyt fustan bedd, sow'd with Incarnat worsett whereoff 15 pieces was of it'. That the needlework was red (incarnat) at this early date is interesting as the majority was of blue-greens. The fifteen pieces would have been four or more curtains, three valances for the canopy, three for the base, a head curtain, a lining for the canopy and a coverlet, with perhaps additional cushions.

Crewelwork was not only used on bed hangings. We see it also on small articles of clothing such as caps, on work bags quite often and even on shoes. A number of panels worked in red wools portray animals, birds, flowers and biblical scenes familiar in smaller pictures but in these cases in a larger format. A hanging in the Embroiderers' Guild Collection may have been a valance. The design is made up of a number of figures and scenes combining Old and New Testament stories including the Nativity. Two other largish pictures, similarly worked, illustrate more conventionally the Judgement of Solomon and King Solomon receiving the Queen of Sheba (Plate 136).

GREAT STATE BEDS

Only a small number of great houses in England, Scotland and Wales had a broad range of textiles and upholstery and there are probably no more than a dozen or so great seventeenth century beds of which the most prized were of silk or velvet and a smaller number were of needlework. It is worth noting that in some cases bedrooms had separate sets of winter and summer hangings. The Queen's bedroom at Ham, furnished in honour of a visit by Queen Catherine, according to an inventory of 1679, had a 'Portugal bedstead' and a set of wall and bed hangings, with twelve chairs to match for summer use. In winter a bed with hangings of blue velvet brocaded with gold were used.

The use of crewelwork and more formal professional needlework was as an alternative to silks and velvets which were used on the more important beds over carved and padded mouldings in the manner of designs by Daniel Marot. Such furniture was suitable for grandiose surroundings and was especially made for royal palaces and other great houses. Several chairs of state, canopies and beds of this kind are still to be seen at Hampton Court Palace, Chatsworth and Knole. Great needlework hangings are well represented by the splendid bed with a wing chair, side chairs and stools en suite at Clandon Park, Surrey. Made in about 1700, the brilliantly coloured silks show a regular pattern of red and blue flowers on a cream background.

The Art of Embroidery

137. This great red satin bed, at Knole, and its accompanying seat furniture, is decorated with appliqué *strapwork and metal spangles or sequins to give a sparkling effect. c.1630.*

The cost of such needlework, probably French, was tremendous. About this time Lapierre, a leading upholsterer, charged the Duke of Devonshire £5 for a large bedstead and as much as £470 for the hangings.

French beds were not usually as grand, tall and important as great English beds but the d'Effiat bed in the Louvre, of c.1640, is perhaps the earliest surviving needlework bed. This is of appliqué in formalised patterns. A bed at Dalemain, Cumberland, is

The Seventeenth Century

probably the earliest English survivor, albeit altered. It has black embroidery on a white ground and was reputedly the gift of Lady Anne Clifford, c.1670. The Spangled bed at Knole, Kent, probably from Whitehall Palace, is one of the finest, being of crimson silk with a buff strapwork design and with silver and gold thread embroidery. Decorative needlework features on several great silk beds. The blue bed at Burghley House, a red bed head at Benningborough and the interior of the great bed at Belvoir Castle which has birds, animals and flowers in tent and other stitches, applied to a white satin ground, are amongst other rare survivals incorporating embroidery.

A remarkable needlework bed of colossal height is at Drayton House, Northamptonshire. It has tall 'paned' curtains and long narrow ones, *cantonières*, at the corners where the main curtains meet. The needlework of these and on a set of six

138. Part of a late 17th century English bed cover of cotton embroidery with a quilted ground, clearly inspired by Indian designs.

The Art of Embroidery

chairs (loose fitting covers) and a sofa is of a formal floral design, probably derived from Dutch engravings, in wool with silk highlights. The bed was made in 1700 for the Duchess of Norfolk and bills show that the needlework was made by Elizabeth Rickson and Rebekah Duffee (Plate 139).[14]

Spectacular beds hung with Chinese embroidery included the great Calke Abbey state bed and one at Erddig, both of the early eighteenth century, are discussed on pages 306 and 307.

Florentine stitch hangings (Plate 81, page 91) offered vibrant decoration, worked in either silk or wool. The bright wavy patterns, and the similar Hungarian *(point de Hongrie)* or flame stitch, the equivalent of the modern bargello, have a timeless quality that has always been popular. The zigzag stripes, or lozenges, were at first of untwisted silks, and later of wools, or of a mixture. They are reminiscent of marbleised paper. A room at Chastleton House, Oxfordshire is hung with Florentine work (Plate 82, page 92) and other splendid examples at Parham Park are on a bed and as hangings. A similar pattern was also achieved in a woven form. There is a technical distinction between Florentine stitch and *point de Hongrie,* the first usually being a vertical stitch over a consistent number of holes while *point de Hongrie* may vary in length and even direction. A further variety of bargello is Irish stitch, worked regularly over several holes but rising halfway each time.

Though on the whole essentially English, crewelwork was also done in America, based on examples taken out to the New World from this country. Good embroidery of this kind was mostly produced in the eighteenth century but there are some earlier examples. A set of bed hangings of the late seventeenth century in the Metropolitan Museum is said to have been worked by the three successive wives of Dr Gilson Clapp. Embroidered in red wool, they show birds, squirrels, stags pierced with arrows, and floral sprays.

American 'Turkey work', needlework imitations of oriental carpets (not woven or hand knotted) were recorded as early as 1670 and were especially used for covering chairs, for table carpets and for bed covers.

It may be mentioned here, in passing, that Persian and Middle Eastern carpets and tribal rugs in general both influenced and were imitated in needlework versions in European countries. One example is a group of carpets of Persian design, attributed to Arraiolus in Portugal, a place well known for designs in the Persian style as well as Anatolian, Mughal Indian, and hybrid mixtures. The use of soft colouring, such as tones of yellow, rose pink, light blue and cigar brown, for example, are delightful.

Quilting had been used for a number of practical reasons and as decoration since the Middle Ages. The stitching bound together several layers to form pocketed insulation. Bed covers of this method[15] were made in mediaeval days and continued to be popular throughout the seventeenth century. For decoration only, however, 'false quilting' was done without padding. The stitching was often in complex geometric, vermicular and foliate patterns (Plate 138). Clothes were also quilted, especially jackets.

Quilting was especially developed in England, but almost certainly had an oriental origin and it is interesting that, while many oriental needlework imports were regarded suspiciously by apprehensive English workshops, Charles I pointedly permitted the importation of 'quilts of China'. In the 1614 inventory of Henry Howard,

139. The Duchess of Norfolk's great state bed at Drayton House of around 1701, the embroidered curtains (together with accompanying chairs) made by Elizabeth Rickson and Rebekah Duffee.

157

The Art of Embroidery

140. A 17th century Italian silk hanging displays the delights of music in an architectural garden filled with flowers, fruit trees, birds and animals.

Earl of Northampton, several 'China quiltes' are listed, including one of a chequered pattern in yellow silk. Yellow, the Chinese imperial colour, was particularly popular and much used in Chinese, Portuguese and subsequent English quilting; often fine work of this kind formed a background for coloured floral embroidery, usually in chain stitch. On other occasions they were plain, displaying the texture of the quilting alone. A fine example in the Victoria and Albert Museum (shown with Abigail Pett's bed hangings) is signed in black on one corner 'III Ward 1680'. It is of linen with yellow in back stitch and with a border of tiered arches, variously infilled. It is of a single thickness with no padding or lining.

Imported Chinese coverlets such as ones at Skokloster Castle, Sweden and Rosenborg Castle, Copenhagen, introduced features that became conventions in England in the eighteenth century, especially a large central medallion, quarter segments at the corners, a running border and Chinese motifs. Couched gold, an especially Chinese feature, became a notable characteristic of some of the grand coverlets of the first half of the eighteenth century. There was no quilting, however, on the Chinese imports which were of silk; that was a particular feature of Indian ones of cotton.

The Seventeenth Century

William and Mary gave their names to the decorative styles prevalent during the last part of the century. It was a period of great building programmes in England, epitomised by Wren, with high quality building, woodwork in large panelled rooms, Dutch and oriental style furniture and porcelain, rich upholstery and luxurious textiles. The court was splendid with costume and uniforms. Even the rat-catcher had a professionally made outfit: 'of crimson cloth lyned with blew serge and guarded with blew velvet Embroidered with their Maties W R M R and Crownes on back and chest and six Rattes Eateing a Wheat-sheave on the left shoulder'.

Queen Mary herself was known for her needlework and was to be seen doing it everywhere, even in her carriage as it passed. The mocking verses of Sir Charles Sedley about Queen Mary compared her with the previous catholic queens:

> *Blest we, who from such queens are freed*
> *Who, by vain superstition led*
> *Are always telling beads;*
> *But here's a queen now, thanks to God*
> *Who when she rides in Coach abroad*
> *Is always knotting threads.*
> *In the meantime dull Phyllis, ignoring the advances of her lover:*
> *Phyllis without frown or smile*
> *Sat and knotted all the while.*

Celia Fiennes in the eighteenth century visited Windsor Castle and noted: 'hangings, chaires, stooles and screen the same, all of satten stitch done in worsteads, beasts, birds, ymages and ffruites all wrought very ffinely by Queen Mary and her Maids of Honour'.[16] There was another set by her at Hampton Court Palace which may have been of knotting as she loved this technique also. Linen threads were knotted with a shuttle and then couched down in complicated patterns, especially suitable for formal furnishings. Red strapwork designs in knotting were applied to yellow silk upholstery on a bed and a large number of chairs and stools at Ham House. Some unused pieces show how brilliant the original effect was. Knotting was also done in metal threads for formal patterns on important canopies, hangings and upholstery. Also at Ham House is an example of couched cord and applied work in the Antechamber to the Queen's Bed-chamber, where a set of wall hangings of damask are bordered with dark blue velvet.

By the end of the seventeenth century canvas work re-emerged as a form for hangings in anticipation of the many uses of this type of needlework on eighteenth century furniture. A series of large panels found in a house in Hatton Garden (now in the Victoria and Albert Museum) show a curious mixture of crewelwork type leaves around columns with the familiar animals below, including lions and unicorn. These follow the continental use of tall panels of needlework, often quite narrow, that were used on tall beds, but also hanging on walls, perhaps as *entre fenêtres* (pier hangings between windows) or within mouldings around a room. Italian hangings were often of floss silk in satin stitch showing columns of floral ornament strapwork and paired birds and other motifs, as the one of about 1700 in the Untermyer Collection, Metropolitan Museum, New York.

CHAPTER SIX

A Note
on Costume

*...the queen in vesture of gold, wrought
about with divers colours*

BETWEEN the extremes of elaborate display and 'modest chic', clothes have always been used as symbols of status and power; a great show of costume was intended both to instil fear in subordinates and to secure the confidence of supporters. At political and social levels an outward appearance of wealth expressed power, but personal vanity no doubt played its part too. In the late sixteenth century Sir John Harrington unashamedly admitted:

*We goe brave in apparell that wee may be taken for better men than
we bee; we use much bumbastings and quiltings to seem fitter formed,
better shouldered, smaller waisted, fuller thyght than we are...*

While mediaeval embroidery in England is famed for glorious church vestments, the *opus anglicanum* renowned across Europe, there was also much secular needlework made of sumptuous quality for court life. Unlike the ecclesiastical robes which were protected and cared for in church treasuries, domestic costumes were worn out, altered and eventually lost. Many were enriched with metal threads, stones and tiny discs of glass, like sequins, to catch the light. Inventories give glimpses into the fantasies and fun of court costume. It is recorded, for example that for Christmas and New Year festivities in 1393-4 two amazing garments were made for Richard II, a white satin doublet embroidered in gold with orange trees, on which hung one hundred silver

*141. Captain Thomas Lee, painted by Marcus Gheeraerdts, 1594, is humorously prepared for a
masque, ready to wade through Irish bogs, and wearing a fine embroidered tunic.*

Facere ci pati Fortia

Ætatis suæ 43
A° D'' 1594

The Art of Embroidery

142. A fine collar of cutwork with complex stitching. Italian, probably Venetian, c.1610.

gilt oranges, and another garment embroidered with water and rocks, amongst which were placed fifteen silver-gilt mussels and fifteen silver-gilt whelks. The French and Italian mediaeval courts were especially sumptuous with magnificent costume. In 1493 the Duchess of Milan, Beatrice d'Este Sforza, wrote in a letter that she was having dresses embroidered in silk designed by Leonardo da Vinci. Even the Duchess of Burgundy's fool had an embroidered costume made for him in 1421 with emblems and pearls on it. Charles d'Orléans had music embroidered on his costume, the notation indicated by 500 seed pearls.

Italian costume was not generally rich in needlework since that country specialised in and preferred to wear fine, woven fabrics. In England however, the Tudor court was splendid with elaborately embroidered dress. Princess Mary Tudor, daughter of Henry VII and later wife of Louis XII, had her footmen dressed in white cloth of gold quilted with a scale pattern. Henry VIII's costumes were renowned for their lavishness and some, like many others of the period, are faithfully depicted in paintings. They are seen to be heavily laden with gold thread, precious stones and pearls (Plate 58, page 65).

Elizabethan dress was equally remarkable and was painstakingly portrayed. Many aspects have already been mentioned, but a further example of the intricate detailing, a description of ruffs by Philip Stubbes, of 1583, may be added. He speaks of them as: '…either clogged with gold, silver, or silk lace of stately price, wrought all over with nedle woorke, speckled and sparkled heer and there with the sunne, the moone, the starres, and many other antiquities straunge to beholde'.

Elizabeth I's costumes were spectacular; it is sad that none has survived but Roy Strong and Janet Arnold have shown us into her wardrobe.[1] A few items from an inventory of 1600 convey the richness of pattern and materials:

> *Item, one fore parte of white satten, embrodered allover verie faire like seas, with dyvers devyses of rockes, shippes, and fishes, embrodrered with Venice golde, sylver, and silke of sondrye colours, garnished with some seed pearle.*
>
> *another…with paunceis, little roses, knotts, and a border of mulberries, pillers, and pomegranets…*
>
> *another…of peach-colour, embroidered all over verie faire with dead trees, flowers, and a lyon in the myddest, garded with many pearles of sondry sortes.*
>
> *a peticoate…like a wilderness*

A Note on Costume

*Item on rounde gowne, of the Irish fashion, of orenge tawney satten,
cut and snipte, garded thicke overthwarte with aish-colour vellat,
embrodered with Venice golde and spangles.*

Mary Queen of Scots' wardrobe was carefully listed, and detailed records were made of her needlework on garments. Significantly, the Queen went to great pains to make a skirt for presentation to Elizabeth I: '…a skirt of crimson satin, worked with silver, very fine and all worked with her own hand, to the Queen of England, to whom the present was very agreeable, for she found it very nice and has prized it much'. Mary had spent three months working on it.

Margaret Laton's remarkable jacket is shown on page 112 but another interesting sixteenth century survival is a bodice known as the Devereux heirloom now in Kyoto

143. Portraits by William Larkin, of about 1615, of Lady Dorothy Cary and Edward Sackville, 4th Earl of Dorset, display fabulous embroidered costume for both women and men. This great high point in English needlework has now almost vanished but is recorded in pictures.

163

The Art of Embroidery

144. This coif, a headdress, opened out, is decorated with silk embroidery of wild animals, birds and monstrous creatures bound by tendrils. Early 17th century. 9in. x 17¾in. (23cm x 45cm).

Museum, Japan. It is of cloth of silver and embroidered in gold, silver and silk thread with a twining design of roses, irises, carnations, peapods, cornflowers, columbine and forget-me-nots, interspersed with caterpillars, birds and butterflies. The garment is said to have been sent to Elizabeth I by the Countess of Leicester (Viscountess Hereford) when her son, the Earl of Essex, was awaiting execution at the Tower.

Dress materials and embroideries were greatly treasured and were unpicked and re-used in various forms until completely perished. For this reason few have survived to the present day. Sometimes costumes were adapted for use as coverings for furniture. An item in Henry Howard, Earl of Northampton's inventory of 1614 includes embroidered slips and borders cut from a cloak 'to imboder some furniture for the howse withall'.

In Charles I's reign a greater availability of fine silk fabrics caused less embroidery to be used for costume. Plainer garments displaying the lustre and colours of the silks were favoured but a man's dress would include ornamental lace collars, cuffs and an embroidered scarf. The last item was originally worn over one shoulder and tied below the opposite arm, and later around the waist. A fine purple scarf worn by Charles I at the Battle of Edgehill is in the Victoria and Albert Museum. A descendant of this form of garment is still worn by soldiers in the army today. Another scarf is at the Nottingham Museum of Costume, where many other early items, including those of Lord Middleton's collection, are to be seen.

Especially fine Swedish royal costumes survive including King Gustavus Adolphus' gold embroidered wedding suit of 1620 and also Paris-made costumes of 1654 made for the heir apparent (later Charles X) for Queen Christina's coronation. The remarkable wedding suit made for the future James II (Plate 145), recently acquired by the

A Note on Costume

Victoria and Albert Museum, displays elaborate gold and silver thread embroidery including the Garter Star, on a 'heather-coloured' cloth ground.

Non-military or ceremonial dress was lavishly fringed and hung with deep collars of needlework and lace. 'Punto in aria', bobbin lace, was so fashionable and expensive that a French nobleman of 1630 boasted 'thirty two acres of the best vineyard...around his neck'. The delicacy of this lace and the charm of pieces such as the 'undress' cap illustrated (Plate 68, page 79), foreshadow the lightness and elegance that was to be the essential feature of the following century. A heavier richness in royal dresses, however, is epitomised in portraits of Queen Charlotte by Allan Ramsay, showing an elaborate dress worn with coronation robes. The tradition of such garments, white silk embroidered with gold, has been continued into the present century by H.M. Queen Elizabeth the Queen Mother and H.M. The Queen (Plate 150).

Eighteenth century dress in England was also highly decorative and pretty needlework was liberally used with a less formalised, flowing elegance. Mrs Delany, in 1738, described both the men's and ladies' costumes worn at the Prince of Wales' birthday party. The Countess of Huntingdon had a petticoat of black velvet with embroidered vases of flowers, shells and foliage. On other occasions petticoats were decorated with crewelwork of amateur workmanship, and even of designs familiar on bed curtains. The *Boston Gazette* in 1749 cited an American example that had been stolen. It was worked with 'Deer, Sheep, Houses, Forrest, etc.' Crewelwork costumes were less formal than the fine silk embroidery worn by older and grander ladies. Other aristocrats were so eager to be dressed in the fashionable Indian and Chinese taste that they sent garments to the East to be embroidered there.

Much needlework on costume was professional work, especially the more sophisticated patterns and varieties with metal threads, the heavier ones being known as bullion. Bugles, spangles, coils, aiglets and beads were used in quantities but were soon snipped off when, with the fashionable craze of 'drizzling' or 'parfilage', every girl robbed old embroidery ruthlessly to sell metals for re-use. Even Prince Leopold boasted earning enough by it to buy a silver soup tureen, which he gave to Princess Victoria on her eleventh birthday.[2]

The embroidering of clothes was a general pastime attempted by all and was not debarred from high-born ladies; Queen Charlotte and her daughters enjoyed doing needlework on their dresses, including silver thread work. The Queen showed her frame for fringe-making to Mrs Delany and a court dress belonging to this last, a celebrated embroideress, survives to this day. It is a

145. The richly embroidered heather coloured suit worn by James II at his marriage in 1673.

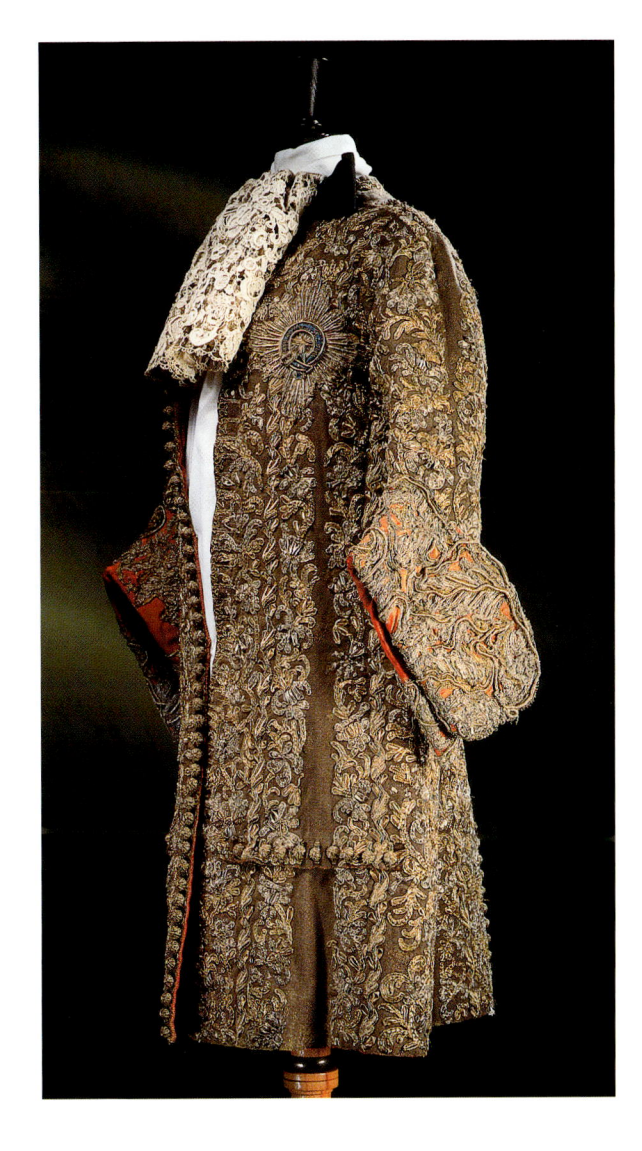

165

The Art of Embroidery

146. This early 18th century outfit includes petticoat, waistcoat and stomacher, all embroidered in silk and gold thread on a vermicular quilted ground.

masterpiece of her own working and the beautiful floral design is reminiscent of patterns for rich woven silks designed by her contemporary Anna Maria Garthwaite for the Spitalfields manufacturers. She used an unusual black silk ground for the embroidery.[3] Metals of contrasting patterns and textures were especially displayed on extraordinary 'mantua' dresses which became fashionable. These protruded sideways from the wearer's hips, supported horizontally by paniers (hoops), and, with matching trains and shoes, were usually of professionally made embroidery (Plate 149). In *The London Tradesman* (1747) Campbell comments on English professional embroidery saying that it is chiefly performed by women: 'It is an ingenious Art, requires a nice taste in Drawing, a bold Fancy to invent new Patterns, and a clean Hand to save their

A Note on Costume

work from tarnishing'. The almost unbelievable lavishness of English mantua dresses was not as extravagant, however, as some French costume. The Marquise de Créqui described the dress of a lady of Louis XV's court. The dress was of rich red velvet; the folds of the ample skirt were held in position by brooches of Dresden china made in the semblance of butterflies; on the front, cloth of silver was embroidered with a design showing an orchestra complete with musical instruments, worked in relief, and the musicians arranged in six rows; within the skirt was a hoop of nearly six yards in circumference.

Huge quantities of metal thread, braids and tassels were used for military uniforms in the eighteenth century and onwards; the weight of the materials contributed to a stiff smartness, the essence of correct turnout. The emblems depicted on grenadier caps and other such accessories called for a high standard of professional needlework.

Royal ceremonial dress continued to be rich in materials and of elaborate workmanship. The purple velvet coronation robe of George III (1761) is exhibited at Kensington Palace. He also had a crimson velvet robe. The suppliers' records show details: 36 yards of each velvet, 116 yards of broad gold lace, 63 yards of open chain lace. George IV's coronation robes (1821) were even more extravagant, characteristically theatrical and influenced by those of Napoleon Bonaparte of 1804 (Plate 245, page 249). The train of his robe (also exhibited at Kensington Palace) is decorated with trophies wrought with gilt metal threads. The *Morning Chronicle* reported that the King was

> *habited in robes of enormous size and richness,*
> *wearing a hat with a monstrous plume of ostrich*
> *feathers out of the midst of which rose a*
> *black heron's plume.*

A gentleman's domestic costume in the second half of the eighteenth century could be bright and flamboyant. Waistcoats and frock coats were of a wide variety of beautiful fabrics, often ornately embroidered with floral or sometimes unlikely designs, even ships. These were often professionally worked and many came from Lyons which had been a centre of embroidery before becoming famous for silk weaving and renowned for a magnificent set of vestments made for the coronation of Emperor Karl VII Albrecht, commissioned by the Elector Clemens-Augustus, Bishop of Cologne. In 1780 a traveller reported that over 6,000 embroiderers were employed in Lyons working on costume and vestments for export 'throughout the world'. A French waistcoat of about 1780 in the Musée Historique des Tissus is decorated with monkeys, flower sprigs and

147. Men's formal costume in the late 18th century was often very rich, in this case of cut and uncut velvet and with fine professional embroidery.

The Art of Embroidery

sprays, symmetrically placed on both sides.⁴ Other equally flippant designs were displayed on the portly figures of eighteenth century gentlemen. An account of the King's birthday celebrations, in *The Times* 5 June 1790, reflects the age of Beau Brummell, and the elaborate decoration of men's costume with a lengthy commentary and description of what was worn. For example 'Earl Weymouth: a very elegant suit of silk with shaded stripes; the embroidery new and pleasing, composed of silver, white and coloured stones, and groups of flowers in silks'.

Regency fashions were similar though less florid, with a tendency towards plainer patterns and the use of limited combinations of colours. But with the introduction of Berlin wool embroidery the range of new opportunities for canvas work led to a mass of ephemera, such as countless slippers made by admiring ladies for their suitors, together with waistcoats and smoking caps.

Outside the world of fashion were the peasant smocks made in English rural areas for use by agricultural and other workers. Of Anglo-Saxon origin, but particularly a short-lived phenomenon of the late eighteenth and early nineteenth centuries, these garments were of plain, homespun linen or twill material, with regional variations of style and colour,

A Note on Costume

ranging from olive green in the Fens to black in Surrey and the Isle of Wight. A few were worked in two colours but most were of a natural off-white. Sussex smocks were the most elaborate. Central panels of 'tubing' on the back and front, surrounded by a 'box' of embroidery and pulled together pleats of material provided a strong area on either side of the garment. Differences in design could signify the trade or skill of the wearer and the embroidery might include indicative devices such as a shepherd's crook or sheep.

Folk costumes with urban associations still seen today are those worn by the Pearlie Kings of costermongering in London. Now an established tradition, though only begun in this century, these are elaborately decorated with mother-of-pearl buttons.[5]

The tradition of magnificent metal embroidery has been continued on Coronation robes. The robe made for H.M. Queen Elizabeth (the Queen Mother), when she and the late King George VI were crowned in 1937, was made by the Royal School of Needlework, following the precedent set by Queen Alexandra and Queen Mary, the two previous Queens Consort (see page 5). In 1953 H.M. Queen Elizabeth II wore the Robe of Estate over a dress designed by Sir Norman Hartnell. This robe was also made by the Royal School of Needlework (Plate 29, page 31). These robes and other costumes relating to the coronations are to be seen at Kensington Palace.

Fashionable dresses of recent *haute couture* were designed as dazzling and sparkling. The designs of Norman Hartnell and Christian Dior for ladies of the Royal Family are characterised by interesting collages of texture and soft-coloured reflective sparkles intended to stand out with appropriate individuality. They also often provide a foil for fine jewels. The wedding dress of H.M. the Queen (Princess Elizabeth as she was then) in 1947 was by Norman Hartnell, who took his inspiration for the rich embroidery for the dress and train from a figure in a Botticelli painting, whilst the bridesmaids' dresses of ivory tulle were inspired by pictures by Winterhalter, Tuxen and Sir George Hayter at Buckingham Palace. The bride's dress was conceived with poetic imagery and appropriately was very much an emblem of its time:

> *Dress of ivory duchess satin, with fitted bodice, padded shoulders, long sleeves and long full skirt. It is ornamented with a design of flower motifs (orange blossom, jasmine, syringa and white roses of York) and ears of wheat richly embroidered in pearls, crystals and beads; the same motifs are used in satin appliqué and embroidery on the long court train.*

Above. 150. Cecil Beaton's photograph of the Queen (then Princess Elizabeth) shows her in an embroidered dress by Norman Hartnell, made for her mother in the 1930s.

Opposite above. 148. Part of an unusual set of appliqué panels of contemporary dress materials, perhaps representing the marriage procession of George III. c.1785. Each band 17¾in. (45cm) high.

Opposite below. 149. Mid-18th century costume, especially wide mantua dresses such as this, provided an opportunity for spectacular embroidery in both silks and metal threads.

CHAPTER SEVEN

THE EIGHTEENTH CENTURY

The pattern grows, the well-depicted flow'r,…
Unfolds its bosom; buds and leaves and sprigs,
And curly tendrils, gracefully disposed,
Follow the nimble finger of the fair.

THE Queen Anne and Georgian periods in England are celebrated for exceptional elegance and quality in almost every field. Architecture, and especially the decorative arts, produced a quantity of perfectly proportioned works, in both standard and unusual forms, and with a progression of varying stylistic treatments, depending on fashionable vogues. Perfect coincidences of stimulus and influence, the man and the moment, made the eighteenth century England's greatest period of decorative creativity. Though the origins of the baroque, rococo, and neo-classical tastes came from outside the country, the styles evolved here were, in essence, distinctly English. This was especially the case with needlework which attained a secular domestic peak, derived from many sources, while retaining its characteristically idiosyncratic nature.

With the Age of Enlightenment there came a renewed sense of fun and gaiety in place of the rich grandeur of previous times and within the first half of the eighteenth century there was a spirit of lightheartedness, frivolity and fun in contrast to ostentatious display. With origins in both Huguenot and Régence decorative forms the Sun King's orderliness was transformed to the smiling whimsies and new extravagances of the rococo taste, which reached its height during the reign of Louis XV. A relaxed and cheerful mood is apparent in the paintings of Claude Gillot and Antoine Watteau and with the introduction of 'rocaille' elements, together with themes from the Italian *Commedia dell'Arte,* singeries, chinoiseries (oriental and a Turkish variety) and gothicism, all sorts of gamefulness brought the joys of gardens, the out-of-doors and far-off lands into places of fashion.

151. Arcadian elegance, a well-dressed lady and her gentleman in an undulating landscape, blessed by the smiling sun, all superbly worked and wonderfully unfaded. English, c.1730.

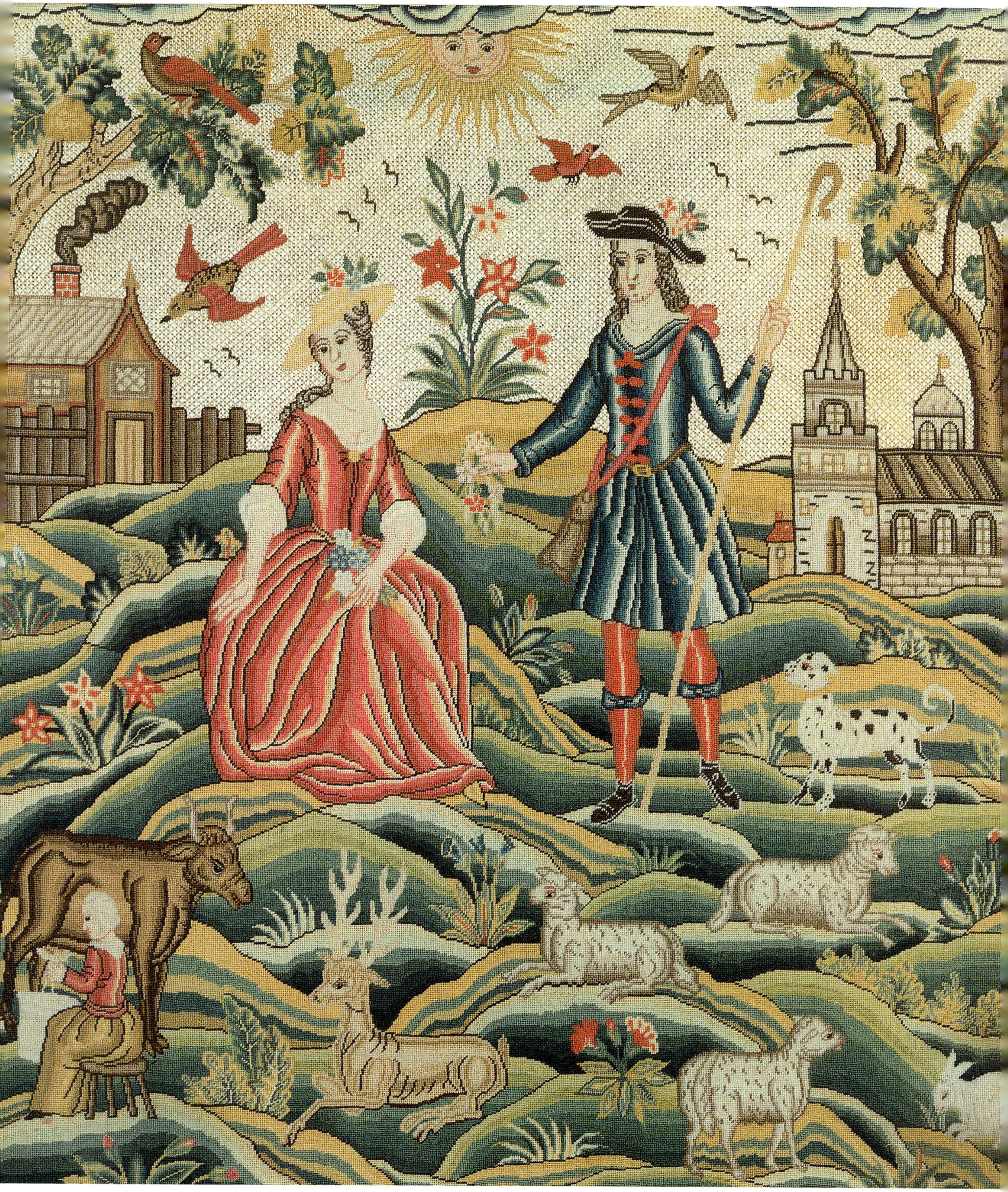

The Art of Embroidery

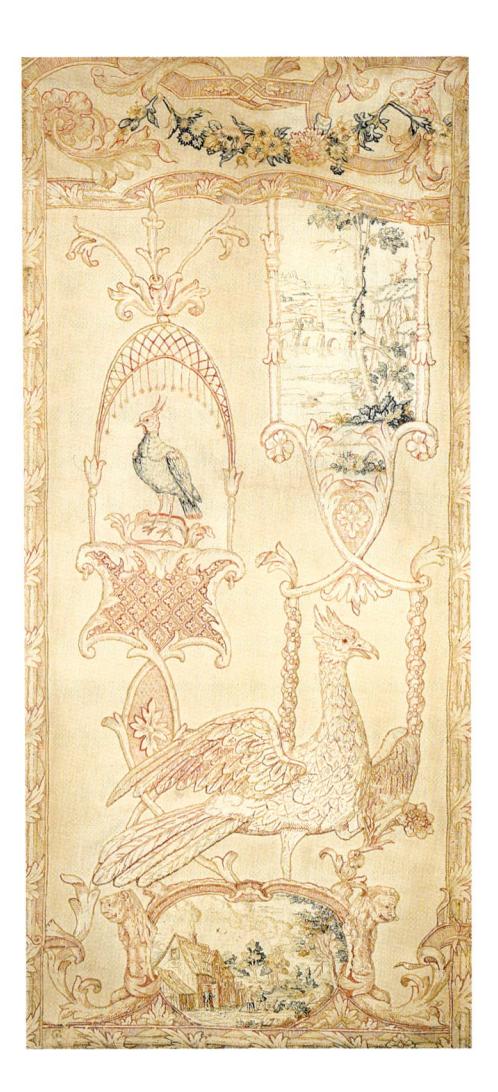

152. Piedmontese wall panels of about 1780 demonstrate neo-classicism with revived forms of 'arabesque' fantasy.

At the outset of the century, however, Parliament attempted to curb the importation of all materials 'of China, Persia, or the East Indies' as these threatened the prosperity of the English silk industry. In 1720 foreign coloured embroidery was prohibited, and even cotton goods were specified in the following year. These restrictions were relaxed in 1736, but in 1749 metal thread embroidery, lace and fringes were forbidden on the grounds of national economy. Venice had inspired a considerable use of metal threads, and 'purl' was much used. This appears in records from early in the sixteenth century and throughout the seventeenth and eighteenth, with a variety of meanings from metal bobbles looking like stringed pearls to gold thread lace. Basically, it was finely coiled gold wire, flexible enough to be couched down in various patterns. The heaviest purl was referred to as bullion. A cheaper form, of copper, was known as silk purl. This did not merit 'drizzling' or 'parfilage', the practice of raiding supposedly old or unwanted garments for reusable materials. Metal threads continued to be fashionable on costume throughout the eighteenth century, often stiffening and weighting the garment. Jewels were not used, partly as silk and metal threads were now

The Eighteenth Century

so lustrous, and partly as there was a tendency for elegance instead of the former studied grandeur. There were exceptions, appropriately, of oriental splendour. We are told, for instance, that Louis XV, at the age of eleven, received the Sultan of Turkey's ambassador 'in a suit of flame coloured velvet, weighed down with nearly 40 pounds in weight of jewels'. The richness of Elizabethan status symbols was continuously practised in eastern countries. French embroidery, however, though consistently more formal in style than English, was increasingly done by amateur ladies. Madame de Maintenon, wife of Louis XIV, founded an embroidery school at the Convent of St Cyr where she retired after the King's death. Daughters of the aristocracy were sent there to learn needlework, especially the canvas embroidery known today as point de St Cyr. Both St Cyr and workshops at St Joseph produced quantities of panels for walls and furniture of very good quality. These featured chinoiseries and 'grotesque' ornament, including the bizarre, like the contemporary woven silks, but more elaborate. An early eighteenth century hanging in the Victoria and Albert Museum with these features is very rich in its density of motifs and variety of stitches, colours and materials. A good deal of French needlework was imported to England for use on furniture; even simple and elegant Queen Anne walnut furniture might be upholstered with fine and complex chinoiseries and singeries in bright colours, such as a set of eight chairs in Brooklyn Museum and a sofa (Plate 227).

Italian vestments, in the meantime, followed the fashion of baroque architecture in which flamboyance was the touchstone of a worldly, almost hedonistic, concept for glorious churches. Workshops in Rome were celebrated for needlework almost exclusively of gold, the patterns being of a bold scrolling form, sometimes with additional bright colours. An Italian altar frontal at Anglesey Abbey is decorated almost entirely with secular motifs – fat spiralling columns richly decorated with flowers, vast urns of flowers, winged cupids holding baskets with more, and a large variety of birds in the air and on the ground. This is clearly professional work, as are French, Spanish and Italian vestments, neatly and perfectly made, and to be seen in museums all over Europe. The luxuriant flowers, scrollings

153. French bed valances and hangings of the early 18th century continue the tradition of petit point scenes linked in a decorative framework of gros point.

The Art of Embroidery

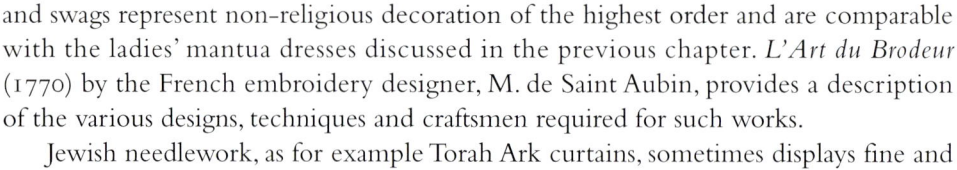

and swags represent non-religious decoration of the highest order and are comparable with the ladies' mantua dresses discussed in the previous chapter. *L'Art du Brodeur* (1770) by the French embroidery designer, M. de Saint Aubin, provides a description of the various designs, techniques and craftsmen required for such works.

Jewish needlework, as for example Torah Ark curtains, sometimes displays fine and complex metal thread embroidery on velvet, somewhat reminiscent of James I ecclesiastical needlework. A fine piece of this kind, c.1775, is to be seen in the Israel Museum, Jerusalem. Others survive in the Victoria and Albert Museum and in America, some of earlier date showing how the distinguished quality and technique were deliberately carried on for continuity of tradition.

Religious subjects were frequently more prominent in domestic eighteenth century needlework than in important ecclesiastical pieces. Carriage seat cushions in southern Sweden were embroidered with Adam and Eve or other religious motifs, and in most countries, throughout the century, Bible stories were portrayed in homely needlework pictures.

After the seventeenth century, the development of English domestic needlework turned from an emphasis on children's work, pictures and caskets, to a preponderance of canvas work. More needlework was done for practical purposes such as covering furniture. It was increasingly adult in approach and designs were based on a wide range of subjects, classical and biblical stories, mythology, fables, chinoiserie and others. Towards the end of the eighteenth century, canvas work was less popular, being replaced by silk embroidery of a purely decorative nature. The bolder tent and cross stitch floral patterns gave way to light silken ones. These, in turn, were followed by plainer geometric designs in canvas work, the simpler lines being more attuned to neo-classicism and Sheraton style furniture.

Throughout the century needlework was held in high esteem as a serious amateur pursuit. Most women did needlework and enjoyed it, and many men as well. Louis XV himself was proud of his abilities in this field. An amusing correspondence in *The Spectator* in 1714 sheds light on the strong views held by the older generation about doing needlework. A woman wrote to that paper on 13 October complaining of her young nieces' lack of desire to do useful and productive embroidery as their forebears had done. She encouraged the paper to take a lead in encouraging its readers in this direction: 'For my part, I have plied my needle these fifty years, and would never have it out of my hand. It grieves my heart to see a couple of proud, idle flirts sipping their tea, for a whole afternoon, in a room hung with the industry of their great grandmother...'. The editor somewhat mockingly replied that he was sure that all ladies would shortly 'appear covered in the work of their own hands... How pleasing is the amusement of walking

154. With the background entirely worked in yellow silk this French hanging, one of four, is filled with upward curling branches of flowers, within a rococo frame. c.1750.

The Eighteenth Century

155. One end of a large silk carpet with the shields of Austria and Mantua. Italian c.1708.

the shades and groves planted by themselves, in surveying heroes slain by their needle…'. He obviously felt that the advocated designs – those dense entanglements of herbage – were inappropriate.

Pictorial subjects were increasingly popular in the latter part of the seventeenth century and in the eighteenth century they show further naturalism. This then led to a decorative, ornamental approach. Garden ornaments such as urns, obelisks, fountains, statues and baskets of flowers were repeated hallmarks. Arrangements of flowers packed closely together, derived probably from Dutch paintings, were often charmingly shown in Chinese or Delft blue and white vases (Plate 190, page 203).[1] Unlike the Elizabethan and Stuart fashion for showing plants growing from the ground, eighteenth century needlework usually shows cut flowers in arrangements or in posies.

The Art of Embroidery

Designs were supplied by pattern drawers, a recognised profession, who in turn derived their subjects from pattern books and published sources such as Robert Furber's 1734 illustrations of flowers, essentially made for gardeners and watercolour painters. Another obvious source was Heckell's *Select Collection of the Most Beautiful Flowers, Drawn after Nature, Disposed in their Proper Order in Baskets, Intended for the Improvement of Ladies in Drawing or Needlework* (undated). Each flower was numbered and named. *The London Tradesman*, 1747, offers an insight into the duties of the pattern drawers' trade:

> *Pattern drawers are employed in drawing Patterns for the Callico-Printers, for Embroiderers, Lace-workers, Quilters, and several little Branches belonging to Women's Apparel. They draw Patterns upon Paper, which they sell to Workmen that want them…for all which they have large Price. This requires a fruitful Fancy, to invent new whims to please the changeable foible of the Ladies, for whose use their Work is chiefly intended. It requires no great Taste in Painting, nor the Principles of Drawing; but a wild kind of Imagination, to adorn their Works with a sort of regular Confusion, to attract the Eye but not to please the Judgement…*

156. A small portrait of Charles I at his trial, still a revered figure when this was embroidered by Anna Skinner in 1716.

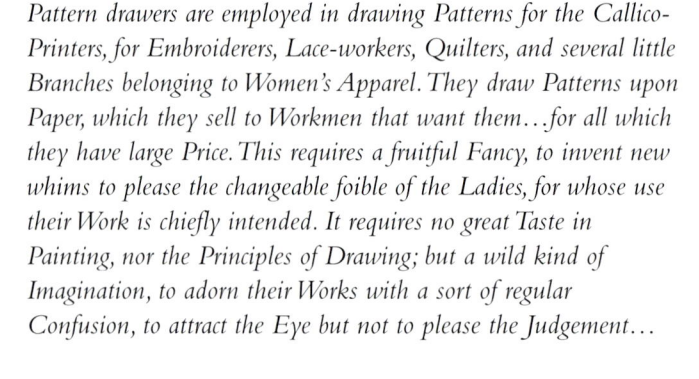

An entry in the diary of a Sussex schoolmaster in 1750-1 notes amongst similar entries that he spent five days drawing out a bed quilt and received 10s.6d. and did another pattern for a handkerchief for which his reward was ' a pint of strong'.

Wool had been much used in crewelwork hangings and Queen Anne pictures were often worked in worsteds, rather than silks, but silks were used for highlighting. The designs, though more realistic, still combined curiously impossible collections of subjects. English landscape hillocks are host to lions, leopards, camels, parrots and oriental pheasants. With these are depicted figures in Eastern or European costume and homely oak trees, sheep and squirrels (Plates 22 and 151). A splendidly documented panel at Mellerstain, Berwickshire is signed with the initials of two Menzies sisters and their governess and dated 1706. A portrait of a lady with flowers, representing the sense of smell, is taken from an engraving. This is surrounded by flower and fruit slip motifs with birds, animals and insects derived from *A Booke of Beast, Birds, Flowers, Fruits, Flies and Wormes…* published by Thomas Johnson in

176

157. Charles I saying farewell to his children with his advice to them, derived from an engraving and signed by Mary Middleton, 1741.

1630. The engraving of Smelling and this book, bound together, are still near the needlework panel in Lord Haddington's collection at Mellerstain.[2]

Needlework portraits of monarchs continued to be made, closely following engravings of official portraits. Charles I was still a cult figure; three similar pictures after Jon Faber's mezzotint (1713) of Bower's painting of the king at his trial, are signed and dated with enigmatic variation (see Plate 156 for one; another, belonging to Sir Richard Carew Pole, Bart, Antony House, Cornwall, is signed 'Anna Skinner in the 68th year of her age, 1715'). A large silk picture of Queen Anne in the Metropolitan Museum, New York, depicts her as she was always represented, wearing her coronation robes. Similar formal portraits were made of the three Georges and their queens.

Though such pictures retained many features typical of the seventeenth century, designs grew more florid as the eighteenth century progressed. Costume, furniture, fabrics and panels became brighter and more elegant. The feeling of tidy woodcuts

The Art of Embroidery

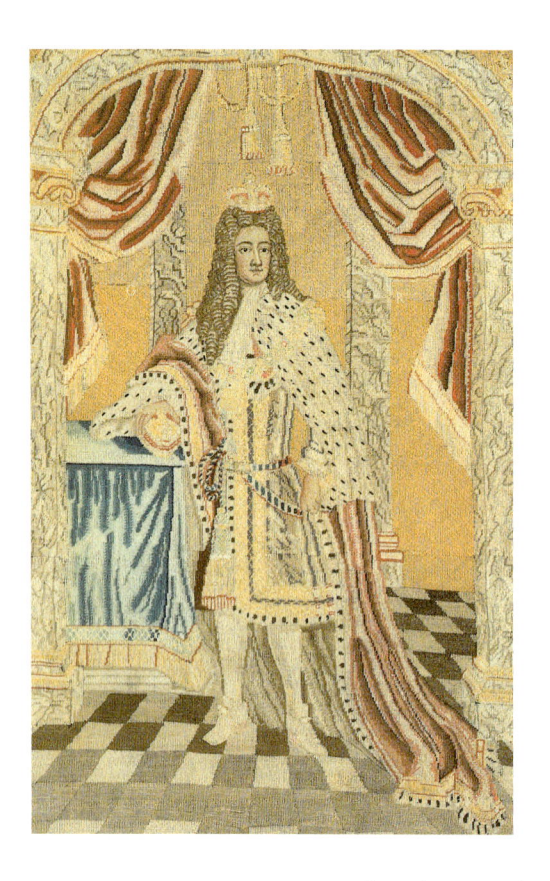

158. George I's state portrait embroidered to a small domestic scale (from an engraving) in fine stitching, the face especially. c.1720.

disappeared and luxuriant garden flowers spread with profusion in needlework for a period of about fifty years. Around 1770 these were superseded by another form of illustration, copper plate engraving and with delicate silky precision. In general, however, a love of natural things was reflected in a passion for 'arcadia'. Elegant rural interpretations were given to old illustrations and, unlike in the previous century, efforts were made to depict figures in the realistic dress of their period. Pastoral subjects were especially popular though others were still drawn from Cleyn's illustrations for Virgil's *Aeneid* and *Eclogues* and *Georgics* (Ogilby's translations of 1658 and 1654). Arcadian scenes, in needlework, were spread throughout the house, interspersed with billowing floral patterns, curling leaves and tendrils. Canvas embroidery was everywhere. Celia Fiennes described a house in Epsom:

> *You enter one roome hung with crosstitch in silks…window curtaines white satin silk damaske with furbellows of callicoe printed flowers, the chairs crosstitch, the two stooles of yellow mohaire with crosstitch true lovers Knotts in straps along and across, an elbow chaire tentstitch…many fine pictures under glasses of tentstitch, satinstitch gumm and straw work also Indian flowers and birds.*

These latter Indian motifs refer us again to continued developments in crewelwork.

CREWELWORK, QUILTING AND OTHER BEDROOM ITEMS

By the second quarter of the eighteenth century crewelwork designs were less crowded, more elegant and colourful; they lost something of their former baroque boldness. Tree tendrils became thinner, more evenly spaced and regularly meandering. They also now had flowers of English or Indian origin with the formalised leaves which were less fat, longer and languidly curling. The range of stitches was limited and simplified and chain-stitch alone sometimes replaced the former complex variety. As an alternative to tree patterns, bed curtains were also decorated with smaller groups of flowers, formalised asparagus leaves and other motifs. Amongst eighteenth century crewelwork bed curtains, of particular note is a splendid pair of curtains assumed to have been made for the Old Pretender, the self-styled James III of England. and his Polish bride Clemantine Sobieska who were married in Italy in 1719 and whose son Charles Edward Stuart, 'Bonnie Prince Charlie', was born in 1720. In wonderful condition, these curtains are embroidered within the centre of a sunflower 'IRCR 1719'. They were acquired by the National Museum of Scotland in 1988 (Plate 160).

Also in Scotland, at Blair Castle, are some altered crewelwork hangings supplied in

The Eighteenth Century

1753 for a mahogany bed by Helen Dallas. Slightly old-fashioned in style, they have a complex pattern with flowers, leaves and tendrils worked in red, blue, yellow and green on a linen ground.

The increasingly popular use of chain-stitch alone was no doubt a reflection of the importation of fine coverlets and yardage of embroidery in this technique from Gujarat which began in the late seventeenth century.

Crewelwork designs and techniques were also used for dresses and bags as well as for beds. Occasionally the same design is found worked on both crewel curtains and

159. Crewelwork of flame colours, red, orange and yellow is rare but several sets of curtains are known.

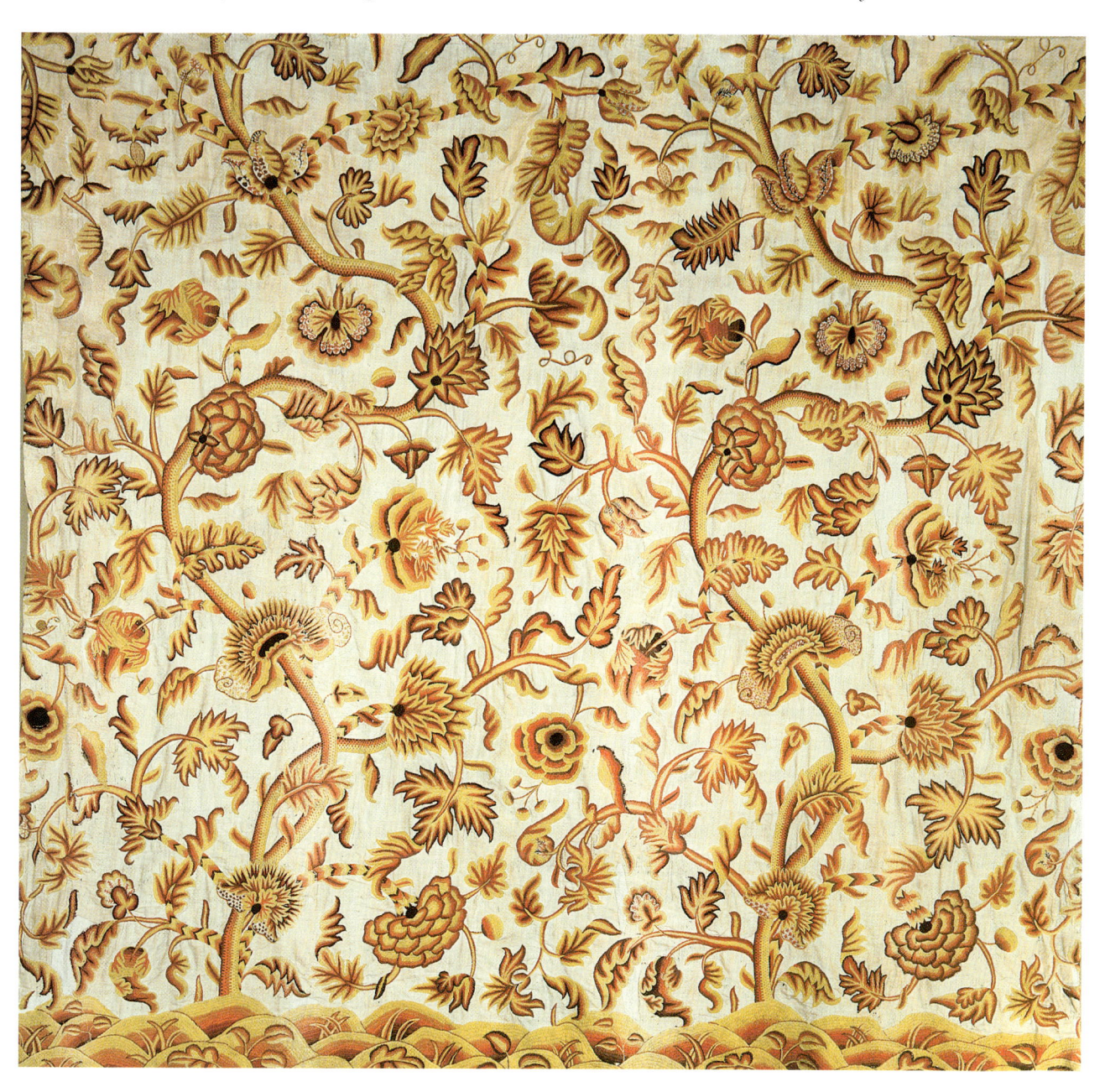

The Art of Embroidery

Right. 160. Part of a set of crewelwork bed hangings, perhaps Scottish, one with the cipher of James Stuart, the Old Pretender. Early 18th century.

Opposite. 161. As if for a child's nursery this crewelwork curtain portrays a glorious jungle of cheerful animals, exotic birds and luscious flowers. c.1720.

in tent stitch embroidery, such as seat coverings. A remarkable series of canvas work panels of crewelwork type designs, but all different, unlike the normally repeated crewel patterns, at St Fagan's, Plate 172, show floral tree patterns against a brown ground and with oriental rockery bases with figures and animals (see also page 191). A set of hangings at Knebworth House, Hertfordshire, is worked in Italian bugle beads in a design typical of crewelwork. They are said to have come from a Medici palace in Florence, having been acquired by Baron Lytton. A crewelwork type design is similarly seen in Russian embroidery of c.1700. A panel in the Victoria and Albert Museum has a tree-flower design with a silver background, gold leaves, and flowers and petals outlined with coloured silk chenille.

American needlework was at its best in the eighteenth century and included fine crewelwork. On the whole, embroidery in the USA was a luxury for those who could afford the time and the materials; most time had to be devoted to productive work

The Eighteenth Century

The Art of Embroidery

162. This French crewelwork curtain retains Régence formality in the strapwork border and exuberant flowers in the centre. c.1730

such as farming the land, while tools and cloth were still relatively scarce. Items made were chiefly of a practical nature with clear household uses. They included rugs, bell-pulls, chair seats and bed hangings but costumes were also sewn with crewelwork designs of a pastoral nature as inappropriate as the English ones *The Spectator* had ridiculed. In 1749 a stolen garment was reported as '…a Woman's Fustian Petticoat, with large work'd Embroider'd Border, being deer, Sheep, Houses, Forrests, etc.…' A large reward was offered for its recovery. American crewelwork designs were usually similar to the English ones from which they were derived but were considerably lighter in feeling; bed hangings especially were less densely embroidered, partly on account of a shortage of wools. Local plants and animals were incorporated sometimes. Indigo was a home product of the American colonies and was much used in shades of dark to light blue, blended with other colours, or by themselves, especially in New England. The apparent simplicity makes many of these works all the more satisfactory and in some ways comparable to the earlier monochrome crewelwork in England. Bed rugs were a speciality of American textiles, early examples being done in a looped pile technique (turkey work) but later ones also in other embroidery techniques. Designs for these were on a bold scale with coarse materials in order to provide maximum warmth. American canvas work embroidery was often especially fine and included flame stitch motifs in bright jewel-like patterns covering items both large and small from wing chairs to wallets. This technique seems particularly timeless (Plate 237, page 242).

By 1750 rich velvets, silks, damasks and brocades were so much more available, and more suitable with elaborately carved and gilded furniture, that crewel hangings became less desirable. The energies of embroideresses were now turned instead to tent stitch carpets, wall hangings and furniture coverings, or to making pictures. Bed hangings of silk were occasionally embroidered with extreme fineness and at great cost. Two sets were made by professional embroideresses for Queen Charlotte. The first was for Windsor Castle and showed accurately depicted flowers on satin. It took Mrs Wright fourteen years to complete. The second was for Hampton Court Palace, where it can still be seen (Plate 209, page 217). Of lilac silk, this was also profusely and minutely embroidered with realistic flowers in brilliant silks. It was made in 1775-8 by Mrs Pewsey, who was also known for starting a school of needlework at Aylesbury.

Sometimes embroidery was added as secondary ornament to silk or velvet

The Eighteenth Century

hangings. Robert Adam's great bed at Osterley Park (Plate 164) is sumptuously hung with velvet but delicate chenille embroidery decorates the valances and the bedcover is of silk with neo-classical ornament. Adam's finely finished drawings for the house show the detailed needlework that was required. He even provided Mrs Child with an 'Etruscan' design for a firescreen, which survives. Another bed, at Spains Hall, Essex, has yellow silk hangings embroidered with the Garter and blue flowers with yellow stalks, by the ladies of Queen Charlotte's court at Kew Palace. For the Yellow Drawing Room at Leeds Castle, Kent, Boudin supplied silk for the walls bordered at the top, below the entablature, with embroidered lambrequins in the form of a valance, with galloon and tassels, somewhat Louis XIV in feeling.

Left. 163. Robert Adam's design for an 'Etruscan' fire screen for Osterley Park, a rare example of English neo-classical needlework. 1776.

Below. 164. Robert Adam's state bed at Osterley Park House is nobly hung with velvet and silk with embroidered decoration, c.1775.

A number of magnificent bed coverlets of the Queen Anne and George I periods were professionally made. Sometimes with sets of pillows in decreasing sizes, these were elaborately worked in coloured silks and with metal threads on silk or satin, the overall background often having a quilted pattern. Dense baroque ornament or lighter chinoiserie motifs were features of some and designs frequently had a central cartouche, medallion or garland with corresponding quarters at the four corners and a complex border around the edge. This symmetric corner and central medallion format together with chinoiserie motifs was derived ultimately from Persia, India and China being also a prominent feature of carpets and book covers. Baskets of flowers, or cornucopias in chain-stitch and long-and-short flat stitches respectively, were other favourite motifs. Many of the less elaborate examples were made by amateurs and a number of beautiful ones survive. Monochrome examples, either professional or amateur, include one of gilt bullion with small coloured silk ovals at Drayton House.

English coverlets varied in size from very large to diminutive. The very big ones emulate the scale of Indian 'summer carpets', the lightweight exquisitely embroidered cotton embroideries that relate closely in design to English bed covers, but which were originally designed as special floor covering. An interesting rust-brown bed cover of huge proportions (Plate 14, page 18) with monochrome scrolling patterns in raised

The Art of Embroidery

work represents a Portuguese derivative of the somewhat earlier yellow silk Bengali 'floor spreads' which were imported during the first decade or so of the seventeenth century (Plate 304, page 316). The smaller English coverlets inherited several features of these pieces such as the border patterns, corner quarterings and yellow quilted pattern backgrounds. The smallest coverlets were presumably designed for babies' beds or cots, but the design formula was also used on series of pillows or cushion covers.

There are good collections of coverlets at Colonial Williamsburg and in the Victoria and Albert Museum. The polychrome silks appear very graceful and delicate in relation to the bold and woolly contemporary crewelwork. Quilted backgrounds (false quilting) were essentially a decorative feature no longer forming a binding of warm layers of material. Professional quilters worked throughout the century for functional and decorative purposes, for furnishings and for costume. A number of patterns were used especially for decorative work. Rope-type twisted threads were sewn in lozenges, squares, roundels, hexagonal honeycomb forms and scale or scallop shell patterns. A wavy, vermicular line was another popular background pattern; it was known as Stormont, having been made fashionable by the whim of Lord Stormont. Quilting was usually done in yellow silks and occasionally overcouched with metal threads. Around the middle of the century more elaborate patterns of flowers, leaves and feather designs were made, but not usually as a background for coloured embroidery. False quilting, as a decorative feature, had originated on imported Indian, Chinese and Persian embroidery. Monochrome patterns were adopted as an excellent foil to colourful embroidery, but were also done without further embellishment. The 'quilts' from Bengal, imported by the Portuguese, were usually worked in undyed tussah (wild silk) which ranged in colour from straw yellow to honey, on white cotton. An interesting use of quilting as a background pattern, but in this case for

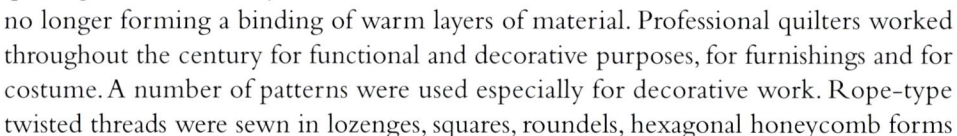

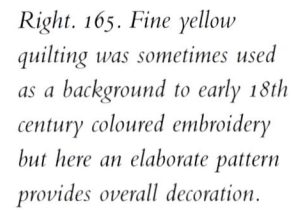

Right. 165. Fine yellow quilting was sometimes used as a background to early 18th century coloured embroidery but here an elaborate pattern provides overall decoration.

Below. 166. A small coverlet for a child's cot embroidered with flowers, birds and animals in fine chain stitch. c.1710.

The Eighteenth Century

Indian embroidery, is to be seen on the magnificent bed curtains at Houghton Hall, Norfolk (see Plate 299, page 311). On these the fine polychrome chain stitch chinoiserie embroidery is worked over an elaborate pattern in natural coloured cotton. The combination of techniques, originally oriental, and with oriental motifs is also seen on a late seventeenth century woman's waistcoat which has the name of the pattern drawer on the lining. On this item, again, we see colourful chain stitch embroidery on a false quilted background.

One of the finest surviving bedsets is at Longleat House, Somerset. It was made in 1733 for the wife of the 2nd Viscount Weymouth, Lady Louisa Cartaret, daughter of

167. A magnificent Queen Anne coverlet in bright silks retains the quartered design of an oriental carpet or book cover.

The Art of Embroidery

Above. 168. This English quilted panel imitates the fineness and elegance of Indian embroidery. c.1730.

Opposite above. 169. A corner of a very large quilted cotton bed cover richly embroidered with repeating floral groups in coloured silks. c.1710.

Opposite below. 170. A corner of a richly embroidered coverlet with extensive use of silver and gold thread, worked over a quilted background. c.1725.

Earl Granville. In wonderful condition it consists of a coverlet, bolster, three cushions and three valances. It is richly embroidered in coloured silks with additional metal thread ornament and quilting.

Despite the extreme differences between crewel and silk bed furnishings in the first quarter of the eighteenth century, some common features can be noticed, such as tendrils of curling leaves, equally satisfactory when adapted to the refinement of silk. Veins in beautifully shaded leaves were often worked in red, a feature of oriental origin. Some coverlets were dotted with small chinoiserie motifs, a feature sometimes seen in the bold fantasies of wool embroidery.

Late eighteenth century patchwork patterns were allied to quilting and were no doubt derived from them; they were also related to earlier traditions of applied and inlaid decoration, long part of the embroiderer's repertoire. Various pieces of fabric were cut and sewn in regular shapes, then applied on a backing in mosaic form giving a brilliant, stained glass, shimmering effect, and often providing an interesting scrapbook collection of plain and printed materials. Patchwork was chiefly made for bed covers but sometimes also for hangings and occasionally garments, perhaps reminiscent of fools and harlequins. American patchwork was notable for a wide variety of designs,

187

techniques and materials. At least 150 printed fabrics were used in one example, in addition to plain and woven materials. The country imported large quantities of printed cottons and even small off-cuts were saved for the purpose. However, American patchwork, as in Great Britain and Ireland, reached its peak at the beginning of the nineteenth century, so more will be said of it in Chapter Nine.

Knotting continued to be popular in the early eighteenth century, the threads being couched-down for hangings, coverlets and for furniture. The hobby was also known as stringwork and many portraits of ladies show them doing this, or with a shuttle, the tool used for it, at hand. A bed-cover made by Mrs Delany of couched knotting on Irish linen has a design of formal flowers in a tight interlacing pattern; this was a birthday present to Thomas Sandford in 1765. Mrs Delany is also known to have made such items as a cot coverlet, bed hangings, window curtains and chair covers alongside her many other industrious activities. A garment of knotting attributed to the King's sister, Princess Amelia (1711-1786). is in the Embroiderers' Guild collection and a piece in the Victoria and Albert Museum is also said to have been made by her. Others in this technique include a man's jacket of about 1630 in the same collection, a bedspread in the Burrell Collection and hangings decorated with flowers and chinoiserie birds at Colonial Williamsburg.[3] Loose knotted macramé fringes were fashionable for several decades. Tatting developed out of knotting and was carried on well into the nineteenth century.

WHITEWORK

Mrs Delany's linen coverlet brings us to the widespread tradition of whitework, spectacularly beautiful embroidery lacking the showiness of colour. Linen industries were deliberately fostered in Scotland and in Ireland, perhaps to discourage either region from competing with the English wool industry. Louis Crommelin was sponsored to set up a manufactory of linen damasks at Lisburn in 1698, a town where there was already a Huguenot colony. Records of the Royal Dublin Society of 1760 refer to the teaching of tambour work in Ireland. From the 1790s this provided a flourishing occupation in the West of Ireland and Belfast. These industries and added whitework techniques led, with the introduction of needle-lace fillings, to sizeable Irish and Scottish industries and the fame of Ayrshire embroidery.[4]

The white embroidery developed out of the necessities of plain sewing but its highly sophisticated ornamental forms owe much to influences from China, Persia, India, Arabia and Turkey, where light costumes of remarkable fineness and delicacy were made for hot climates. Muslins were blanched with lemon water and given poetic descriptions – 'dew of light', 'running

171. Detail of an Irish linen coverlet of knotted and couched cord made by Mrs Delany in 1765. 8ft.4in. x 5ft.6½in. (254cm x 169cm).

172. One of a series of early 18th century canvas work wall hangings having much in common with crewelwork, worked in wool and silk.

The Art of Embroidery

Above. 173. An appliqué panel, the wool ground worked with shaded petals of cloth, partly embroidered. English, c.1720. 13½in. x 39in. (34.3cm x 99cm).

Opposite. 174. One of a set of long panels worked with hanging ropes with flowers and ribbons. English, c.1720. 5ft.4½in. (164cm) high.

water', 'woven wind', 'scorched tears'. They were so diaphanous that a Dutch visitor to India in the seventeenth century wondered if the wearers of these fabrics were not naked! An Indian historian, describing a period c.400 wrote:

> *She wore a gown of white bleached 'netra' cloth [a net with gold thread interwoven] lighter than a snake's slough, flowing down to her toes. Underneath gleamed a petticoat of saffron tint…a divine woman wearing a dazzling muslin robe embroidered with hundreds of diverse flowers and birds gently rippled by the motion of the breeze.*

Vasco da Gama brought back to the Queen of Portugal a 'white embroidered canopy for a bed, the most delicate piece of needlework, like none other that has ever been seen; this has been made in Bengal, a country where they make wonderful things with the needle'. The Rig-Veda in an invocation to Raka (goddess of the full moon) refers to the divine industry: 'With never-breaking needle may she sew her work and may she bestow on us a son…' According to the Roman poet Lucan, Cleopatra had what sounds like a whitework semi-transparent robe:

> *Her snowy breast shines through Sidonian threads*
> *First by the court of distant Seres struck*
> *Divided then by Egypt's skilful toil*
> *And with embroidery transparent made.*

Fine cottons imported from several sources were decorated in self-coloured embroidery or worked in the various techniques that imitated or competed with the lace industry. The finished products were mostly related to costume and, like the substantial whitework embroidery industry that developed out of the many

The Eighteenth Century

seventeenth and eighteenth century strains in Ayrshire work, it was focused on baby clothes and trimmings for ladies' costume.

CANVAS WORK

The transition from the homely techniques of crewelwork developed in several ways through the century. The tent-stitch hangings from Hatton Garden were mentioned earlier; they mark the beginning of the move from woolly baroque hangings towards pictorial embroidery that eventually developed into the neat but unspirited silk pictures of the early nineteenth century. The series already referred to in relation to crewelwork (page 180 and Plate 172) is a set of canvas work hangings (twelve widths) from Brynkinalt, Clwyd. Now at the Welsh Folk Museum at St Fagan's Castle, they show much of the mood of crewelwork design, having a mostly continuous panorama of trees, wonderful leaves, flowers, birds and, on hillocky ground below, both elegant and pastoral figures, including a horseman, St Michael, a lutenist, with sheep, a cow, dogs, a stag and geese; also a castellated building and a timber-framed house. Made by or for the Trevor family, this tent stitch embroidery with a brown background and all these delightful subjects anticipate many characteristics and motifs that were to be part of the vocabulary of smaller tent stitch panels throughout the eighteenth century. The designs of these large hangings is conceived in pairs of canvas widths with the basic form of the foliage repeated in each pair and augmented with variations. A more familiar and more pictorial series of ten wall panels worked by (Lady) Julia Calverley, dated 1717, is preserved at her later home, Wallington Hall, Northumberland. They are mentioned in her husband's memorandum book: 'my wife finished the sewed work in the drawing room, it having been three years and a half in the doing. The greatest part has been done with her own hands'. She must in fact have had helpers to achieve so much in addition to living an active life. The designs would have come from London: these also are of a crewelwork form with undulating hills, tree patterns and exotic birds. Lady Calverley went on to embroider a screen, of pictorial form with scenes from engravings for Virgil's *Georgics* and *Eclogues*. Pictorial hangings are also represented by three at Castle Ashby, Northampton which incorporate thirteen large pastoral panels, each within a border and under a trompe l'oeil curtain valance, and a magnificent large pair of pictorial hangings in fine tent-stitch, from Stoke Edith (Plate 181), now at Montacute House, Somerset, depict formal garden scenes with tidy precision:

We see the Marks of the Scissars upon every Plant and Bush
THE SPECTATOR 1712

The Art of Embroidery

Above. 175. A French Régence panel, fairly formalised with decorated strapwork and exotic chinoiserie elements. c.1720.

Right. 176. One fold of a Régence screen of wool with a high proportion of silk, including the background, in a flowing tree of life design. French c.1720. 36¼in. x 19¼in. (92cm x 49cm).

Parterres, tulips, clipped yew trees, ponds and garden ornaments, a summer house and an orangery are shown. Figures and dogs on the pathways are thought to be slightly later additions. These glorious hangings epitomise the charms of architecture, gardening and needlework of the Queen Anne period. This needlework is reputedly amateur but perhaps follows a continental form, for example Italian silk embroidery such as the seventeenth century garden scene shown in Plate 140 which has similar features (Ashmolean Museum). In the professional field, tapestries still had an elder brother influence. A panel at Alnwick Castle is in the style of a Soho tapestry by Joshua Morris in fine stitches and depicting baskets of flowers, parrots and strapwork against a buff and yellow background. A further large pair of canvas work hangings, together with a carpet en suite (Plate 186), are at Aston Hall, Birmingham; they are signed by Mary Holte, aged sixty, and dated 1744 and are chiefly floral, though the wall hangings depict Holte family houses, Aston Hall and Brereton Hall.[5]

A delightful hanging, signed 'Anne Grant 1750', at Monymusk, Aberdeenshire shows vases and pots of flowers under an arcade, with trees, and swags of flowers hanging above. Also in Scotland, at Wemyss Castle, Fife, there is a set of four bed curtains worked by Janet, Lady Wemyss, dated 1727-30, with the initials of her children, as they were born, on each respective curtain. They are of fine linen and blue satin, in broad vertical stripes, and are embroidered with small vases of flowers, delicately arranged. These are interspersed with small chinoiserie birds and sprigs. As was often the case, the patterns are largely repetitive but the colours are varied. The clear-cut stripes of blue and white might be thought more typical of late eighteenth century forms or a throwback to the paned hangings of mediaeval times. In the second half of the eighteenth century a desire for plainer lines grew out of the search for a 'back to basics' campaign and to a revival of Greek and Roman decorative principles, in neo-classicism.

Neo-classical needlework is fairly rare. Relatively little was made, probably because the technique did not lend itself especially well to the style. But two panels made to designs of the most important English exponent of neo-classicism, Robert Adam, at Newliston, Midlothian, are of interest. Neat formations

The Eighteenth Century

of urns, sphinxes, and hanging baskets of flowers are depicted in felt appliqué, partly tinted with watercolour, on a yellow moiré woollen fabric. The hangings were made about 1792-5. Twelve others of the same set, in poor condition, were sold at Sotheby's in 1928. A bed with curtains in a similar technique, from Newliston, is at the National Trust for Scotland's house at 28 Charlotte Square, Edinburgh. All these were probably made by Lady Mary Hogg. A large number of felt appliqué pictures were also made from about this time depicting birds, flowers, fruit (especially strawberries) and also more ambitious subjects. Fruits were often padded and suspended in three dimensional form. A series of felt flower pictures at Gwsaney, North Wales was made by Helena, Countess of Mount Cashel (Mountcashel) (d.1792), perhaps inspired by Mrs Delany's paper mosaics.[6] Perhaps earlier than the Newliston bed but of the same material, moreen, a popular watered woollen repp, are the hangings on a mahogany bed at Castle Fraser, together with window curtains, pelmets, a sofa and four chairs. Crewel embroidery on this fabric is decorated with nosegays of flowers tied with ribbons. By tradition these were worked by Miss Elyza Fraser (1734-1814) and her friend Mary Bristow (d.1805).

177. Pomegranates, as in this French screen, and other unusual fruits are a feature of French needlework not seen in English patterns. c.1720.

The Art of Embroidery

178. Of the earlier part of the 18th century, this hanging has recognisable French features, a white background and curious exotic fruits amongst the boldly curling leaves.

ROCOCO FANTASIES

The middle decades of the eighteenth century saw confidence in political stability, established wealth and a new determination to enjoy life and be seen to be doing so. Within this framework the rococo spirit of joyous decoration pervaded the decorative arts. The mood is symbolised by outwardly cascading and scrolling motifs and endless fantasies including chinoiserie and gothic (gothick) extravagances. Chinoiserie was a charmingly frivolous fashion, playing a part in both baroque and rococo tastes. Early in the eighteenth century, John Vanderbank's Soho tapestries with dark blue and brown backgrounds, perhaps derived from lacquer, depicted isolated oriental vignettes, as imagined through European eyes. The subjects were treated with a certain quaintness and lack of distinction between Chinese, Persian or Indian figures, and with a charmed quality characteristic of the Chinese taste that had pervaded art from the early seventeenth century. The playfulness of 'China work' was associated with the extremes of rococo, in which naturalistic forms became exotic and fanciful. Both were exemplified in the furniture designs of Thomas Chippendale whose influential book *The Gentleman and Cabinet-Maker's Director* was published in 1754. Sir William Chambers' *Designs for Chinese Buildings* (1757) reflected the fascination of such projects, and even if they were mostly temples of the air they stimulated the fashion generally, inspiring even needlework. Other books of Chinese designs for many uses, including textiles, were produced by J.A. Fraisse (1735), Matthew Darly (1754) and Paul Decker (1759). Pattern books of the seventeenth century continued to be used or have influence but with a new interpretation of frivolity replacing the exotic and bizarre. The various kinds of chinoiserie motif are not always found together. While the ubiquitous Willow pattern, known in every household in the Western world, combines figures, trees and pagodas, much decoration showed either playful figures in amusing pursuits, pagodas, temples etc. and oriental birds, curious animals, or blue and white porcelain. Many of these were caricatured. Professional French needlework for chair and sofa coverings from the St Cyr workshops, for example, displayed Chinese figures at ridiculous activities, figures of fun in a playful scheme of decoration. Chinoiserie was just one but perhaps the ultimate in the delights of arcadia, the out-of-doors brought inside.

The Eighteenth Century

Wonder was blended with exotic fantasy in the imported Chinese wallpaper and porcelain which continued to be both direct and indirect sources of inspiration, as were lacquerwork designs. Yellow, the imperial colour of the Ching dynasty, became a favoured background colour for needlework. Chinoiserie scenes tended to be done in tight pictorial patches on uncluttered backgrounds, within reserves, as in lacquer and porcelain, and were depicted in considerable detail. Other less obvious oriental forms were adopted such as elegant feathery leaves and blocks of in-filled trellis pattern, a crisscross, with studs on the intersections. This was especially used on costume. Countless oriental birds, pheasants usually rather than phoenixes, were intermingled with mythological, curious and homely local species in charming harmony: '...birds praising Our lord without discord, the popyngay, the mavys, partryge, pecocke, thrushe, nyghtyngale, larke, egle, dove, phenix, wren, the tyrtle trew, the hawke, the pelly cane, the swalowe, all singing in quaint blending of Latin and English the praises of God' (as described in a pamphlet entitled *Wild Flowers and Birds as Seen on 18th Century Needlework*). Real foreign birds were accurately embroidered in picture form, individually or in small groups, perhaps with a moth or two, in the manner of William Hayes' engravings or the embossed paper versions painted by Samuel Dixon and following the popular engravings of Edwards and others like him.[7]

There must have been many pattern drawers who would supply designs already made up or combining personally chosen motifs. Professional embroiderers did this as well as undertaking the sewing if required. Roger Nelham (d.1654) and John Nelham (d.1684) were professional embroiderers in the parish of Christ Church, Newgate Street, London, and their trade must have continued. In 1732 Marmaduke Smith offered 'an entirely new collection of Patterns for Ladies' Work' that included canvas work chair seats, screens and carpets.[8] A rarely seen repetition of a design, made up of vignettes including St Philip's baptism of the Ethiopian Eunuch, a chinoiserie pheasant and a blue and white vase, is seen on a firescreen panel and a wing armchair in the Metropolitan Museum. The two panels must have come from the same drawing source (Plate 179).

Early eighteenth century books were published with the intention of being useful – for gardening, painting and needlework – and, con-

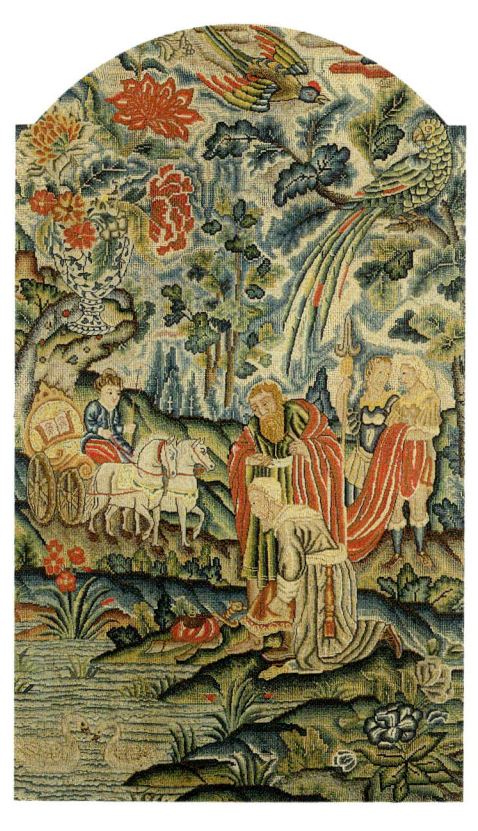

Above. 179. English eclecticism: a firescreen panel with subjects drawn from several sources includes the baptism of the Ethiopian eunuch by St Philip. c.1710.

Left. 180. Rebekah at the well, the English oasis with camels, a black sheep and colourful birds, all in strong unfaded colours. Mid-18th century.

195

The Art of Embroidery

The Eighteenth Century

Left. 182. This small picture is minutely worked in silks. 14½in. x 13¾in. (37cm x 35cm).

Opposite. 181. One of two large early 18th century tent stitch hangings originally from Stoke Edith, Herefordshire, depicting formal gardens with figures and buildings.

versely, designs were undoubtedly taken from other sources. The idea, at very least, behind the many panels of flowers embroidered for firescreens and pictures must be in part derived from Robert Furber's *The Twelve Months of Flowers,* 1730. Fletcher's engravings in this work are themselves derived from paintings by Peter Casteels. A *palampore* from India, for example, made for the English market, is linked to a specific engraving. Pattern drawers still carried out individual commissions: Abraham Pinhorn, married in 1731, is known to have drawn 'all sorts of Patterns for Needlework, French Quilting, Embroidery, Cross and Tent Stitch'. He also supplied 'shades of silk and Worsted'. In 1732 Marmaduke Smith advertised 'an entirely new Collection of Patterns for Ladies' Work' including designs for chair seats, screens and carpets. Walter Galle, the schoolmaster of Mayfield, Sussex, noted in 1750, amongst similar activities, supplying patterns:

> *I finished the bed-quilt after five days close application. It gave satisfaction, and I received 10s 6d for the drawing...*
> *Went to Mr Baker's and did the drawing for Miss Anne's handkerchief. I took for my reward a pint of strong.*

197

The Art of Embroidery

Right. 183. One of a set of mid-18th century unused stool covers worked by Lady Helen McDonnell in patterns influenced by French designs. 31in. x 28¼in. (79cm x 72cm).

Below. 184. Dated 1741, this panel with curling plumes has great movement and provides splendid opportunities for interesting shading. Approx 3ft.3in. x 2ft.6in. (100cm x 80cm).

From about the middle of the century women went out to the American colonies to teach sewing of every kind including samplers, and to draw and sell patterns and canvas. They advertised their services in local newspapers. In the *Boston Newsletter* of 1738 Mrs Condy offered: 'All sorts of beautiful Figures on Canvas, for Tent Stick; the Patterns from London, but drawn by her much cheaper than English drawing'. She also supplied 'Silk Shades Slacks Floss Cruells of all Sorts, the best White Chapple Needles, and everything for all Sorts of Work'.

CARPETS

Needlework carpets and smaller floor rugs of canvas work continued, in the eighteenth century, a form that began in the sixteenth century and flowered in the seventeenth. Those earlier ones were mostly table carpets but the basic pattern structure was the same, a central panel framed by a border and often incorporating central medallions and corresponding ones at the corners. Usually made in professional workshops, but

The Eighteenth Century

increasingly by amateurs, they could vary greatly in scale and design. They were predominantly in designs of leaves and flowers, though some of the earliest were of leaves only, in stylised form like crewelwork. Gradually they became more fluid with frayed, curling leaves, and a greater oriental feeling and more colour. Further varieties of foliage followed in a smaller scale and with an increasing number of flowers. Eventually a mass of larger or smaller blooms displaced the leaves and filled the whole design. Contrasts of pattern were maintained with a fairly deep borer and a central motif, sometimes shaped as in oriental carpets. Some designs showed an increasing naturalistic tendency while others depicted vases or baskets from which sprang huge sprays of flowers. Backgrounds were of blue, red, cream, yellow, brown and purple (Plate 189). An unusual example in the Metropolitan Museum has a variety of patterns, chiefly geometric, but also includes a text. It is dated 1764. Rococo, chinoiserie and Georgian Gothic ('Gothick') designs were all practised on carpets as overall patterns, or in pictorial forms. Table carpets usually had concentric designs

185. A large French table carpet, a tour de force of colourful shading on a black background, entirely of wool, is bordered with elegant plumes in single and mixed colours.

The Art of Embroidery

around the border, though the central panel might lie in a horizontal plane. A splendid large sized carpet in the Fitzwilliam collection, and a rug, are both signed by Mary, wife of the second Marquis of Rockingham, who died in 1761.[9] Two very interesting carpets at Raby Castle, Co. Durham represent unusual forms.[10] The first has a 'gothick' design; only a fragment survives but it was presumably round as it was made for a circular drawing room in about 1785 and it has architectural tracery on a pink ground, similar to a rose window. This is a knotted carpet but the other at Raby is of needlework, done by the Countess of Darlington and measures no less than 26ft.6in. by 17ft. (8m by 5m). It was made in about 1745, when payments were made for 'worsteds for the Great Carpet'. Possibly designed by the architect Daniel Garrett, it combines French Régence formalised ornament, totally removed from contemporary English floral patterns, with architectural motifs of great sophistication, and a key pattern edge. Both this and Lady Rockingham's large carpet owe more than a little to Aubusson patterns and colouring.

From about 1760 geometric designs tended to replace floral patterns, being featured either in the border, or the main part, or as a background to flowers and leaves. Key patterns, octagonal bamboo patterns and trellis designs were also incorporated. The many variations were made as alternatives to the increasingly popular woven carpets produced at Kidderminster, Wilton, Kilmarnock and Axminster. Moorfields hand-knotted carpets were in demand during the second part of the century and were especially favoured by Robert Adam. Few needlework carpets were made in the neo-classical style; the technique and texture was somewhat incompatible with the hard lines and smooth steely sheens of the period. However, a good example worked to an Adam pattern for Lord Coventry's London house and later at Croome Court was recently seen in the salerooms, and the original designs for this and others of its kind are in the British Museum and Soane Museum, London.

English and French canvas work was often virtually indistinguishable. A set of four large hanging panels at the Musée Nissim de Camondo of c.1740 are very close in style to English carpets. Each panel shows a vase piled high with flowers, leaves, and with large bouquets above, on

186. A carpet with the Holte family arms at its centre made for Aston Hall. The carpet was probably professionally made. English, c.1760.

The Eighteenth Century

an off-white background, within a border of similar foliage on a blue background. An early eighteenth century French bed in the Untermyer Collection (Metropolitan Museum) is of canvas embroidery with six valances and two side curtains, on which are depicted classical myths and Aesop's fables, these with light coloured backgrounds, and borders with a black background. The valances have the characteristic French scalloped and lambrequin shaped lower edges (Plate 153, page 173). Pomegranates are a feature of French rather than English needlework having been adopted from Ottoman textiles, probably through woven silks. The background colour of French needlework is often white, unusual in England. Early Savonnerie carpets had a black ground, later ones a yellow one and textiles generally took on lighter and brighter colouring (Plates 154 and 178). Naturalistic fashions in the silk weaving industry were introduced at Lyons from about 1730, the trade having originally been brought to France from Italy, and in turn especially free designs were woven at Spitalfields in London.

187. A large early 18th century embroidery depicting one of the mosaics found on the site of the Roman villa at Stonesfield, Oxon, based on a contemporary engraving.

The Art of Embroidery

Many other sizeable needlework projects in tent stitch of an ambitious and original nature were undertaken. At Wallington Hall there is a black lacquer six-fold screen, already mentioned, signed by (Lady) Julia Calverley, 1727. It incorporates large panels depicting scenes adapted from an edition of Virgil's *Eclogues* and *Georgics* published by John Ogilby in 1654, with illustrations by Francis Cleyn who was also a designer at the Mortlake tapestry factory, or by Wenceslaus Hollar and Pierre Lamport in 1658. An unusual panel formerly at Littlecote, Wiltshire, of about 1730, depicts the Roman pavement that was discovered in the park but was subsequently reburied to avoid crowds of curious visitors. Very fine sewing delineates every detail of the archaeological remains which are now being excavated again. (See also Plate 187 for another.)[11]

A large number of smaller canvas embroideries were carried out for the seats and backs of sets of chairs. Many were of a floral design, others pictorial, derived from illustrations, and some heraldic, as for example on a set of gilt furniture at Berkeley Castle, Gloucestershire. Further discussion of needlework for furniture is included in the next chapter.

SAMPLERS

In the seventeenth century samplers were worked by teenage girls and sometimes by adults but by the eighteenth century they were exclusively done by younger children. They were technically simpler and more decorative. Many from around the middle of the century show the age of the child and it is not surprising that they were not expected to use metal threads or do raised work as in the previous century. A few samplers were, however, done by older women, as examples for their children.

By about 1725 the usual shape of samplers was squarer and a variety of fabrics was used. Linen was the chief one, sometimes of a coarse weave and of a yellowish colour. Tammy, a fine wool cloth, became an alternative for a short period. Satin and tiffany (a fine glazed muslin material) were used for map and darning samplers. Threads of silk and linen were used, occasionally wool, especially in Scotland and Ireland. The old format of a large number of short bands was replaced by wider ones of increased interest, more like pictures, and by the middle of the century borders are seen around a panel containing lettering, texts and motifs. These borders were usually of a formal pattern or sometimes wide with delicate scrolling flowers of all colours. Sometimes this last form stemmed from a basket at the base, perhaps resting on undulating hillocks. In other instances there was a landscape scene at the bottom with shepherdesses, houses,

Above. 190. A finely worked carpet or hanging with a wealth of flowers, some in Delft pots, within a strapwork border with unidentified arms. c.1750.

Opposite above. 188. Another Georgian carpet displays a riotous overall pattern of flowers and leaves within a deep border and narrow bands.

Opposite below. 189. A mid-18th century carpet or hanging of wool highlighted with silk filled with flowers shown against a sky blue ground.

The Art of Embroidery

191. A rare Scottish sampler is worked in two colours only with bands of pattern, the Annunciation and curiously decorated lettering. 25½in. x 10½in. (65cm x 27cm).

trees, etc. Some girls, especially in America, were expected to do two sorts of sampler: firstly, a plain one of alphabets and numerals, which was good practice for the marking of linen, a normal task on entering into service in a household; and secondly, a more decorative one to be regarded as a peak of sewing achievement. Middle-class families were justly proud of the charming little works that their children learned to do in schools and at home and many samplers were framed, glazed and hung on parlour walls. The sizes varied greatly as did the fineness of the stitching. Some large samplers were made, up to 30in. (76cm) wide, and divided into sections with texts, patterns and animal motifs; but the sewing on these usually lacks the grace of smaller ones.

An unexpected form of sampler with an earlier lace-like appearance was that of the holy-work or hollie-point. Always of white, and invariably on a small scale, these represented work done on baby clothes and caps. The name was derived from a needlepoint lace stitch of three centuries earlier. Patterns were made of small pinprick holes, being in fact gaps in a build-up of buttonhole stitching over an area where the fabric had previously been cut away. On samplers the technique is usually combined with whitework borders, drawn thread or cutwork. The designs were always simple, showing stylised flowers, an occasional bird or animal, and a number of crowns, hearts, geometric patterns, and often a date.

Other whitework samplers, or parts of samplers, included features derived from earlier Italian sources – cutwork (reticello), drawn thread work and needle lace including punto in aria. They were sometimes mounted on coloured paper.

As stylised bands gradually disappeared from eighteenth century samplers they were replaced by pictorial motifs. Some of these were adapted from the spot samplers of the previous century but others of an angular nature also developed and soon became standard conventions. Adam and Eve under a fruit tree, boxers, crowns, stags and hearts had all featured before and continued to do so, while houses, other animals including dogs and sheep, and human figures were introduced together with a naturalistic portrayal of flowers. Seven year old E. Philips depicted her entire family in 1761 but on the whole the combination and composition of motifs was formal and conventional. Occasionally topical interest is reflected. A sampler at Cullodon Moor (National Trust for Scotland) commemorates the battle in 1746, the last fought on British soil (Plate 192). Another at Bethnal Green Museum, signed 'Mary Hall. Wye 1786', shows a hot air balloon rising from the ground, clearly alluding to the Montgolfier brothers.

The use of a continuous border pattern framing the main part of the sampler began around 1720, the zig-zag form enclosing flowers derived from bands on seventeenth century samplers. Vine-like chains were filled with single or alternating floral

The Eighteenth Century

motifs, especially honeysuckle, but these became increasingly stylised and ultimately a rather weak convention. However, the awkward turning round corners betrays, charmingly, the child's difficulties.

Samplers taught not only sewing but also alphabets and numerals, in a variety of scripts. Several kinds are sometimes included in one sampler. John Brightlands' *Grammar of the Englishe Tongue* (1711) contained an alphabet of 'sampler letters' and was much used as a pattern book. As they progressed, children were sometimes required to undertake lengthy texts in needlework and many examples can be seen of small lettering in fine stitching, usually in monochrome, red, black, green or blue, and surrounded by other motifs in several colours. The ten commandments (*Exodus* Chapter 20) on two tablets were a favourite. An example in a private collection in red, green and blue is signed 'Jane Brain Iuly the 6th 1738'. The Lord's Prayer was similarly worked and essays on virtues such as 'Meekness'. Another sampler has two poems 'Of Love' and 'Of Sincerity' in red on panels within a flower border, signed 'Sarah Maggee her work 1729'. Later examples, usually worked in black alone with no decorative features, spelled out painfully slowly educative lessons such as 'Geography' (1797).[12]

Many samplers had shorter texts of four to eight lines, sometimes Bible quotations, but more often moral verses or proverbial sayings, of a puritanical and priggish tone. They were full of terrifying warnings of the imminence of death, pious persuasions to virtue and self-righteous warnings against human temptations, adapted from writers such as the non-conformist churchman Dr Isaac Watts, author of *Divine and Moral Songs for Children* (1720). Morbid reminders of the shortness and uncertainty of life were indelibly stamped into tiny children's minds as they spent days slowly stitching them:

Above left. 192. Commemorative samplers are unusual. This one records the British defeat of the Scots at Culloden in 1746.

Above right. 193. Almost a picture, this London sampler of 1754 by Ann Stibbs shows an ambitious basket of flowers.

The Art of Embroidery

194. An elegant sampler of 1752 may be noted for its well-balanced layout.

*Let not the Morrow your vain Thoughts employ
But think this day the Last you may enjoy.*

Poignant verses told the children that their lives were frail and transitory. Mary Wakeling's otherwise charming sampler (Victoria and Albert Museum) of 1742, worked when she was ten, includes a gloomy rhyme:

The Eighteenth Century

195. As more often with American samplers, this English one consists of a densely embroidered picture with a central panel of lettering. Signed and dated 'Margrett Clare, Aged Twelve, 1734'.

Gay dainty flowers go swiftly to decay,
poor wretched life's short portion flies away,
we eat, we drink, we sleep but lo, anon,
old age steals on us, never thought upon.

Some texts commemorated the feasts of Christmas, Easter and Ascensiontide. Though the Crucifixion appeared on samplers from continental Europe, particularly in Germany, it was not common on English ones. Occasionally special prayers were embroidered; some were simple and pious, but others were ridiculously trite:

The Art of Embroidery

> *Oh may thy powerful work*
> *Inspire a breathing worm*
> *To rush into thy Kingdom Lord*
> *And take it as by storm.*

Samplers were even used to drum into children the dangers of thoughts of love and other aspects of evil imagination. Elizabeth Bock, in 1764, was made to sew into her work:

> *And if I should by a young youth be*
> *Tempted*
> *Grant I his schemes defy and all*
> *He has invented*

Proverbial texts were more reasonable and, displayed on the wall, provided for periodic reflection:

> *Be not hasty in thy spirit to be angry: for anger resteth in the bosom of fools.*

Sarah Grimes' text of 1730 is a little prim but none the less a sensible and neatly composed nursery text:

196. Exceptionally finely embroidered, this sampler includes the various crowns and coronets of the nobility, useful symbols for marking linen.

The Eighteenth Century

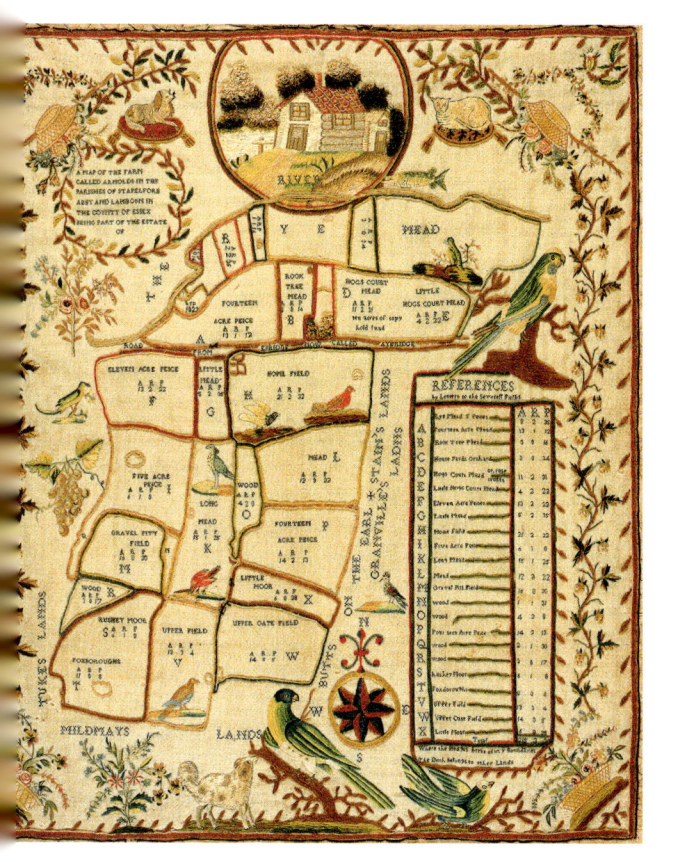

Keep a strict guard over thy tongue, thine ear and thine eye, lest they betray thee to talk things vain and unlawful. Be sparing of thy words, and talk not impertinently or in passion. Keep the parts of thy body in a just decorum, and avoid immoderate laughter and levity of behaviour.[13]

Above left. 197. A late 18th century embroidered sampler of Arnolds Farm in Essex.

Above right. 198. More interesting than wordy texts were map samplers, this one of Ireland being dated 1791.

This must indeed have drawn her attention not only to bodily care but also to long words she had not used before. A fascinating sampler by Mary Dudden of Cardiff, 1780, is a moral lesson true to Langland's or Bunyan's mysticism, enough to keep the sewer thinking for a lifetime:

THE LIFE OF A HAPPY MAN
The happy Man was born in the city of Regeneration, in the Parish of Repentance unto Life, was educated at the School of Obedience, and now lives in the Plain of Perserverance, he works at the Trade of Diligence, not withstanding he has a large Estate in the County of Christian Contentment and many Times does Jobs of Self-denial.

A note attached to the backboard of the sampler informs us: 'Mary Dudden were 12 years of age when this sampler were worked, and some part of it by moonlight'. Some

209

The Art of Embroidery

Below left. 199. A most unusual 18th century sampler with formalised emblems entirely embroidered with glass beads by Jane Mills.

Below right. 200. This darning sampler, dated 1788, incorporates many examples of darning patterns, even in the flower leaves and petals.

Opposite. 201. A fine and decorative sampler of 1784 with many little features including the seated stag, an historical motif and the badge of Richard II.

texts were in the form of acrostics, where the initial letters of each line spelled out a word or name. A pleasant verse of 'Anno Dom: 1749' in this form is:

   A virgin that's Industrious, Merits Praise
   N ature she Imitates in Various Ways,
   N ow forms the Pink, now gives the Rose its blaze.

   Y oung Buds, she folds, in tender Leaves of green,
   O mits no shade to beautify her Scene.
   U pon the Canvas, see, the Letters rise,
   N eatly they shine with intermingled dies,
   G lide into Words, and strike us with Surprize.

Other samplers were worked in the form of a rebus, some words being replaced by pictograph images. Perpetual almanacs in table form and genealogical charts showing family birth dates were also made towards the end of the century, usually in black with little coloured ornament.

Map samplers, combining experience in sewing with geography, were popular in the last two or three decades of the century. Sometimes they were drawn out individ-

Tell me, ye Knowing and discerning few,
Where I may find a Friend both firm and true;
Who dares stand by me when in deep Distress,
And then his Love and Friendship most express.

Jane Corona
1784

The Art of Embroidery

202. A mid-18th century French panel depicting the pleasures of hearing in small stitches, within a floral border of larger tent stitch. 34in. x 26¾in. (86cm x 68cm).

ually and on other occasions they were worked over printed patterns. The sewer often marked her own native village prominently amongst the familiar landmarks. Great Britain and Europe were frequent subjects, as were single and double hemispheres. Individual maps of Ireland and countries far afield perhaps indicate personal connections; they often show quaintly inaccurate or unknown boundaries and territories, as for example in Canada and large parts of America. Australia was often marked 'New Holland'. A map of Africa dated 1784 'Done at Mrs. Arnold's Fetherston Buildings' shows markings such as Grain Coast, Tooth Coast and Slave Coast alongside the more familiar Gold Coast.[14]

English darning samplers have special charm and were probably inspired by Dutch originals. Earlier ones consisted of adjoining squares of fairly coarse darning patterns while others were of finely worked vertical crosses of darning scattered over an area. Both were worked in a variety of coloured silks, sometimes with additional decorative motifs including flowers and birds. A popular format consisted of a posy of flowers tied with a ribbon with crosses of plain and coloured darning alongside, surrounded by a border of intertwined flowers (Plate 200).

Individual and rare samplers include a beadwork one by 'Jane Millf', about 1760, showing spot motifs including many birds, trees, vases of flowers and squirrels (Plate 199). Another interesting curiosity is a diminutive sampler of only 5½in. x 5in. (14cm x 12.5cm). It is very finely worked with a verse and motifs, including cats on cushions, Adam and Eve under a tree with the snake, and baskets of flowers, within a conventional border pattern.

The tradition of sampler making was naturally taken to North America but eighteenth century examples made in that country, of which a large number have been preserved, were significantly independent in style. Unlike their European counterparts, they were primarily decorative, and instead of having the characteristic angular features were densely covered with naturalistic, flowing embroidery, more like needlework pictures. Pictorial subjects often filled part of the canvas and sometimes the entire background was worked over. The depiction of foliage was not stylised as in England and the conventional border patterns were not common. Texts were less prominent but a border of flowers often framed a central panel in which were lettering, a scene with a house, a church, figures, animals, trees, etc. Human figures were depicted and also two specially American hallmarks, the eagle and weeping willows. Enough good samplers have survived for some to be identified in groups or even as

The Eighteenth Century

the work of particular schools, or as made under the direction of a specific teacher. Samplers done by girls in schools in Pennsylvania often have a border within a border and a picture in the centre, neo-classical in feeling, showing a doleful and high-waisted lady standing under a willow tree. A group from Providence, Rhode Island, supervised by a teacher called Mary Balch, often portray a public building in considerable detail. A pair of pillars flank the main panel of the sampler, and outside this is a floral border. The background canvas was frequently totally filled in with stitching. Samplers from Salem, Massachusetts, worked at Miss Sarah Stivour's school, show the distinctive use of a long stitch of crinkled silk for backgrounds. They also have a landscape at the bottom.

Samplers from continental Europe were less decorative than English or American ones but often technically superior, with a greater variety of stitches and colour combinations. They were less pictorial, more a collection of patterns and of a less personal nature, usually without texts and not showing the age of the sewer. French ones were nearest in form to the English but often more tightly filled with motifs. Spain, Portugal, Italy, Switzerland and Holland all produced samplers. Denmark was renowned for fine whitework and this was reflected in samplers. An example dated 1758 (Victoria and Albert Museum) shows no less than ninety-eight neat squares of varying drawn thread

203. A mid-18th century French picture depicting men and women working in a garden by a monumental staircase with fountains.

The Art of Embroidery

204. An unusually fine large panel entirely worked in minute beads. French, c.1760.

and embroidered patterns. Dutch samplers were broad rather than long with patterns worked horizontally, and consisted of a fairly haphazard collection of motifs without formal composition. Spanish samplers show densely packed rows of intricately worked border patterns, sometimes with a heraldic device in the middle. They were not usually dated. Alphabets were not used much. German ones, on the other hand, were often made up of alphabets and numerals only, usually in red. I have seen one with continuous rows of alphabets in nineteen different scripts, with numerals also and two tidy columns of border bands. Other German samplers show a Crucifixion motif with the Instruments of the Passion, ladder, nails, scourge, hammer, sponge, hour-glass, dice, cock and the crown of thorns. Adam and Eve, wild animals and exotic birds were amongst other motifs. The arrangement of these symbols had a certain unity but never had the decorative form so characteristic of American samplers. Some English ones were also devised almost as pictures with a signature squeezed in at the top or bottom. A delightful example shows principally a large basket of flowers resting on hillocky ground. Above it is a saying from *Proverbs* and below: 'Ann Stibbs Workt This Piece of Work at Mrs Rea Bording School Tower Hill, London Finisht Iune the 25 1754'. It is not surprising that details are given in full since needlework was taken very seriously and the art and pleasure of it were frequently a lady's chief accomplishment and interest. From childhood, the skill required was linked with the morals, discipline and hopes provided by religion:

> *Jesus permit thy gracious name to stand,*
> *As the first effort of an infants hand,*
> *And while her fingers on the canvas move,*
> *Engage her tender thoughts to seek thy love,*
> *With thy dear children let her have A part,*
> *And write thy name thyself upon her heart.*

Though it had to be expressed in terms of relative humility, the inference is that needlework was a close second to godliness (Mary Cole, 1759):

> *Better by far for Me*
> *Than all the Simpster's Art*
> *That God's commandment be*
> *Embroidered on my heart.*

LATER GEORGIAN COSTUME, FURNISHINGS AND PICTURES

By the middle of the eighteenth century male and female costume was immensely decorative and embroidery at the zenith of fashion; a considerable industry based at Lyons generated and coordinated fashionable styles and dispensed products to the high societies of many European countries. In England professional artists, designers and embroiderers supplied an extensive market in decorative coats, waistcoats and dresses, but some of the finest specimens were home produced. Mrs Delany was an archetype of the period and its tastes in general and, having been born in 1700, even her age coincided with the years of the century. She was twice married, lived at Glasnevin, near Dublin, and in London and Windsor. She knew the King and Queen and many celebrities of the day, and was a diarist and accomplished practiser of a variety of domestic arts including needlework. She was astonishingly industrious: her husband Dr Delany commented 'She works even between the coolings of her tea'. Other than the knotted coverlet, illustrated on page 188, she began a quilt in 1747 and worked on it for three years, presumably alongside other things, but often for sessions of four hours. It was of white cotton with borders of flowers, bows of ribbon and with white knotting. We gather she made all her own designs for this, aprons, a court dress, stomacher, over-shirt, handkerchiefs and many domestic furnishings.[15] Lady Llanover described a petticoat of Mrs Delany's as:

205. Another French panel illustrates the season of Harvesting within a border of formal decoration. c.1750.

> *Covered with sprays of natural flowers, in different positions, including the burgloss, auriculas, honeysuckle, wild roses, lilies of the valley, yellow and white jessamine, interspersed with small single flowers. The border at the bottom being entirely composed of large flowers in the manner in which they grow, both garden and wild flowers being intermingled where the form, proportions and foliage rendered it desirable for the effect of the whole.*

A letter from Mrs Delany (25 November 1752) shows how she even kept less fine embroidery to do when light failed:

> *My candlelight work is finishing a carpet in double-cross-stitch, on very coarse canvass, to go round my bed.*[16]

The Art of Embroidery

Right. 206. A small picture in fine wool and silk stitches with a cornucopia of flowers neatly filling the frame. c.1750.

Far right. 207. 18th century dress was sometimes heavy with variations of gold embroidery, perhaps set off with bright colours in addition.

Mrs Delany was a keen gardener and clearly enjoyed both cultivated and natural beauty. She also recorded details of the individual tastes of celebrated contemporaries. She noted 'Lady Dunkerron's sedan is yellow velvet, embroidered and imbossed with silver' and commented on fashion:

> *The Duchess of Queensberry's clothes pleased me best. They were white satin embroidered, the bottom of the petticoat brown hills covered with all sorts of weeds, and every breadth has an old stump of a tree that ran up almost to the top of the petticoat, broken and ragged, and worked with brown chenille, round which were twined nastertiums, ivy, honeysuckles, periwinkles, convolvuluses, and all sorts of twining flowers, which spread and covered the petticoat.*

This same Duchess did not however please that princeling of taste in Bath, Beau Nash, when she wore an embroidered apron at the Assembly Rooms. He tore it off her, protesting that only servants wore white aprons, but she reacted in good humour apparently, despite the fact that the garment was of fine needlepoint lace, and said to have cost 500 guineas. An earlier apron at Nottingham Museum of Costume, signed and dated 'EW 1721', is of fine whitework with exotic oriental birds and flowers. Short decorative aprons had been introduced to England from France where they were worn in the late seventeenth century. They derived from a passion amongst court ladies for a pretence of rustic pursuits, an imitation of dairy maids, and early feelings of Romanticism. English aprons were often of heavy silk in plain rectangular form or with a scalloped lower edge. Some had pockets, others were trimmed with lace or

The Eighteenth Century

gold lace. They were either delicately embroidered with light porcelain-like flower sprigs or heavily embroidered with metal threads and colourful vases, baskets or cornucopias of flowers. Chinoiseries and other exotic fantasies provided further variations. An alternative type of apron was of fine muslin, decorated with traditional whitework, or tambour embroidery.[17]

The old skill of tambouring was brought from China to France in about 1760 where it quickly became fashionable. Even Madame de Pompadour was painted doing it.[18] The technique involved sewing with a hook on to material stretched on a hoop (tambour meaning drum); it is recognisable by a continuous line of stitches on the back. The ground material was usually cream silk or satin and the relatively fast stitching could be quite fine. The most popular subjects were those typical of Louis XVI's reign – architectural remains such as broken classical columns, rustic figures, birds, butterflies fruit and flowers and groups of musical instruments with tambourines and music books. The bright silks have invariably faded to soft pinks, ochres and greens. The technique was much used for French chair coverings.[19]

The Louis XVI style was the most significant influence in a wave of neo-classicism that swept across Europe as a kind of second Renaissance. There was a new attempt to turn from rococo frivolities and within an intellectual pursuit going back to classical beginnings in a search for ancient, basic truths and the ornamental forms of Greece and Rome. With recent excavations at Pompeii and at Roman sites, a sense of new learning led to widespread remodelling of architecture and decoration and a new

Left. 208. A Louis XVI neo-classical panel largely embroidered in twisted 'chenille' silk with a trompe l'oeil of an incense burner under a suspended mantle. French, c.1770.

209. English neo-classicism: the underside of the canopy of a fine silk bed made for Queen Charlotte to a design by Robert Adam.

The Art of Embroidery

Right. 210. A neo-classical carpet has a central heraldic shield on a mosaic ground framed within key-pattern and flower chain borders.

Opposite. 211. Motifs from chintz and printed cottons are appliquéd on a coverlet dated 1782, possibly American.

academic taste. Urns, swags of husks, sphinxes and such motifs, the new vocabulary of architect designers such as Robert Adam, were incorporated with classical pediments and columns to the exclusion of the previous feathery scrollings. But the new vogue did not combine naturally with the techniques of needlework, as mentioned earlier, and as a result the craft was less used with a preference for plain or striped silks. Neo-classicism was more noticeable in costume than in other forms of sewing. Hepplewhite and Sheraton furniture had light elegant lines that called for plain or simple coverings rather than the fussy ornament of embroidery. Needlewomen therefore turned their attention once again away from practical works to incidental decorative pictures. They did not attempt anything too serious but were content to sew lightweight designs in keeping with the antiquarian mood of the times. In addition, pictures depicting oriental pheasants had much in common with porcelain

The Eighteenth Century

The Art of Embroidery

The Eighteenth Century

painting, for example first period Worcester, but many subjects were derived from prints and worked in fine silks that resembled engravings and even imitated them in certain cases. Though silky and smart, they lacked the originality of earlier needlework, though sometimes the same subjects were portrayed. Seventeenth century themes, Old Testament stories and familiar tales from the classics and mythology were retold in more sentimental renderings, often following the mezzotints of Francesco Bartolozzi (1727-1815), Angelica Kauffmann (1741-1807) and others. The paintings of Wheatley and Cipriani were further sources and given a similar stamp of mellow gracefulness, often in an oval format. Details of faces and hands were painted and sometimes much of the backgrounds, the sewers having given in to Mrs Delany's understandable complaint: 'It is provoking to have the ground take up so much more time than the flowers'. The painting of faces had an old precedent for this was done in mediaeval embroidery (for example an early fourteenth century altar frontal at Château Thierry). Chenille was used for some parts especially in pastoral scenes where it was appropriate for sheep and trees. Often a sense of delightful melancholy prevailed in these pictures. 'Fame Strewing Flowers on Shakespeare's Tomb' was a particularly popular subject, embroidered countless times with little originality. Symbols of mourning, derived from Greek and Roman models, provided 'a reflection on decayed magnificence'[20] – urns, tombs, follies, sylvan glades with Flora, Bacchus and other gods and classical figures beside ruined temples and grottoes. These were also aspects of the impending

Above. 213. Long embroidered pictures such as this, by Hannah Otis, were made in Boston incorporating a number of narrative scenes joined in a landscape. c.1750. 24¼in. x 52¾in. (61.5cm x 134cm).

Opposite. 212. Mary Knowles (1733-1807) copied prints and paintings with stitches resembling brush strokes. This self portrait shows her embroidering a version of Zoffany's portrait of George III. 1771.

221

The Art of Embroidery

Above. 214. Essentially English, but also very American, pastoral scenes such as this large one would illustrate a shepherd and shepherdess with flocks of wild animals and buildings united in a landscape. c.1760. Approx. 39in. x 31in. (100 x 80cm).

Opposite above. 215. An English neo-classical silk picture, a pastoral image with a lovelorn shepherd. c.1770.

Opposite below. 216. This large silk and hair picture of Burghley House, Lincolnshire, is directly imitating a contemporary engraving. c.1790.

birth of Romanticism. Joan Edwards identified four signed silk pictures worked by Elizabeth Farran.[21] She lived in Dublin and recorded the dates and times she took to work four subjects between 1790 and 1792. Derived from unknown prints they depict romantic themes: 'Charlotte at the Tom [sic] of Werter', 'Griselda returning to her Father', 'Ferdinand and Miranda' and 'Lord Thomas and Fair Elinor'. Religious pictures now also included more New Testament scenes such as the Resurrection, Christ and Mary Magdalene, and Christ with the lady at the well. Romantic literary themes were popular too, illustrations of subjects from Goethe being a favourite.

Monochrome pictures, sometimes in hair but more often in black silks with some lighter shades, had a sober smartness and seriousness. Worked on silk or satin, these imitated engravings, etchings and drawings and have been termed 'printwork'. Sometimes on a larger scale than the polychrome silk pictures, they depicted imaginary or real topographical subjects such as Burghley House. Occasionally they were signed, as were versions after engravings of Cambridge colleges by Lamborn, for example one showing the Wren Library and the river at Trinity College, 'H.B.WELLS. '89' (Plate 217). Smaller rustic landscapes in a similar technique followed in the nineteenth century, and were known as etching embroidery.

The designs for embroidery were to be acquired in printed pattern form on paper or ready drawn out on material in most instances, and the repetitive nature of these

The Eighteenth Century

last were the beginnings of what we know now as kits. Some pattern books, however, continued to be published as, for example, by Johann Friedrich Netto of Leipzig at the end of the eighteenth century. Netto was an accomplished artist who turned his skills to needlework patterns and provided in 1800 *Self-Study Book of Drawing, Painting and Embroidery for Ladies Occupied with the Fine Arts*.

But many ladies, perhaps more old-fashioned in taste and temperament, continued to do needlework that was useful rather than decorative only. Mrs Delany reports again, that on her visit to Holkham Hall in Norfolk in 1774:

> *Lady Leicester works at a tent-stitch frame*
> *every night by one candle that she sets upon it,*
> *and no spectacles.*

Some women required the assistance of a spherical lens or water-filled glass or 'lacemaker's lamp' to intensify the flame.

Late eighteenth century American pictures differed slightly in spirit, often having a certain stiffness and charming naïvety. Designs included landscapes, pastoral scenes, views of architecture and ships, maps, portraits, biblical and mythological subjects, memorials, flower pieces and allegorical compositions. A good many were worked in schools including scenes from Shakespeare, after prints by John and Josiah Boydell.[22]

223

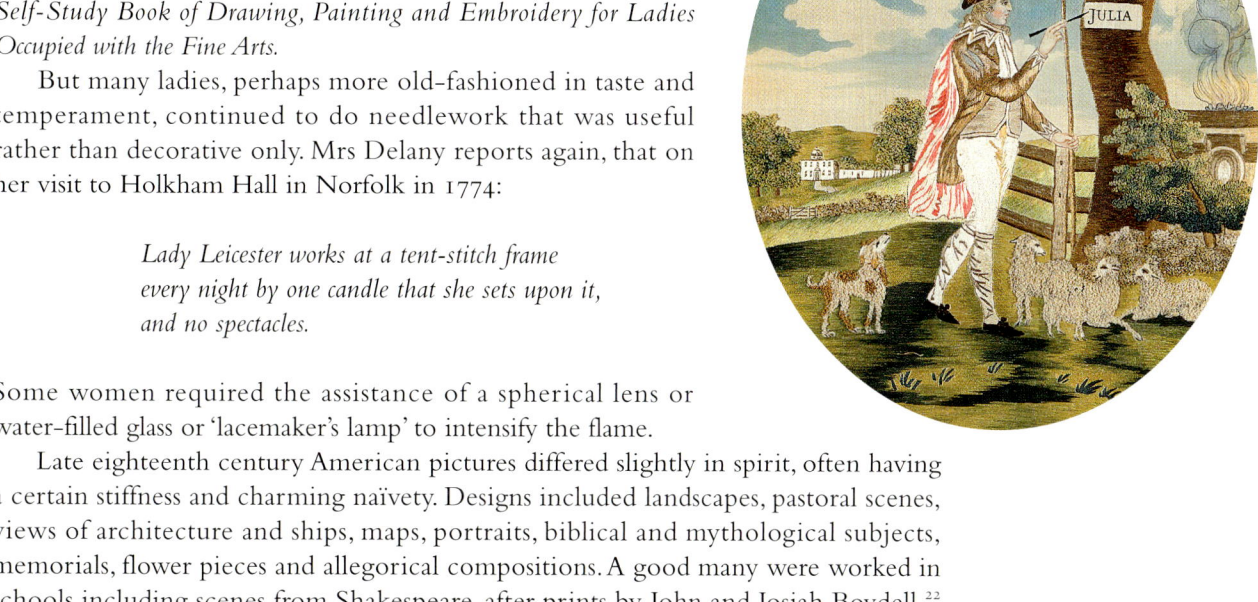

The Art of Embroidery

217. Engravings of Trinity and Kings Colleges in Cambridge are derived from known prints and each is dated 1789.

Some commemorated George Washington. They were embroidered with a variety of stitches in floss or twisted silks. As in England, the sky and faces were usually painted and they were often given a blackened glass mount with a gilt frame, very much a feature of Regency taste. Also as in England these were usually closely based on contemporary prints. Further embroidery pictures generally had an atmosphere of melancholy gloom with titles like The First, Second and Last Scene of Mortality, an example worked by Prudence Punderson c.1775 (Connecticut Historical Society, Hartford).

Sentimental but fine quality pictures were worked in schools. The Moravians, a religious group from Germany, founded two institutions in Bethlehem near Philadelphia in 1749 and here girls were taught the silk picture embroidery, tambour work, ribbon work, crepe work and flower embroidery. In addition they made banners, including a surviving example from the American Revolution, known as the Pulaski Banner, that now belongs to the Maryland Historical Society, Baltimore. Of canvas work, some thirty-six panels in tent stitch from New England are generically termed the Fishing Lady pictures in reference to a central motif.

Larger imitations of oil paintings in wool embroidery were another development which was immensely admired following the successes of several professional and semi-professional embroideresses. In 1771 Arthur Young described in great detail needlepaintings after old masters by Miss Morritt of Rokeby, Yorkshire.[23] They included two Zuccarelli landscapes, two Gaspar Poussin landscapes, an unfinished picture after Rubens and a picture by Salvator Rosa entitled Democritus in a Contemplative Mood. Mary Knowles (1733-1807) was a friend of Dr Johnson and herself a noted conversationalist. She too was famed for elaborate needlework copies of paintings. Queen Charlotte commissioned her to copy Zoffany's portrait of George III (Victoria and Albert Museum) and another large scale embroidered picture commemorates the event, showing Mrs Knowles working the portrait (Kew Palace) (Plate 212). Mary Linwood (1756-1845) exhibited similar works, with great success, at permanent displays in London and in Edinburgh and Dublin. At Hanover Square in 1798 she showed a hundred copies after artists such as Raphael and Rubens, and many other painters and portraitists of the period from continental Europe and England. Her exhibitions became a social phenomenon like Madame Tussaud's wax models, though the popularity did not last in the same way. A London guidebook describing the pictures concluded: '…in a word, Miss Linwood's exhibition is one of the most beautiful the metropolis can boast and should unquestionably be witnessed, as it deserves to be, by every admirer of art'. She laid out her shows with the greatest theatrical panache, even with gas lighting, an enterprising novelty in those days, so that viewing could continue throughout winter afternoons. A Stubbs lioness appeared to be nothing short of the real creature emerging from a cave. She also delighted in narrative subjects such as James Northcot's *Lady Jane Grey visited by the Abbot and Keeper of the Tower by Night*. Miss Linwood was generally celebrated and was received by the Royal Family, the Empress of Russia, the King of Poland and Napoleon, whose portrait she embroidered twice. She left what she considered her masterpiece, a picture after Carlo Dolci, *Salvator Mundi,* to Queen Victoria. Other works are now at the Museum of Leicester, her birthplace. These include a large scene showing a woodman and a dog, after a lost painting by Thomas Gainsborough.

Whitework embroidery was continuously made since its origin in lace costume accessories. Denmark was especially famed for it, on fine lawn, a semi-transparent linen, with linen thread or imported cotton. Hedebo and Amager embroidery was renowned, combining floral decoration and drawn-thread work, on locally woven grounds.

Indian muslins were much admired in the early eighteenth century for their fineness and transparency and they temporarily ousted lace for dress accessories. Fine plain ones were the rage, as can be seen in portraits, and they in turn perhaps stimulated the challenge by very fine bobbin laces made in Flanders. Needlework imitations of these then followed throughout northern Europe and were almost indistinguishable. Muslin was ideal for embroidery as the threads could be pulled apart easily. Dresden in Saxony was the centre of the professional production of this work giving its name to the whitework. It was soon to be taught to all young girls in schools.

The development of Arkwright's and Crompton's looms meant that fine muslins and cottons no longer had to be imported from India. This led to a development of Britain's whitework industry and included the techniques of tambour embroidery and broderie anglaise. Embroidery of this form was known throughout the country – in London a tambour workshop master faced a trial in 1801 for cruelty to apprentices – but it was in Scotland and Belfast that 'sewed Muslin' whitework became an important industry at the end of the eighteenth century. It was known as 'Ayrshire' embroidery, though the first design workshops were centred around Edinburgh. An Italian, Luigi Ruffini, set up a workshop in 1782 and successive ventures led to a massive production of flowered muslin or sprigged muslin, two further names for it, in the nineteenth century. Agents co-ordinated the manufacture of intricately embroidered children's robes, caps, dresses and cuffs by women in their own homes and in factories. Several mechanical developments led to groups working together. Designs included imitations of French lace which was difficult to procure during the Napoleonic wars. The American Civil War eventually threatened the supply of cotton but the agents had built up a thriving industry. They exported products to Europe in a needlework trade of an importance that had not been enjoyed since the production of *opus anglicanum* in the fourteenth century.

CHAPTER EIGHT

A Note on Furniture

…we have twice as many firescreens as chimneys.

MINUTELY detailed illuminations in mediaeval manuscripts often show rich canopies, beds and hangings. The fact that they were prominently portrayed indicates how much they were valued. These textiles were undoubtedly treasured as highly as ecclesiastical vestments. The latter were stored flat, and thus preserved, in great chests, such as the magnificent half-round one for copes at Gloucester Cathedral, but few secular materials have survived, so details must be gleaned from inventories. Fragments of information such as the fact that Edward VI's gown of 'black velvet embroidered very richly' was later used on a footstool help to make up a historical picture. An instance where church vestments were relegated to furnishing fabric is cited in the Westminster Abbey accounts for 1571:

> *Thomas Holmes upholster for*
> *Thaltering of certain coapes*
> *Into Quisshions Chaires etc*
> *And for the workmanship…*

The word 'furniture', until recently, was used more generally to include all decorative and useful 'movables', but in many early records the term was used specifically to refer to bed curtains, upholstery and textile fittings in general. These were amongst the most valuable items of a house and are often listed in inventories, beginning with

218. Supplied by Thomas Phill for Canons Ashby, Northamptonshire, in 1720, these chairs display flowers in fashionable Chinese blue and white or Delft jars.

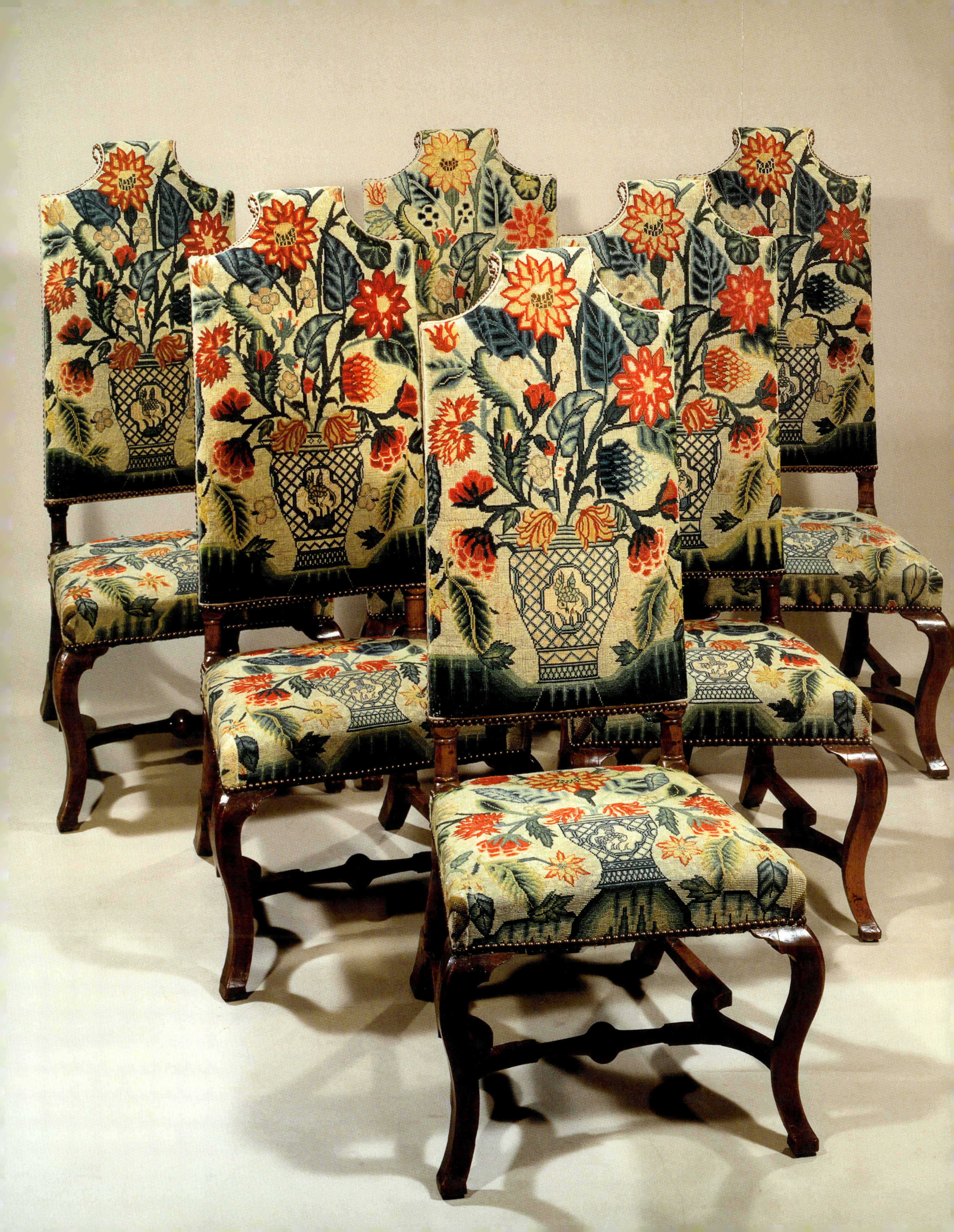

The Art of Embroidery

Right. 219. The interior of a walnut cabinet of c.1670 is lined with embroidered panels following the painted interiors of Flemish versions. The finding of Moses, the four elements, and classical stories, are depicted.

Opposite above. 220. Part of a blue crewelwork hanging with stylised leaves worked in satin stitch on a closely woven wool ground, c.1700.

Opposite below. 221. Made to complement Plate 220, an unused canvas work panel of the same design made for seat furniture, these two matching varieties for a room perhaps being a unique survival of their kind.

cloths of estate or throne canopies. The bed was, after all, the stage of life, as nicely expressed by Margaret Swain.[1] It was where the drama of birth and death was enacted, in it the new generation was hailed and celebrated and around it mourners gathered at death. Like a stage it had curtains and a backcloth, with valances around the canopy or tester. Elaborate state beds were of symbolic importance in a house as well as the focal point of official and social activities. They were lavishly furnished with hangings fitted by an upholsterer (or French tapissier), considered the most important craftsman until the full emergence of woodwork in the eighteenth century, when carving, gilding and painting became important. Fine beds displayed status and wealth and many were of costly needlework. Heavy metal threads, silks and velvets were used on the most important. Crewel embroidery on others was less expensive and more durable, so as a result more of these have survived. These were often worked by their owners. Lady Anne Drury of Hardwicke, Suffolk, for example, bequeathed in 1621 'a cloth bed of my own making'. Beds became less important towards the end of the eighteenth century when bedrooms were considered private places and were smaller and less prominent in the architecture of the house. Bedroom accessories including

A Note on Furniture

magnificent coverlets, hangings, quilts and patchwork, British and American, continued as symbolic bed furnishings however into the nineteenth century and modern times.

The magnificence of early beds is clearly indicated in wills, and the descriptions are poetic: 'one large bed of black satin embroidered with white lions and gold roses and escutcheons of the arms of Mortimer and Ulster'. This reference of 1380 recalls the heraldic creatures so often featured in hangings. An item in a will of 1434 records the colourfulness of late mediaeval textiles: 'my bed of silk, black and red, embroidered with woodbined flowers of silver, and all the costers[2] and apparel that belongeth thereto…'.

A century later Mary Queen of Scots returned to her kingdom to find the royal residences rough and bare. She immediately brought from France embroiderers and tapissiers and had many beds erected for herself, her attendants and her fool. Some were embroidered, others were of appliqué and trimmed with silk braids and some were of warm wool with worsted fringing. Wool linings were essential as insulation against the cold and damp. Mary's excellent chamberlain, Servais de Condé, recorded many interesting details and we know for example that of twenty sets of hangings and canopies of estate brought to Scotland in 1561, twelve were embroidered, some with the ciphers of her French relations and some with 'histories', that is, narrative illustrations of stories. One bed was described as having 'six pands [i.e. valances] roof, headpiece and three underpands' showing the labours of Hercules. This was probably the bed inherited by James I and recorded at Hampton Court in 1659. Tent-shaped beds were also listed at this period and field-beds, still elaborate but more easily packed and moved. In 1562 Mary Queen of Scots confiscated a number of possessions from the rebel Earl of Huntly including yellow damask bed hangings 'made like a chapel' and altered into a four-poster. She also took many vestments which the Earl had in safe keeping for Aberdeen Cathedral and had no qualms about adapting these to secular use. Some were given to Bothwell and 'a cope, chasuble and four tunicles to make a bed for the King [i..e. Lord Darnley]. All broken and cut in her own presence'. A green velvet set was used for a bed, a high chair, two seats and a chaise percée.

Cushions were an important feature of the furnishing of a room and many were listed of various materials, often needlework. An inventory made at

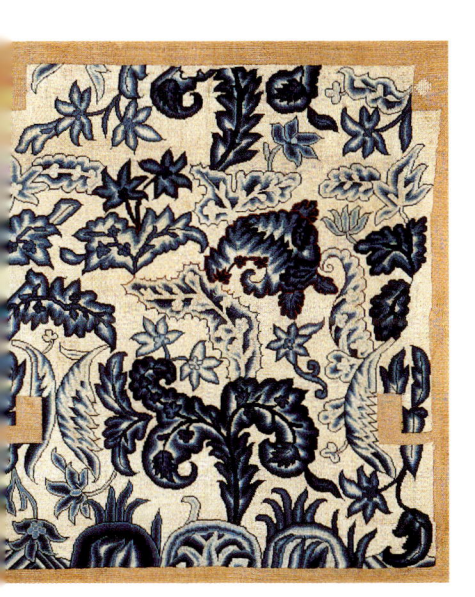

229

The Art of Embroidery

222. A pair of candle sconces backed with charming naïvely worked needlework panels, c.1720.

Edinburgh Castle in 1578 lists ten chairs and as many as forty cushions. Two stools 'coverit with sewit werk of divers culloris' are in the same inventory but chairs and stools were far less numerous than soft furnishings and were reserved for the most important visitors or the chief members of the family. Like beds they were invariably covered with luxurious fabrics. In 1543 Princess Mary gave her father Henry VIII a chair which cost about £4, but the needlework covering for it cost no less than £18. A splendid painting at Sherborne Castle depicts Queen Elizabeth I going in procession to Blackfriars. She is being carried in a litter, the canopy of which is embroidered with flower slips, clearly depicted, though probably in a larger format than the actual sewing. Meanwhile James I's horse-drawn carriage, now in the Kremlin, is upholstered with a needlework interior.

An increase in comforts in the seventeenth century called for further hangings and upholstery; Knole and Ham House are two great houses where one can still see how rich textiles and furnishings were extravagantly employed to create magnificence. Curtains were not used for windows until the eighteenth century but 'coverlets' were sometimes hung over windows and doors; Daniel Marot's designs of 1702 for portières illustrate the latter. The Hardwick Hall inventory of 1601 lists 'a coverlett to hang before a dore' and 'thre coverlets to hang before a windowe'. These may have been tapestry or needlework. Bed hangings were made, often of needlework, with great elaboration and at great cost. The Countess of Salisbury had a set made professionally in time for the birth of her daughter in 1612. They were of white satin embroidered with silver and pearls, and were said to have cost a fortune. James II ordered a bed, two armchairs and six stools to be made in Paris by Simon Delobel at a cost of £1,515. A number of fine seventeenth century beds have survived and eighteenth century ones, the most remarkable of which is the sumptuous green velvet bed at Houghton Hall which cost Sir Robert Walpole a fortune in 1732. It is embellished with gold thread embroidery (over vellum) in lace-like ornament, architectural detailing and braid on the great shell headboard (Plate 224).

The uses of needlework became greatly extended; it was made for considerable quantities of seat furniture in addition to beds and wall hangings. Canvas embroidery was much more durable than crewelwork for upholstery, and the same design in both techniques is occasionally seen together on complementary furniture (Plates 220 and 221). In other cases designs are clearly related: a wing chair and five other armchairs at

A Note on Furniture

Boughton House are covered with needlework of a red leaf design reminiscent of crewelwork. In France professional needlework was made for a large amount of seat furniture and a good deal survives from the seventeenth century. In England however, chairs covered with needlework were exceptional, though there are good numbers of surviving examples from the early eighteenth century. This form of covering was relatively tough and was perhaps especially saved if associated with amateur workmanship. Velvets eventually perished; dining chairs were often covered in leather or 'horse cloth' (horsehair) and chairs in public rooms were most likely to be covered with woven fabric, often matching curtains, wall hangings etc. Needlework presented an element of informality sometimes, and each piece was individual. Florentine needle-

223. Much grander, this gilt gesso double sconce wall bracket contains an embroidered scene of sophisticated arcadian pleasure. c.1715.

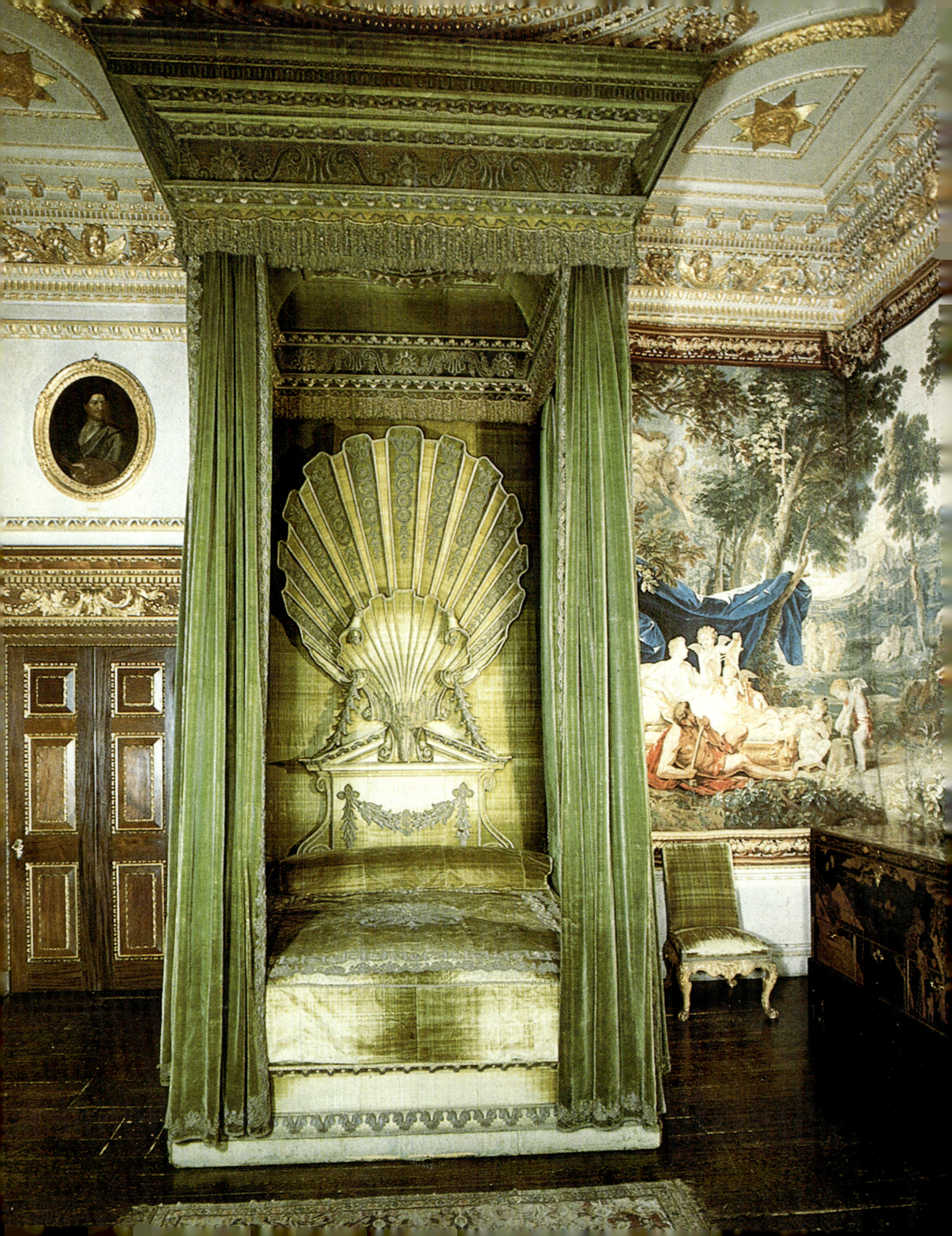

A Note on Furniture

work was used on walls and on beds as well as for covering seat furniture. Another set of chairs and stools at Boughton House and a bed at Parham, Sussex, illustrate this, even if not original to the particular pieces. The pattern was especially popular for use on furniture in America, early examples being a late seventeenth century wing chair at Historic Deerfield in kalem or knitstitch of Florentine zig-zag form and an early eighteenth century one in the Metropolitan Museum in so-called Irish stitch (Plate 237).

Most furniture coverings, including this last example, were of canvas work. 'Canvas' would nowadays be termed linen, an unstiffened, unbleached plain-weave material, whether closely or loosely woven. The word derives from 'cannabis' so is theoretically hemp, but in fact not necessarily so.

A closer consideration may now be made, however, of the various forms of needlework on furniture. By the end of the seventeenth century a wide range of decorative items were either wholly embroidered, or incorporated pieces of needlework. In Antwerp pictures were made for use in the doors and drawer fronts of cabinets.[3] This technique was similarly carried out from time to time in England; a splendid walnut cabinet on stand, formerly at Groombridge Place, Kent, is inset on the interior with panels of needlework, typical of embroidery of the period but rarely seen mounted in this manner in England (Plate 219). An interesting mahogany cabinet, c.1745, acquired by Temple Newsam in Leeds, incorporates floral panels of tent-stitch with chenille on the outside and twenty-two small silkwork drawer fronts on the inside.

A form of furniture closely associated with the more familiar embroidered pictures, but still essentially decoration, is wall sconces for candles, with framed embroidered back panels. A number of these, often in pairs, have survived, mostly dating to the last years of the seventeenth century and first decades of the eighteenth century. They are usually of walnut, gilt gesso or parcel gilt walnut and I have seen one pair with ivory frames and needlework that was probably imported from China. Others, for example in the Metropolitan Museum and in the Mulliner collection,[4] are glazed and with a glass or brass arm for a candle. A pair of c.1735 was seen at Sotheby's[5] with silk and chenille embroidered portraits of George II and Queen Caroline, the first with an Indian servant and the second including the king, both after engravings of paintings by Sir Godfrey Kneller.

After grand beds, seat furniture was the next most significant category with wide

224. Opposite. The truly extravagant green velvet bed at Houghton Hall is richly embroidered with details in 'galloon', metal threads, now tarnished to grey.

Below. 225. Needlework for covering furniture often incorporated a pictorial panel in fine tent stitch enclosed within a decorative frame of coarser work, as this French example of about 1720.

233

The Art of Embroidery

variations of style between the seventeenth century and modern times. The more formal furniture, especially in the greatest houses, was usually upholstered with rich woven fabric – velvet, brocade, damask, plain silk, and occasionally woven tapestry. Needlework was mostly put on furniture for less formal rooms. But even in formal instances velvet might be enriched with monograms, as in the case of a Charles II carved walnut settee at the Palace of Holyrood, which has ducal coronets and monograms of gold appliqué embroidery (now remounted on modern material). Such devices have always been pleasing decorative emblems as well as prestigious. A settee of canvas work, with a crown and intertwined initials, in the Royal Collection is reputed to be the work of Princess Amelia (1711-1786). A number of chairs are covered with embroidered arms, a notable example being a suite of giltwood furniture at Berkeley Castle, Gloucestershire.

Representational designs in needlework on seat furniture tend to fall into two types, floral and pictorial. Perhaps the most famous early ones of the floral kind are the detachable covers on Lady Betty Germain's chairs at Drayton House, Northamptonshire (see pages 155-157). These are of a dense floral pattern in the Dutch manner, similar to marquetry of the period and very different from the less grand curling leaf patterns of crewelwork. Flowers tightly packed into a vase became larger and more spread out. A

Above. 226. The floral design here is that of an English flower garden, in full bloom. c.1720.

Right. 227. Imported needlework from Paris was used on this Queen Anne sofa. It depicts exotic chinoiserie figures within 'bizarre' patterns.

234

set of chairs made for Canons Ashby, Northamptonshire, has a spray of large colourful flowers and leaves springing from a blue and white vase, one each on the seats and backs of these high back side chairs. A sofa and firescreen were also made at the same time and loose covers (otherwise known as case or false covers) were supplied, which no doubt partly accounts for their excellent condition today. They are recorded in the accounts of the house and were supplied by Thomas Phill who in 1719 was 'at the sign of The Three Golden Chairs in the Strand'. Five years earlier he had supplied Edward Dryden of Canons Ashby with six walnut-back chair panels 'of ye newest fashion' with green sage for the backs and gold serge for false cases. He also charged for making 'ye needlework covers and fixing ym on ye chairs' (Plate 218).

Pictorial subjects had in the meantime become increasingly popular, based on classical, religious, allegorical stories and fables. They were more formal in mood and a good many came to London from Paris workshops. As with floral needlework, pictorial themes formed the basis of seat backs for single chairs or sets of furniture. They were rarely seen on seats and backs together (flowers and birds were preferred for a seat below an upholstered back), though chairs with wooden backs did occasionally have seats with pictorial subjects. Some eighteenth century seat furniture was still covered with needlework depicting Bible stories but these diminished in favour of novel French sophistication with classical themes. The set of seven walnut chairs made for Stoneleigh Abbey, Warwickshire to mark its completion in 1726, for example, have well drawn designs for Ovid's *Metamorphoses,* as have a French Régence settee and two chairs in the Royal Ontario Museum, Toronto. A scene was often portrayed in a reserve, worked in fine tent-stitch, and with a surrounding border of flowers, worked in coarser stitches. Many good pieces of this format have survived; examples can be seen at Waddesdon Manor, Scone Palace, Seaton Delaval, Northumberland and in the Frick Collection, New York. The use of gros point around pictorial motifs worked in petit point was partly for effect but also for economy, being quicker to work. In some cases the entire panel was of one or other type of stitch with corresponding extremes of appearance. In many cases, even in petit point work, certain small areas, particularly representing faces and other flesh parts, were worked in finer stitches on a separate

228. An early 18th century wing chair covered with its original needlework, the flower and leaf forms inspired by Indian design and the background worked in unusually fine stitch.

The Art of Embroidery

229. A settee seat cover embroidered in silk and wool on canvas worked after an illustration to John Gay's Fables. c.1750.

small piece of linen, worked into the surrounding area. This method could also give a slight padded relief to faces, adding to the liveliness of the work (Plate 225).

Two pairs of large Régence armchairs and a sofa in the Frick Collection are covered with good tent stitch work in excellent condition (though some of it is of a later date). One pair has a light blue background decorated with polychrome motifs including Venus, cupids and small mythological landscapes amongst animals, masks, shells, ferns, flowers, swags, scrolls and lambrequins, reminiscent of Bérain. English and French tent stitch work were similar; the latter is sometimes distinguished by a tendency to set the design against a white or black background, and to depict more exotic plants, especially pomegranates.

English wing chairs of the first half of the eighteenth century, often termed 'easy chairs', were particularly favoured as a vehicle for elaborate canvas embroidery and many good examples have survived. The designs ranged from pictorial forms to general or specially arranged floral patterns. Queen Anne and George I wing chairs could display particularly well large expanses of fine needlework (Plate 228). Almost invariably made individually, each one was highly personal and as the form was so comfortable this type of chair continued to be made up to the mid-eighteenth century, though seldom with needlework after about 1740. A beautiful chair at Mompesson House, Salisbury is shown on page 24, Plate 20. At Aston Hall, Birmingham there is a wing chair with Jonah and the Whale, dated 1738, by Rebecca Hornblower. Another in the Burrell Collection, Glasgow shows Elijah and Susanna and the Elders. There are two at Clandon Park. In the Metropolitan Museum, New York, a fine wing chair shows St Philip meeting and converting the Ethiopian Eunuch on the seat back, the scene

A Note on Furniture

further enriched with oriental birds and pots. The chair has numerous other vignettes on the arms and seat cushion. Interestingly a firescreen panel of exactly the same design as the chair back must have been drawn out by the same provider of patterns (Plate 179, page 195). The chair has numerous other vignettes on the arms and seat cushion. In the same museum there is another Queen Anne style walnut wing chair, signed 'Newport 1758', entirely covered with needlework in a diamond-shaped flame pattern in Irish stitch but the back of crewelwork with a landscape with birds, deer, sheep, people, trees and hillocky ground (Plate 237). Fine needlework on squarer, Chippendale period wing chairs is rare, but a pair from Hornby Castle, embroidered by members of the Godolphin-Osborne family, are notable. These and a pair of large sofas are decorated with a great variety of flowers in sprays and growing up a trellis, with a cream background (Plate 238).[6]

Though relatively little furniture of the style made famous by Thomas Chippendale seems to have been upholstered with needlework, that most famous of furniture

230. The interesting needlework fitted to these chairs depicts prized blue and white pots on a red ground and within dividing compartments, c.1700.

237

The Art of Embroidery

Above. 231. This English chair seat, one of a set of variations, shows exuberant blooms in fine and coarser tent stitch. c.1730.

Right. 232. A French chair seat depicts a variety of flowers and creatures on a black ground, using silk and wool and different sized stitches.

suppliers and designers is in fact known to have supplied Lady Knatchbull with patterns for large 'Barjair' chairs. Additionally he gave specific instructions for the design of canvaswork he considered suitable for certain furniture. A chair in Lord Pembroke's collection has covers worked with figures in exotic costumes, animals, urns and flowers, closely following suggestions in the third edition of Chippendale's *The Gentleman and Cabinet-Makers Director* (1754).

Many ambitious projects were undertaken. The Great Parlour Chamber at Weston Hall, as already mentioned, has an impressive quantity of needlework made by Mrs Jennens c.1731, including a bed and six chairs, while at Nunwick, Northumberland, there is a set of furniture by Lady Allgood, c.1750, consisting of a settee, six chairs, stools, card tables and firescreens. She was married in 1739 and a portrait of the embroideress shows her holding a needlework seat. She is also reputed to have had a spinning wheel fitted in her coach.[7] Furniture was made for her by William Greer in 1752. This is at Arbury Hall, Warwickshire, where there is also a pair of stools for which Sophia Conyers, first wife of Sir Roger Newdigate, did needlework in trompe l'oeil fashion, supposedly showing objects that she left lying about.[8]

Chair backs and seats were frequently, even usually, made first and then an appropriate chair was ordered for them. The Duke of Atholl ordered from William Gordon a famous set of eight mahogany armchairs for Blair Castle, with carved scales on the legs, for needlework which had been worked by the Duchess. Gordon's bill for these is dated 1756. In a number of cases the shaped panels of needlework and corresponding shapes of the furniture suggest that one was specially made for the other rather than the needlework purchased or worked as an afterthought. The Copped Hall suite of twelve chairs and a sofa (Leicester Museum and Victoria and Albert Museum) have fine needlework of a stiff formal nature with pictorial scenes framed within borders of flowers. Another remarkable set of settees and six chairs from Chicheley Hall (now to be seen at Montacute House, Somerset) are of a grand scale and

A Note on Furniture

worked in gros and petit point, reputedly by a member of the Chester family.⁹ Likewise of specially shaped form is the needlework on a sofa and set of chairs worked by Ann Northey, c.1745 and now at Marble Hill House. The scenes depicted on the seats are clearly amateur work, the genre subjects being of a homely though charming rustic nature. Another series of seat covers, on several different chair models, also show rural themes with domestic animals. Plate 239 shows two of these related to a set of six chairs from the Duke of Buckingham's house, Stowe, which were illustrated in Mallett's catalogue of 1931.¹⁰

A further pictorial theme has a rococo flavour like the chinoiserie frivolities of the St Cyr workshops. Actors, dancers and opera singers, from engravings by Jean Mariette of Paris are portrayed on English, French and Italian chairs, firescreens etc. *Commedia dell'Arte* figures (Harlequin, Columbine, Punchinello and Pantaloon) also feature. Harlequin is shown on the wing chair in the Metropolitan Museum mentioned above (together with St Philip and the Ethiopian Eunuch, shepherds, attendant gentlemen and an oriental potentate) and also in a screen at Wallington Hall. In both cases he is derived from a print published by Nicholas Bonnant in Paris. Italian comedy figures

233. This panel of needlework with trompe l'oeil playing cards was made for lining the top of a games table in about 1740.

The Art of Embroidery

234. The needlework on this early Georgian sofa displays an overall pattern of rich garden blooms gloriously packed together.

also feature on twelve long narrow hangings in the Germanisches National Museum, Nüremberg, made in Dresden, c 1711 and 1718.[11]

Amongst further notable needlework coverings in the greater houses are, for example, several sets at Arundel Castle, Sussex, particularly a suite of large gilt gesso armchairs with differing designs, one chair signed 'DHG 1762' and traditionally said to be from Worksop Manor.

The redoubtable Mrs Delany made two sets of covers for drawing room chairs: her winter ones were of worsted chenille with groups of flowers and her summer ones were of brilliant blue linen with husks and leaves in white linen, sewn down with five varieties of knotting. For the chapel she did work with a black background 'which gives it a gravity' but without roses ('too gay') and with 'cross-stitch in diamonds which looks rich and grave'. At Culzean Castle, Ayrshire, there is part of a set of twelve chairs believed to have been worked by the mother of the Duke of Wellington, Anne Lady Mornington, 1742-1831. The designs include rustic card players and mythological scenes on a yellow background. The National Trust for Scotland also owns ten chairs sewn by Mrs Ivory of Tipperary and a set of chairs from Lady Abercrombie.

Tradesmen offered their services in all possible forms; they would draw out patterns for embroideresses, supply the materials, or undertake to design and carry out

A Note on Furniture

the work in its entirety. Thomas Hill's trade card, London 1747 (Huntington Library, Pasadena), is ornamental and advertises such services in English and French.

Professionally made needlework chair seats and backs are represented by a set of ten giltwood fauteuils at Scone Palace. Depicting mediaeval, mythological and oriental scenes in yellow reserves surrounded by a red foliate pattern, these were probably supplied by the tapissier Planqué at St Cyr. The chairs were made by Pierre Bara in 1756.

Needlework is by nature elaborate and textured and therefore usually looks best on chairs of a simple line, but Chippendale, whose furniture designs of 1754 are generally noted for considerable rococo ornament, recommended 'tapestry' coverings 'or other sort of Needlework' for chairs in the French style. A pair of chairs in the Untermeyer Collection, Metropolitan Museum, New York, are upholstered with needlework, and a number of other rococo mahogany chairs retain their original needlework seats. Though not the case in England, in Europe generally needlework

235. A pair of walnut side chairs of c.1730 have cascading leafy plumes worked on canvas with masterly shading.

241

The Art of Embroidery

was usually regarded as the poor relation of tapestry and used in less formal circumstances. A set of ten mahogany chairs of Chippendale form at Dunster Castle have good needlework seats.

Chair coverings of plainer forms, and in a limited range of colours were also made. These sometimes imitated or echoed damask with bold formal leaf patterns in red, blue or green. From the seventeenth century, needlework of this type would have been an alternative to the prohibitively expensive imported cut velvet and, later, damask. Examples are settees illustrated in *The Dictionary of English Furniture,* Macquoid and Edwards (2nd edition, 1954) from Hampton Court, Herefordshire, and Burley-on-the-Hill. An early wing chair at Drum Castle has cross stitch needlework in a damask pattern with red and green on a yellow ground.[12] There are further examples at the Bowes Museum[13] and at Temple Newsam, Leeds. At Temple Newsam, also, there is an extensive set of gilt furniture consisting of twenty chairs, four sofas and a day bed upholstered in bold and colourful over lifesize blooms of floral work in tent stitch and French knots. It is interesting that such an extensive and magnificent suite of furniture, supplied in 1746, was covered in needlework rather than damask, or even tapestry. Another remarkable set of mid-eighteenth century English mahogany chairs with fine needlework covers was sold in New York in 1981.[14] It consists of twelve side chairs, two armchairs and a sofa (plus a stool, when previously sold), all with floral needlework. The designs are repeated on pairs of chairs, with alternating colours for the backgrounds to the

A Note on Furniture

flowers and surrounding formalised borders. In such large quantity, this was presumably made professionally.

A later form of plainer upholstery needlework, usually all wool, and often in 'rice stitch', is seen in many mid- and late eighteenth century country house rooms. This is of geometric form worked in squares, octagons, or basketwork design in a limited range of colours. A set of six chairs at Drum Castle, for example, have a plain basketwork design in shades of yellow and green. These called for no skills of drawing, just counting. Others can be seen at Mellerstain, Blair Castle and Leixlip Castle, Co. Kildare. Similar work, of the same period, was done in Pennsylvania. Between ornate designs and plainer ones is a suite of chairs from Cusworth Hall, Yorkshire which have intersecting roundels with bosses in the centres.[15]

Simpler designs were increasingly preferred from about 1770. Silk weaving and embroidery could be combined to great and sympathetic effect, such as in Marie-Antoinette's bedroom at Fontainebleau where work was carried out by Mme Baudonin in 1791. The tidiness of tambour embroidery on silk suited elegant French furniture; this was also used for large screens. Good examples of tambour work and other needlework are to be seen at the Musée Nissim de Camondo, Waddesdon Manor and the Metropolitan Museum, where there are two pairs of chairs by George

Opposite above. 236. The early 18th century drop-in seats for two walnut side chairs have bordered roundels with idyllic pastoral scenes.

Opposite below. 237. An American wing chair of 1758 has a crewelwork hunting scene on the back and an overall pattern of Irish stitch on the other sides.

Below. 238. A pair of mid-18th century wing chairs are unusually upholstered with a realistic garden of different plants growing up a trellis.

The Art of Embroidery

239. A set of chairs associated with Stowe, Buckinghamshire, depict rural scenes, framed in formal roundels. c.1760.

Jacob, c.1775, upholstered with tambour embroidery in the style of the textile designer Philippe de la Salle. Another suite of French seat furniture in the same museum has satin coverings with embroidered baskets of flowers, and posies (not tambour stitch). In bright condition, the panels are bordered with a twisted ribbon pattern. The furniture is of gilded mahogany and this is an instance of needlework being employed on the highest quality saloon furnishings.

Neo-classical embroidered coverings are relatively scarce, particularly in England, but a set of furniture, including two sofas and twelve armchairs at Syon House, London, were made to designs by Robert Adam, c.1769. The needlework was executed by French nuns in 1810. An interesting firescreen at Robert Adam's Osterley Park, designed in 1777 for the Etruscan room, contains a relatively rare example of true neo-classical needlework,[16] very different from the classical figures depicted on shield-shaped and oval pole screens (see page 183).

Throughout the history of interior decoration and furniture-making table carpets, firescreens and other items offered endless opportunities for displaying needlework and from the first many unexpected or smaller items were decorated with embroidery. Two early eighteenth century objects at Parham, Sussex, are random examples. The first is an early eighteenth century baby's or doll's cot which has a quilted coverlet and upholstery of cream satin. The second is a banner firescreen of delicate and brilliant workmanship; like contemporary pictures, it depicts a shepherd and shepherdess on hillocky ground, with a dog, a sheep, a house and trees, within a floral border. Cushions continued to provide scope for needlework. Martha Washington made twelve squab cushions (pads) for windsor chairs over a period of thirty-six years with a scallop shell design in red on a yellow ground. Of worsted, they were highlighted with some yellow floss silk. Some can be seen at Mount Vernon.[17]

Some nineteenth century needlework lent itself to complementing furniture. Berlin wools were used for fairly traditional floral coverings for chairs, even large sets, as at Burghley House, while new formalised Berlin type patterns added to the richness that the Victorians sought; bright colours and complex designs contributed to a density of atmosphere and the best of it was impressive. The work was undemanding technically and as it was done with strong materials much has survived. At Mapledurham House, Oxfordshire, there is a large suite of furniture of various periods with Berlin rice stitch needlework in geometric forms, crosses and roses, that is bold, colourful and decorative. There is also a pretty hexagonal Berlinwork ottoman there. Prie-dieu chairs and hanging firescreen banners offered opportunities for a wide variety of designs, techniques and materials. A round conversation sofa at Wallington Hall and curtains at the Bowes Museum, with bold relief flowers, especially roses and lilies in plush stitch, represent Victorian delights. Couched chenille silks are combined with Berlin woolwork on curtains at House of Dun, near Montrose.

Berlin woolwork seems indeed to have been applied to every household and personal article, appropriate and inappropriate. Though carried to extremes in the nineteenth century this manic 'work' followed a tradition of domestic industry, from which a relatively small quantity survives. In late seventeenth century furnishing and decoration, for instance, many smaller items, even bellows, might have embroidered embellishment. Bellows dated 1673, with a female figure in beadwork on one side and a vase of flowers on the other, are in the Burrell Collection.[18]

Above. 240. Informality is the essence of the variety of the rococo decoration of this English mahogany chair of about 1770.

Left. 241. The needlework seats and backs on a set of chairs from Glemham Hall were reputedly worked by Lady Barbara North (died 1755) and relate to a surviving design.

The Art of Embroidery

Above. 242. One of a pair of giltwood sofas covered with elegant early 19th century needlework.

Below. 243. In pristine condition, this English stool cover, worked in wools and silks, is partly closely defined and partly worked in simpler block colours.

Interesting formal embroidery of the gothic revival period is on the throne chairs designed by Augustus W.N. Pugin for the House of Lords, Palace of Westminster. Two of them were given as perquisites to the Lord Great Chamberlain, the Marquess of Cholmondeley, and are therefore normally to be seen at Houghton Hall, Norfolk. The velvet upholstery is richly embroidered with the royal arms and Prince of Wales feathers.

Art needlework was not suited to upholstery, the designs and workmanship being too random and fragile, but it was favoured for large screens and wall hangings. Table cloths, furniture runners, curtains, portières, piano covers and bell-pulls were amongst the many other articles on which it could be displayed with pride.

A revival of crewelwork in the first decades of the twentieth century is represented without great originality in the furnishings of many country houses. It was sometimes, however, effectively and charmingly used on beds and as upholstery, as can be seen on two very long sofas at Osterley Park, London, where any other form of needlework would have been extremely daunting.

A large amount of needlework has been done in recent years for covering furniture, usually old and treasured pieces. Most of it is of a traditional form appropriate to the age of the furniture. Its success always depends on the quality of the design and the dyes of the threads. Unfortunately, good patterns are still difficult to obtain. The late Lady Victoria Wemyss worked an impressive number of seats and backs to an old design showing blue and white pots on a red background similar to Plate

A Note on Furniture

230. Designs supplied by most retailers are deplorable and it is sad that many hours are wasted on mediocre kits. But the leading needlework organisations and a growing number of businesses foster the interest in doing furniture coverings and will hopefully stimulate good work. For old furniture, if a suitable pattern is not available the only satisfactory solution is to create, adapt or copy a good design, consulting any source whatsoever, from printing to pottery, have it transferred correctly to canvas, and seek out wools or silks of especially good quality, and magically beautiful dyes. It is in doing this that the art lies, the rest depends on an industrious spirit.

244. The mid-18th century coverings on these chairs, part of a set of six, are of wool embroidery worked in naturalistic flowers in satin stitch on an entirely worked rust-red ground.

CHAPTER NINE

The Nineteenth Century

Sad sewers make sad Samplers. We'll be sorry
Down to our fingers'-ends and 'broider emblems
Native to desolation —cypress sprays,
Yew tufts and hectic leaves of various autumn
And bitter tawny rue, and bent blackthorns.

REGENCY England and Napoleonic France shared in their arts aspects of a general formal stamp, a semi-political style, often Grecian, or Egyptian in idiom. This was developed from the refined and academic neo-classicism of the late eighteenth century but it now had a new vigour and severity that was partly inspired by reports of motifs and emblems seen by military campaigners in North Africa. Architecture and interior decoration were subjected to the vogue but, on the whole, embroidery was unsuited to the style and surviving pieces in the manner are rare. Plain or woven fabrics and materials with striped weaves or small motifs, such as laurel crowns or Napoleonic bees, were more generally favoured.

There was relatively little professional embroidery for private use in the nineteenth century; what was supplied was consciously 'imperial' in order to demonstrate political strength and show a dignified continuity. Napoleon commissioned hangings for Versailles, St Cloud, Compiègne and Fontainebleau, decorated with the familiar emblems, trophies and symbols of his reign – laurel leaves, key pattern, Greek, Roman and Egyptian motifs and bees. Following the French Restoration, hangings for the bedroom of Louis XVIII in the Tuileries palace, of about 1815, were made of blue figured silk velvet embroidered with a heavy design in couched gold thread, showing elaborate scrolls, wreaths, swags, fleurs-de-lis, crowns and ribbons.

In England, the lively and theatrical decoration extravagantly carried out by the Prince Regent included consideration of embroidered elements. In 1798 he ordered

245. Imperial neo-classicism. Sir Thomas Lawrence's portrait of George IV shows the king's elaborate and costly Coronation robes which he designed himself, interestingly influenced by Napoleon's Imperial robe.

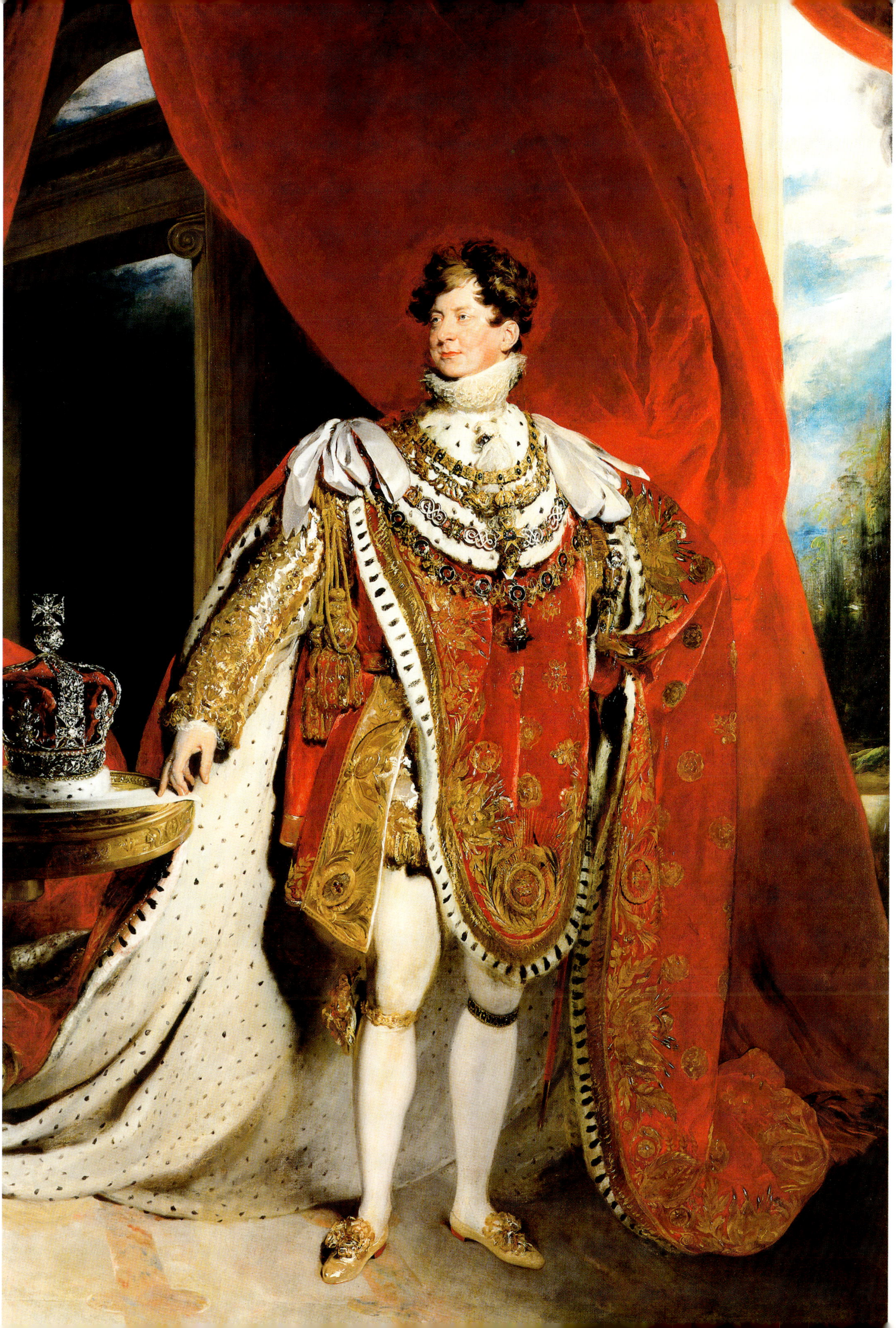

The Art of Embroidery

Right. 246. Derived from an engraving, this neo-classical silk picture shows Christ and Mary Magdalene. c.1810.

Below. 247. French silk pictures of about 1800 depict in moss stitch and chenille a ram, ewe and lamb on a silk ground.

from Peter Chomel French gold embroidery to be applied to velvet hangings and coverings in the Drawing Room and Throne Room at Carlton House but the project was abandoned. Regency chinoiserie, epitomised by the Royal Pavilion in Brighton, lent itself occasionally to needlework but not extensively. Imported Chinese embroidery from Canton was increasingly popular for hangings and for use in smaller

248. French Empire neo-classicism is epitomised by this embroidered satin by Cousin and Bony, Bissardon, Lyon, 1811.

situations. A suite of eleven silk wall hangings and two pairs of curtains with trees, flowers and birds in the manner of Indian palampores was sold at Christie's about twelve years ago. Ludwig II of Bavaria (1864-1886) patronised costly embroidered hangings for his castles, especially Herrenchiemsee, in the grand manner of Versailles. Hangings for the state bed there took seven years to make and depict the story of Venus and Cupid.

Despite those fashionable innovations of interior decoration, however, conventional forms, following those of the eighteenth century, continued to evolve in conservative circles. Pictures in silks and wools were enormously popular, becoming increasingly stereotyped and less skilled in workmanship. The rise of a relatively prosperous middle class with a desire to emulate the comforts and cultural activities of their superiors led to a sudden expansion in embroidery which was no longer the preserve of privileged ladies. Needlework indeed became a general, and somewhat standardised, hobby with sizeable business repercussions. Large-scale, colourful 'fancy' embroidery of coarse, simple workmanship was produced in unrestrained quantities. The plain sewing of

The Art of Embroidery

clothes was usually a morning occupation, while coloured work was done in the evenings, on Sundays and at times of social visiting. Tatting, a form of knotted work, continued to be a pastime. Jane Austen in a letter to her sister, Cassandra, in January 1808 wrote of her father: 'His working a footstool for Chawton is a most agreeable surprise to me…I long to know what his colours are – I guess greens and purples'.

Mary Linwood's needlework copies of contemporary oil paintings encouraged many amateurs to attempt pictures on a smaller scale. These were usually in wools in long and short stitches, but many varieties were tried out (Plate 251). Two examples by Lady Danesfort in the Victoria and Albert Museum, depicting Chichester Cathedral (after Turner) and The Avenue (after Hobbema), are worked in tiny tent stitch. Almost any canvas was considered for reproduction in needle-painting. George Morland and Francis Wheatley were frequently copied with the sentimental appeal of children and farmyard pets. As in silk pictures, the faces were often painted. Religious subjects were an alternative, frequently following an old master style. Silk 'printwork' embroidery was established in the previous century, and done in black, brown, cream and white silks, sometimes wholly, or partly, with hair. The pictures became smaller, often in an oval format, and took on the appearance of etchings. F.V. Tanner, from Switzerland, exhibited examples of 'etching' embroidery at the Great Exhibition in 1851 and boosted interest in the technique (Plate 249).

Before considering specific developments of nineteenth century needlework, a look at the samplers of the period will indicate trends affecting changes in the basic conventions established in the eighteenth century.

Left. 251. A needlepainting worked in wools after Favourite Chickens, Saturday Morning, Going to Market *by W.R. Bigg, 1791, and engraved 1797.*

Opposite above. 249. A pair of etching embroideries, only 7⅛in. (20cm) long, imitate cleverly varied tones in Dutch engravings of rural scenes.

Opposite below. 250. A large early 19th century flower-piece worked in silk chenille depicts a basket packed with garden flowers. 39¼in. x 27½in. (100cm x 70cm).

SAMPLERS

Fine stitchery was no longer an important part of a child's education and, unlike in the two previous centuries, was certainly no longer required for practical needlework. Latterly, however, there was a considerable interest in variety of technique, encouraged by a weariness of dull and repetitive work. This culminated in, for example, the popularity of Thérèse de Dillmont's *Encyclopaedia of Needlework* (English edition 1870).

Nineteenth century samplers were fairly stereotyped; in many cases ordinary and rather sad products of schools or nursery classes, they recorded the misery that went into their making. But others display pride, and a few show considerable originality, breaking away from standard conventions. An example measuring 26in. long by 22in. wide (66cm x 56cm) shows, in a number of panels, flocks of sheep, horses, black swans, sailing ships and human figures as well as alphabets, a text and an extraordinarily large vase of flowers (Plate 253).[1] Most samplers, however, were made up of a limited variety of alphabets, motifs, texts and borders, some with ridiculous rather than endearingly disproportionate scale relationships. A huge bird perching on a house was commonplace; human and animal figures in stylised, angular stitching often appear as repetitive caricatures. However, a fair number of charming, decorative and even, at times, amusing samplers are worthy little works.

The Art of Embroidery

252. Eleven year old Elizabeth Irlam Barlow commemorated the death of King George III's wife, Charlotte, in her sampler of ten years later, 1827.

Children were sometimes required to attempt several kinds and an interesting series worked by Elizabeth Gardner of Glasgow (born 1806) indicates her progress. At the age of twelve she did one in worsteds, and two years later completed one in silks. In 1821, the following year, she did a most unusual one on drawn fabric of Dresden whitework. Finally, in 1822, aged sixteen, she completed a white sampler with squares in blue ribbon bands, a hollie-point centre, darning patterns and needlepoint lace fillings.

Many nineteenth century samplers had no alphabets or numerals, nor even a name or date, but consisted solely of either symmetrical or random motifs spaced regularly over the linen canvas. The motifs were considerably more varied than in the previous century and increasingly included small, shaded vignettes in the romantic

The Nineteenth Century

mood of full-scale Berlin pictures, to be discussed shortly. Little scenes of ruins, children and pet animals, derived from engravings, depicted in naturalistic shades with faded backgrounds are often seen (Plate 257). Shading had been used in seventeenth century spot motifs but was entirely absent in eighteenth century samplers.

A large sampler at Bethnal Green Museum by 'Elizabeth S. Musto Age 14' shows a fine scrapbook composition of characteristic subjects. A largish pastoral scene is flanked by two smaller views with an elegant gentleman and lady and a dog in a garden setting. A conventional border pattern encloses a poem and dozens of small motifs including a lion, an elephant, a tiger, a goat, a fox, a parrot, a peacock, shells, red ensign flags, a horn, a sword, a parasol, a boat, a gun, a key, a caduceus staff, rabbits, butterflies, books, scales, scissors, fighting cocks, a candle and fruit. The combination is typical of the haphazard selection of emblems chosen for semi-decorative, semi-educational purposes. Sometimes the outside zig-zag floral border was replaced by a Greek key pattern, a char-acteristic element of Regency decoration.

Many samplers were worked in classes at schools and orphanages. Some similar examples, reflecting varying ability, have survived together, perhaps because they were the work of sisters. Others show the names of class mates or friends, listed in differing colours, and a good many record the name of the school in a signature, for example, 'Worked at Mrs Ertights School by Mary Morgan April the 15 1805'. Many institutional samplers were notably of a practical rather than ornamental nature and

253. A small group of samplers (this one of 1825) has a similar combination of ships, flocks of sheep, horses and other vignettes around a vase of flowers and alphabets and texts.

The Art of Embroidery

254. Jane Howard's sampler of 1830 records the members of her family and includes a favourite verse of embroiderers.

Opposite. 255. This accomplished monochrome sampler is typical of a type worked at Bristol Orphanage in about 1865.

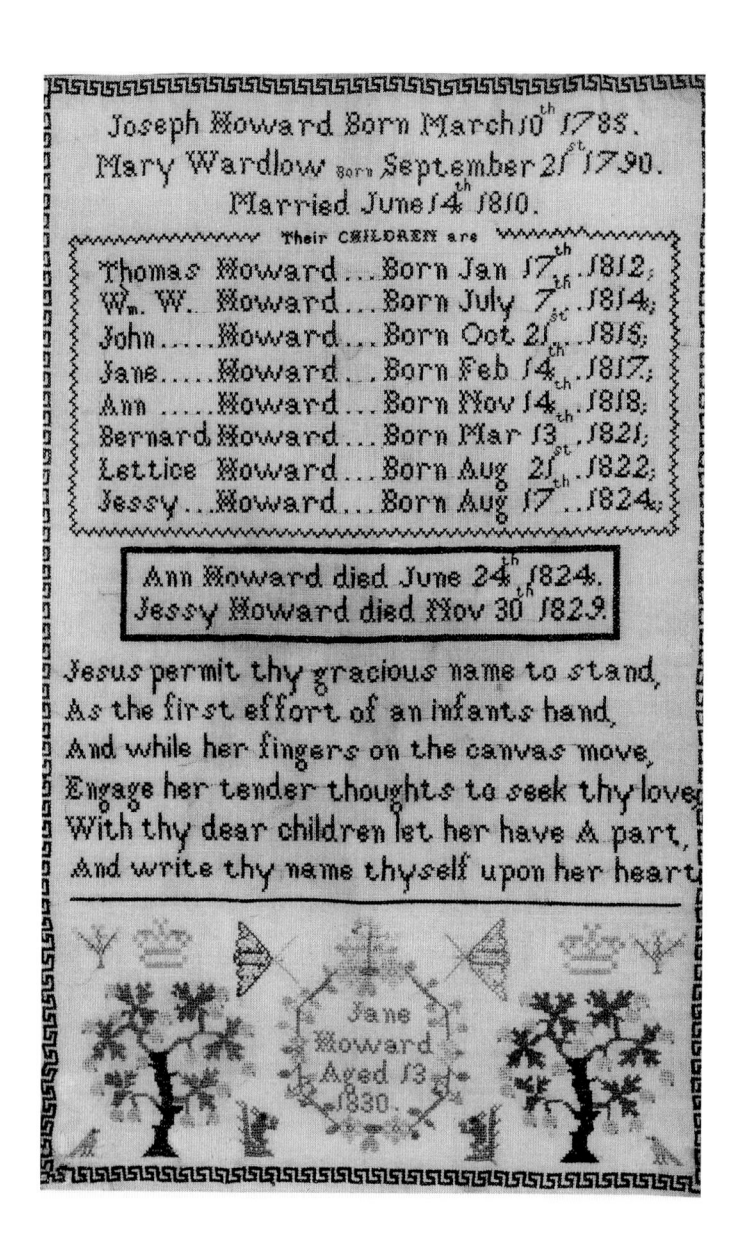

were worked with great precision in preparation for tasks to be done when the girl entered into service. Rows of red or black alphabets in many scripts, sizes and numerals were practised, no doubt in preparation for marking linen. Border patterns and a few corner patterns, roundels and stars might be combined with other small motifs. An individual type of sampler associated with pupils of the Quaker Friends' school at Ackworth, Yorkshire, is characterised by monochrome or polychrome wreaths, circles and octagons containing sprigs of flowers or initials. Mary Gregory's of 1807 was entirely of brown silks, made up of a combination of these geometrical forms. These patterns were also used on small pillows as gifts to friends. Other school samplers attempted to teach multiplication, money and calculation tables as well as incorporating useful and perpetual almanacs. But very often the main message was contained in a solemn moral verse:

The Nineteenth Century

> *While you my dear your needlework attend*
> *Observe the counsel of a faithful friend*
> *And strive an inward ornament to gain*
> *Or all you needlework will prove in vain.*
> ELLEN SHEPHERD KESGRAVE SCHOOL 1856

Many were grim and morbid with frightening texts emphasising the horrors of hell, original sin, purgatory, rotting of bones, the jaws of death and the prospect of being suddenly thrown into an unknown world. Moreover the texts took a long time to do, enabling the content to be soundly assimilated:

> *When I was young*
> *And in my prime*
> *Here you may see*
> *How I spent my time.*

The sewer often wept bitterly over her endless task but even this was regarded as morally strengthening:

> *Patience will wipe away the streaming tear*
> *And hope will paint the pallid cheek of fear.*

An otherwise charming and fine sampler at the Welsh Folk Museum, St Fagan's Castle, signed 'Margaret Morgan Aged 14 Years 1839. S. Westbrook's School', contains Isaac Watts' terrifying saw, typical of many others:

> *There is an hour when I must die.*
> *Nor can I tell how soon twill come.*
> *A thousand children young as I.*
> *Are calld by death to hear their doom.*

On other occasions, however, the sewer got away with shorter and happier epithets such as: 'Home Sweet Home, be it ever so humble, there's no place like home'. This particular one was used, ironically, on samplers worked in an orphanage. Bristol Orphanage samplers were usually uniformly worked in a single colour, red or black, with neat rows of alphabets, numerals and patterns, clearly related to their purpose, a training for household stitching, including the marking of linen. Emma Barnet and Mary Jeffries are each immortalised by their industrious and tidy samplers done in the New Orphan House, North Wing, Ashley Down, Bristol in 1865 and 1867. (See also Plate 255 for an unusual one with an elephant.)

Other samplers, as earlier, consisted of long texts of an instructive nature, without decoration. A curious one of about 1830 in the Victoria and Albert Museum has a long text worked in red silk with an autobiographical tale of a housemaid:

> *As I cannot write I put this down simply*
> *And freely as I might speak to a person…*

The Nineteenth Century

It ends with a lengthy prayer. The three Brontë sisters in 1829 and 1830 embroidered passages from Proverbs in green-black silks, within a plain key pattern border. These historic but otherwise unremarkable works have survived.[2]

Other kinds of sampler making, already practised in the eighteenth century, such as maps, continued with little change; acrostics and family records were also made. The former showed a verse, the initial letters of each line spelling out a name or 'Christ', etc., while the latter showed members of a family, alive and dead, in coloured and black threads. They were sometimes in the form of a family tree issuing at the root from heart-shaped plaques bearing the names of the parents. These were done especially in America. However, American samplers were generally not as elaborate as previously, less in the manner of embroidered pictures and often relatively simple. The Quaker schools, for example, taught a plainer form, often oval, with an uncomplicated vine leaf border. In the States mourning pictures were done as samplers, combining a variety of needlework subjects (figures, trees, architecture) and therefore suitable for schools. Many are attributable to individual institutions or mistresses, and also to specific engravings. These all date from the nineteenth century, especially around 1815, though they often celebrate the famous of earlier times such as George Washington or Shakespeare, or family ancestors. Shakespeare was also sometimes commemorated in England in this way, alongside a few other 'memorial' pictures.

Berlin woolwork samplers in a new format were done on long ribbons of canvas about 5-8in. wide (13-20cm) and of various lengths, up to as much as 16ft. (4.9m). Kept rolled up in the sewing box, they were close to the original purpose of samplers being true records of patterns, techniques and colour combinations for easy reference (Plate 256). They were not popularised as an achievement in themselves since they were neither decorative nor easy to display, but they had a certain charm, being embroidered with ingenious variety, colour, shading and frequently random spot motifs. An interesting hanging known as the Dowell-Simpson sampler consists of a large number of 'visitor's book' pieces of similar form, made between 1848 and 1896. The total size is 41ft. long by 18in. high (12.5m x 46cm).

256. A late 19th century woolwork sampler reverts to the true purpose of recording patterns and techniques.

The Art of Embroidery

257. Sampler of 1849 with an interesting combination of subjects and little scenes, all within a rosebud and honeysuckle border.

The Berlin embroidery illustrates a large number of patterns and motifs, some of topical interest, and also marking the introduction of 'gas colours', the bright synthetic aniline dyes which were developed around 1860.

Some children learning basic sewing were taught to make miniature garments with a wide variety of stitching and seaming. These charming little apprentice pieces were kept together in albums for reference. They were remarkable technically and utterly different in quality from the coarse wool samplers so proudly framed and hung on parents' walls.

The Nineteenth Century

BERLIN WOOLWORK

Berlin woolwork basically displaced sampler making and no other occupation is more emblematic of the Victorian age. Queen Victoria's reign began in 1837 and spanned two-thirds of the nineteenth century; her name is rightly associated with all the vicissitudes of imperial expansion, the achievements and shortcomings of a long and varied period, good, bad and middling. Berlin woolwork was largely middling, despite it being hugely popular.

Significantly, a number of chemical dyes were introduced around the middle of the century. Earlier there was a reliance on the familiar tones of vegetable and other natural dyes from insects etc. There was nothing earthy about these; they could be surprisingly bright as unfaded eighteenth century needlework shows. Blues had been derived from woad and indigo from Egypt and Mesopotamia thousands of years ago. Red from madder was known in the Indus valley equally long ago and then from insects, kermes and cochineal, a form known to the classical world. Purple from purpura and murex, whelk-like molluscs, was famed from Tyre and Sidon for Roman Imperial use. In the eighteenth century a purple or violet dye was prepared from lichens. Yellows came from various vegetable sources (weld, saffron, sunflower and annetto) from prehistoric times and also from fustic (wood) and in India from myrobalam (plums). The accidental discovery of Prussian blue (in the preparation of quinine) in 1856 and other synthetic dyestuffs by Sir William Perkin was a breakthrough. He patented the first aniline dye and started producing it commercially in 1857. This made a brilliant violet and was known in France as mauve. Queen Victoria wore a dress of this colour at the Great Exhibition of 1862 and it was also used for the penny postage stamps. Other aniline dyes followed: magenta (1859), sulphonated blue (1859) and black (1863). A number of other synthetic dyes followed these.[3]

A feature of art in the early part of the Victorian era was an interest in romantic, mediaeval subjects, *le style troubadour*, incorporating castles, ruins, chivalry and

Left. 258. Tropical birds and great birds of prey continued to provide interesting subjects for embroiderers, sometimes adapted from coloured engravings. This one includes an unlikely bower of exotic flowers.

Below. 259. In the manner of a Landseer portrait, this Victorian Berlinwork picture shows the Prince of Wales dressed in tartan in a romantic Scottish setting.

The Art of Embroidery

the 'scenery' of Sir Walter Scott's heroic novels. This was at the heart of the phenomenon of Berlin woolwork which enjoyed a colossal vogue from the 1830s for half a century. The craze appealed to the growing number of women who had time and money to spend on sewing; simple patterns and kits for doing it became a social appendage even to be carried around on visits to each other's houses. A picture of Florence Nightingale with her sister by W. White in the National Portrait Gallery, London, shows her at this form of embroidery. At a tea party at Brighton at which King William IV and Queen Adelaide were present, it was reported that the Queen sewed with the other ladies, and M.T. Morrall in *A History of Needlework* (1852) observed:

> *If any lady comes to tea, her bag is first surveyed,*
> *And if the pattern pleases her, a copy there is made.*

With the simple technique of working soft-coloured wools to squared patterns in plain tent or cross stitch, often with coarse threads, Berlin work displaced almost every other form of sewing. It alone became virtually synonymous with the word needlework; Mrs Henry Owen started *The Illuminated Book of Needlework* (1847) with the words: 'Embroidery, or as it is more often called Berlin wool-work…'. The new form of needlework originated in 1803 in Berlin when A. Philipson, an engraver and landscape painter, produced a book of patterns printed on a chequered grid with different symbols indicating colours. Colours were later painted in. Another Berliner, Frau Wittich, took up the idea and soon led the market in printed patterns.

Originally, the technique was done in silks on fine mesh canvas for smallish items such as firescreens or a pair of face screens, as in the Museum of Costume in Bath, made by Queen Victoria for the Duchess of St Albans. It was made for accessory objects, including purses and bags. But wool as an alternative to silk on a coarser canvas became more general and, being easier to work and fairly inexpensive, was soon more favoured. By 1840 some fourteen thousand designs were in use, printed and then hand-coloured by armies of women earning pin money in publishers' warehouses. At least 1,200 were employed by the larger companies alone. The chief outlet was a shop in Regent Street, London where a Mr Wilks sold his imported patterns and bright 'Zephyr' or Berlin wools. These original designs with hand-coloured

260. Queen Victoria's pets, painted by Sir Edwin Landseer, were worked in canvas embroidery, sometimes with additions, as here with Osborne House.

The Nineteenth Century

261. Eos, a Favourite Greyhound, the Property of HRH Prince Albert *by Landseer in a finely stitched canvas work version, c.1850. 25in. x 33½in. (63cm x 85cm).*

shading, and overprinted with stitch squares, both appealing innovations, were issued by a print seller in Berlin. The Merino wool from Saxony was spun in Gotha, dyed in Berlin and exported. Later, wools were produced in England, Scotland and France. Several kinds of canvas were used; silk canvas of a fine mesh was usually left partially unsewn. It was made of silk-bound cotton and was available in several colours but as it was not suitable for wear it was limited to pictures, firescreen panels, table screens, banners and bell-pulls. Jute canvas was tough for cushions, carpets, upholstery and heavy pelmets. Cotton, woollen, Java and Double (or Penelope) canvases were also used, of various degrees of coarseness. Designs were highlighted with silks and use was made of silk chenille in two thicknesses. Glass beads from France added lustre, and were sometimes used extensively in mixed or single colours; the weight of them helped banners to hang well. Bugles (long pipe-shaped beads), metal beads and pearls were also used, but less frequently. Plush-stitch raised work provided further variety, being made of long woolly threads trimmed down to form an embossed and shaped surface. The technique was used to depict parts of a picture such as a bird, an animal or flowers. Glass eyes were often used. Plush stitch was both sculptured and soft looking, the former aspect perhaps reminiscent of stumpwork and early padded embroidery, though much coarser. It was used for birds or flowers, within a composition (Plate 269, page 271). At Dorney Court, Buckinghamshire, there is a banner firescreen with a handsome leopard in this technique.

The colouring of earlier Berlin work was soft and natural but with the use of

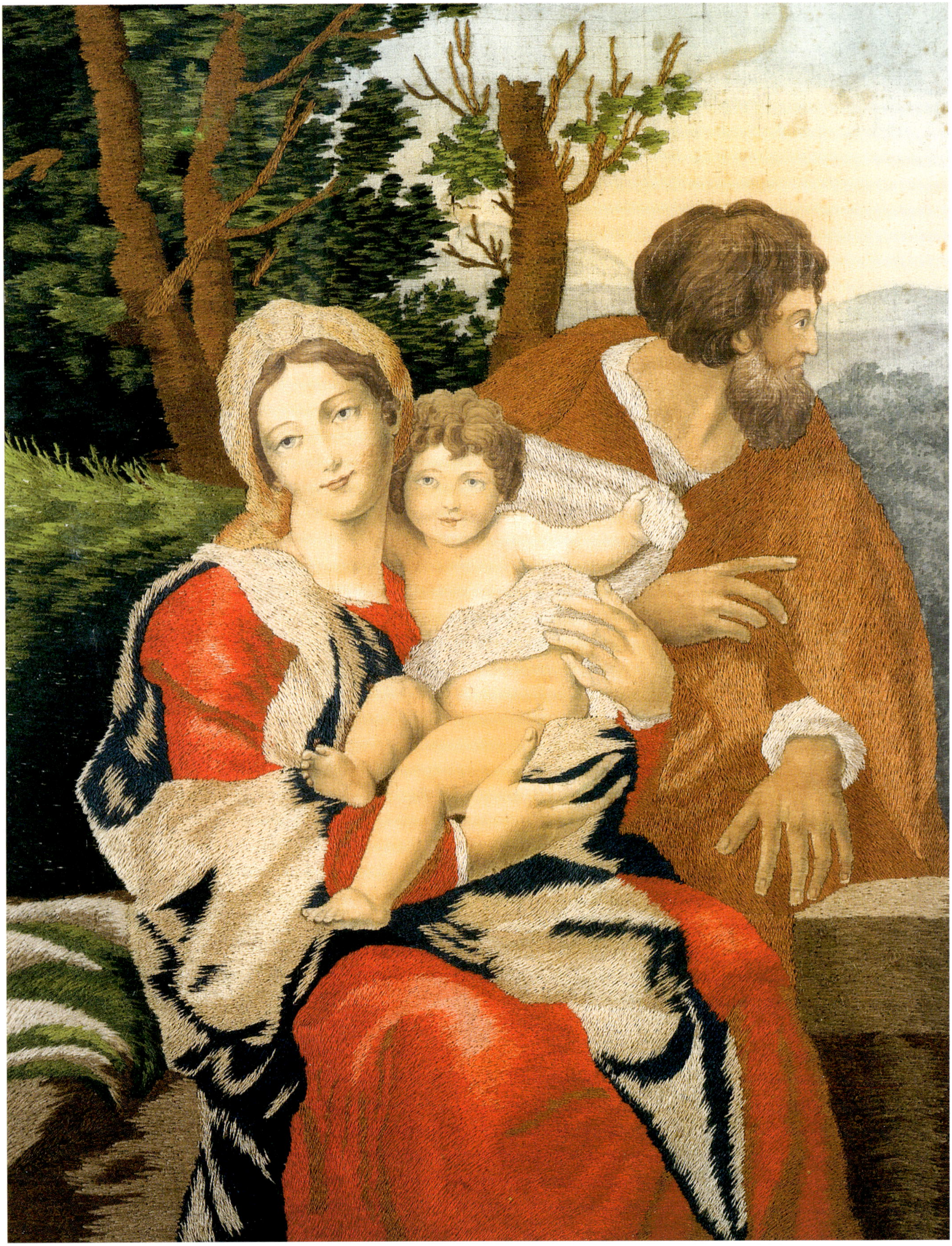

The Nineteenth Century

aniline chemical dyes from the late 1850s it became hard and exaggerated; gaudy parrots were perched in over-abundant wreaths of flowers, each depicted with garish luminosity. But eventually colours improved again and more interesting tones and pattern combinations were used. Background tones were of crucial importance; there was a great fondness for black from around 1850 but purple, red, green and lighter colours were also used. Birds, cabbage roses and lilies were scattered through every household. Some were inspired by the publication of fine books delineating species; Edward Lear's coloured lithographs of the parrot family, Gould's and Audubon's bird books and the opening of the Zoological Gardens at Regent's Park in 1828 all contributed ideas while Curtis's *Botanical Magazine* and *The Botanical Register* gave inspiration for garden flowers and also new and exotic plants from far off lands. Earlier pieces tended to depict traditional flowers reasonably discreetly, but these were gradually crowded out by larger, brighter blooms, in many cases overblown, blowzy specimens created in hothouses rather than typical of English gardens.

Berlin pictures were however sometimes of more substantial form and continued the tradition of imitating great or popular paintings; some of the Bible stories that had earlier been embroidered in silk and wool forms were transposed directly to the counted square technique of Berlin woolwork. Well-known masterpieces such as Leonardo da Vinci's *The Last Supper* were popular in various sizes; six versions were exhibited at the Great Exhibition in 1851. Countless identical kits depicting *The Flight into Egypt*, *The Expulsion of Hagar*, *Moses in the Bulrushes* and similar themes were sold and worked without a stitch of originality. Many designs were derived from original paintings, reproduced by the German factories without permission or royalties since no law prevented this until 1842. Paintings by living artists were often 'improved'. Landseer's charming animals were popular and were unashamedly altered or transposed into different settings. Many patterns were given away with ladies' magazines such as *The Englishwoman's Domestic Magazine*, *The Young Ladies' Journal*, *The Ladies' Treasury* and the *Girls' Own Annual*. These of course were dated. Large and often complex historical subjects provided the greatest challenge and were sometimes worked in relatively small stitches. Finer stitching was sometimes used for faces and other flesh parts amidst thicker sewing, and also for details within bolder decorative patterns. Historical and contemporary subjects often showed royal events or members of the Royal Family. A huge picture (6ft. x 5ft.) (1.8m x 1.5m) of Mary Queen of Scots is reported to be in a

Above. 263. The Young Ladies' Journal, 1872, published a squared pattern for this Berlinwork picture of a woman gathering holly and mistletoe. 28in. x 20in. (71cm x 51cm).

Opposite. 262. Also worked in wool, on a silk ground with some body parts painted, this panel imitates an old master painting.

The Art of Embroidery

private collection. Favourite themes were Mary Queen of Scots mourning over the dying Douglas at the Battle of Langside, and Charles I bidding farewell to his family. Queen Victoria, the young Prince of Wales, wearing tartans, or the latter as a sailor, and the Queen's pets were frequently portrayed, often with charm (Plate 259). An example now at Kensington Palace showing royal dogs. *Islay and Tilco with a red Macaw and Two Lovebirds,* was after the picture by Sir Edwin Landseer painted in 1839 and placed in the drawing room at Osborne. This version shows the group out of doors with flowering bushes, trees and a castle, all additions to the oil painting (cf. Plate 260). King Charles spaniels and cats sitting on tasselled cushions were often embroidered in pictures, on stools and on cushions.

Baxter prints were another source for needlework, especially views of the royal castles at Windsor, Balmoral and Osborne as well as portraits of members of the Royal Family. They also provided famous, romantic scenes, and a snow scene from the Alps celebrating the new sport of mountain climbing. American Berlin work was similar to English but, in addition to the usual subjects, portraits of George Washington, Benjamin Franklin and topographical designs were embroidered.

In 1880 Russian embroidery or *broderie Russe* helped to displace the popularity of Berlin woolwork. It was propagated by the Broderie Russe Company of Regent Street, London, with cross stitch embroidery worked to patterns.

CARPETS

Victorian woolwork carpets are amongst the most satisfactory of nineteenth century embroidered works. In general, after experiments with older forms, Berlin designs were firstly pictorial, then also boldly floral and, lastly, geometric. The last two styles

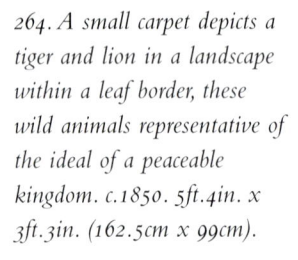

264. A small carpet depicts a tiger and lion in a landscape within a leaf border, these wild animals representative of the ideal of a peaceable kingdom. c.1850. 5ft.4in. x 3ft.3in. (162.5cm x 99cm).

The Nineteenth Century

were applied to carpets which, being of a large format, were happily suited to the technique. Late eighteenth century carpets already had formalised patterns, mostly geometric, in shaded colours, and sometimes with optical effects. A revival of leaf designs with a predominance of bright flowers followed and then there were 'tile' designs made up of squares, roundels and octagons fitted together and often containing flowers or rosettes (Plate 265). The Victorian taste for large blooms in cluttered groups was somewhat restrained by this method of making up carpets of a number of joined squares. Huge examples were made, some consisting of individual panels with varied motifs or vignettes, contrasting backgrounds, differing borders and corner patterns. Screens were similarly made with all the expected subjects of Berlin work pieced together in a scrapbook formation that lacked much artistry but was none the less effective. Sentimental rural scenes, garlands, birds, animals, children with hoops or kites, real or imaginary butterflies and heraldry provided colourful combinations. A large carpet given to Queen Victoria and shown at the Great Exhibition was made by 'The Lady Mayoress and 150 ladies of Great Britain' to a design by John Papworth, the architect, and others of squares made by contributors were designed as suitable for presentation purposes.

The ladies' passion for woolwork almost drove husbands mad since its application

265. A colossal French carpet made up of squares (tiles) of a repeated design. c.1850. 22ft.4in. x 14ft.10in. (680cm x 452cm).

The Art of Embroidery

seemed endless: 'Two hearth rugs and an ottoman, seven chairs and after that I hope to do some groups of flowers, and a handsome carriage mat'.[4] It was applicable to many smaller items too, such as blotters, watchpockets and 'carpet' slippers for the men, as well as for furnishings. The technique could not, however, be used for garments as it was too heavy. It was the social conditions that required women to show abilities in certain kinds of activities, such as needlework, that led to the endless quantity of indifferent work and inappropriate ornamentation in every possible form, of various techniques and often in ill-chosen colours. Needlework of this kind is still done. An amusing collection of slippers with a wide variety of patterns and emblems worked by the Marchioness of Tavistock has been exhibited at Woburn. Embroidered slippers with monograms or crests have remained a fashionable accessory of evening dress, endorsed by the Prince of Wales in conjunction with a velvet smoking jacket. Modern 'tapestry' kits continue the tradition of Berlin woolwork, with simple repetitive stitches, rarely highlighted with silks unfortunately, and seldom with fine detailing, small stitching or clever colour shading. An associated form, still done, is the small handbag, especially Viennese. The designs for these are repetitive but the workmanship is very minute in many cases.

PATCHWORK AND QUILTING

Second only to woolwork amongst popular needlework was the making of patchwork coverlets or 'quilts', especially in America, where the terms 'pieces' and 'piecework' are also used. The hobby was barred to none since the materials could be gleaned from

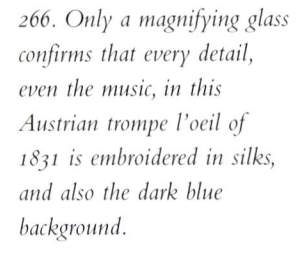

266. Only a magnifying glass confirms that every detail, even the music, in this Austrian trompe l'oeil of 1831 is embroidered in silks, and also the dark blue background.

The Nineteenth Century

267. American patchwork was finer than any other. This 'Rising Sun' or Star of Bethlehem quilt by May 'Betsy' Totten was made in New York, c.1830.

available scraps; however, more ambitious attempts were made to collect interesting fabrics for original and elaborate designs. As in the eighteenth century, fragments cut to various shapes were artistically assembled to make up a unified whole and the best examples were also quilted. Patchwork largely depended on the quality and charm of the fabrics used and the identification of these helps to date quilts. Silks, printed materials and velvets were used independently or together. As the century progressed, the designs tended to be plainer or less orderly; good early coverlets had essentially a Regency feel with geometric effects akin to parquetry or Tonbridge ware. Optical tricks, such as the log cabin pattern,[5] gave an interesting, lively appearance. American patchwork was especially sophisticated and a popular art form; it lacked the dull, commercial sameness of so much of the English needlework of the period. A circulation of patterns was carried out privately and each example was subject to personal variation. The height of American 'quilting' was reached in the first half of the century by which time 'quilting bees', parties at which ladies gathered to do their sewing, were a social institution, and a feature even recorded in song:

The Art of Embroidery

> *'Twas from Aunt Dinah's quilting party*
> *I was seeing Nellie home…*

It was expected that a girl should have as many as twelve quilts in her dowry, one of which, the Bride's Quilt, would have had the most time and attention devoted to its design and making.[6] Some three hundred named designs have been recorded, some with loose religious connections such as 'Star of Bethlehem'. Album quilts were also made, usually of squares contributed by individuals, often signed and sometimes dated. The pieces were embroidered with a variety of decorative, topical or factual details, and the finished article was often for presentation, such as a fine Baltimore album quilt, dated 1848, made for John and Rebecca Chamberlain, probably by Mary Evans (108in. x 108in. – 275cm x 275cm).[7] Good patchwork was also done in England, Wales and Ireland,[8] and delightful examples have been preserved as heirlooms. A large number of lesser ones of ordinary materials were made for plain practical purposes; even 'a patchwork quilt made from socks' was listed in a recent saleroom catalogue.[9]

Crazy patchwork, also known as Japanese patchwork, was deliberately made of irregular pieces, often of bright and deep-coloured fabrics, with embroidered feather stitch joining (often in yellow) and sometimes superimposed with motifs of embroidery or appliqué. The jagged edges resembled broken pieces of stained glass. Kits for making these were available towards the end of the century. In America coverlets of this humbler nature were termed 'slumber throws' and were kept downstairs for an occasional nap.

Felt patchwork made from soldiers' uniforms or tailors' trimmings were done by men, and frequently included appliqué or embroidered pictures, military motifs, flags, arms or regimental badges (Plate 271). Others were composed of a number of small portraits, scenes or animals around a central subject or device. Embroidered details and captions were added. Three major examples shown at the Great Exhibition were worked by a Scotsman (who allegedly spent eighteen years on his), an Irish policeman and a man from Lancaster.[10] Two at Town House, Biggar, were made by a local tailor, Menzies Moffat (1829-1907). One is entitled *The Royal Crimean Hero Tablecover* with war leaders depicted, also Queen Victoria, Prince Albert and various court ladies, together with Italian comedy figures and actors. Theatrical figures, a ship, arms and regalia are shown on another felt patchwork in

268. Wool canvas embroidery for the border and centre of this Victorian bed cover are effectively combined with silk patchwork in geometrical form. Signed 'M.L. Wilson'.

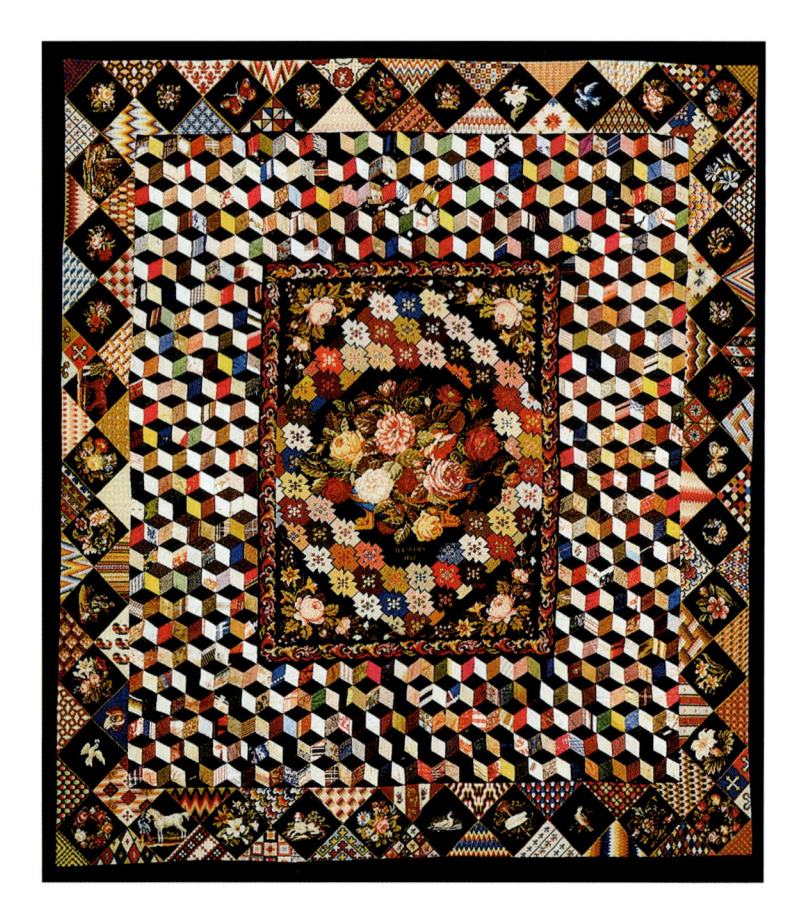

The Nineteenth Century

Glasgow Art Gallery and Museum by David Robertson, Falkirk, Stirling, and dated 1853.

True quilting was sometimes combined with patchwork but was mostly used in a humbler role in the nineteenth century, being a local, traditional craft in South Wales and the North of England; Scotland was in the meantime largely busy with her whitework industry. Professionals sometimes drew out the designs for quilting in these country areas, and the materials used were inexpensive cottons. Regional examples can be seen in the Welsh Folk Museum, at St Fagan's Castle. Candlewick bedcovers were embroidered with soft bulky cotton (like the wick of a candle).

Another country needlework craft was smocking (see page 168). Strong, natural coloured working garments of linen had complex gatherings of material at back and front, worked in patterns with regional or occupational variations. Distinctions denoting a trade may have made the wearer's skill recognisable at farmers' hirings, but such marks were probably worn partly out of professional pride, like uniforms.[11] By the end of the century a decorative form was adopted for women's and children's costumes, using coloured threads.

269. *Perhaps someone's special friend, a spaniel worked in petit-point and plush stitch, c.1840.*

The term 'Fancy Work' included all sorts of needlework done for amusement. Amongst these were sewing with ribbons and aerophanes (coloured gauzes) popular in the 1830s and then again in the 1880s. Narrow China ribbon, usually shade dyed across its width, was used. Fish scale embroidery and the use of iridescent beetle wings from India offered opportunities for the decoration of small articles and for glamorous costume, such as muslin evening dresses, in the 1820s and 1830s.

Ayrshire and Other Whitework

The quick, chain-stitch technique that originated in India and China and developed into tambour work was brought to France in the eighteenth century. It was immediately popular and by the middle of the nineteenth century was practised by half a million workers of white embroidery in Ayrshire and Northern Ireland. The fashion for light, embroidered muslin had grown since the 1790s, especially for children and babies. Known as 'sewed muslin', the fine quality embroidery, so contrary in spirit to Berlin work, was sewn with a hook instead of a needle, in cotton on cotton, and parts had holes filled with semi-lace devices. The embroidery now included padded stitch and other stitches, in addition to chain stitch or tambour work. A French christening robe imported in 1814 greatly influenced the styles developed, and very soon the designs were exclusively of small flowers, decorative filling patterns

The Art of Embroidery

and light foliage. The embroidery was sometimes done in factories but more often by women at home. R. Samuel, and Thomas Brown of Glasgow in 1857 employed two thousand staff in Glasgow and twenty to thirty thousand outworkers in Scotland and Northern Ireland. A colossal business grew around Glasgow and Paisley but Ireland soon produced strong competition; a large proportion of lower paid women in both countries were efficiently employed by astute organisations on charming and skilled, but repetitive and demanding work. It is indeed well to recall when we admire the delicate 'flowerings' of endless christening robes, frocks and caps, that the 'flowerers', as they were known, were sadly impoverished women who undertook the work to boost their families' meagre wages. The wives of lowly paid miners, smelters and farm labourers, they were given printed patterns with instructions and time limits by co-ordinating agents. At first each woman worked a complete item but later mass produced single pieces which were collected for manufacture into garments, laundering and packing at a factory. The women sometimes met in small groups and a child might be paid a small wage to keep up a supply of threaded needles. It was hard labour:

> *With fingers weary and worn,*
> *With eyelids heavy and red,*
> *A woman sat in unwomanly rags,*
> *Plying her needle and thread –*
> *Stitch! Stitch! Stitch!*
> *In poverty, hunger, and dirt.*[12]

270. Ayrshire embroidery combines contrasting stitches and techniques with pleasing effects, as on this part of a baby's robe, c.1860.

No doubt working in poor light, the flowerers strained their eyesight terribly; James Morris in *The Art of Ayrshire White Needlework* (1916) reported that women would bathe their aching eyes in whisky to revive them.

Much of the industry was for export to the United States and Europe but some was for sale in Britain. The cotton used was imported, largely from America, and the Civil War (1861-1865) was chiefly the cause of the collapse of the business towards the end of the century. But the technique was already being superseded by successful ventures in machine embroidery.

A number of less fine but interesting white-work techniques were continued, developed or revived, usually from Italian sources, during the century. They were partly associated with lace making and were mostly heavier than Ayrshire work and for household purposes rather than costume.

Guipure d'Art or *Filet Brodé* was inspired by sixteenth century lace and a return to Vinciolo's pattern book of 1588. It involved darning on hand- or machine-made net, imitating the old style. A blunt needle was used to make a variety of stitches to designs advocated in books such as Madame Goubard's *Patterns of Guipure Work* (London 1869). Large items such as bed covers were made up in squares, often alternating with contrasting ones of another type of work, such as broderie anglaise. This was a coarse cutwork that became fashionable c.1825 and developed into a coloured variety known at the end of the century as 'Madeira work', the technique having been most successfully established on that island by nuns from England. Holes in stylised floral patterns were cut out and then edged with buttonhole stitch. 'Richelieu' embroidery also reflected the Italian Renaissance with a heavy lace effect; leaves and flowers were outlined in buttonhole stitch, were joined with bars, and then the rest of the material was cut away. Coloured materials were again sometimes used. Various other *guipure* forms were of similar techniques.

'Coggeshall' embroidery from Essex was a light, white tambour work on muslin and chiefly characterised by designs of wild flowers continuously trailing over the fabric, for costume use, and in imitation of lace.

A number of whitework techniques were fostered in Ireland to give employment and utilise cheap labour. 'Carrickmacross' was another simulated lace and made throughout the century. Cut-out flower sprigs of thin cambric were applied to net and infilling patterns were made by drawn-thread stitching. 'Mountmellick' was initiated by Johanna Carter at the village of that name near Waterford in about 1825, and consisted of embroidery in heavy white cotton on strong shiny cotton. The designs were again of wild flowers, with oak leaves, blackberries, corns and ferns in textured contrasts of stitching. A quilt of this work dated 1855 is in the National Museum of Ireland. 'Limerick lace', made from the 1830s, was tamboured on net and then sewn over with infillings of various lace stitches.

Particularly fine and laborious sewing, resembling lace, was done on handkerchiefs. Beautiful examples from continental Europe inspired imitation and variation. A remarkable handkerchief probably made in Belgium around 1840 for Queen Sophie of the Netherlands is now in the Rijksmuseum. On it are eight different drawn-thread background patterns and delicate flowers, a crowned monogram, armorial shields and

271. This feltwork appliqué panel is attributed to a soldier who used military tailors' cuttings to great effect and with Daniel in the lion's den at the centre. c.1850.

a scalloped edge in leaf pattern. In America, wedding handkerchiefs called for painstaking white embroidery.

In 1828, Josué Heilmann of Mulhouse, France invented a multi-needle embroidering machine that threatened the whitework industry of Scotland and Ireland, but also in some respects encouraged a new interest in hand work. The machine could be operated by 'one grown-up person and two assistant children' with up to 140 needles. It was in Switzerland that the techniques were perfected but the English patent rights were bought by Henry Houldsworth of Manchester in 1829 and by 1859 his textile firm had twenty machines producing economic trimmings for dresses and table cloths. The patterns were repetitive but accurate and effective, being traced from a design by the operator with the aid of a pantograph. The products were exhibited at the Great Exhibition in 1851 and at the Dublin Exhibition two years later. Similar machines were used in Switzerland and Germany. Simultaneously, the domestic sewing-machine with a shuttle and continuous thread action was developed by Isaac Singer in New York. By the end of the century, most repetitive work was done by machinery leaving embroideresses free for individual or specialist work. Those employed in the skill still had uniforms, ceremonial and exclusive 'fashion' costumes and a revival in ecclesiastical needlework to turn to; but many were ready for new inspiration and a return to artistic creation in embroidery.

ART NEEDLEWORK, THE ROYAL SCHOOL, WILLIAM MORRIS AND REVIVALS

By the 1870s there was a strong reaction in England against the lack of inventive style in Berlin woolwork. Branching away from this middle class pursuit, indignant upper class ladies sought more ambitious and interesting projects. Surprisingly quickly they turned to Art Needlework (or Art Embroidery) and this became highly fashionable for a relatively short period of about twenty years. The somewhat self-confident term 'Art Needlework' was applied to a new artistic approach to designs and materials, but it was significant that embroiderers looked to artists for their designs rather than to mere pattern drawers. This had not happened since mediaeval times. Obvious pictures and posies worked in garish synthetic colours were dismissed in favour of natural forms relating to drawing and painting. Alongside this a revival of interest in old embroidery, a close examination of it and attempts to repair it led in particular to a revival of crewel embroidery. Seventeenth century hangings, referred to as 'Jacobean' (James II 1685-1688), were newly admired and these influenced modern leafy patterns which incorporated woodland and wild plants and flowers; larger foliage was often shown as a surround to smaller plants and each subject had a sense of seriousness; 'every flower that sad embroidery wears'[13] was depicted in natural herbal colours. Used in preference to bright aniline dyes, these were realistic and sober, perhaps a little too sombre and, being natural dyes, many surviving pieces have faded badly (Plate 275).

Art Needlework was intrinsically English in mood and though novel when it was created may now be seen to have had antiquarian roots. Natural and garden foliage was blended with a mediaeval historicism, elegance and romance, as cultivated by Sir

272. William Morris' Artichoke hanging of 1877 shows a design inspired by Islamic patterns and baroque silks based on similar forms. 7ft. x 5ft. (213cm x 150cm).

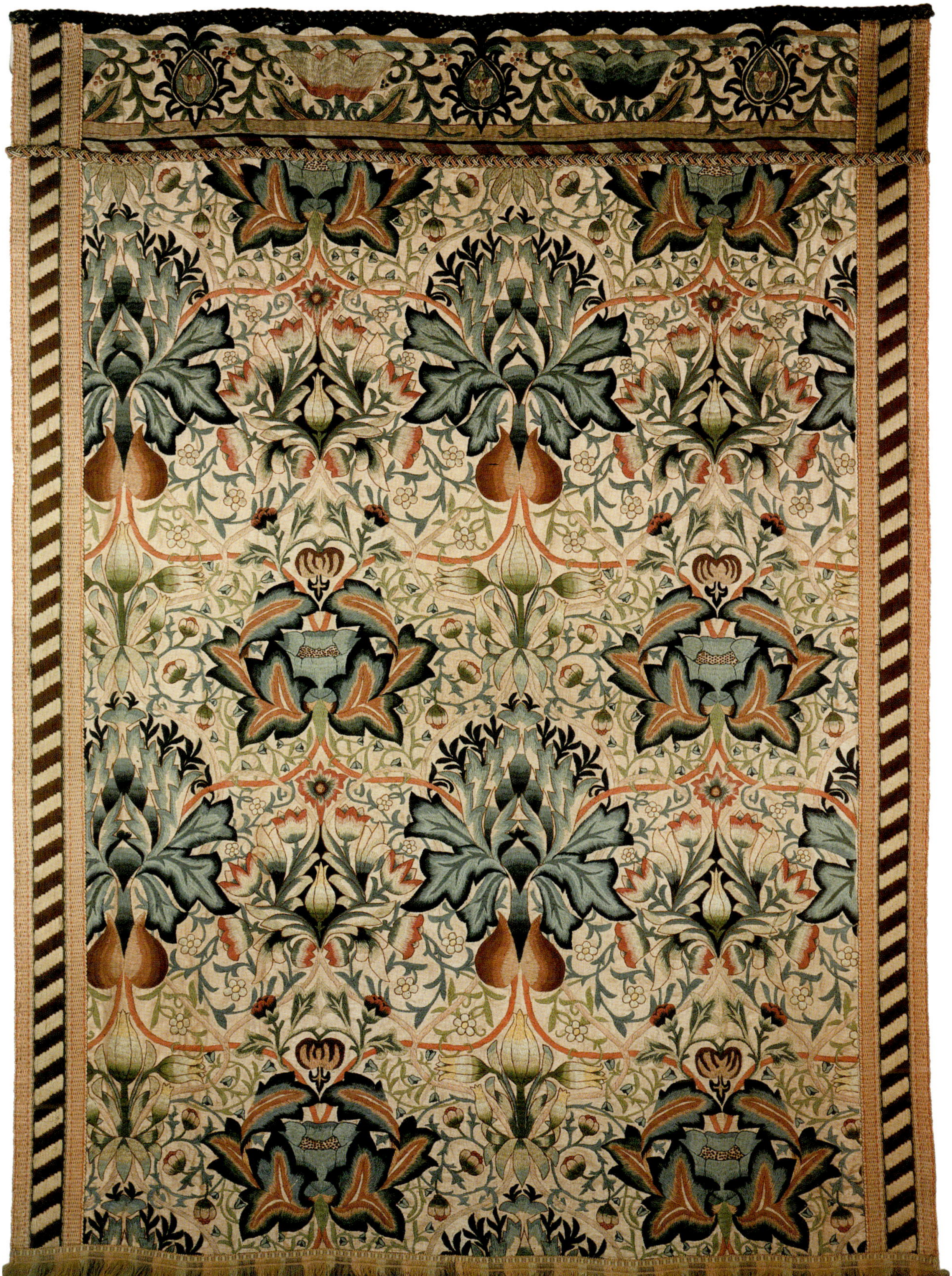

Edward Burne-Jones and contemporary painters. It also borrowed features from oriental designs and incorporated the development of a Japanese style, as a form in itself. Walter Crane had admired the 'fineness, firmness and precision of workmanship' in Japanese embroidery and the American painter James Whistler decorated his studio with Japanese lacquer and embroidery. Water birds, large leafed plants, sprigs of blossom, clouds and other motifs found their way into all European decorative arts, including English embroidery.

These new fashions in needlework developed largely in conjunction with the School of Art Needlework, founded in 1872, and later known as the Royal School of Needlework. Under the presidency of Queen Victoria's daughter, Princess Christian of Schleswig-Holstein, its aims were 'for the twofold purpose of supplying suitable employment for Gentlewomen and restoring Ornamental Needlework to the high place it once held among the decorative arts.' It was involved both in the restoration of old needlework and the creation of new. The committee consisted of distinguished and high-minded ladies such as Lady Marion Alford whose book *Needlework as Art* (1886) epitomised the serious approach to the subject. The school employed over a hundred women and undertook commissions, working to designs by leading painters including Burne-Jones, William Morris, Lord Leighton and Walter Crane. Prepared works were supplied for ladies to do in their own homes and the provision of set pieces soon became a substantial business and source of income. An 1880 advertisement[14] indicates the practical nature of the articles chosen for art needlework. Hangings, bedcovers, curtains, screens, tablecloths, cushions, chair back covers, and all sorts of borders were advocated, but the school also listed designs and materials for more curious accessories:

Tennis Aprons, Folding Screens, Kettledrum d'Oyleys,
Photograph Frames, Bellows, Opera Cloaks,
Piano Panels, Babies' Head Flannels, Knitting Pockets.

In fact the craze for art needlework would seem to have almost eclipsed the abundant Berlin work. An amusing cartoon in *Punch* entitled 'Sweet Little Buttercup, or Art Embroidery 1879' depicted a languid female dressed in a garden of embroidery and surrounded by admiring animals in human clothes. In the following year, Elizabeth Glaister described how the new passion for crewelwork made the rooms of many houses look more like laundries, the furniture being draped with embroidered linen. Another lifelong embroideress apparently followed each trend of needlework and had many results to show for it: '…she wrought the whole Bible in tapestry, and died in a good old age after having covered three hundred yards of wall…'.

Other needlework societies were formed, many of them stemming from the Royal School. The Decorative Needlework Society, The Ladies' Work Society and, amongst smaller establishments, the Wemyss Castle School provided constructive employment for gentlewomen. Organisations in Scotland and Ireland stimulated more embroidery. The Donegal Industrial Fund encouraged a type of needlework known as 'Kells Embroidery', the designs being derived from the famous eighth century manuscript, the Book of Kells, and worked with soft russet and green vegetable dyes, in shades of blue or in whitework.

The Leek Embroidery Society was founded in 1879 by the wife of Thomas Wardle, a textile producer and friend of William Morris. Using his specially dyed silks, the society produced fine embroideries for church use, 'Anglo-Indian' needlework (sewn over imported silks or printed materials made by Thomas Wardle's business) and a full-scale copy of the Bayeux Tapestry, now owned by Reading Corporation.

Following the success of the Royal School of Needlework's pavilions at the Philadelphia Centennial Exhibition in 1876 and at the Paris International Exhibition in 1878, a similar institution was instigated in Philadelphia. This led to further organisations being formed in Boston, Chicago, New York and other American cities. Teachers were sent out from London and they naturally propagated styles developed here but distinct efforts were made to achieve an independent American quality. In New York, a Society of Decorative Arts was formed by Louis Comfort Tiffany and Mrs Candace Wheeler to encourage the production and sale of a wide variety of arts

273. Three embroidered panels depicting Chaucerian Goode Wimmen (Lucretia, Hyppolyte and Helen), designed by William Morris for his Red House c.1861.

The Art of Embroidery

and crafts; related organisations also produced needlework. One project was a set of embroidered gauze bed hangings made for the actress Lily Langtry's hotel bedroom in London; another was a striking curtain designed by Tiffany in 1879 for Madison Square Theatre, depicting a woodland scene with an immense depth of field – a sunny foreground stretching through dense, misty trees to a blue distance. It was worked in appliqué of many materials. 'American Tapestries, made by embroidery alone' were offered by Associated Artists, after early tapestry designs such as Raphael's *Miraculous Draught of Fishes*. In Deerfield, Massachusetts, two New York painters, Margaret Whiting and Ellen Miller, set up an industry in 1896 making blue and white crewelwork, based on simplified seventeenth century designs. Flax thread was dyed with indigo and embroidered on linen imported from Russia. Other colours were used later. The works were signed with a 'D' within a spinning wheel.

Of the English artists already mentioned, William Morris (1834-96) was the most

274. An altar frontal worked to a design by Charles Kempe, c.1865, shows in the centre Christ enthroned flanked by lutenist angels revived from Renaissance art, here richly portrayed within palm tree arcading.

significant, being directly concerned with the development of needlework. An apprentice in the office of the celebrated architect, G.E. Street, with Philip Webb, another enthusiast, Morris led the cultural reaction following the technical and commercial successes of the Great Exhibition, which had firmly established England in a strong trading position. Architect, poet, designer and true socialist, he was dissatisfied with the complacency of the mechanised achievements that served mass production and resolved to pursue better and more interesting designs linked with a revival of old techniques and craftsmanship. His commitment was vocational but was also tied to practicality. In 1883 he explained his earlier search for finer objects of a general commercial kind:

> *I got a friend [Philip Webb] to build me a house very mediaeval in spirit in which I lived for 5 years, and set myself decorating it, we found… that all minor arts were in a state of complete degradation especially in England, and accordingly in 1861 with the conceited courage of a young man I set myself to reforming all that.*

Despising the mass production of machine processes, he turned with almost fanatical emphasis to hand skills which were superior in some respects but inevitably lacked certain advantages. This specialist approach produced many fine works, at best sharing feelings akin to other noble arts in Victorian England, with a sweet and dark richness. But in other respects it perhaps led to a restricted branch line in artistic development for a major factor was that it was essentially backward-looking in attitude. With other architects and painters he sought to conjure up again qualities of the bygone age of mediaevalism, largely following Street's embroidery and views on textiles, in a gothic revival. From this he progressed to pattern making of Islamic inspiration (Plate 272), but throughout his designs there are fascinating fusions with several strands of antiquarianism turned into modernity. While mastering an understanding of ancient and modern techniques, Morris also nurtured an understanding and love for natural things – flowers, trees, insects, animals and birds. He combined the two in his role as designer and his overriding legacy was a 'heaven-sent gift', as his daughter Mary described it, to see design in mass (repeating), not in line, and to be able to create numerous original patterns in swift succession.

Morris and those who worked with him or followed his teaching were extremely thorough in attention to detail; with painstaking enthusiasm they unpicked early pieces of needlework to learn stitches, worked out methods of dyeing and Morris himself embarked on a major project depicting Chaucer's *Goode Wimmen* for his Red House at Bexley Heath, Kent (Plate 273). An eclectic interest in mediaeval facets, such as stained glass and tapestry weaving, were incorporated in his approach to design, contrasting strongly with silk or wool needlepainting of the earlier part of the century. He saw embroidery design as 'midway between that for tapestry and that for carpets' and subsequently it is not surprising that many of his pieces have an oriental flavour. Languid leaves in formal swirling patterns, often flat and feathery, are strictly disciplined, with something of a Persian feeling, such as the 'artichoke' hanging at Standen, Sussex. Couched down wools led to a heavy, dense, textured feeling like tapestry. Morris and Co. catalogues often erroneously called needlework 'tapestry', but Morris' embroidery

The Art of Embroidery

275. One of a series of season hangings, Autumn, represents Art Needlework with naturalistic embroidery with vines and wild plants, even blackberries. c.1870. 11ft.6in. x 3ft.9in. (351cm x 114cm).

was not the canvas work often referred to today as tapestry; he favoured straight stitches such as darning, running, long and short, and satin as they permitted mass freedom of interpretation and were not distracting in themselves. Real plants and flowers were advocated but he warned against 'cheap and commonplace naturalism', preferring an adapted artistic style. A major contribution of his teaching was an awakening of interest in fine quality materials with rich and glistening colours and textures, intricately worked. No doubt thinking of Berlin work, he pointed out that embroidery 'is not worth doing unless it is very copious or very delicate – or both'. A sense of cultivating beauty was to be remembered: '…and also since we are using especially beautiful materials, that we shall make the most of them and not forget that we are gardening with silk and gold thread'.[15] Morris did not particularly seek precious qualities, but an honest, genuine, correct use of each material with 'primary beauty':

> *I have tried to produce goods which should be genuine as far as their mere substances are concerned and should have on that account the primary beauty in them which belongs to naturally treated substances; have tried, for instance, to make woollen substances as woollen as possible, cotton as cottony as possible, and so on; have used only the dyes which are natural and simple, because they produce beauty almost without the intervention of art…*

Lady Marion Alford, however, a pillar of art embroidery enthusiasts, objected to the foliate carpet patterns on account of their 'repetition of vegetable forms as being reminiscent of a kitchen garden in a tornado'.

William Morris's firm, Morris, Marshall, Faulkner and Co., was founded in 1861 and announced that it carried out 'Embroidery of all kinds'. This included a considerable amount for church use, a natural consequence of the prolific church building

The Nineteenth Century

of the period. The Catholic Emancipation Act of 1829 contributed to the building of many new churches and Street had been a believer in Tractarianism, with a reawakening of interest in the decoration, pomp, and regalia of religious ceremony. Morris' church needlework was not particularly ecclesiastical in design but was characterised by tight, intricate patterns of leaves of contrasting sorts as, for example, in a large wool hanging behind the altar at Lanercost Priory, Cumbria, which was probably designed by Morris and possibly made by his firm. Figures, when incorporated, were largely inspired and sometimes actually designed by Burne-Jones. Vestments were usually of damask, perhaps with additional embroidery; Philip Webb was influential in the design of these. Morris himself designed needlework hangings for his firm, as well as coverlets and other articles for various craftsmen, including Catherine Holiday, the wife of a designer of stained glass and mosaics. She was given a free range of colours and worked in partnership with Morris, discussing with him fine details for things which were to be sold through the business. Linda Parry has illustrated the development of Morris' and the business's embroidery styles and techniques.[16] Morris' embroidery was extremely influential in its

276. Aesthetic Movement walnut and embroidered screen designed by Selwyn Image and worked by the Royal School of Art Needlework. 5ft.8¾in. x 7ft.9in. (174.5cm x 236cm).

The Art of Embroidery

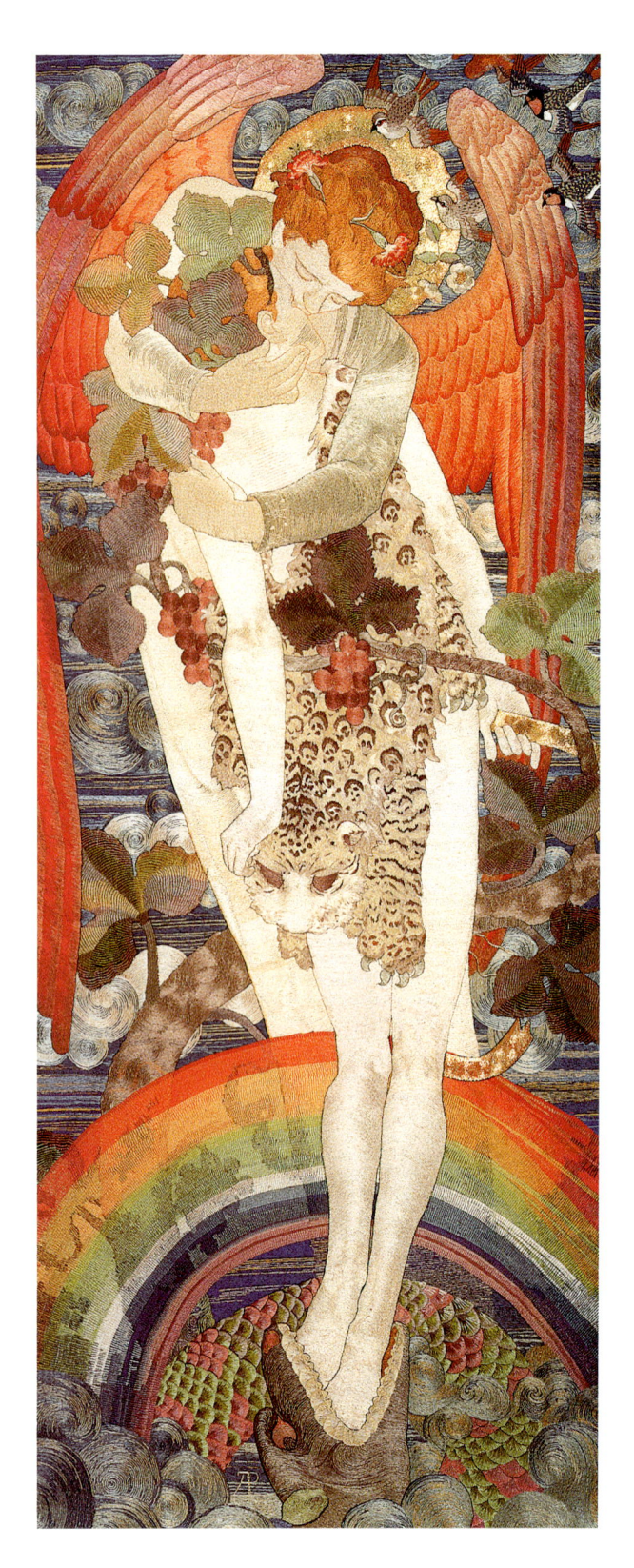

field but not as much so as his carpets, tapestries and woven fabrics.

The Arts and Crafts Society was founded in 1888 and was a significant sponsor of exhibitions of modern decorative arts, supported by leading artists. Embroidery was one of its chief concerns. Many craftsmen exhibited through the Society, including Phoebe Anna Traquair whose fourfold allegorical screen of 1895-1902 in the National Gallery of Scotland is a significant work of the period. Of exceptionally fine quality the panels depict, after an essay by Walter Pater, the four stages in man's spiritual life – the Entrance, the Stress, the Despair and the Victory (Plate 277).

Another screen, of five folds, at the London School of Economics was designed for the Royal School of Needlework by Walter Crane. The designs are similar in style to his well-known wallpaper *Peacocks and Amorini* and his book illustrations. An elaborate neo-Renaissance type pattern incorporates peacocks, swans and other birds, with monkeys, cupids, fruit and the god Pan. A Greek inscription from Theocritus is quoted at the bottom (see epigram, page 32).

By the end of the century the Royal School was generally esteemed as a national institution, holding extensive exhibitions and having a wide influence. The starting of a new building for it in 1899 was celebrated as something of a minor state occasion. The Prince of Wales laid the foundation stone, the Life Guards were paraded, the Royal College of Music performed and the Bishop of London offered a prayer before a rendering of The Old Hundredth. But in due course the originality of Art Needlework inevitably became weakened; reformers started questioning its value suggesting that it was too much an eclectic mixture of 'museum-inspired' styles. There was some truth in this. J.D. Sedding asked for a return to nature and to garden subjects, even suggesting Sutton's seed catalogues as a source for real flowers.

In the meantime the revival of ecclesiastical needlework continued. From about 1840 it was chiefly led by the prestigious architects of the period, whose ambitions were to restore many aspects of mediaevalism. They built colossal numbers of neo-Gothic churches, hoping to decorate and furnish them in an appropriate vein and reinstate ceremonies with rich vestments.

G.E. Street, an Anglican High Churchman, with the

The Nineteenth Century

help of his sister and Agnes Blencowe, founded in 1854 the Ladies' Ecclesiastical Embroidery Society to provide altar cloths based on old examples, or made to modern designs supplied by architects. Amongst these was G.F. Bodley whose drawings were closer to mediaeval origins than many others, in that they were largely pictorial, with figures rather than pattern alone; most designs were not especially religious, being of naturalistic flowers and leaves. Bodley also commissioned work from Morris' firm and from Watts and Co., a business still operating today. There is a banner worked to his design at Peterborough Cathedral. In 1841-2, A.W.N. Pugin, a Roman Catholic, and prominent architect and partner of Sir Charles Barry in designing the Houses of Parliament, attacked in the *Dublin Review* the 'prettiness' of domestic needlework and urged a return to serious work with 'an appropriate meaning'. He designed vestments for the Roman Catholic Church and preferred a rich background of velvet or cloth of gold.

Supporters of the Oxford Movement had also called for more elaborate liturgy and church ornament in the Anglican Church. In 1848 The Cambridge Camden Society published *Ecclesiastical Embroidery* with floral patterns derived from mediaeval embroidery. From 1841 their magazine had provided designs for church furnishings. *The Episcopal Prayer Book* stated:

> *Ceremonial is not mere show. It is symbolic language by which the heart of man expresses his sense of the mystery and holiness and splendour of the Godhead, his aspirations after higher things, his reverence, his hope of glory.*

Vestments underline the fact that the clergy act not as individuals but as representatives. The various items have allusive associations with Christ's garments and the colours worn and used in church furnishings have symbolic significance. The most important are as follows:

> *White: festivals of our Lord and our Lady; of saints who were not martyrs; of all Saints; the Pope.*
> *Red: blood and fire; martyrs; Good Friday; Holy Spirit at Pentecost; the cardinals.*
> *Violet, purple: penitence; Advent; Lent; St Paul; bishops.*
> *Green: nature; for ordinary days; The Trinity.*
> *Black: funerals, shot through with gold sometimes for Christian hope; All Souls.*
> *Blue: feasts of the Virgin.*

Pugin's set of vestments made for St Chad's Cathedral, Birmingham, have a feeling of mediaeval richness with elaborately patterned damask and a liberal use of silver and gold thread. Sir Arthur Blomfield, another prominent architect, also designed embroideries, including some for the Radcliffe Infirmary Chapel in Oxford. Street provided designs for Newton, Jones and Willis of Birmingham, a firm that produced catalogues of designs that were popular for church furnishings for many years. But he

277. In terms of both design and colouring the dawn of modernism is clearly seen in Victory, *part of* Progress of a Soul *by Phoebe Anna Traquair, 1902.*

The Art of Embroidery

also saw the potential of amateur embroideries and spoke of the '…happiness which must result from employing their fingers and their eyes upon something fair and beautiful to behold instead of upon horrid and hideous patterns in cross-stitch, for foot stool, slippers, chair-covers, and the like too common objects'.[17]

Several other organisations for church needlework included the Church Extension Association and the School of Mediaeval Embroidery. The serious devotion to this work was epitomised in *Church Embroidery, Ancient and Modern* by Anastasia Dolby, 'Late Embroideress to The Queen' (1867), which was produced more like a prayer book or Bible than an instruction manual, being printed in Gothic script and with red lines framing each page. Whether devout or luxuriant, there was scope for religious needlework in contrasting forms. An example of the occasional continuance of an old form is a Missal of 1809 made for the Duchess de Berry. Approximately 12in. x 10in. (30.5cm x 25.5cm), it has an embroidered binding and contains thirty-four embroidered 'plates' of minute workmanship. A century later a banner was made for Ely Cathedral with gold thread heraldic embroidery, cordwork, damasks and a central figure of St Etheldreda. This too is a fine example of its kind, comparable with stained glass of the period, and both demonstrate aspects of the neo-mediaevalism that spanned more than a hundred years.

278. Even into the late 19th century, an Italian chasuble from Rome maintains an official grand style of embroidery, unchanged for two hundred years.

TOWARDS MODERNISM

At the end of the century, a highly secular trend in design, leaning towards twentieth century modernism, became apparent in Art Nouveau. Languid and nebulous shapes of a semi-foliate, dreamy nature were adopted in many forms. A considerable stimulus for needlework was further fostered in Great Britain through the initiative of the Glasgow School of Art and its Principal, Francis H. Newbery. The emphasis was on simplicity and originality at all costs. Plain embroidery, or applied work, was taught to children in preference to the basic grammar of white sewing, which was said to be bad for the eyes. Materials also had to be simple. Mrs Jessie Newbery and Ann Macbeth advocated the use of the many beautiful fabrics of a cheap kind instead of costly silks or glistening threads. Backward-looking historicism and eclecticism vanished in a single-minded, novel clarity. The former now appeared somewhat unoriginal and the latter was daringly fresh and simple in shape. Sinuous forms were contrasted with strong vertical and horizontal lines; simplified plant motifs; black

The Nineteenth Century

279. *Finely worked in silks and metal threads, this 'Peace' panel was exhibited at the Arts and Crafts Exhibition Society. 17in. x 13in. (43cm x 33cm). c.1918.*

and white and pastel shades were incorporated into original patterns which were never copied. Whether these really have lasting artistic qualities and are beautiful or not remains secondary to their importance as a transitional phenomenon on the way to modernism. It was at Glasgow also that Charles Rennie Mackintosh led a distinctive movement that was influential in many parts of Europe, its chief essence being in those simple contrasts of curves with vertical and horizontal straight lines.

285

CHAPTER TEN

CHINA
A LONG HERITAGE
OF SILK

*...embrodered with antiques of golde and silke of
sonderie colours, called china worke*

THE two materials silk and wool are of towering significance in the world of needlework and embroidery. While England was famous for wool from the mediaeval period, silk production in China is even more ancient. Silk has a most remarkable history and magical properties: strength, flexibility, variety, lustre, an inexplicable allure and natural beauty. Use of the cocoons of the silk moth, *Bombyx mori,* has been known in China for five thousand years. Hemp and other bast fibres were plied in the Neolithic period but wool was noticeably absent, being a feature of nomadic peoples further west. Cotton was introduced relatively late to China and only became generally available in the twelfth century. In the meantime Chinese silk farming, sericulture, was active from the fifth century B.C. and a certain amount of finished silk had arrived in Rome by the first century B.C. Sericulture only reached the West in the Middle Ages but since then the much admired natural thread and woven textile has been prized as one of the wonders of the East. Silk has remained the essential ingredient of oriental costume, for fabric, for elaborate weaving and for embroidery from ancient times up to the present.

Chinese textiles are important as part of the background to any study of the arts of the West, but particularly in relation to the textile arts developed along the Silk Route. Dr John Feltwell has shown how this legendary flow circuits the whole world[1] and just as silk was introduced to every country from China so also were fabric methods, dyes and pattern-making developed for craftsmanship from that ancient civilisation.

*280. This detail of an 18th century robe
demonstrates richness of both embroidery and symbolism.*

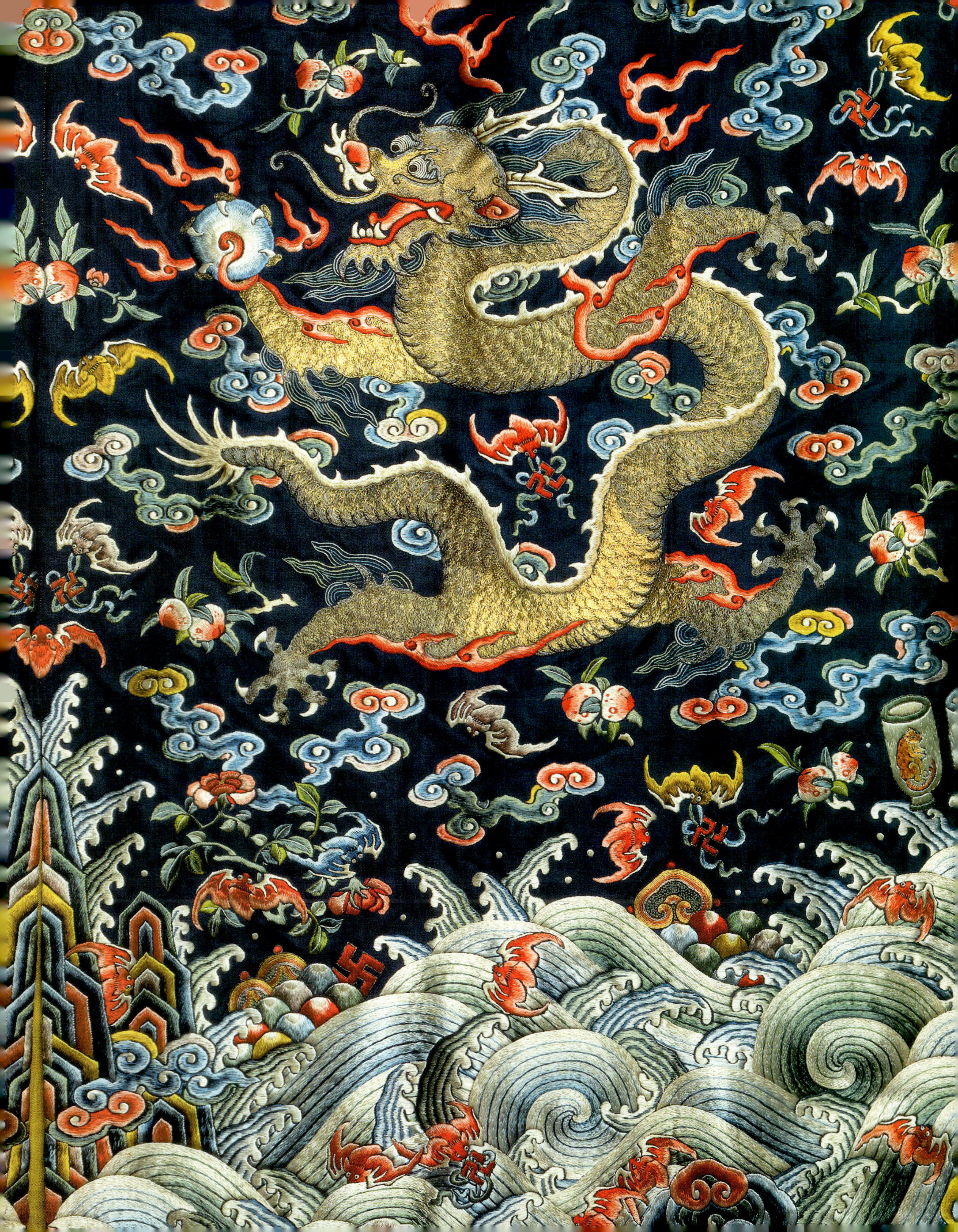

The Art of Embroidery

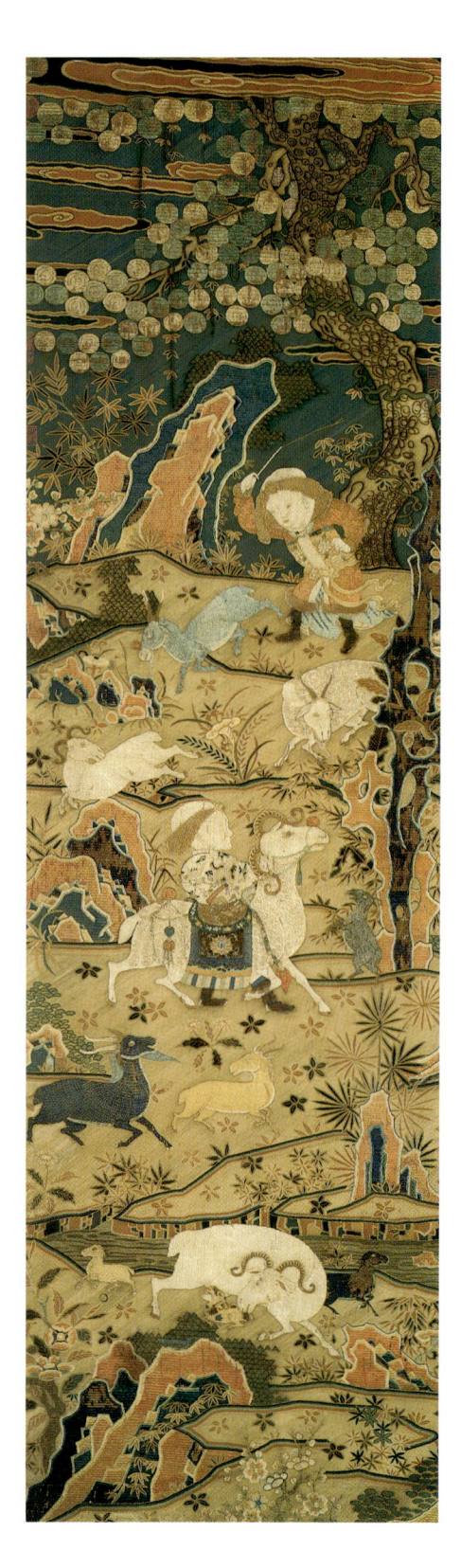

Within the spectrum of the decorative arts, Europeans may have derived more from the Chinese than they inherited from the Greeks and Romans though these civilisations did introduce much from the Far East, even pheasants. Silk goods, porcelain and tea are obvious but on a metaphysical level is a whole language of motifs and thought patterns that seems to percolate every facet of semi-symbolic and purely ornamental decoration. Furthermore an inter-relationship of ideas was built up after Marco Polo's communications with the Chinese which caused a mutual growth of taste, trade and manufacture for over three hundred years, from the sixteenth century onwards. Many beautiful artefacts owe their charm to a happy combination of Oriental and European features, as in 'export porcelain' on the one hand and chinoiserie on the other.

I shall now therefore outline key aspects of Chinese needlework and will illustrate how Chinese embroidery influenced English and European needlework. Many idioms were adopted purely as decoration, though sometimes retaining a degree of symbolic metaphor and always carrying an element of exoticism. Sometimes the age-old language of the ornament became obscure even before its use passed westwards and it would seem that by the Qing period (1644-1912) some of the many symbols still used ceremonially were confused in meaning and had already become in some respects semi-superstitious decoration, however venerated they remained, partly in a conscious effort to emphasis historical continuity.

Chinese textiles can be either of woven tapestry, *kesi* or *kossu* (split tapestry), or of needlework in counted stitch form or embroidery on fabric. The style and subject matter of each is similar and there is a general overlap of usage and motifs. I must limit myself to concentrating on needle-wrought techniques rather than *kesi* which is the product of a loom. Needlework was by no means the cheaper or less noble cousin of tapestry, as in Europe; indeed it would seem to have been considered the more highly valued form of workmanship, being used almost invariably for the Emperor's most formal robes.

Needlework has been practised in China for three thousand years for two main purposes: for secular use at court and for religious use by priests and in monasteries. The principal function of secular needlework was as the official ornament of state costume. The importance of robes made for the Emperor, his family and court officials can not be overestimated for these garments were intended to display status according to prescribed rules and to set a formal basis to political hierarchy. The robes combined the functions of graduated uniforms and heraldic vestments. They displayed rank with clearly shown differences and shone with didactic emblems of power, security and goodwill. They were designed to be both terrifying and comforting. In these respects they may be seen to share qualities with other pinnacles of needlework,

China: A Long Heritage of Silk

mediaeval Christian vestments and the elaborately embroidered iconographical costumes shown in the portraits of Elizabeth I. Chinese, church and Tudor garments are all heavily charged with easily recognisable symbols which showed messages that could be 'read' easily by fearful or adoring courtiers and laity. As in Christian imagery, where references to Old Testament and Gospel stories were repeatedly represented in stonework, glass, woodcarvings, book illumination and needlework vestments, so in China a wide language of symbols was adopted from ancient and less old sources as a convention based on archetypal anthropological beliefs with motifs which give it a lasting meaningfulness. This may be somewhat obscured by changes of relevant emphasis but the overall heritage of the metaphors creates security in its continuity. This was a feature that was distinctly exploited by the Manchu Emperors who ruled China during the Qing dynasty. Strict formats advocated by these foreign governors imposed the ancient symbols partly for their potency and partly as a kind of heraldry giving them historical authority.

Early dynasties had ornamented their ceremonial robes with symbols that identified them and personified them as central to elemental powers. The late fifteenth century Ming Emperor Hsiaotzung was, for example, hierarchically shown in his ancestor portrait in a voluminous robe using an extravagant quantity of rich yellow silk wonderfully embroidered with a number of clearly defined symbols, especially imperial dragons. The motifs are instantly recognisable from a relatively standard vocabulary of iconography.

MANCHU DYNASTY ROBES

Perhaps the most impressive of all Chinese needlework are the imperial robes of the Qing dynasty. These superb embroideries of the eighteenth and nineteenth centuries display wonders of needlework worked in clean and clear dyes but they also have in their decoration a relatively small but interesting vocabulary of symbols. A general recognition of these helps to understand other textiles in Asia and Europe. In 1759 the Manchu Emperor commissioned a comprehensive illustrated catalogue of the ceremonial garments worn according to strict hierarchical and seasonal regulations by members of the court.[2]

The generous use of fabric, as shown in Ming portraits, was a symbolic and prestigious feature of early Chinese *pao* long coats, a form established during the Han dynasty and revived by the Ming in 1368 following the Mogul Yuan dynasty, when tighter fitting garments relating to horsemanship were preferred. The generous cut of the Ming robes emphasised grandeur and lent themselves to imposing slow movement suitable for court pageantry. The long sleeves honoured the Chinese aversion to displaying hands in public on formal occasions.

The Manchu rulers, however, imposed different forms of costume, again associated with horsemanship and traditional garments reminiscent of their origins in a nomadic way of life. These robes were more closely cut. An important government ministry, the Board of Ritual, commissioned imperial costume on a regular basis from factories that also supplied private orders. The official needlework factory was at Suzhou, a city renowned for its embroidery. The Dyeing and Weaving Office in Peking provided the

281. A delightful panel, Welcoming Spring, of about 1300, represents fine Chinese embroidery contemporary with the famed opus anglicanum of mediaeval England. 84in. x 25in. (213.3cm x 63.5cm).

The Art of Embroidery

282. A Kangxi period (late 17th century) couched gold thread nobleman's surcoat.

necessary dyestuffs and pattern drawings for this factory and for the one at Nanjing which produced woven robes and fabrics.

The two principal male robes of the imperial court were the *chao fu* and *ji fu*. Many of each kind, of specific colours, were made for the Emperor and I shall examine examples of these to describe important features that were echoed in other robes. The *chao fu* was the most important ceremonial court garment. The character *chao* means 'court' or 'dynasty'. Gary Dickinson and Linda Wrigglesworth in *Imperial Wardrobe*[3] have written:

> The right-hand side of the written character depicts the moon and
> the left-hand side symbolizes the rising sun. The overall impression
> of the character is one of light in the early morning, the time at
> which the Chinese believed the mind to be at its greatest clarity
> and when the most important court ceremonies took place.

The *ji fu* or 'dragon robe' was slightly less formal but still devised with great attention to its embroidered iconography. It was a festive garment, used for some of the major ceremonies. The term *ji* stands for 'happy' and 'auspicious'.

The most prominent motif on each form of robe was the dragon which reflected, represented and referred to the Emperor himself on every person, place and object under his jurisdiction.

China: A Long Heritage of Silk

From time immemorial the ancient kings of China were associated with rain-making and were responsible, as fierce but also benevolent embodiments of natural forces, for the control of water and the necessary irrigation of crops. Each early Emperor was said to have been an incarnation of a dragon born out of water or at least descended from a dragon as a deity of clouds and rain, a good omen bringing power, prosperity and the beneficial rejuvenation of nature. He was referred to equally as the 'Son of Heaven' or 'True Dragon', an earthly spirit linking heaven and earth, and this role was central to the ornament on the robes of the Emperors until the end of the Qing dynasty in 1911.

The dragon was visibly the imperial emblem at least from the Tang dynasty (618-906). Early dragons had three claws. The Manchu Emperors' personal symbol had five *(lung)* and this could only be used by the Emperor and his immediate family. Other nobles used a four clawed dragon *(mang)*. In a tenth century encyclopaedia Wang Fu described dragons as having:

> *Horns like a stag, forehead like a camel, eyes like a demon, neck like a snake, belly as a sea monster, scales like a carp, claws like an eagle, footpads like a tiger, ears like an ox.*

Dragons of this character were meticulously worked by the most highly skilled profes-

283. A red silk summer gauze dragon robe made for a Manchu noblewoman, decorated with dragons and cosmological designs. Late 19th century.

The Art of Embroidery

284. A 19th century chao fu robe with dragons at all four points around the head and protecting every edge.

sional embroiderers on the Emperor's *chao fu* and *ji fu*. Earlier robes had a single large dragon surrounding the neck opening of the garment, later ones had a large dragon over the whole front of the robe, but by the Manchu reign smaller dragons were placed systematically over several zones above and below the waist level. A splendid ancestor portrait painted by the Italian Jesuit, Castiglione, shows the Qianlong Emperor wearing his *chao fu*. We know that the portrait illustrates the robe accurately and indeed this picture and surviving robes illustrate clearly the formalised design and disposition of motifs. A bright yellow *chao fu* of silk gauze was made for summer use[4] with silk and gold embroidery including the depiction of no less than forty-three gold dragons, the principal ones being the four arranged symmetrically around the neck and the others in concentric circles around the lower parts of the garment. Each band is arranged as a kind of protection.

The second type of robe, the *ji fu* dragon robe was made in greater numbers and was worn by the Emperors, the court and all civil and military officials. It was even more elaborate in decoration, within strictly regulated conventions, but only the Emperor's dragon robe carried the full complement of twelve symbols in addition to the overall emblematic design (Plate 285). In shape the garment was based on a nomadic riding coat, with tight sleeves and horsehoof cuffs, but in ornamentation it was designed to display the concept of universal order upon which the principles of Chinese imperial power rested. John Vollmer has summarised this aspect of the robe as:

China: A Long Heritage of Silk

A schematic diagram of the universe. The lower border of diagonal bands and rounded billows represents water; at the four axes of the coat, the cardinal points, rise prism-shaped rocks symbolizing the earth mountain. Above is the cloud-filled firmament against which dragons, the symbols of imperial authority, coil and twist. The symbolism is complete only when the coat is worn. The human body becomes the world axis, the neck opening, the gate of heaven or apex of the universe, separates the material world of the coat from the realm of the spiritual represented by the wearer's head.[5]

285. Only the Emperor wore yellow. This dragon robe of the early 18th century bears all the traditional iconographic motifs.

As the Son of Heaven, the Emperor thus became a physical and spiritual link between human society and universal order. In a cosmic diagram he would be seen at the centre, wearing a robe of yellow representing earth, the symbolic fifth element and fifth point of the compass. Colours were very significant. Yellow was particularly reserved for the Manchu Emperor but he also used other colours for specific ceremonies and according to the season. Red was the colour of the great bird of the South, was associated with the element Fire and was used for family celebrations, particularly weddings and births. It had been the dynastic colour of the Ming Chinese and was therefore avoided by the Manchu conquerors. North, governed by the element Water, and with the tortoise symbol was linked with Black. The West was influenced by Metal and linked with the tiger emblem and the colour White which was worn for mourning and associated with autumn. The East was dominated by the element Wood, for growth, vitality and vegetation (with the millet seeds emblem) and was represented by a dragon for Spring. Blue was associated with this part of the order of things.

The 1759 edicts for rituals stipulated that the clouds on imperial robes should have five colours as happy omens: blue, red, yellow, white and black, for the five activities *(wu xing)*, the elements, compass points and seasons. The shades and tones would be considerably varied for interest, in one case, for example, to pale blue, pink, dark yellow, light green and violet. The chief colour was always yellow. The heir apparent was to wear orange, members of the imperial clan would wear brown, other nobles blue, and lesser ranks were assigned black.

SYMBOLS ON THE EMPEROR'S DRAGON ROBE

Only the Emperor's *ji fu* was charged with the full variety of symbols. A significant feature of later robes, that is those of the Qing dynasty, of the eighteenth and nineteenth centuries, was an accumulation of auspicious decoration introduced at the expense of larger dragons. Clouds diminished in size and in boldness, the wave border at the base increased in depth and there was the addition of extra good luck emblems. In general the robe became more heavily laden with decoration, each motif inevitably on a smallish scale. However the overall effect is embroidery of jewel-like richness both in quality and in subject matter. The symbolic meaning of the motifs invariably has an interesting history, the potency of each pictograph often having altered in emphasis from a specific to a general wish of happiness, good luck or longevity.

Long life was considered infinitely desirable in Taoist belief and old age was venerated. It was considered possible to find the secret of long life by visiting the immortals on the Isles of the Blessed in the Eastern Sea. They were said to have flesh as smooth as ice and skin white as snow. They were gentle as young girls and needed no food but inhaled the wind and drank the dew. Because they were endowed with great wisdom and were invested with special powers it was believed that the Emperor might be granted the opportunity to commune with them and be a personal link with his people in general. The Chinese were not so much concerned with what happened after earthly life as in continuing in a perfect happy state of longevity. Many symbols refer to this wish, including the swastika which is an aspect of the ubiquitous variations of key pattern that borders, protects and adorns almost everything Chinese.[6] The swastika was, however, in one central identity a mystic symbol of Buddha's heart, and a Sanskrit term, adopted into Chinese in 693 having the meaning 'ten thousand', and thereby alluding to longevity. Many symbols had meaning suggested by punning allusions in similar sounding or similarly written names. Typical Chinese short word rebuses called for abstract word-play messages. A simple example is the word *'lu'* for 'deer' which could also be read or depicted as a symbol for 'riches'. Another very familiar one is the image of a bat, a rebus on the word *'fu'* for happiness.

China: A Long Heritage of Silk

Several stylised characters were themselves used as calligraphic decoration with messages of longevity, joy and luck or double happiness, a favourite wedding symbol.

A focal image on dragon robes is the flaming pearl which is variously described as an orb, a thunder disc or the pearl of wisdom, an allusion to the Buddhist notion of Enlightenment. It has prominence in front of each large dragon, being either pursued or closely guarded by it.

Particularly featured on the Emperor's dragon robe *(li fu)* were the 'twelve symbols' which had been long associated with the principal annual sacrifices offered by the Emperor in rituals linked with astronomical, seasonal and important agricultural events in the year. The symbols were systematically arranged in three concentric circles around the Emperor's body, at his neck, his chest and his knees. Below are sketches of these important emblems with aspects of them summarised as follows:

Sun: a red disc with a three legged cockerel, a prime symbol of yang, the active male aspect in Chinese cosmology, the bird that heralds dawn.

Moon: a blue disc with the legendary white hare pounding the elixir of life beneath a cassia tree.

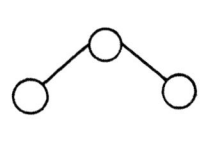

Three star constellation: the third astrological link of the Emperor in orientation with the planets.

Mountains: representing stability and the earth.

Dragons: ascending and descending, adaptability; animals.

Pheasant: literature; birds, and with the previous symbol, the world of nature.

Sacrificial cups: with a tiger and monkey in them. Linked with the element metal and together with the next three symbols and the mountains, representing the five elements.

Waterweed: water, purity.

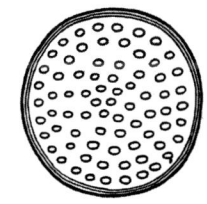

Grain: (wood), sixty grains of millet, traditionally the first cereal crop raised in China.

Fire: flames of the element fire.

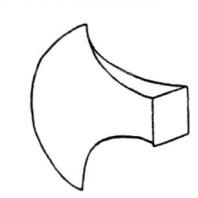

Axe: imperial power.

Fu: the power of judgement, opposing blue lines of mysterious significance but with word name associations.

The Art of Embroidery

In the cosmic sea of waves and clouds on the dragon robe were further auspicious symbols, the Eight Precious Objects:

Coral	Scrolls
Jewels or pearls	Ingots
Musical stones	Gold ornaments, square and round
Rhinoceros horns	*Ruyi* sceptre

Alongside these are the scrolling motifs, perhaps related to the fungus of longevity on which the fairies lived in the Isles of the Blessed.

In other circumstances, in addition to those on the imperial robes further familiar symbols used included the attributes of the mythological Eight Immortals; a fan, sword, double gourd, castanets, basket of peaches, bamboo tube, flute and lotus pod. Another set of eight Buddhist emblems consisted of four royal tokens of Buddha himself and four symbols of the religion:

1. Canopy	1. Wheel of the law
2. Conch shell	2. Endless knot
3. Sacred vase	3. Lotus flower
4. Royal umbrella	4. Pair of fish

286. Even a sceptre (rui) might be embroidered, in this case with coral and pearls. 18th century.

These various groups of symbols are inanimate objects linked either to mythological figures or simply suggestive of status and wealth in society. Further robes, that is in addition to the two male garments already described, and particularly women's garments were embroidered more decoratively with semi-symbolic motifs. Less formal in design the robes are glorious in their variety, subject matter and workmanship.

Such costumes show further birds and flowers representing pleasant and auspicious qualities. Paramount amongst them perhaps was the phoenix, the *simurgh* of the Persians, one of the Four Fabulous Beasts of mythology. This was the female, *yin*, counterpart to the dragon and was reserved for the empress but was also used by brides who were honoured as an empress on the day of their marriage. The *feng-huang* hermaphrodite form (male-female) is a mixture of pheasant, peacock and bird of paradise. White cranes with red crestings (and other white beasts) were auspicious as they were inhabitants of the realm of the immortals and lived to a great age. They are often seen repeated in an overall pattern.

Mandarin ducks, and also geese, were symbols of marital fidelity and conjugal happiness as they were said to mate for life. Birds and animals are frequently shown in pairs. In decoration they often appear with lotus flowers, symbols of fruitfulness and offspring. Magpies symbolise a happy meeting.

287. A dragon roundel, tightly drawn and finely worked, for an Emperor's robe. 19th century.

The Art of Embroidery

288. An informal woman's robe with auspicious peonies and the character shou, *in stylized seal form, for long life. Late 19th century.*

Other birds and creatures were included in the rectangular badges of rank that were required on dark surcoats worn over dragon robes for all ranks of officials as insignia of position. Civil officials wore birds while the military had the fabled *qilin* and various real animals. The former group, with the ability to fly, had a closer connection with heaven and were linked with literary talent and wisdom while strong terrestrial animals were more appropriate for the more earthly tasks of the army. In each insignia badge there was also a sun. The practice of wearing badges dates from the Yuan dynasty (1279-1368).

Ordinary coats worn by women of prosperous rank were decorative and in some respects reflect a weakening of formal design in costume but show a slow acceptance of, and new vitality in purely aesthetic considerations with chosen colour combinations, fabrics, designs and seasonal variation.

Many flowers and plants suggested Spring, especially fruiting trees – plums, prunus etc., and multiple repeats of these suggested a wish for longevity. The name for 'rose' also stood for 'flower of lasting springtime' and the marigold was 'flower of ten thousand years'. The plum tree was the first to bloom in winter and therefore an omen of rejuvenation while pines, being evergreen and very long living, exuded similar virtuous and desirable qualities. Chrysanthemums were flowers of Autumn and were worn by older ladies particularly but were often combined with summer peonies in a linking of motifs where opposite seasons again emphasised the repeating cycle of the year. The peony was also seen as the flower of riches and honour, and thereby a wish for success (Plate 288).

The cicada, which emerged from the ground, was seen as representing the life cycle and the regeneration of eternal youth while the butterfly, an immensely popular image, the name of which is *'tieh'*, was a rebus for 'seventy or eighty years of age'. Butterflies are also treasured as the spirits of our ancestors.

Another group of suggestive emblems were seeding fruits: double gourds carried subtle wishes for fertility, as did seeding melons and pomegranates. These last fruit were another potent and decorative symbol carried through to French and English eighteenth century needlework with receding meaning.

NUMBERS

Combinations of motifs in pairs or sets added meaning to symbols and the numbers themselves often had significance. The most important of all was the duality of *yin* and *yang* which pervaded every aspect from male and female to the seasons. Even and odd numbers were reflective of further characteristics of *yin* and *yang*, the static and dynamic. Depicted as a solid or broken line, compositions of trigrams in each of the eight possible combinations like semaphore (i.e. dot and dash) formed part of an ancient system of philosophy and divination. Decoratively, they are often found together with the *yin yang* double lob symbol.

Other significant numbers indicative of the high regard for auspicious groupings included, for example:

> The Three Sages Lao-tsu, Shakamumi and Confucius –
> the patriarchs of Taoism, Buddhism and Confucianism.
> The Four Accomplishments poetry, calligraphy, music
> and chess
> The Five Elements earth, water, fire, metal and wood
> (paralleling the five directions, north, south, east, west
> and centre)[7]

Eight was important, as we have seen, as the number of precious objects, of Buddhist emblems representing the immortals, and of trigrams.

EAST-WEST RELATIONSHIP

The above summary of symbolism displayed in the decoration of Chinese costume is valuable for a general appreciation of similar motifs used and adapted in other Asiatic and European textiles. The strength of Chinese influence was great and it must be remembered that even during the eighteenth century China was the most populous and powerful country on earth and was much feared and respected. The Manchu rulers imposed their will over Tibet and spread their influence and respect far afield.

The Art of Embroidery

289. A 19th century silk hanging filled with figures including 'young boys' and many auspicious elements, rocks, flowers, fruit and courtiers before the emperor.

George III's emissary to their court was expected to 'kow-tow' and the Emperor made it clear that China needed no favours of the British. On the other hand there was considerable Western influence even as early as the seventeenth century when, for instance, the Kangxi Emperor (1654-1722) learned arts and sciences from European Jesuits serving in his court. By that time printing and the production of books had helped Europe advance very much faster than China.

More than costume, other aspects of Chinese needlework have clear parallels with European textiles of similar forms. These included secular hangings for furniture such as sets for tables and chairs, examples of which are shown at the Victoria and Albert Museum, worked in counted thread technique. Beds were an important part of a Chinese bride's marriage symbols. Massive structures would be hung with curtains and pelmets, and furnished with fine quilts and pillows. Even more so than in Europe, the beds would have been used during the day as well as for sleeping at night. Bridal hangings and trousseaus are a universal and age old custom: in China, as elsewhere, these were worked by the bride together with other female clan members long before betrothal negotiations were carried out. A wedding hanging at the Victoria and Albert Museum shows happy boys (rather akin to cherubs) riding a dragon and a phoenix amongst blossom and clouds while another at the Edmonton Art Gallery depicts dozens of small boys, symbols of the successful production of male children, in continuous festive procession (see also Plate 289).

China: A Long Heritage of Silk

RELIGIOUS EMBROIDERY

Turning now from the highly stylized professional robe embroidery and conventional secular needlework we can note the often rather massive textiles made for temple hangings and priests' vestments. The type of needlework used for these seems usually to have been of long satin stitches of lustrous untwisted floss silk. The advantage of this bolder embroidery, other than being faster to work, was that carefully shaped motifs such as rounded faces would from different perspectives take on naturalistic shading giving great life to the needlework. The silks were more vulnerable to wear but unlike robe use, temple-hangings, hung for distant illustrative effect, just as stained glass windows, were safe from immediate damage. A huge hanging in the Victoria and Albert Museum features an embroidered mandala, a mystic diagram of the Womb Treasury World and owes, as such, much to Tibetan religious art.

Many devotional banners and scrolls were executed in needlework, some of a boldly embroidered floss silk variety, but others are of fine single threads worked with extraordinary delicacy. Again some of the finest of these are Sino-Tibetan (Plate 291).

Amongst religious vestments is an interesting Taoist priest's robe of 1650-1700 in the Victoria and Albert Museum which is embroidered with tiers of immortals, like saints on a mediaeval English chasuble. Other vestments were more pictorial and were sometimes decorated with the familiar dragons of court robes, clouds, waves, *yin* and *yang* and trigrams. Buddhist and Taoist robes are derived in shape from the Greek toga that had reached India with Alexander the Great but the eighteenth century Taoist

290. The voluminous form of a Taoist robe (early 19th century) is reminiscent of European mediaeval vestments.

301

decoration was notably varied and colourful. The Taoists were originally alchemists and their all-embracing accord with the forces of Nature called for a wide appreciation of decorative and symbolic motifs (Plate 290).

CHINESE INFLUENCE WITHIN ASIA

Chinese embroidery has numerous aspects despite at first sight seeming to have a limited vocabulary of techniques and subject matter. Court costume appears to have become relatively conventional in form, though rarer examples show variation including enrichment with pearls or coral, for example. Large religious hangings tended to be of untwisted floss silks with a lustrous effect of natural shading and particularly showing light faces. Small shrine hangings and other costume were, however, also worked in fine intricate stitches of thin twisted thread sometimes including Peking knot technique, loop stitch embroidery, and even single strand silk embroidery. Some of these finer techniques are best seen on pieces for places where Chinese influence was adopted. The variation in styles is as wide as the geographical and historical context of the huge country and population of China. The great land mass of Tibet, also Japan, Korea, Indonesia and India, all influenced and were influenced by China.

Discoveries are still being made of early survivals of textiles. The most recent date to the fourth century B.C. of the Warring States period. Embroideries have been found in underwater tombs at Han Lu showing extraordinary fineness of workmanship. Less ancient but incredibly fascinating, and often wonderfully preserved, are a number of Chinese embroideries recently revealed and available to museums of the Western World, from Tibet. Preserved in the now persecuted monasteries there, these mediaeval textiles, though sometimes fragmentary, have been carbon dated to dates around the thirteenth century. Many items incorporate gleaming gold foil and there are a number of extensive survivals. Many pieces are particularly impressive in their rich technique (Plates 291, 292 and 293).

TIBET

While even earlier embroidery is still being excavated in China, the 1980s were marked by the re-emergence of 'mediaeval' Chinese textiles preserved in Tibet. They had been sent to monasteries there in the Tang, Sung, Yuan and Ming dynasties – the eighth to the fifteenth centuries.

Tibet is a large country equal to one third of the land mass of the People's Republic of China. Artefacts in the many monasteries in this great religious state enjoyed, at a high altitude with thin air, a museum-like safe environment. The atmosphere contains little bacteria or ultraviolet light and there are no moths. The air is also dry. Unlike in India or China conditions on the Tibetan plateau are near perfect for the preservation of textiles, which were in any case safeguarded as sacred and precious. From the first millennium the finest fabrics were taken to Tibet from China.

China: A Long Heritage of Silk

In the thirteenth century Kublai Khan (1216-94), who was a student of Sakya Lama, virtually gave the land of Tibet to this Buddhist teacher and thereby created the theocratic government. Subsequently, he and successive Emperors gave huge quantities of precious textiles to the Buddhist monks. Many of these were highly treasured and were only rarely brought out of safe storage, for annual festivals.

Jacqueline Simcox has written about magnificent fragments and larger items that appeared on the art market.[8] Many of the textiles are of *kesi* (or *kossu*), the woven tapestry technique referred to earlier. This is of single colour combinations, related to and perhaps derived in parallel with kelim flat weaving. Other pieces are of

291. Fierce, but in fact benignly protective, this Chinese embroidered thanka *of the 16th century was probably an imperial gift to a Tibetan lama.*

303

The Art of Embroidery

needlework in several varieties of stitch, often combined, on woven silk, damask or silk gauze. Considerable use is made of laid gold thread and gold covered paper is used behind areas worked in unattached needle-loop embroidery, a remarkably rich and especially characteristic feature of these precious religious textiles.

While some pieces show overall designs of a secular or semi-secular nature, with repeated birds, animals and flowers, many others, particularly the embroideries, depict votive motifs associated with Buddhism. The central mood of most Tibetan artefacts is a satisfactory combination of such elements with the decorative imagery so familiar in Chinese art in general.

The largest and most impressive survival is a Buddhist priest's robe (Plate 292) made in China during the early Ming dynasty (fourteenth-fifteenth century). In patchwork form, as was traditional, this magnificent rectangular garment (9ft.9in. x 3ft.10in., 297cm x 117cm) is of red silk gauze embroidered in tent or counted stitch with a lotus flower and swastika pattern while Buddha figures, set on clouds, are worked separately

292. Vaishravana, guardian of the North. A small detail on a Buddhist priest's robe of the early 15th century.

China: A Long Heritage of Silk

in satin stitch on yellow silk and applied to the gauze, in the same manner as used on European vestments. The colours are remarkably unfaded (Cleveland Museum of Art, Ohio).

Even earlier, of the Yuan dynasty (1279-368) is a purple gauze canopy in the Metropolitan Museum of Art, New York, which is square (4ft.7in. x 4ft.9in., 140cm x 145cm) with two dissimilar phoenix birds amongst clouds and pursuing a pearl, forming a central medallion, while from four vases at the corners many different flowers issue from continuous curling tendrils. The satin stitch needlework is executed in thin strands of untwisted silk.

It is thought that only about forty such early textiles have been recorded so far. A *thanka* (Plate 293) is also at Cleveland Museum.[9] Confirmed by carbon 14 dating to the early Ming dynasty this votive hanging (1ft.5¼in. x 7⅝in., 44cm x 19.4cm) is worked on a dark blue ground. It depicts a Buddhist deity *(bodhisattva)* seated on a lotus in an arbour of lotus flowers stemming from animal *(makara)* heads. Above is a symbolic canopy while below lotus flowers stemming from a vase support various auspicious Buddhist objects. This magnificent early Chinese icon incorporates intricate decoration worked in couched gold thread.

CHINESE EXPORTS TO EUROPE

Chinese embroidery of exquisite fineness, fascinated early travellers and successive merchants. It was inevitable that Europeans would try and acquire it, would adapt it for furnishing uses and ultimately would attempt to imitate it. European embroidery, however, took on a distinctive character, never seriously heeding the religious or philosophical significance of Chinese forms and symbolism. Nor did Europe attempt to emulate the minuteness of workmanship. As early as the second century the Chinese were a source of wonder for embroidery and became known to the West as the Seres or Silk People. It was the monk Dionysius Periegetes, at about the end of the third century, who wrote:

The Seres make precious figured garments resembling in colours the flowers of the field, and rivalling in fineness the work of spiders.

293. An early Ming thanka *(1368-1424) with the Seventh Bodhisattva, preserved in pristine condition in Tibet.*

Over the centuries Chinese styles and techniques have changed relatively little; a classical tradition emerged early on and in essence took on a revered status not subject to changes brought about by fashion. It was essentially independent and uncompromising to Western influence except for items specially made for export once travellers had opened up commercial exchanges.

The Art of Embroidery

Temple embroideries and costumes were not suitable for European markets but plain silk and subsequently painted and embroidered fabrics were made in large quantities for trade with India and the West. Silk is of course prone to deterioration when exposed to light so most of the popular imports, fashionable all over Europe from the seventeenth century, throughout the eighteenth and periodically during the nineteenth century, have long since disappeared. What remains has survived mostly by chance, having been saved by lack of use, and inevitably it is mostly later works such as nineteenth century bed covers and shawls that we see in country houses today.

Exports of Chinese silks, plain, embroidered and painted, were prolific as early as 1631 as specified in a proclamation by Charles I. In 1679 the Duchess of Orléans had furnished an outer chamber for her eldest daughter's apartments with:

294. The remarkably well preserved bed at Calke Abbey is entirely of Chinese export silk embroidery with the additional lustre of peacock feathers. c.1710.

> *tapisserie de satin blanc remplie de quantités de figures de la Chine, travaillées toutes avec d'or, d'argent, de la soye.*

A rare seventeenth century survival at Hatfield House is a red silk bed cover embroidered with galloping horses and floral motifs in coloured floss silks with gold thread. Queen Mary, who ruled with William III, is famous for her love of porcelain but she also had a bed of oriental embroidery at Windsor, presented to her by the East India Company. Described by Celia Fiennes as 'Indian' this is in fact more likely to have been Chinese than Indian.[10]

Perhaps the most remarkable survival of Chinese needlework is the state bed preserved at Calke Abbey, Derbyshire which, happily for posterity, was never assembled but remained in storage for two hundred and fifty years (Plate 294). Thought to have been made for the marriage of Anne, daughter of George I, to the Prince of Orange in 1734, it was probably given by her to one of her bridesmaids, Lady Caroline Manners, when she married Sir Henry Harper of Calke Abbey later in the same year. No room at Calke was tall enough for the bed and it thus remained in boxes in the attic. The superb embroidered silk hangings are of blue for the outside and white on the interior worked in brightly coloured floss and twisted silk threads depicting narrative and decorative subjects including trees, flowers, birds, animals, Chinese

China: A Long Heritage of Silk

people and buildings. The work includes couched gold thread and the use of twisted peacock feathers, also couched down, for the knots on gold tree trunks and the eyes in butterflies wings.

The Chinese had a curious method of using gold and silver on leaves of paper, rolled into scrolls, around silk, and their use of spun peacock feather is an old technique. The earliest record of this skill dates back to the Southern Ch'i in the latter part of the fifth century. The medium was very popular in the reign of Kangxi (1662-1722) for the mandarin squares applied to officials' robes, as badges of rank.

Two other magnificent beds must be mentioned. The first is the splendid 'angel' bed (or 'lit à la duchesse') at Erddig, near Wrexham, with its flying tester canopy, suspended without the use of front supporting posts. This bed, which was purchased in 1720, is entirely upholstered and hung with early eighteenth century Chinese silk needlework (Plate 295). The delicate embroidery is worked on a cream-white silk background and covers upholstered panels, with gilt gesso carved mouldings for extra ornament. Long curtains of the same needlework are hung from the tester. This elegant tour de force of early Georgian furniture was rescued and restored when Erddig was in a near state of collapse and rainwater was dripping through the bed. The house has now been saved by the National Trust. The embroidered silk covering the bed is composed of a number of coverlets and hangings of the type imported by the East India Company in the early eighteenth century.[11]

295. The great bed at Erddig, made in 1720, is hung with Chinese embroidered silk made for export.

The Chinese needlework of that bed may have been acquired by the purchaser through his neighbour who was Governor of Fort St George in India, as Chinese textiles were frequently imported through India. On account of such circumstances materials were often incorrectly referred to as 'Indian'. 'Indian' is the true description of a great bed at Houghton Hall, Norfolk that appears at first to be Chinese (Plate 299). The spectacular hangings were made in India specially for Sir Robert Walpole and are remarkable. The English fascination for China has here been indulged in happy imitation, through Indian merchants, even incorporating Sir Robert's heraldic arms. The Houghton bed and another set of comparable hangings were clearly made by the same professional workshop. In each case the overall 'Chinese' designs are derived from oriental 'coromandel' lacquer and painted wallpaper. They show a wide variety of European and oriental flowering shrubs with magnificent birds.

The Art of Embroidery

FURTHER CHINESE NEEDLEWORK IMPORTED TO EUROPE

Amongst the more interesting survivals of Chinese needlework used for furnishing purposes are window curtains, pelmets and chair backs which formed part of a gift in 1791 to the Dutch King, William V, from a Dutch East India Company representative. At Het Huis Ten Bosch, The Hague, these survive from the original 'suites of furniture for two or three rooms of satin embroidered in colour on a white background.' The designs include chinamen at various pursuits including hunting on horseback, with bows and arrows.[12]

Panels of Chinese needlework are fitted to the walls of a room at Ombersley Court, Worcestershire. These were probably supplied by Marsh and Tatham, c.1812. At Buckingham Palace, the Centre Room, which opens on to the balcony (also known as Balcony Room), was largely redecorated by Queen Mary in the 1920s. Here there are six Chinese yellow silk embroidered hangings and also curtains applied with Chinese embroidery, together with pelmets.

From the middle of the eighteenth century bedrooms were often furnished in the Chinese manner with Chinese painted wallpaper and with chinoiserie furniture. Four-poster beds were usually hung with damask but Chinese needlework coverlets were frequently seen on large beds. At Nostell Priory for example, a Chinese silk embroidered bed cover is shown on a chinoiserie Chippendale bed in a room hung with Chinese wallpaper.

Plate 296 shows a silk coverlet with a design that owes as much to Indian palampores as to China. A tree of life design in the central panel is cleverly echoed in the border by wistaria-like trees which grow out of stylised rocks. The leaves and flowers combine a mixture of realism and the exotic, with red veins. Much Chinese silk embroidery of the nineteenth century exhibits a richer and more crowded combination of plants, flowers, birds and butterflies and is worked on a variety of coloured silk backgrounds varying from cream, pale blue and yellow to dark reds and even purple late in the century. Most of this export work was made in Canton where the embroidery industry alone must have

296. This 18th century Chinese bed cover of satin with silk embroidery made for the European market follows an exotic tree of life pattern that originated in Indian painted cottons.

China: A Long Heritage of Silk

been extensive. A splendid Cantonese panel of about 1860 is typical (Plate 297). It displays pairs of exotic birds with brilliant plumage standing on the branches of a pine tree and amongst peonies. The fine thread in Chinese silk embroidery lends itself to a wonderfully lustrous and life-like representation of birds' feathers. Pheasants and mandarin ducks, for example, were portrayed in naturalistic golden tones to great effect.

Amongst smaller items of Chinese export needlework were shawls. An attractive example in the Victoria and Albert Museum (Plate 298), c.1800, is of buff coloured silk with polychrome embroidery in a design made up of archetypal Chinese images. Far removed from the serious iconography of both early and later costumes, the continuous garden scene with boats and pavilions, it represents work that the Chinese factories knew was expected of them by Europeans. Though strictly Chinese in origin, the feeling of the decoration is close to the ubiquitous 'Willow pattern' and the distinctly European chinoiserie that portrayed the orient as a decorative panacea in preference to the complicated visual imagery that was heavily charged with symbolic meaning and a part of China's governing culture in imperial times.

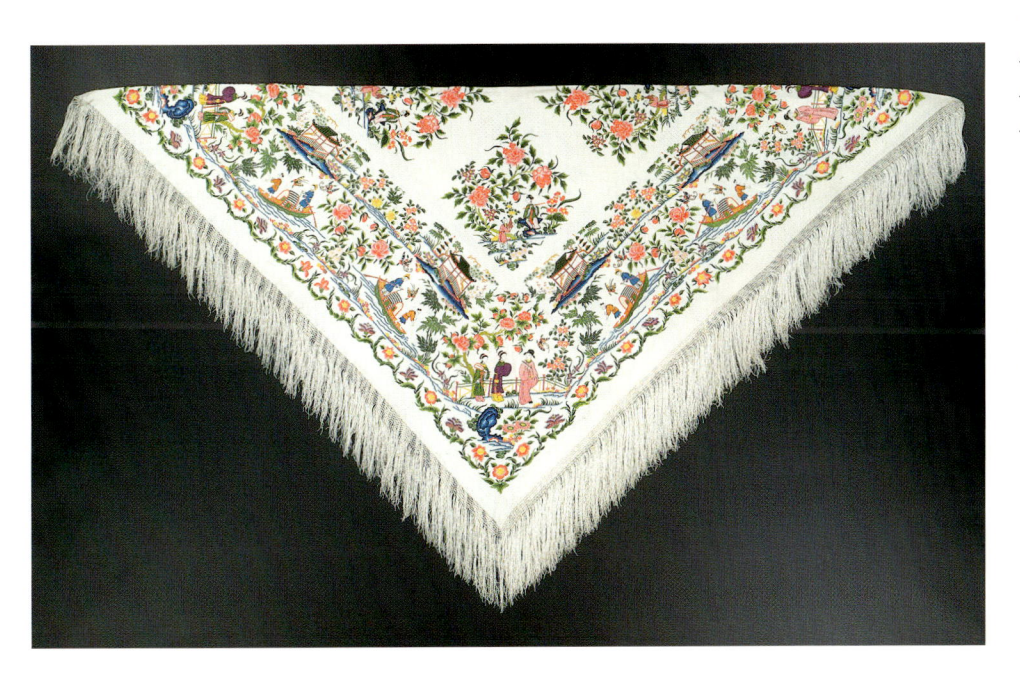

Above. 297. 19th century embroidery made in China for the European market is frequently dense in detail and finely worked in silk on a satin ground.

Left. 298. A late 18th century Chinese export shawl with vignettes typical of those adopted in English chinoiserie crockery of today.

309

CHAPTER ELEVEN

INDIAN EXPORT NEEDLEWORK

A foretaste of paradise

Some of the most beautiful of all embroidery in Western collections is Indian. Amongst a variety of imported textiles, this needlework was supplied commercially from the subcontinent from the seventeenth century onwards. Still today Indian crewelwork is popular and is available by the yard in department stores. This decorative but relatively crudely worked woolwork is not, however, comparable in quality to the minutely worked and beautifully coloured lustrous silk embroidery from which it is derived. Indian needlework of the Mughal period and up to the eighteenth century was amongst the finest and most charming of all textiles.

I have already mentioned the importance of Anglo-Indian trade which was established as early as 1600, when the East India Company was incorporated by charter by Elizabeth I; its headquarters were set up firstly in Surat on the west coast of India and were transferred to Bombay in 1687. Portuguese, Dutch and French merchant travellers also did business in India and soon trade was carried out more generally and textiles were exported from many parts of the huge country including places now in Bangladesh and Pakistan and from Southern India. Above all the provision of lustrous silks met with a burgeoning taste for new costume fashions and household textiles and they differed from the familiar home-made woollen stuffs.

While old inventories refer to imported textiles, and other artefacts, as 'Indian', this term was regularly used in a general sense to refer to exotic materials of all kinds from anywhere in the East; little distinction was known or acknowledged between

299. The embroidered bed at Houghton Hall is hung with Indian chain stitch needlework of a design imitating Chinese lacquer with flowering trees and birds, c.1725. See Plate 17 for a similar hanging.

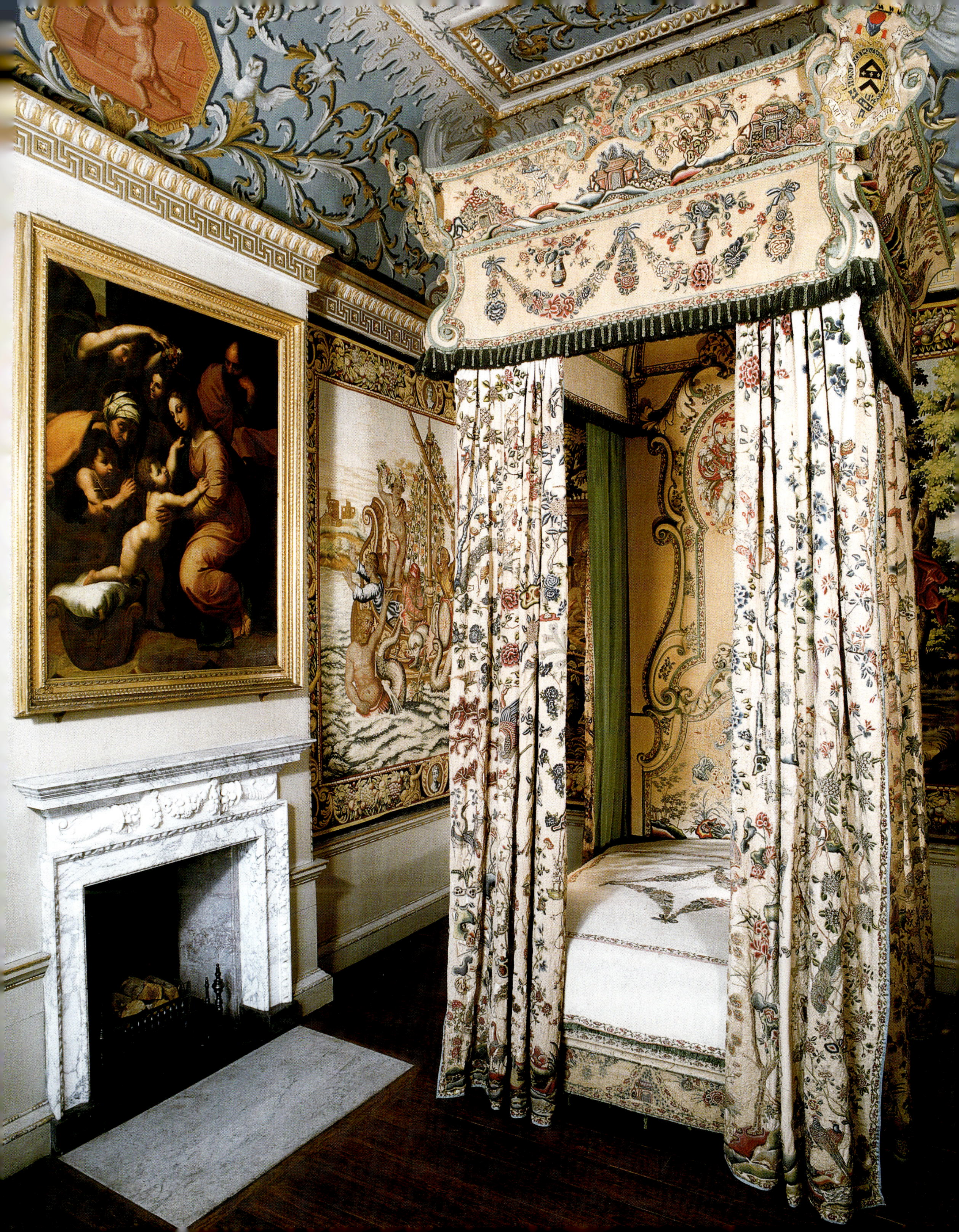

The Art of Embroidery

300. This late 17th century Indian bedcover is further enriched with earlier Chinese and English motifs in a curious and unusual manner. 7ft.8in. x 7ft.8in. (233cm x 233cm).

China, India or other distant lands whether East or West. Treasured exotica were brought from overseas by men in ships, or overland along the silk route which reached from the edges of the world, and these were termed 'Indian'. The same was used to describe the equally fascinating treasures brought from the unknown shores of the Americas. Part of the confusion stemmed from the fact that many Chinese exports were shipped to Europe via India. A well-known form of Chinese lacquer, with engraved decoration, for example, is generally known as coromandel lacquer, because it was shipped from the Coromandel coast of India having already been brought from China. There was a good deal of inter-trading between China and India which meant that merchants could acquire Chinese artefacts in India for re-sale in England. Complicating terminology further, market makers in England in the eighteenth century sent orders to their agents in India for textiles 'in the Chinese taste'.

The great embroidered bed of about 1725 at Houghton Hall (Plate 299) is of Indian needlework, though for long was described as 'Indian' in the sense that it represented an imitation of oriental design. The hangings are of Chinese design, the

Indian Export Needlework

patterns derived from Chinese lacquer, textiles and wallpaper. They are not chinoiserie in the English manner which tended to be more whimsical. The needlework on both the curtains and the complicated fitted upholstery is of finely worked polychrome cotton embroidery, chiefly in chain stitch on a cotton material that is also finely quilted. *Simurgh* birds, peacocks, cranes and pheasants are displayed flying in a continuous tree garden of magnolias, roses, peonies, hydrangeas and prunus. At the base of the curtains a multicoloured undulating ground is the feeding place for further waterbirds amongst characteristic Chinese rock formations. The Duke of Lorraine is said to have slept in the Houghton bed on his visit to the house in 1731. At that time it was in the great green bedroom, but perhaps because it was old-fashioned in shape was subsequently replaced by the equally remarkable but very different colossal velvet bed (page 232). The embroidered bed, though essentially Indian, remains a high point in the story of English embroidery. One of another set of bed curtains of the same design and workmanship, though now rebacked and lacking the original quilting is also illustrated (Plate 17, page 21). As early as 1743 Horace Walpole in *Aedis Walpolianae* remarked on the fineness of the Indian needlework made for Sir Robert's bed at Houghton. It was supplied after Sir Robert's appointment as Knight of the Garter in 1726.

Textiles have always been particularly significant in Indian civilisation and many forms are based on ancient traditions of cotton growing and sericulture. Fabrics of both substances, vegetable and animal, have almost always been manufactured and greatly admired by travellers and traders alike. Wool, which was plentiful in Europe, was not much developed for export from India until recent times. Kashmir embroidery,

301. Part of a Gujarati floorspread displays the neat sophistication of Mughal design, the silks mostly limited to pink and green. c.1700.

313

The Art of Embroidery

especially of the nineteenth century onwards, is the chief exception. Ironically the early English entrepreneurs who travelled to India took out broadcloth, the famed woollen fabric, in the hope of bartering this in the procurement of the spices for which there was such a demand. They were not successful in this exchange but, as the Arab traders before them discovered, they could acquire Indian cottons and barter these for Malayan and Indonesian spices and trade with them elsewhere. Even from ancient times Indian cotton fabrics were famed far afield and were highly regarded. Locally, the bodies of the great, even Buddha, were wrapped in it for burial, while in Europe the Romans greatly prized it and paid high prices for what came to be known as 'woven winds'; similarly poetic terms referred to muslins as running water or morning dew – it was said to be invisible when wet and stretched on grass.[1] English traders quickly discovered that there was a considerable potential in marketing Indian cloth to the Arabs, to North and West Africa, to Turkey and the Levant, as well as in London. In this business they soon faced competition from the Portuguese and Dutch but in the process there developed a distinctive artistic genre in embroidery and other techniques.

302. Part of an Indian export coverlet, finely worked in silk chain stitch on a quilted cotton ground. (It also has English added borders.) c.1690.

Indian Export Needlework

In many parts of India white cottons were the standard form and were often of superb quality. In Gujarat and Rajasthan, however, colour always seems to have been important and even today colourful costumes seem like wondrous blossoms in the dry desert lands. 'Raga' is a word for both 'mood' and 'dye' and indeed specific colours are linked with subtleties of meaning. It is said that red is for lovers and a local Hindi couplet numerates three tones of this colour for three stages of love, madder being the most secure. The basic colours were derived from madder, indigo, and myrobalan ochre (from the medicinal plum). Pomegranate rind combined with indigo produced a dark green, iron shavings with vinegar made black and turmeric was used for yellow. This last colour had associations with Spring, as in many cultures. Indigo provided the blue colour of Krishna, who is likened to a rain-filled cloud, while another blue is the colour of water, reflecting the sky. Saffron is the colour of the earth and of the yogi, the wandering minstrel seer and poet. Each colour reflects seasons and moods.

Indigenous needlework traditions of India were the basis of all the sophisticated subsequent textile arts and traditional ethnic embroidery still enjoys great and widespread relevance as an important domestic art, perhaps more so than in any other country. With the Mughal invasion of India in the sixteenth century, however, courtly designs derived from both Persia and China became infused with Indian workmanship in the production of superbly fine embroidery for the ruling classes. Their courts employed boundless quantities of fine textiles for forts and palaces, for costume and for travelling in a semi-nomadic way of life. It was from this juncture that Indian textiles grew beyond their local relevance with truly cosmopolitan design and appeal. In each stage of Mughal and European development outside demands for textiles were combined in a happy fusion though manufactured with the basic Indian techniques and materials.

A magnificent Mughal coat in the Victoria and Albert Museum is very finely decorated overall with silk embroidery depicting hunting animals, trees, birds and flowers (Plate 303). Of the early seventeenth century, this represents magnificent costume while equally fine tent hangings and floor carpets reflect the luxury and elegance of courtly and travelling standards that are often depicted in miniature paintings.[2] A panel in the Victoria and Albert Museum, embroidered with red lilies on blue-green stems within an overall pattern of the same characteristic colours under a mihrab arch, is typical of a form that traditionally hung around tents and is seen on carpets. The silk is worked on a cotton ground and dates from the second half of the seventeenth century (Plate 312, page 322).[3] Many variations of this characteristic

303. Detail of a Mughal jacket with fine chain stitch embroidery reminiscent of miniature painting, and depicting both wild animals and distinct flower species. c.1630.

The Art of Embroidery

304. A small detail of a large cover or floor carpet made in India for the Portuguese market, with a combination of European and Indian motifs finely worked in natural tussah silk. c.1610. 9ft. x 10ft.9in. (275cm x 327cm).

pattern can be seen in different textures and techniques, some of velvet embroidered with silks or with metal threads, others with gilding, or in appliqué.

From surprisingly early times Indian embroideries were treasured in English households; the inventory made in 1600 for the Countess of Shrewsbury ('Bess of Hardwick'), herself a redoubtable needlewoman, at Hardwick Hall, Derbyshire, includes Indian embroidered quilts. From early in the seventeenth century Portuguese traders brought fine embroidery from their trading post at Satgaon near Calcutta in Bengal, especially 'Bengalla quilts'.[4] They had established there a business relationship based on the local tradition of embroidery using wild tussah silk. This was applied to the manufacture of huge floorspreads densely decorated with complex chain stitch needlework in forms combining European figurative arabesques, related to engravings for the decoration of silver, plasterwork and wood carving, together with a local flavour with ingredients of Mughal hunting incidents and also European travellers. The result of this curious mélange was a short period that produced glorious

Indian Export Needlework

lightweight 'summer' carpets or floorspreads, later regarded as oversize bed covers embroidered in a single colour, usually the natural undyed yellow, with designs showing mythological, religious, traditional and topical subjects, even incorporating sailing ships of the travelling merchants. An example, is shown in Plate 304. No less than 129in. x 106in. (327cm x 265cm), this spectacular quilted floorspread is embroidered with tussah silk in a variety of stitches, mainly chain stitch, on an undyed cotton ground. The design consists of a central medallion, four quarter medallions and three borders. The imagery includes classical stories (Diana and Actaeon, the Judgement of Paris, Hercules, etc.) together with hunting scenes, fishermen, winged musical mermaids and double headed eagles. The overall background of the central part of the carpet displays a chaotic panorama of Portuguese horsemen and other hunters on foot and with guns, amongst a variety of wild animals. Another, worked in red silk, in the Victoria and Albert Museum, has the arms of a Portuguese family at the centre, indicating that it was a special commission, together with sailing ships and Jacobean musicians within Mughal-style borders of animals, trees, flowers and birds. Export needlework based on this type was subsequently carried out in other parts of India; it would certainly seem probable that the Portuguese developed the manufacture of similar items in their western territories of India, such as Goa. As a general rule it may be noted that Portuguese exports from India have more elements of local Indian design and ethnic motifs than did the decorative embroideries cultivated by English merchants. Stylized animals are a feature of Indo-Portuguese furniture and embroidery while those made for the English market were essentially elegant and floral.

As early as 1611 hand-drawn painted cloths were made in Masulipatam for export to England through an agency set up by the East India Company. These proved both popular and influential in England and led to a mutual exchange of design that was to be immensely important in both countries. I have already indicated how important was the influence of India on English needlework in the seventeenth century. The popularity of Indian painted, printed and sewn textiles, both hangings and floor carpets, was widespread and the interplay of design and craftsmanship between the two cultures was extremely fortuitous and fruitful. The commercial aspect of the East India Company's trade was balanced at home with professional supplies of fabric, pattern drawers for crewelwork hangings and the private and very personal production of needlework by ladies in their households. All were inspired by the charm and technique of Indian chain stitch

305. An Indo-Portuguese embroidered coverlet probably made in Goa, for export to Europe, c.1720.

The Art of Embroidery

306. This hanging of lustrous silk worked in chain stitch is closely related to painted cotton hangings made in India for the European market. c.1650. 8ft.6in. x 5ft.1in. (260cm x 155cm).

embroidery. There are many survivals of each kind of work, even joined together, in English country houses today. At Saltram, Devon, for example, there is a bed upholstered with three varieties – English needlework, Indian needlework and painted textiles from India. The large quantities of textiles imported to Britain was despite legislation prohibiting trade introduced to protect local business. This seems to have made the fabrics all the more coveted in fashionable circles. They were also relatively inexpensive, durable and wonderfully cheerful in Europe where brightly coloured textiles were still not readily available to a broad section of middling rich people.

The tree of life design, so familiar in its evolved form in English crewelwork hangings, is of course of oriental origin. The well-known Ashburnham hangings from India at the Victoria and Albert Museum show the archetypal pattern with an exotic tall plant form rising up to its full height effortlessly supporting large and decorative flowers, curling leaves and tendrils that are home to elegant and playful chinoiserie birds, while at the base, amongst a wild land of cavernous rocks (more representative of China or Persia than India), huntsmen pursue wild animals. These hangings are of painted and dyed cotton, made in Gujarat, Western India, c.1700. A related embroidered hanging of almost identical design, from the same origin and in extraordinary condition, is another great treasure of the museum. It has pairs of love birds, small squirrel monkeys and diving paradise birds amongst the luscious floral vegetation. Another fragment of similar embroidery in a private collection has upright borders with floral twisted columns (Plate 306). Cambay, in Gujarat, was probably the original centre of this fine needlework; merchants of the East India Company were particularly instructed to buy 'quilts made about Cambay' and the name Patania also occurs,

Indian Export Needlework

probably referring to Patan, in northern Gujarat. After the silting-up of the Gulf of Cambay, Surat probably became the centre of trading. While English crewelwork hangings were, from their earlier origin, always of wool embroidery, and continued to be so, Indian embroidered hangings were of finely worked silk. The former had a base material of linen-cotton home-spun twill while the Indian used finely woven cotton and occasionally silk. A common feature latterly, however, derived from the Indian work, was the predominant use of chain stitch.

While English crewelwork designs clearly took on aspects of Indian palampores (the hangings and, more literally, the bed covers made for export), embroidered textile patterns in the eighteenth century became less baroque, the design more uniform overall and smaller in scale. Notably consistent, however, was the colour palette of the silks and this remains the most recognisable distinguishing feature of Indian embroidery. The predominant colours were a darkish red and a greenish blue with dark blue, green and yellow being the supporting secondary colours. The reds, more properly deep pinks, were derived, as indicated above, from madder, combined with a necessary fixing agent (mordant), while the other principal colour, blue, was indigo, which bonds naturally in dyeing without an added agent. Curtains of Indian embroidery formerly supplied to Drayton House, Northamptonshire, in the early eighteenth century, show an all over design with relatively small decorative leaves and flowers (Plate 308). Mention has already been made of a bed at Saltram. At Osterley Park, Middlesex, two beds exemplify admirably the late eighteenth century taste for Indian silks in bedrooms particularly. In one there is a bed hung with painted silk hangings supplied by John Linnell for a bed designed by Robert Adam. It once had an embroidered counterpane of 'rich Satin Decca work lined and fringed'. Decca work

Above. 307. Fine Indian export needlework in a repeating pattern, less Mughal and more French in style. c.1740.

Left. 308. Part of a set of silk embroidered curtains imported to England from India in the mid-18th century.

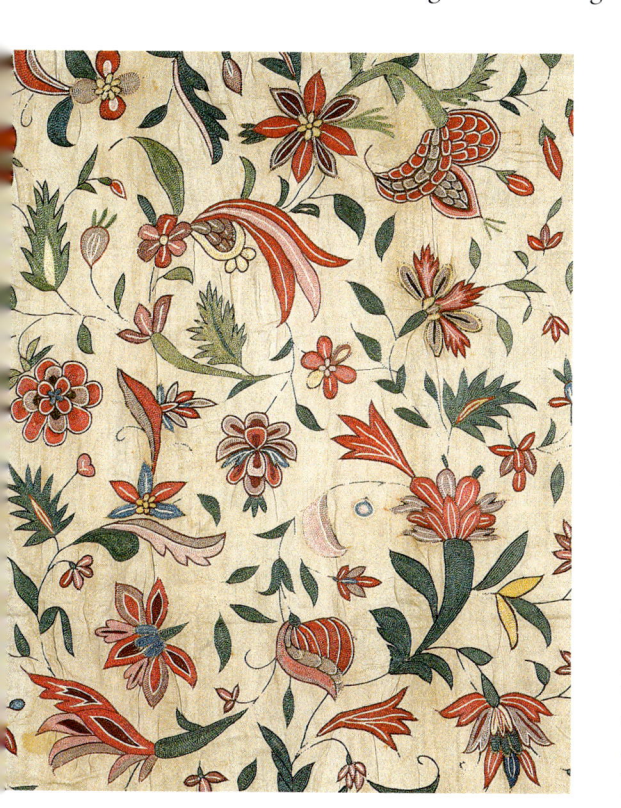

319

The Art of Embroidery

309. Based on chintz designs, palampores of cotton finely embroidered with silk chain stitch were made in Western India for export to England and Holland in the 18th century.

(embroidery made in the Deccan states of southern India) is not to be confused with Dhaka, now in Bangladesh, which was famous for fine cotton, exceptional muslin and white embroidery. In Mrs Child's bedroom at Osterley is another bed, this one hung with silk embroidered hangings of cotton (only partially surviving), matching festoon window curtains and chair covers (not surviving). The embroidery is typically delightful and principally in shades of blue-green and red with flecks of yellow.[5] Celia Fiennes visited Windsor Castle on one of her eighteenth century journeys around England and noted: 'next is the Queen's Chamber of State all Indian Embroidery on white satin [*sic*] being presented to her by the Company [East India Company] on it is great plumes of white feathers'. 'Indian' in this case might have meant Chinese.

In the meantime, another principal import was bed covers, in actuality, or adapted in scale from, Indian floor spreads. Mughal miniatures of the sixteenth century show princes seated on floor carpets the design of which is clearly the prototype of Queen Anne English needlework bed coverlets. The Islamic features with arches, borders, medallions and corner decorations are each seen to be gradually adapted with the shared love of floral decoration providing the principal feature (Plate 302, page 314). A superb Mughal floorspread of about 1700 in the Victoria and Albert Museum (Plate 301) has a well-balanced and fully filled overall pattern in predominantly dark pink colouring with oft repeated flowering plant forms, familiar in mosaic decoration, as on the Taj Mahal. The usual quarter medallions of the corners in this instance are transformed to vases of flowers and there is no central medallion. The flowers depicted include tulips with the familiar oriental favourites lilies, peonies, jasmine, and other stylized varieties. While this carpet is entirely floral, another contemporary example (Plate 310) is notable for its border with wild animals, paired Chinese birds entwined in the corners, and the main field dotted with floral sprays and an entertaining array of birds, beasts and fish including blue elephants, scaly fish with legs, gazelle, tigers and cranes.[6] Another cover or canopy, from Gujarat, c.1700, in the Calico Museum, Ahmedabad, is decorated with the familiar Chinese birds, derived from the legendary Persian *simurgh,* with eagle-like heads, strong wings, and either long peacock tails or feathers with serrated edges, sometimes the last two combined. The corners show fierce lion dogs and the overall design is essentially Chinese.[7]

Less 'native' and highly luxuriant in design and quality are two comparable palampores that appear to be related in design to Dutch marquetry with densely crowded arrangements of flowers in vases as a repeated principal motif. In the Victoria and Albert Museum and at Colonial Williamsburg, these two pieces of about 1725 are related to chintz designs and indeed such needlework was sometimes referred to as 'worked chintz' (Plate 309). The border pattern repeats an elegant floral tree form reminiscent of the tree of life design while a delicate full scale version fills the main field of the palampore around the 'Dutch' vases, which are in the customary medallion locations. A feature of these two embroideries is a more colourful palette and greater closeness to reality in floral depiction. An interesting curiosity of the period shows a rare combination of Indian, Chinese and English embroidery (Plate 300, page 312). This is an Indian quilted coverlet, with simple embroidered borders, on to which have been applied, in the late seventeenth century, a variety of old (perhaps older) Chinese spot motifs and further English ones.

In other English imports, and indeed in English imitations or versions, the Indian feature of limited and repeated single colour patterns was continued. Bed covers were thus decorated, usually on a quilted ground, with sprig-like trees worked in single colours, and repeated in turn, red, green, blue or brown in any regular combination. In some instances it takes close inspection to identify the difference between English and Indian varieties, both being finely stitched. The first recognisable feature is usually the ground material, the Indians having used a fine cotton and the English linen, but in essence design and technique are seen to have come together perfectly across the two distant cultures (Plate 302).

Returning to more distinctly Islamic textiles, mention must be made of the spectacular tents and tent hangings of which there must have been many magnificent variations. Susan Stronge has described how, in Akbar's reign, the court would travel with a vast city of tents, in duplicate so as to have a continuous relay, furnished with hangings and carpets.[8] Surviving tents, as in the Maharajah's Palace at Jodhpur, have walls with arcaded panels of traditional Islamic form, sometimes of velvet with gold embroidered decoration.[9] Others were of appliqué or painted or gilded: every variety of textile was to be seen on walls, on tent roofs, on the ground and indeed in the costumes and headdress of the court and myriad supporters. A late eighteenth century dark blue cotton tent hanging in the Victoria

310. This Mughal floorspread of c.1700, with a central medallion and corners of Persian origin, is alive with wild animals and numerous semi-mythical creatures. 10ft.6in. x 9ft. (320cm x 274cm).

The Art of Embroidery

Right. 311. A small Punjabi coverlet or rumal of cotton embroidered with Hindu motifs in a characteristic range of colours. c.1880.

Below. 312. A cotton hanging embroidered with silk consists of an archetypal mihrab arch containing an elegant Mughal tree of lilies. c.1650-1700. 3ft.10in. x 2ft.8in. (117cm x 81.25cm).

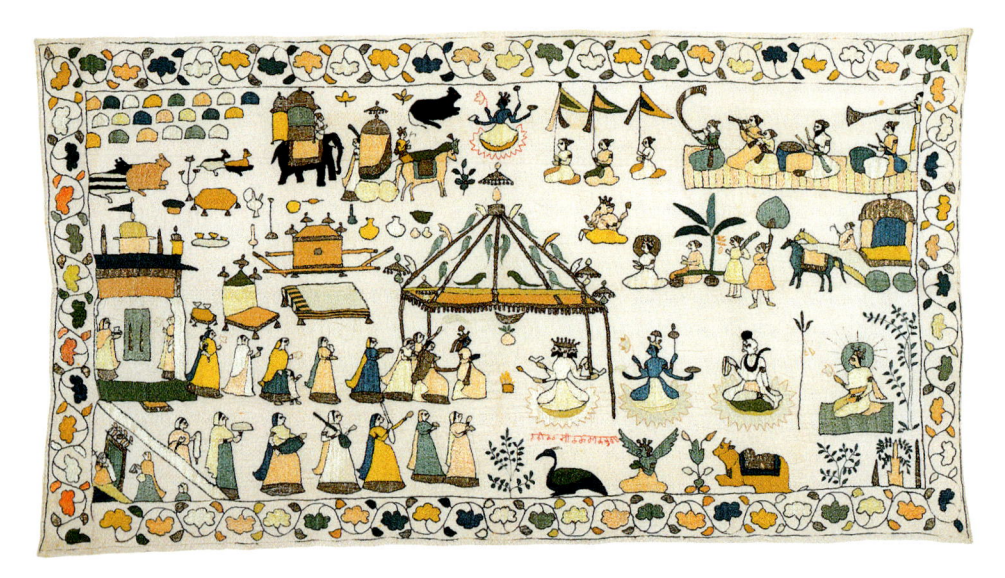

and Albert Museum is embroidered with a tree of life design under a mihrab arch in pink, yellow and other shades.

Further floor carpets, exported regularly to Europe as bed covers or hangings, included those from the Deccan and specifically from Goa. These are somewhat more Islamic in design with a close overall pattern of floral palmettes within scrolls, sometimes with gold thread stems and sometimes on a gold thread background. Border patterns might have the familiar small flower sprigs within rows of round-topped arches. Plate 305 shows a typical example and others can be seen at Waddesdon Manor, Berkshire and, especially beautiful, one which came from Tippu Sultan's palace at Seringapatam at the Victoria and Albert Museum. This has a luxurious variety of curling leaves and flowers embroidered in contrasting coloured silks, metal thread stems and a bold pattern, unlike the more familiar dense repeated design.

Hindu religious and mythological motifs are incorporated in many forms of decoration including some export embroidery. They are particularly a feature of late eighteenth century rumals, small coverlets for gifts or temple offerings, from Chamba in the Punjab Hills. This needlework shows lively subjects such as Krishna and his cow-herding lady attendants and other traditional themes in story telling, worked in blue and yellow silks especially and metal thread.

From the highlands of Kashmir very good quality wool weaving and embroidery was famed from ancient times. Shawls with Persian inspired patterns and other textiles have enjoyed popularity for hundreds of years, originally made for men. For women in Europe they became a

Indian Export Needlework

passion in the nineteenth century, both embroidered and woven (Plate 313), and imitations were made in England, France and at Paisley in Scotland. They were particularly characterised by the lobe-shaped tree or cone form that dominated many designs, and which subsequently became known as paisley pattern.

As in Europe, official court embroidery often incorporated the use of impressive gold work. A saddle cloth from Hyderabad, of the early eighteenth century (Victoria and Albert Museum), is of red velvet profusely decorated all over with silver-gilt thread in a flame-like foliate pattern and with other herbal forms disciplined into ornament like the damascene of Renaissance armour. In this formalized professional embroidery we see again a special sophistication in Oriental and European decoration, united in style, grandeur and workmanship; origins and functions were shared and adapted across the continents.

313. An early 19th century Kashmir shawl elaborately embroidered with a map of Srinigar.

CHAPTER TWELVE

THE TWENTIETH CENTURY

*...thy mind
Shall be a mansion for all lovely forms*

PAST generations did not have the unlimited access, as we do, to the resources of the world and all the experience of techniques generated through time. The richness of the heritage from which we can so readily seek inspiration and counsel, and the availability of both natural and man-made materials, should in theory enable us to create today great needlework equal to anything of the past. But the trends of the twentieth century have unfortunately not produced works of that excellence. Although it is still too early to judge, it would appear that since the end of the nineteenth century, needlework, like most other art forms, has been feeling for a course and journeying through experiments to discover satisfactory expression. A number of styles have shone with varying qualities, a few with distinction, but truly remarkable embroidery with new and lasting virtues cannot as yet be identified. The Embroiderers' Guild, an educational charity founded in 1906 to promote the craft to the highest possible standards, has however been influential in co-ordinating new ideas of design and technique. The Guild also has a substantial historic collection which is housed at its headquarters at Hampton Court Palace. This is conveniently close to the Royal School of Needlework which also moved to Hampton Court. The Textile Conservation Centre, which from the first was a pioneering organisation with an important influence on scientific preservation of our textile heritage, was also there, but is now at Southampton University.

The art of needlework from mediaeval times progressed in multiple ways, identified and co-ordinated by a unity of purpose and character which disciplined and con-

*314. A detail of the Queen's Silver Jubilee cope,
designed by Beryl Dean. (See Plate 322.)*

The Twentieth Century

The Art of Embroidery

315. Lady Evelyn Murray, daughter of the Duke of Atholl, worked this remarkable whitework in the early 20th century.

tributed to skills and designs. A certain lack of integration originated only in the last century when no permanent form emerged after a series of revivals. William Morris was the principal pioneer of the modern movement but no definite style emerged from the wide scope of historical and cultural forms which had influenced him. He was perhaps too retrospective in his approach, neglecting aspects of contemporary technical achievements, and unable to accept the benefits they had to offer. Lewis Day (1845-1910) was an industrial artist with different views and he also designed for embroidery amongst other crafts. His *Art and Needlework* was published in 1900. He believed in division of labour and in the value of the machine. He took a less idealised view of needleworkers' skills than Morris and saw that ability in design and workmanship does not necessarily come together in one person. He promoted collaboration. But major artists and designers in the twentieth century have not chosen to design for embroiderers and the craft has become polarised largely on the 'home made' on the one hand, and kit forms on the other, with various degrees of originality.

It is said contentiously that younger people tend to be governed by fashions while others of greater maturity seek style. All, however, delight in pattern-making and creativity. In addition, in all the arts much the most pleasant is to be enveloped by illusion, at least in part. The portrayal of basic reality is relatively dull while there is charm in fantasy. Equally, as in painting and so many disciplines, in the best embroidery the art often lies in what is left out rather than what is put in. Elimination of the unnecessary concentrates the value of the chosen theme. Selection is all, but that is not to say that there should not be plenty of scope for ornament and variety in needlework.

The Twentieth Century

Machinery superseded many domestic crafts but did not seriously influence or threaten needlework since its products replaced only what had already become artless. Some forms of mass-produced embroidery were still carried out by hand, as at Arthur H. Lee and Sons of Birkenhead, Cheshire, where decorative crewelwork curtains were made to old designs with coarse wools and using up to four threads in the needle at once. These and other traditional designs were carried on timelessly as long as fashion demanded. Crewelwork made in Kashmir for the European market is still available by the yard in London department stores and more refined crewel embroidery imitating eighteenth century English work is also now being made in India for sale in London and elsewhere.

Carpets, likewise, have continued to be made following set forms, particularly of nineteenth century design, and reproductions are now manufactured cheaply in India and China for sale all over the world. A traditional pattern was adopted, as one would expect of Edwardian England, for the huge carpet made by Queen Mary that travelled the world for charity exhibitions. A carpet made by the Gladstone family at Hawarden

316. Of baroque-rococo inspiration, this panel by Peter Maitland is worked with many shades of silks and wools.

The Art of Embroidery

Above. 317. One of a series of needlework panels designed by Beryl Dean for St George's Chapel, Windsor Castle, shows the three Magi.

Opposite above. 318. A section of the massive Overlord Embroidery showing King George VI, Eisenhower, Montgomery, Alanbrook and Churchill.

Opposite below. 319. Phoenix by Zara Merrick, a large hanging of wool tent stitch rivalling a woven tapestry, as large scale embroideries have done since the 17th century. 3ft.4in. x 8ft.4in. (99cm x 254cm).

Castle was another post war collaboration, this one a copy of a Savonnerie original. While Lady (Sarita) Vansittart made a good copy of a magnificent needlework carpet from Hatfield House, others sought original patterns. At Bulbridge House, near Wilton, Lady Juliet Duff worked rugs in gros point from designs by Rex Whistler and for Send Grove, Surrey, Loelia Duchess of Westminster made a stair carpet of her own design.[1]

More ambitious attempts at originality with a wide range of materials were tried out simultaneously. Ann Macbeth's designs were distinctly simplified, light and consciously not overworked. She enjoyed considerable success supplying designs to Liberty's and other shops. Elaborate stitching was not much favoured until after the influence of Cubist painters in the 1920s, when texture was again considered important. Three-dimensional effects reminiscent of stumpwork, but much less intricate, were attempted and quick appliqué became fashionable again, often on a huge scale.

Appliqué (applied work) where pieces of different fabric are superimposed or joined in pictorial or patterned forms is a very old and universal technique and often very sophisticated. It is closely related to patchwork and is especially effective on large scale works. From East to West it has been fashionable in religious and secular circumstances. It is seen in *opus anglicanum* and mediaeval Chinese needlework. A large seventeenth century Tibetan thanka in the Metropolitan Museum, New York, of appliqué, couched cord and embroidery, is a tour de force of the technique. Even in the late eighteenth century felt appliqué was effectively used for pictures and for the bed hangings at Newliston. Formal strapwork in applied form is represented by the sixteenth century panel illustrated (Plate 61, page 68) while at the other extreme George III's wedding procession (Plate 148, page 168) exhibits in relief a wide variety of textures. The technique is timeless and seems to have been well suited to the twentieth century. Vestments designed by Matisse for the chapel at Vence are of applied work in a strong, bright design. The celebrated Overlord Embroidery,[2] commemorating the Second World War and the culminating invasion of Normandy in 1944, for which the code name was Operation Overlord, was commissioned by Lord Dulverton. It was made by the Royal School of Needlework and is of appliqué and on a massive scale, being 272ft. (83m) long, reminiscent of the mediaeval saga hangings, besides having an obvious parallel with the Bayeux Tapestry. Its artistry is in reflecting the illustrative techniques of the period such as newspaper photography; it does this remarkably, and very much with the favoured colours and textures of the times. The theme depicted is suitably momentous and eminently worthy of such a large-scale work and the subjects are varied and interesting (Plate 318).

328

The Twentieth Century

A less serious but charming hanging of three panels, totalling about 28ft. (8.5m) in length, was designed by Belinda, Lady Montagu, to mark, in 1979, the 900th anniversary of the New Forest. It combines, in a rich variety of textures, appliqué work, canvaswork and embroidery, and depicts vignettes of historical and social interest within a general theme of natural history.[3] This work is representative of many multi-technical embroideries, some worked on a large scale.

A number of embroideresses have been prominent in attempting to stimulate fine needlework: The Hon. Mrs Rachel Kay-Shuttleworth (d.1967) was a collector and teacher founding a centre for study at her home, Gawthorpe Hall, Lancashire; Mrs Theodore Roosevelt Jr. (d.1960), daughter-in-law of the American president, was another notable and versatile embroideress. Her pictorial designs for screens and pictures contain an element of humour; one picture portrays a 'Sea Serpent' while a screen depicts monkeys swinging about in tropical vegetation. The tradition of patchwork quilting was also carried on throughout the twentieth century in America and in England, where it has taken more the form of a revival.

In canvas embroidery, however, the emphasis has been on novel designs and interesting stitches, a prominent contribution of needlework teachers. A large amount of amateur work has been directed to hassocks and cushions for churches; many cathedrals have impressive quantities of neat and bright needlework standing out against stone and woodwork in majestic settings. Some of this is rich in design and intricate in workmanship. Good examples can be seen at Lichfield, St Albans, Wells and Exeter cathedrals. At Iona there are cushions in the

329

The Art of Embroidery

Above. 320. A contemporary work, Leaf, *by Louise Baldwin.*

Opposite. 321. The 14th century stalls at Wells Cathedral are decorated with fine wool embroidered cushions and hanging panels, c.1937.

choir stalls embroidered with verses from the Benedicite. At Winchester a body of about two hundred embroiderers was co-ordinated by Louisa Pesel, a student of Lewis Day, on a project known as *A St Swithin's Day Enterprise,* making kneelers and cushions.[4] Miss Pesel had previously done needlework for the private chapel of the Bishop of Winchester at Wolvesey, based on seventeenth century sampler designs. Artistically and technically she adhered to two fundamental rules that are crucial to successful embroidery. If the work is to be multi-coloured, the variety of stitches must be reasonably limited; conversely, if a variety of stitches is to be displayed, a limited range of colours should be use. In monochrome embroidery a variety of stitches gives shading and textural interest.[5] This was especially a feature of blackwork and early crewelwork. Some good modern needlework is derived from ethnic or tribal sources, an endless field which I have not been able to consider here.

Nowadays 'serious' modern needlework is conceived as an art form but in traditional formats such as pictures or hangings. Divorced from utilitarian characteristics, it often lacks subtleties. Some pieces show bold strokes of originality, sometimes in an exciting way but often unduly self-conscious, undisciplined, and with little true content. Neither brash variation nor conventional decoration are interesting; change for its own sake is not enough and is the limited scope of popular decoration and ordinariness is the dullest of all. Subtlety and illusion must be part of the equipment of a true artist. Fritz Feller, the designer of the Rolls Royce Silver Spirit, speaking in 1980, expressed these concepts neatly:

> *Nothing in this life is so dull and miserable as the 'average' or 'the mean'. Once we throw away the concept of excellence and perfection we take away the excitement and incentive for living. Once we regard dreams as a waste of time magic also dies.*

Beryl Dean has been responsible for some remarkable works which combine a feeling of the times with interesting technical innovations and, above all, appropriateness. She trained at the Bromley School of Art, the Royal College of Art and the Royal School of Needlework. Her cope, stole, mitre and morse made for the Bishop of London on the occasion of the Queen's Silver Jubilee in 1977, echo in a collage effect of specific architectural motifs a sense of binding unity which is embodied in Church and State. The design includes St Paul's Cathedral, seventy-three London churches and two Royal Peculiars. Many modern vestments draw our attention by the use of brilliant colouring but these Jubilee pieces are especially attractive, being worked in subtle and

The Twentieth Century

The Art of Embroidery

harmonious shades of yellow-golds and silver-greys (Plates 314 and 322).

Colour judgement is one of the most important factors of needlework and one of the least understood. The softness, subtlety and brilliance of good dyes are perhaps more crucial even than a good design. Dr Johnson quoted a useful extract from Addison in his *Dictionary*:

In a curious brede of needlework, one colour falls away by such just degrees, and another rises so insensibly, that we see the variety without being able to distinguish the total vanishing of the one from the first appearance of the other.

This may have been referring specifically to Florentine embroidery but a keen consideration of tones is important for all needlework.

Colours have always had significance beyond their decorative associations to mood and feeling. In music there are distinct relationships to colours and shades of colour (for example Sir Arthur Bliss' *Colour Symphony*), while in religion and philosophy unknown ancient origins have led to rules and traditions linking colours to seasons and hierarchical significance. Chinese costume and the textiles of Christian worship are two obvious examples of this. In modern times the significance of colours worn in church or state ceremonial or even in fashionable costume are important in the language of communication. Historically all

The Twentieth Century

such traditions have governed and continue to influence suitable colour use in needlework and embroidery in an ever shifting and relevant way.[6]

That modern works are often charmless may be justified as reflecting circumstances of the times, but that they are frequently soulless is indefensible. It must be hoped that the position will be rectified by constant re-examination of the invaluable and inestimably beautiful works bequeathed by previous generations. A willingness to value a degree of continuity and to derive an essence from the best of any age is the crux of creating works that will uplift and adorn the present and future. We have a natural urge, and indeed an important responsibility, to contribute to the world's artistic achievements; the resources at our fingertips are tremendous; we can travel almost anywhere to consult wonderful designs and can see countless ideas through photographs, books and modern technology. A new style, neither brutal nor twee, will help to restore self-confidence and interest in the wake of 'post-modernism'. There are, happily, signs in architecture and in many fields of a strong new form, with a more sensitive language of historical nurture, coupled with a richer depth of expression. Bald functionalism has had its day and, unashamedly, the age-old grammars are at last being adapted and extended as the basis of exiting new achievements. Surely, the treasury of historical needlework will ensure that the future of the craft shall be continuously alive to engender many more fine works in the art of embroidery.

Opposite above. 322. A cope created to mark the Queen's Silver Jubilee in 1977 for the Diocese of London, designed by Beryl Dean. It depicts St Paul's Cathedral and many churches in a formalised design.

Opposite below. 323. Wish you were here, *by Linda Miller, 1995.*

Below. 324. Haymakers *by Alice Kettle, 1989.*

333

NOTES

INTRODUCTION

Epigram: *Spectator,* 1714
1. Early weaving techniques are seen in Bronze Age basket fragments and other primitive 'luxury' items such as mats, containers and sieves as well as in pattern-making, as on Celtic crosses, now reflected through knitting in Aran pullovers.
2. *Apollo,* January, 1977, p.57.
3. Ibid.
4. M J Mayorcas, *English Needlework Carpets,* 1963, p 9.
5. Chaucer, *The Miller's Tale.*
6. Queen Anne was also an embroideress. See a sale catalogue of Hall, Waterbridge and Owen, Auctioneers, in the Music Hall, Shrewsbury, 18 Sept. 1875, Lot 1151:' A fine piece of Old Silk tapestry – a garden scene, the offerings of Flora to Venus …etc. This screen, the work of Queen Anne, was presented by Her Majesty to the Rt. Hon. Richard Hill, Ambassador Extraordinary to the court of Turin, 1703.' Mentioned by a correspondent to *Country Life,* 29 Nov. 1956.
7. James II bought a cravat of Venetian 'gros-point' lace for his coronation in 1685.
8. John Taylor, *The Prayse of the Needle,* 1640.
9. Ibid. For a fuller account of The Royal School of Needlework see *The Royal School of Needlework,* Winefride Jackson and Elizabeth Pettifer, 2nd ed., 1986.

CHAPTER ONE

Epigram: Theocritus, Idyll XV. Embroidered on a screen designed by Walter Crane.
1. 'Beautiful, young and talented was Arachne – but boastful. She claimed she could spin and weave better than anyone in the world – even the goddess Athene. When Athene visited her, disguised as an old woman, Arachne unknowingly challenged her to a duel at tapestry weaving which of course the goddess won. Athene, as a warning to all conceited mortals quickly changed her into a spider so that she could spend eternity perfecting her stitches.' Erica Wilson's *Embroidery Book,* 1973.
2. Noin-Ula, Mongolia. Illustrated in *Chinese Art* vol. 3, R. Soame Jenyns, 1981, p.64.
3. St Etheldreda was daughter of Anna, king of the East English, and twice married, secondly to King Egfrid, but after twelve years with him she became a nun and founded a monastery for monks and nuns on the island in the fens which had been part of the dowry of her first marriage, to Tonbert, Prince of the South Gyrwas (Pitkin, Pictorial History of Ely).
4. Erica Wilson's *Embroidery Book,* New York, 1973.
5. Quoted in 'The Bayeux Tapestry in the hands of Restorers', Charles Dawson, F.S.A (*The Antiquary,* August 1907) and by Margaret Jourdain, *English Secular Embroidery,* 1910.
6. A.F. Kendrick, *English Needlework,* 1933.

CHAPTER TWO

Epigram: Dame Dorothy Selby's tomb at Ightham, Kent, 1641.
1. Matthew Paris records Pope Innocent IV (1243-1254): 'having noticed that the ecclesiastical ornaments of certain English priests, such as choral copes and mitres, were embroidered in gold thread after a most desirable fashion, asked whence came this work. From England, they told him. Then exclaimed the Pope, "England is for us such a garden of delights, truly an inexhaustible well; and from there where so many things abound, many may be extorted." Thereupon the same Lord Pope, allured by the desire of the eye, sent letters, blessed and sealed, to well nigh all the abbots of the Cistercian order established in England, desiring that they should send to him without delay, these embroideries of gold which he preferred above all others, and with which he wished to decorate his chasubles and choral copes, as if these acquisitions would cost him nothing. This command of my Lord Pope did not displease the London merchants who traded in these embroideries and sold them at their own price.' Quoted by Donald King in *Age of Chivalry,* Royal Academy of Arts, 1987.
2. *Apollo,* July 1972, Philippe Verdier, 'Arts at the Courts of France and England (1259-1328)'. Birds and animals are shown in Queen Mary's Psalter (1310-20), British Library. God creating birds and beasts. Such creatures are seen throughout English needlework: hawks, crows, swan, squirrel, goat, monkey, cattle, griffin, seated lion, seated stag, seated unicorn.
3. This shape was often used at later periods. See, for example, the inlaid decoration on the front of a scriptor with silver mounts, c.1675, in the Duke's Closet, Ham House, Surrey. It became an archetypal form.
4. Daroca Cope and Melk Chasuble: see illustrations in *Apollo,* October 1963: *Opus Anglicanum, a Study of the Melk Chasuble,* Pauline Johnston.
5. The use of script as a decorative pattern is an important and beautiful feature of embroidery in the Near and Middle East. Elaborate calligraphy is also seen in Russian needlework.
6. Kunsthistorisches Museum. See also *The Connoisseur,* March 1977. Robert L Wyss, 'The Dukes of Burgundy and the encouragement of textiles in the Netherlands.'
7. Ibid.
8. The Worshipful Companies of Merchant Taylors (2), Fishmongers, Ironmongers, Parish Clerks, Brewers, Saddlers and Vintners. The pall from Dunstable Priory is in the Victoria and Albert Museum.

*325. A panel with bizarre patterns and chinoiseries,
St Cyr, France, c.1730.*

9 This true coat of arms was part of two sets of insignia carried in front of the procession, on his instructions at his funeral: 'two destriers covered with our arms and two armed men in our arms and in our helms… that is to say, one for war with our full quartered arms and the other for peace with our badges of ostrich plumes…'. The arms for peace were for the tournament.
10 Quoted from a document by Margaret Swain, *Historical Needlework,* 1970.

CHAPTER THREE

Epigram: Chaucer, *The Book of the Duchess,* 252-3
1 The everlasting knot of life pattern is also one of the auspicious symbols of Buddhism, found throughout Asia.
2 These are discussed by Santina Levy, 'Rich and rare in silk: A little-known embroidery in the grotesque style', *Apollo,* April 1994.
3 George Wingfield Digby, *Elizabethan Embroidery,* 1963, lists pattern books.
4 Shakespeare, *Othello,* 3,iii.
5 See Janet Arnold *The Secrets of Queen Elizabeth's Wardrobe Unlocked,* 1987.
6 Inventory of Royal Wardrobe at the Palace of Holyrood, Edinburgh, February, 1562.
7 An inventory of the wardrobe of Queen Catherine includes; 'item: One paire of shetys of fyne Hollande clothe, wroughte with Spanysshe worke of blacke silk upon the egies'.
8 A splendid portrait of Captain Thomas Lee by Marcus Gheeraerdts, dated 1594, shows him dressed in masque costume, as an Irish Knight with bare legs for walking through bogs. He is however wearing a shirt of elaborate and beautiful blackwork. (Tate Gallery, London.) (See Plate 141.)

The Art of Embroidery

9 Shakespeare, *Titus Andronicus,* 2.iv.
10 Wife of Henry VII.
11 Margaret Swain, *Figures on Fabric,* 1980.
12 See examples in Landes Museum, Zürich, including one dated 1533.
13 Heylin, *History of the Reformation,* 1661.
14 *Travels in England,* 1598.
15 Hangings of a similar technique are at Berkeley Castle, Gloucestershire.
16 Roy Strong, *Mary Queen of Scots,* 1972.
17 Calendar of Scottish Papers II, 632, no. 1020.
18 An early example with intricately worked European figures and oriental animals is in the Isabella Stewart Gardner Museum, Boston. Another is in the Cooper-Hewitt Museum, New York. See also Irwin Hall *Indian Embroideries,* Calico Museum. Another with red embroidery is in the Victoria and Albert Museum.
19 Kremlin Museum, Moscow.
20 Macramé fringes had earlier been established in Italy, being derived from those on Turkish towels, the Turkish word 'macrama' meaning towel.

CHAPTER FOUR

Epigram: crewelwork bed curtains in honour of the Old Pretender, the self-styled James III of England, married in 1719, and father of 'Bonnie Prince Charlie'.

326. A firescreen panel with a vase full of delightfully rambling flowers. English 1750.

1 See John Fowler and John Cornforth, *English Decoration in the 18th Century*, for this and other funeral decorations.
2 Hugh Roberts, *Journal of Furniture History Society*, 1989.
3 *Country Life*, 29 January and 5 February 1981. Judith Banister 'Rewards of High Office'.
4 Illustrated *Country Life* 11 July 1987.
5 *The Dictionary of English Furniture*, Ralph Edwards, 1954, 'Settees', fig.6.

CHAPTER FIVE

Epigram: Samuel Pepys
1 A similar panel in the Cooper-Hewitt Museum, New York is thought to be Italian or Spanish.
2 Therle Hughes, *English Domestic Needlework*, n.d., p.21.
3 *Apollo*, August 1988.
4 Other hangings of this type are in the Benaki Museum, Mount Athos Museum and the State Russian Museum, St Petersburg.
5 Bought by Lord Yarmouth for George IV in 1815, silk embroidery on linen. At Buckingham Palace, *The Annunciation*, at Hampton Court, *The Massacre of the Innocents* (after Tintoretto), *The Rest on the Flight into Egypt* (after Bourdon), *Christ in the House of Simon the Leper*, and one more.
6 The Metropolitan Museum of Art, *Bulletin*, Spring 1989, 'French Decorative Arts during the reign of Louis XIV'.
7 Howard Coutts 'Hangings For a Royal Court', *Country Life* 13 October 1988.
8 Quoted on the endpapers of *The Needleworker's Dictionary*, Pamela Clabburn, 1976.
9 Marcus B Huish, *Samplers and Tapestry Embroideries*, 1900.
10 *Apollo* February, 1977. Margaret H. Swain, 'Embroidered Pictures from Engraved Sources', citing examples in the Burrell Collection.
11 Royal Scottish Museum, Edinburgh, Fitzwilliam Museum, Cambridge, Victoria and Albert Museum, London respectively.
12 Bacon's awareness of needlework is reflected in his Essay no.V Of Adversity: '…Prosperity is not without many fears and distastes; and adversity is not without comforts and hopes. We see in needleworks and embroideries, it is more pleasing to have a lively work upon a sad and solemn ground, than to have a dark and melancholy work upon a lightsome ground: judge, therefore of the pleasure of the heart by the pleasure of the eye'.
13 A modern bed hung with early coral-red crewelwork is at Stonor Park, Oxfordshire.
14 See guidebook to Drayton House by Gervase Jackson-Stops and his article, *Country Life*, 13 October 1988. Also *Apollo*, January 2000, Geoffrey Beard and Bruce Bailey 'Two State Beds: Belvoir and Drayton'.
15 Quilts are listed in spellings varied from *cowltes* to *qwhiltez*. The word is derived from the Latin *culcita*, a stuffed sack mattress or cushion.
16 Queen Mary was followed also, according to Tindal, 'by all sorts of ladies of distinction throughout the kingdom, and so fashionable was labour of a sudden grown that not only assembly rooms, but the streets, the roads, nay the very playhouses were witness to their pretty industry.'

CHAPTER SIX

Epigram: Psalm 45 'My heart is inditing of a good matter' (Coronation anthem).
1 Roy Strong and Julia Trevelyan Oman, *Elizabeth R*, 1971
2 *Country Life*, 6 February 1953. Sylvia Groves, 'The Practice of Parfilage'.
3 *Letters from Georgian Ireland:* The Correspondence of Mary Delany, 1731-68.
4 The design is in the Cooper-Hewitt Museum.
5 Margaret Lambert and Enid Marx, *English Popular and Traditional Art*, 1946, p.34.

CHAPTER SEVEN

Epigram: W Cooper, *The Task*, 1784.
1 *Country Life* 22 January 1976. Michael Archer, 'Pyramids and Pagodas for Flowers'.
2 *Apollo* (date unknown) Margaret H. Swain, 'The Mellerstain Panel'.
3 'Knotting and Stringwork', Margaret Swain, *Embroidery*, Summer 1982, p.38.
4 *Textile Collections of the World* Vol.2, Natalie Rothstein.
5 The carpet, though similar, was probably made professionally and somewhat later. Another remarkable achievement may be noted, a set of bed hangings, six chairs, a carpet and window curtains made by Mrs Jennens, c.1731, for the great Parlour Chamber at Weston Hall, Northamptonshire. Partly illustrated in *Country Life* 22 January 1976 in an article on the house by Francis Barnford.
6 *Country Life* XCIII, 21 May 1943, Fig.8, p 927.
7 George Edwards, *Natural History of Uncommon Birds and Gleanings of Natural History*, 1776, but earlier in parts.
8 Margaret Swain, 'Stitching Triumphant', *Country Life*, 21 March 1991.
9 *Country Life* CXXIX, 1 June 1961, p.1271, Fig.4.
10 *Country Life* 31 May, 1990, p.148.
11 This larger example, also derived from an engraving, and also incorporating a lengthy inscription, is illustrated in a catalogue, Jonathan Harris, *Works of Art*, June 1995 (Plate 187).
12 Christie's South Kensington, 4 December 1979, Lot 61.
13 Quoted by Anne Sebba, *Samplers*, 1979.
14 Illustrated by Huish, op.cit.
15 Hayden, Ruth, *Mrs Delany, Her Life and Flowers*, 1980.
16 *Letters from Georgian Ireland:* The Correspondence of Mary Delany, 1731-68. There are several other interesting references to embroidery etc.
17 There is a group of five aprons at Dyrham Park, Avon.
18 Francis Drouais' portrait of her (1763) shows her in a fine embroidered dress and working at a tambour frame (National Gallery, London).
19 See for example a finely worked sofa cover at Waddesdon Manor, Buckinghamshire.
20 William Shenstone.
21 *Embroidery*, Winter, 1991.
22 Margaret Swain, *Figures on Fabric*, p.69.

The Art of Embroidery

23 Anne Elizabeth Morritt (d.1797), see *Country Life* CXI, 7 March 1952.

CHAPTER EIGHT

Epigram: Francis North (1637-1685), first Baron Guildford, concerning his industrious wife's needlework.
1 Margaret Swain, *Treasures In Trust,* HMSO for National Trust for Scotland, 1981.
2 'Costers' were wall hangings.
3 A Flemish ebony and tortoiseshell cabinet inset with needlework panels appeared, for example, in a sale at Christie's, 11 December 1980.
4 Illustrated, H.H. Mulliner *The Decorative Arts in England,* 1923.
5 Sotheby's, 16 November 1984.
6 See Christie's catalogues Thursday 27 March 1958 (lot 101), 23 May 1963 and Thursday 30 June 1977 (lot 31a) for details and references. Also described and illustrated by H. Clifford Smith, F.S.A., *Connoisseur* April 1957, p172.
7 *Country Life* 21 March, 1991, article by Margaret Swain.
8 *Country Life* CXX 28 March 1957.
9 *Country Life* LXXXIX 23 May 1936, p 534.
10 A cabriole leg chair (ex Percival Griffiths collection) with similar needlework was sold at Christie's, 7 April 1983, amongst others known.
11 Margaret Swain, *Figures on Fabric,* p.69.
12 Illustrated by Margaret Swain, *Treasures in Trust,* p.64.
13 Eight chairs and a sofa from Faulkbourne Hall, Essex, with a red floral pattern on a blue background.
14 Sotheby's Parke Bernet, 25 April 1981 (lot 71). See also *The Connoisseur* March 1964, J.F. Hayward, 'An English Suite of Furniture with embroidered covers'.
15 Illustrated, Fowler and Cornforth, *English Decoration in 18th Century,* p.158.
16 Ibid. Adam, in his provision for every element of a room, even designed a needlework bag for Mrs Childe of Osterley, to contain her knotting shuttle (Soane Museum).
17 One illustrated on a chair, Hope Hanley *Needlework Styles for Period Furniture,* p.63.
18 Macquoid and Edwards *The Dictionary of English Furniture,* 'Chimney Furniture', figs.20 and 22.

CHAPTER NINE

Epigram: Lord de Tabley, *The Soldier of Fortune.*
1 Mallett & Son, 1979. A similar sampler of the following year was clearly worked under the same instructress, though the family names are different.
2 Brontë Parsonage Museum, Yorkshire
3 E. Mairet. *Vegetable Dyes,* London, 1939. Also S. Robinson, *A History of Dyed Textiles,* London 1969, and *Penguin Guide to the Decorative Arts.*
4 M.T. Morrall, *A History of Needlemaking,* 1852.
5 The log cabin pattern is made up of bars of material graded in length, and sewn together around a smaller square piece.

6 Rosemary Ewles, in The Royal School of Needlework *Book of Needlework and Embroidery,* ed. Lanto Synge.
7 Sotheby's *Art at Auction,* 1987-88.
8 Irish Patchwork exhibition and catalogue, Kilkenny Design Workshops, 1979.
9 Christie's South Kensington, 29 April 1980.
10 There is a curtain of felt patchwork at Bamburgh Castle, Northumberland. For further examples see Margaret Swain, *Figures on Fabric.*
11 One of two fine smocks made for the Great Exhibition (1851) is to be seen at Abingdon Museum, Oxfordshire.
12 Thomas Hood, *The Story of the Shirt.*
13 John Milton, *Lycidas.*
14 *Handbook of Embroidery,* 1880.
15 William Morris, *Hints on Pattern Designing,* a lecture given in 1881.
16 Linda Parry, *William Morris Textiles,* 1983.
17 G.E. Street, lecture to Durham Architectural Society. Printed in *The Ecclesiologist,* vol. XXI 1863.

CHAPTER TEN

Epigram: Inventory of Elizabeth I's wardrobe, 1600.
1 *The Story of Silk,* Dr. John Feltwell, 1990. The author explains how silk was brought not only from East to West but was taken across the Pacific to the Americas, and from Europe was introduced to the English colonies in North America by James I shortly after silkworms were brought to England.
2 *Huangchao liqi tushi: Illustrated Precedents for the Ritual Paraphernalia of the Imperial Court,* 1759. In 1766 there was a printed edition with 6,000 illustrations and 5,000 pages of text. Finely executed paintings on silk form the original work in the Victoria and Albert Museum and in other collections illustrate the requirements of the robes with great accuracy.
3 Gary Dickinson and Linda Wrigglesworth, *Imperial Wardrobe,* 1990, definitive in this field.
4 Summer robes of gauze were worn over a light white undergarment of 'grass linen' (ramie) made from a stingless nettle. Winter garments were sometimes lined with fleece and were often trimmed with mink or sable around the opening edges.
5 John E. Vollmer, *In the Presence of the Dragon Throne,* Royal Ontario Museum, Canada 1977.
6 In a repeated joined-up form it makes a fretwork pattern. A yellow embroidered version of this on a fine blue robe in the Victoria and Albert Museum gives the garment the overall impression of being yellow.
7 The five specific colours used in Qing imperial robes: blue, red, yellow, black and purple (or white) also represented the five 'activities' – the elements.
8 *Hali* 43, February 1989: Jacqueline Simcox, 'Silks from the Middle Kingdom'.
9 *Hali* 58, August 1991: Sailer, p.64.
10 John Cornforth, 'A Role for Chinoiserie', *Country Life,* 7 December 1989, describes and illustrates examples of Chinese, Indian and English chinoiserie decoration at Milton, Northamptonshire; Saltram, Devon; and Osterley, Middlesex.

11 *A State Bed from Erthig,* John Hardy, Sheila Landi and Charles D. Wright, Victoria and Albert Museum, London, 1972. The conservation of the bed is described.
12 Illustrated *Country Life* 25 November 1982.

CHAPTER ELEVEN

1 *Treasures of Indian Textiles,* Calico Museum, Ahmedabad, 1980, p.59, Pupul Jayakar 'Indian Textiles through the centuries'.
2 See John Guy and Deborah Swallow (eds.), *Arts of India 1550-1900,* Victoria and Albert Museum, 1990.
3 The Mughal emperor Aurangzeb (1658-1707) is shown at prayer on a very similar carpet in a miniature painting illustrated in *Hali,* December 1990, 'Textiles in Indian Miniatures', Valerie Berinstain. The relatively simple design reflects the austere ideals of the emperor.
4 See John Irwin and P.R. Schwartz, *Studies in Indo-European Textile History,* Calico Museum of Textiles, Ahmedabad, 1966.
5 Included in the 1782 Osterley Park inventory and illustrated in a guidebook, *Osterley Park,* Eileen Harris, National Trust, 1994, p.49.
6 There is a comparable coverlet at Hardwick Hall, Derbyshire, of similar format. Cf. *Art and the East India Trade,* John Irwin, Victoria and Albert Museum, London 1970, pl.4.
7 *Arts of India,* op.cit. The Age of the Mughals p.75.
8 The early eighteenth century tent of Maharajah Abhaisinghji of Jodhpur is illustrated in Charles Allen and Sharada Dwivedi, *Lives of the Indian Princes,* 1984, p.146.
9 John Irwin and Margaret Hall, *Indian Embroideries,* Vol. 2, Calico Museum Ahmedabad, 1973 – a seminal work.

CHAPTER TWELVE

Epigram: W. Wordsworth, *Lines composed a few miles above Tintern Abbey.*

1 See *Latest Country Houses,* John Martin Robinson.
2 To be seen at the D-Day Museum, Portsmouth.
3 New Forest District Council, Lyndhurst, Hampshire.
4 There was a similar scheme at Guildford Cathedral.
5 Further good examples of needlework cushions and hassocks can be seen at Girton College, Cambridge and in many churches. At the Community of the Resurrection, Mirfield, there is a 'tapestry' derived from a mediaeval manuscript.
6 Note colours in flowers as gifts and symbols of seasons. See *English Liturgical Colours,* Sir W.St.J. Hope and E.G.C.F. Atchley, SPCK, 1918. Also catalogue, *Korean Embroideries,* Victoria and Albert Museum, 1984. C.f. also the symbolism of colours in heraldry.

327. Turkish metal and silk embroidery, c.1830.

GLOSSARY

ACUPICTURA Needlepainting; embroidery representing subject in as accurate detail as possible and resembling painting, or imitating it.

ALBUM QUILT Patchwork, usually American, made up of a number of sections contributed by various individuals, each designed by the sewer and sometimes signed. Often for presentation.

AMICE White linen band worn by priests at the service of the Eucharist. At the collar sometimes embroidered. *See* Apparel.

APPAREL 1. Clothes in general. 2. Bands of embroidery for decorating ecclesiastical garments.

APPLIED WORK, APPLIQUÉ Cut out pieces of fabric laid and stitched on to another in patchwork form. An ancient and continuously popular technique.

ARABESQUE Low-relief decoration in form of scrolls, interlacing strapwork, curving lines, sometimes with animal and leaf motifs. Of oriental and Moorish origin, especially introduced through carpets.

ASSISI EMBROIDERY Needlework that originated in Assisi in north Italy characterised by formal designs, the motifs left unworked against a background entirely filled in with cross-stitch.

BARGELLO *See* Florentine stitch. Said to be so called on account of four chairs in Bargello Museum, Florence, covered with zig-zag needlework. Others link it with work done at Bargello prison. A modern term.

BAROQUE Grand classical and sculptural style of the second half of the seventeenth century, sometimes heavily ornate, always lively; aspect of late-Renaissance florid flourish in contrast to earlier strict classicism. Associated with lavish use of metal thread work and with bold crewelwork designs.

BEETLE WINGS Used as sequins for luminosity, in ethnic, American and English costume embroidery.

BIZARRE pattern Very exotic forms, originally in silk weaving c.1700, with highly asymmetric and irregular shapes, curious flower and fruit forms, creatures and colours.

BLACKWORK (SPANISH WORK) Monochrome embroidery usually in black, sometimes enriched with metal threads, fashionable in sixteenth century and brought to Europe through Spain by the Moors.

BLANKET STITCH Similar to button hole stitch (q.v.) but with the loops spaced out; often used for edging as on wool blankets.

BOKERAM (Mediaeval) Derived from Bokhara, original source, fine cotton cloth.

BROADCLOTH Famed English wool cloth, given the softness and appearance of felt by brushing.

BROCADE Woven textile with varied materials and pattern, with metal threads, silks etc.

BRODERIE ANGLAISE Mid-nineteenth century cutwork, white embroidery characterised by oval and round holes in light cotton fabric, closely edged with stitching, and with some additional padded satin stitch embroidery. A coloured version adopted in Madeira.

BURATO Whitework darning on gauze or net. Compare with net laces, filet or lacis (q.v.).

BURSE (Corporal case) Ecclesiastical: stiff, square pocket to contain linen cloth (corporal) used at Holy Communion; also formal bag, as carried by the Lord Chancellor, for example, often elaborately embroidered, in which a seal is carried.

BUTTONHOLE STITCH Simple loop-stitch, one of the oldest and most popular, especially suited for edgings, but its chain form has been applied to all forms of embroidery.

CALICO Cotton cloth, originally from Calicut on the west coast of India.

CAMBRIC Linen material, originally from Cambrai in Flanders; also more generally applied to cotton, or cotton and linen fabric.

CAMOCA Fabric with combination of fine camel hair and wool.

CANVAS Strong, unbleached cloth of hemp or flax, as sailcoth, for tents and for painting on. Open mesh variety of wool, linen, hemp, cotton or jute used for needlework. Berlin canvas was of a silk covered weave as the background was left unworked. A canvas of double threads was introduced in the 1830s (*see* Penelope), though multiple threads had been used in the seventeenth century.

CANVAS WORK All over embroidery done in regular counted stitches over the threads of a ground fabric.

CHAIN STITCH The chief of many linked, loop stitches. Ancient and universal, it has been used for outlines and infilling, and is done either with a needle, or hook ('ari' in India), and in France on a drum frame ('tambour'). Quickly made, it is frequently the only stitch used in sizeable hangings; in small workmanship lends itself to shading. Also made by early sewing machines.

CHASUBLE Vestment worn by priest officiating at the Eucharist; a large, almost circular garment, in the Middle Ages often magnificently embroidered. In the sixteenth century the shape altered to a long round-ended vestment, leaving the arms free of the heavy material.

CHENILLE Soft, fluffy thread, usually silk, though also of cotton or wool, with furry appearance like a caterpillar (French *chenille* = caterpillar). Used from about 1770, chiefly for small contrasting areas in conjunction with plainer canvas and embroidery stitching.

CHINOISERIE European imitation of Chinese decoration in lacquer, needlework etc., often recognisable by caricatured features.

CLOTH OF GOLD Rich fabric, generally of silk, with gold threads woven into it.

COIF (QUOIF) Close-fitting cap worn by men and women

340

from the Middle Ages to the early seventeenth century, latterly finely embroidered; worn on semi-formal and domestic occasions.

COLIFICHET Floss silk embroidery on paper.

COPE Ecclesiastical cloak worn by dignitaries on festal occasions, a large semi-circular garment often of rich materials or fine embroidery. *See also* pluvial.

CORNUCOPIA Horn of plenty. Motif showing a curved horn filled with an abundance of flowers, fruit, etc.

COUCHING Technique whereby a thread is laid over fabric and attached to it by an additional one sewn over it. Technique especially used for metal threads. *See also or nué,* underside couching.

COUNTED THREAD STITCHES As opposed to freehand embroidery stitches, these are regular ones based on a build-up of simple stitches over an equal number of threads in canvas or fabric.

CREWEL (CRUL, CRUEL, CREWELS ETC.) -WORK, -WOOL Strong, two-ply, lightly twisted, worsted yarn of home manufacture, extensively used for domestic embroidery of hangings, furnishings and costume since the Norman Conquest.

CROSS-STITCH *(gros point)* Simple and ancient double stitch in the form of an X, used in almost every part of the world.

CUTWORK *(opus scissum)* Forerunner of needlepoint laces in sixteenth and seventeenth centuries and extensively revived in the nineteenth century. Parts of white fabric are cut away and then infilled by patterns of crossed threads, with elaborate variations.

DALMATIC Ecclesiastical vestment worn by deacon at Eucharist, normally a short tunic. A historic garment also worn by the sovereign at coronation ceremony.

DAMASK Fabric of silk originally, but also of linen etc., with woven design in same colour. Originally associated with Damascus.

DARNED EMBROIDERY Simple oversewing, popular especially in the eighteenth century for silk pictures of birds, fruit, flowers etc.

DARNING SAMPLER Sampler specifically exercising varieties of darning methods and patterns; popular in England in the late eighteenth century, perhaps introduced from Holland.

DIMITY Stout cotton fabric, usually having a stripe pattern in the weave, used undyed for hangings.

DOSSAL Curtain, or hanging, placed behind altar or around chancel, sometimes embroidered.

DOUBLE RUNNING (HOLBEIN) STITCH The chief stitch of blackwork (represented in Holbein drawings) whereby lines of embroidery are made up by measured stitches in one direction and completed by infilling stitches in the return. *See* running stitch.

DRAWN-THREAD WORK Needlework that forms patterns by pulling threads of fabric aside or out, the resulting holes forming design.

DRESDEN EMBROIDERY *(point de Saxe)* Fine, drawn-thread work on muslin as less expensive alternative to lace in the eighteenth century.

ERMINE STITCH A detached stitch for speckling background, consisting of a long stitch superimposed with a cross-stitch, often in metal thread, on velvet, silk or satin.

EYELET STITCHES Small stitches worked outwards from a central point, forming little rings. Often seen forming lettering in samplers.

FEATHER STITCH A coral or fern-like stitch, composed of blanket stitches forming zig-zag links along a line. See also long-and-short stitch for a different variety of the same name.

FILET Hand knotted cloth, like traditional fishnet, with darned designs.

FLORENTINE (HUNGARIAN, BARGELLO, FLAME) STITCH Work in wavy, zig-zag design on canvas in shaded colours. Forms effective pattern for wall hangings, bed curtains and upholstery. Originated in Hungary in the late Middle Ages, and later practised in Italy and most of Europe. Modern varieties equally timeless and effective.

FLOSS SILK Soft, untwisted silk of fine strands from the outer part of a silkworm's cocoon.

FRENCH KNOT Knot-like stitch usually used in close formation for flower centres, depicting sheep etc. Chinese Pekin knots are similar; this 'forbidden stitch' was so finely worked that the sewer would eventually go blind, especially so with whitework perhaps.

FUSTIAN Thick, cotton twill, sometimes with linen warp, woven like velvet with a sheared surface brushed with teasels. Probable origin of velvet. Name derived from Fostat, suburb of Cairo.

GALON or GALLOON Trimming braid used for uniforms, upholstery etc., of silk, wool or metal threads, or of lace.

GOBELIN STITCH An almost vertical stitch which in rows gives the semblance of woven tapestry.

GOLD THREAD Is made of finely beaten-out gold, wrapped around silk thread. Pure gold was used in the early Middle Ages but later silver-gilt replaced it, the expanding silver carrying a sufficient coating of gold to a greater extent. An alternative was the use of fine gold leaf laid on thin animal tissue.

GROS POINT Cross stitch (q.v.). Loosely used as term for coarser canvas work.

GROTESQUES Derived from Roman ornamental decoration, revived by Raphael, related to arabesques (q.v.). Linear and curvaceous fantasies with animals, figures, birds, flowers etc. developed by Jean Bérain.

GUIPURE D'ART Darned net. *See* lacis.

HASSOCK Church kneeler, especially favoured object for modern needlework.

HOLBEIN STITCH *See* double running-stitch.

HOLLAND Linen

HUNGARIAN STITCH *See* Florentine stitch.

IRISH STITCH A long and short stitch, as Florentine stitch, a term particularly used in U.S.A.

KNOTTING Craft carried out with a shuttle, producing knotted threads of string, linen or other materials, then laid and couched on a ground fabric in border form, or in patterns. Practised in the late seventeenth and early eighteenth centuries for hangings, chair coverings etc.

LACIS Handmade netting darned with patterns, with coarse lace-like appearance, but very ancient in itself, and often highly complex. Designs often in squares, of a stylised nature, following pattern books. Also known as *filet, guipure d'art,* etc.

LAIDWORK Long threads, sometime floss silk, laid on fabric and fixed at points by couching threads, at regular or irregular intervals. *See* couching.

LAWN Fine, light-weight, white fabric, originally linen, more recently cotton, used for baby clothes, handkerchiefs, bishops' sleeves, etc.

LINEN Age-old type of cloth of exceptional comfort and durability made of flax fibres.

LONG-AND-SHORT-STITCH Old and continuously used simple stitch used in silks and wools. The outer row is of alternately longer and shorter stitches, but rows built within this, in brick fashion, are of equal sized stitches. Also known as feather stitch *(opus plumarium),* etc.

LONG-ARMED CROSS-STITCH Cross-stitch where the first of the two stitches is twice the length of the second. Hence a series of stitches gives a woven effect.

MANIPLE *En suite* with a stole, a shorter strip of material, sometimes embroidered, worn by a priest over his left forearm at the Eucharist. A symbol of the towel used by Christ at the washing of the feet of His disciples.

MANTLE Cloak, sometimes ceremonial. Heraldic mantling, like foliage, around a coat of arms represents a mantle shredded through gallantry in battle. Also, the richly decorated cover placed over the Scroll in Jewish ceremonies.

NACRE WORK Embroidery with small pieces of mother-of-pearl.

OPUS ANGLICANUM Very fine English needlework for vestments, especially c.1250-1350.

OPUS CONSCUTUM Appliqué.

OPUS PECTINEUM Woven or combed work.

OPUS PHRYGIUM Gold work.

OPUS TEUTONICUM Mediaeval German whitework, in contrast to the bejewelled and colourful embroidery of other countries, especially England.

OR NUÉ Shaded gold embroidery. Technique whereby gold threads are laid horizontally, couched-down with coloured silk threads at densely close intervals where dark shades are required, and sparsely for lighter areas, forming shading in a pictorial design.

ORPHREY Band, usually of embroidery, superimposed in cross or 'Y' formation, or as border, on chasuble, cope, etc.

PAISLEY PATTERN Takes its name from Paisley in Scotland where imitations of Indian fabrics were made in the nineteenth century. The characteristic motif of a tapering and curved lob is anciently derived from a buta, a pine cone, mango or kind of plant.

PALAMPORE Indian dyed, painted (latterly printed) cotton hangings or cover for export to Europe.

PANE(S) Jointed widths of materials in strips as for hangings, or in making up a counterpane. Also the formal slashes in sixteenth century costume, allowing under-fabric to be seen.

PANED Striped, as in curtain hangings. (French: *pentes.*)

PASSEMENTERIE Earliest narrow pointed edgings which appeared in fashion after the development of punto in aria (q.v.)

PEKIN KNOT Like French knot (q.v.), but more loop-like in appearance.

PENELOPE CANVAS Canvas of threads woven in parallel pairs invented in 1830s and named after the wife of Ulysses who spent nights unpicking work done during the day, in the absence of her husband.

PETIT POINT Tent-stitch (q.v.). Usually applied to finer work only.

PIQUÉ Embroidery where the design is outlined with cord and infilled with stitches resembling a figured fabric.

PINKING Decoration of material by cutting, or punching holes or pattern in it, to reveal under material, or along edges to prevent fraying.

PLUSH STITCH Loop-stitch, taking its name from plush fabric, which has a long nap in excess of that of velvet. Loops may be left or trimmed to various degrees to give sculptural effect.

PLUVIAL Ceremonial cloak or cope (q.v.)

PORTIÈRE Curtain or hanging to cover a door, sometimes of needlework.

POPLIN A plain woven fabric, usually cotton, with a corded surface.

POUNCE Method of transferring design (and the powder used), whereby pattern is 'pricked' out and charcoal dust, or another kind, is rubbed through the perforations on to fabric, to mark it.

PUNTO IN ARIA Earliest form of needlelace made on a parchment pattern (literally, 'stitches in the air').

PURL Seventeenth century metal thread embroidery, and the thread itself.

RATIONAL (PECTORAL) Metal or embroidered panel worn by bishop at church ceremonies, derived from Jewish High Priest's breastplate.

RICHELIEU Late nineteenth century openwork white linen embroidery where some of the material is cut away.

ROCOCO STITCH Groups of about three of four straight stitches tied together by a binding stitch across the middle producing the effect of small holes between each group.

RUNNING STITCH Simple continuous linear weaving in and out of fabric at regular intervals. *See* double running-stitch.

SAMITE Prized mediaeval fabric, probably a heavy silk with twill weave, often embroidered.

SARCENET A fine, light silk fabric, first made by the Saracens.

SATIN Twill-weave fabric of silk or other materials made flossy by being calendered (passed through heavy rollers), which process could also produce a moiré, or watered appearance. Originally from Zaitun in China.

SATIN-STITCH Straight parallel stitch, a mass of them giving a flat, shiny, satin appearance.

SCRIM Fine, open-weave, brown linen canvas, much of it imported from Russia.

SERICULTURE Silk farming.

SLIP Motif derived from a gardener's cutting; a sprig with flowers, buds or fruit with a few leaves and often a heel for planting. Used as a spot motif (q.v.).

SPANGLE Small glittering object of various materials, usually metal, attached to embroidery for sparkling effect.

SPLIT STITCH Very fine stitch worked in untwisted silk thread

where each stitch pierces the thread giving a tiny, fine chain-stitch appearance. Used for delicate detailing, as of facial features in *opus anglicanum*.
SPOT MOTIF Individual motif such as floral slip (q.v.), animal, insect, etc., usually on linen or canvas, to be cut out, often for applying to another material.
STEM STITCH Outline stitch where continuous back stitches each partly overlap in following the line.
STOLE Long narrow band, often of needlework, worn by priests at Eucharist and other church services.
STRAPWORK Type of decoration in form of interlacing curved and angular bands in regular patterns, derived from Moorish and oriental sources. *See* arabesque.
TABARD Herald's garment blazoned with the sovereign's arms.
TABBY Watered fabric, especially silk, brindled, streaked – as cat.
TABBY WEAVE Plain over and under weave.
TAFFETA Thin silk cloth, sometimes now of other materials, even man-made.
TATTING A form of knotting or stringwork, done with a shuttle, eighteenth and nineteenth centuries.
TENT-STITCH Plain, diagonal stitch across one thread of canvas or other material. May be worked in horizontal rows or diagonally, usually the former.
TESTER Originally the part of a large, canopied bed at the head end, reaching from the pillows to the roof; later the canopy itself, whether suspended over the bed or supported by four posts, also sometimes listed as the 'celour'.
TICKING Closely woven, twill fabric of linen or cotton, chiefly used for containing down in pillows, and hair in mattresses. For the former it is soaped on the inside.
TRAM Weft (q.v.) Also preparatory laid-thread on canvas to pad out stitches and to cover rawness of canvas where it might show between stitches.
TRAPUNTO Form of quilting where a soft padding is inserted through the under material, after the quilting stitches have been done, to emphasise a relief design. In Italian quilting a cord is inserted in the same way between parallel lines of stitching.
TROMPE L'OEIL Pictorial deception making the spectator think he is looking at the actual subject depicted, rather than a representation. Playing cards, counters, etc. are sometimes embroidered on the lining of card tables, for example.
TURKEY WORK Post-mediaeval wool knotting in carpet form, in imitation of imported oriental ones, used for upholstering furniture etc.
TWILL Fabric in which weft threads pass over one warp thread and under two or more, producing diagonal lines in the weave.
UNDERSIDE COUCHING Mediaeval method of attaching laid threads whereby no couching threads are visible on surface or prone to wear. The securing threads are stitched over the metal one and then pulled back to the underside of the fabric holding a loop of thread.
WARP AND WEFT The interlaced threads in weaving, the former fastened lengthways in the loom and the latter woven at right angles through them.
WHITEWORK General term applied to needlework of white threads on white or natural ground; Ayrshire embroidery, etc.
WORSTED Yarn of sheep's wool, where long-stapled fibres are combed parallel and closely twisted.
ZARDOSI Metal thread embroidery.
ZEPHYR MERINO WOOL Berlin wool, firstly produced in Gotha, Germany, and dyed in Berlin for woolwork; popular in the nineteenth century. Later also made in England.

328. A small satin cushion with silk embroidery, English c.1660.

BIBLIOGRAPHY

Reading good descriptions of old textiles can be nearly as enjoyable for a reasonably experienced enthusiast as seeing them. I have referred to the following and am indebted to all of them.

Alexander, Jonathan and Paul Binski (eds.), *Age of Chivalry Art in Plantagenet England. 1200-1400,* Royal Academy of Arts, London 1987 (article by Donald King).

Alford, Lady Marion, *Needlework as Art,* London 1886, republished 1975.

Armstead, K.M., *English Samplers and Embroidered Pictures,* Bristol (City Art Gallery), n.d.

Arnold, Janet, *The Secrets of Queen Elizabeth's Wardrobe Unlocked,* W.S. Maney, 1987.

Ashton, Leigh, *Samplers, Selected and Described,* London 1970.

Baker, Muriel, *Stumpwork: The Art of Raised Embroidery,* New York and London 1978.

Bath, Virginia Churchill, *Needlework in America,* New York 1979.

Baumgarten, Linda R. 'Costumes and textiles in the collection of Cora Ginsburg', *Antiques,* August 1988, p.261.

Beard, Geoffrey, 'Some Eighteenth-Century English Seats and Covers Re-Examined', *Antiques,* June 1994, p.842.

Beck, Thomasina, *The Embroiderer's Flowers,* London 1992.

Beck, Thomasina, *Embroidered Gardens,* London 1979.

Benn, Elizabeth (ed.), *Treasures from the Embroiderers' Guild Collection,* David and Charles 1991.

Bridgeman, Harriet, and Elizabeth Drury (ed.), *Needlework: an Illustrated History,* London 1978.

Brown, Deborah and Margaret Fawdry, *The Book of Samplers,* London 1980.

Browne, Clare and Jennifer Wearden, *Samplers from the Victoria and Albert Museum,* London 1999.

Butler, Anne, *The Batsford Encyclopaedia of Embroidery Stitches,* 1979.

Carbonell, Dorothy, *Winchester Cathedral Embroideries,* Winchester 1975.

Caulfield, S.F.A., *The Dictionary of Needlework,* 1882.

Christie, Mrs A.G.I., *English Medieval Embroidery,* Oxford 1938.

Christie, Mrs A.G.I., *Samplers and Stitches,* London 1921.

Christie, Mrs A.G.I., *Embroidery and Tapestry Weaving,* London 1909.

Clabburn, Pamela, *Samplers,* Shire Album booklet, 1977.

Clabburn, Pamela, *The Needleworker's Dictionary,* London 1976.

Colby, A., *Patchwork,* London 1958.

Colby, A., *Samplers,* London 1964.

Cornforth, John, 'Stitching in Time', *Country Life,* 25 November 1982. (about conservation of textiles in major country houses). Also other articles on needlework.

Davis, Mildred J. (ed.), *The Dowell-Simpson Sampler,* Richmond, Virginia, 1975.

Dickinson, Gary and Linda Wrigglesworth, *Imperial Wardrobe,* 1990.

Dolby, Anastasia, *Church Embroidery, Ancient and Modern,* London 1867.

Earnshaw, Pat, *A Dictionary of Lace,* 1972.

329. A lutenist and a lady approached by cupid. English panels of about 1720.

Bibliography

Edwards, Joan, *Crewel Embroidery in England,* London 1973.
Edwards, J., *Bead Embroidery,* London 1966, New York 1972.
Edwards, Joan, *Sampler-Making 1540-1940,* Dorking (Bayford Books) 1983.
Edwards, Ralph, *The Dictionary of English Furniture,* 2nd revised ed., London 1954. Articles: Beds, Boxes, Carpets, Chairs, Cushions, Mirrors (Toilet), Needlework, Sconces, Screens, Settees and Sofas, Stools, Tables (Card and Gaming).
Eve, G.W., *Heraldry as Art,* London 1907.
Ewles, Rosemary (ed.), *One Man's Samplers,* The Goodhart Collection Exhibition, London 1983.
Fassett, Kaffe, *Glorious Inspiration,* Needlepoint Source Book, 1991.
Feltwell, Dr. John, *The Story of Silk,* Ian Sutton 1990.
Finch, Karen and Greta Putman, *Caring for Textiles,* London 1977.
Finley, R.E., *Old Patchwork Quilts and the Women who made them,* Philadelphia and London 1929.
Fitzrandolph, Mavis, *Traditional Quilting,* London 1954.
Fowler, John and John Cornforth, *English Decoration in the 18th Century,* 2nd ed., 1978.
Freeman, Margaret B., *The St Martin Embroideries,* Metropolitan Museum of Art, New York 1968.
Gibbs-Smith, Charles, *The Bayeux Tapestry: a comprehensive survey,* 2nd ed., London 1965.
Gilbert, Christopher, James Lomax and Anthony Wells-Cole, *Country House Floors 1660-1850,* 1987.
Girouard, Mark, *Life in the English Country House,* Yale University Press, 1978.
Gloag and Hackenbrock, *English Furniture,* Irwin Untermeyer Collection, 1958.
Gostelow, Mary, *Blackwork,* London 1976.
Gostelow, Mary, *Embroidery, Traditional designs, techniques and Patterns,* London 1977.
Grierson, Roderick (ed.), *Gates of Mystery, The Art of Holy Russia,* Lutterworth Press, Cambridge, 1993.
Guy, John and Deborah Swallow (eds.), *Arts of India 1550-1900,* Victoria and Albert Museum 1900.
Hackenbrook, Y., *English and other Needlework, Tapestries and Textiles in the Untermeyer Collection,* London 1960.
Hake E., *English Quilting, Old and New,* 1937.
Hall, Maggie, *Smocks,* Shire Album booklet, 1979.
Hanley, Hope, *Needlework Styles for Period Furniture,* New York 1978.
Harris, Eileen, *Osterley Park, Middlesex,* National Trust, 1994.
Harris, Jennifer (ed.), *5000 Years of Textiles,* British Museum 1980.
Hedlund, Catherine A., *A Primer of New England Crewel Embroidery,* Stourbridge, Mass., 1975.
Heynes, A., *Quilting and Patchwork,* Leicester Dryad Press, 1928.
Higgin, L., *Handbook of Embroidery,* ed. Lady Marion Alford, Royal School of Art Needlework 1880.
Howe, Margery Burnham, *Early American Embroideries in Deerfield,* Massachussetts, 1963.
Hughes, Therle, *English Domestic Needlework 1660-1860,* London n.d.
Huish, Marcus B., *Samplers and Tapestry Embroideries,* London 1900.
Humphrey, Carol (ed.), *English Samplers at the Fitzwilliam,* Exhibition 1984.
Irwin, John and Katherine B. Brett, *Origins of Chintz,* London 1970.
Irwin, J.C., *Indian Embroidery,* London 1951.

Irwin, J.C., and Hall, M., *Indian Embroideries,* Ahmedabad 1973.
Jenyns, R. Soame, *Chinese Art: Textiles, Glass…etc.,* Oxford 1981.
Johnstone, Pauline, *Three Hundred Years of Embroidery, 1600-1900 Treasures of the Embroiderer's Guild of Great Britain,* 1986.
Jones, Mary Eirwen, *A History of Western Embroidery,* Studio Vista, London 1969.
Jones, Mary Eirwen, *English Crewel Designs,* London 1974.
Jourdain, M., *English Secular Embroidery,* London 1910.
Jourdain, M., *Chinese Export Art in the 18th Century,* 1950.
Kendrick, A.F. *English Needlework,* 2nd ed., revised by Patricia Wardle, London 1967.
Kendrick, A.F., *Victoria and Albert Museum Catalogue* (4 vols.).
Kew, Rose (ed.), *Chinese Art and Design,* Victoria and Albert Museum, 1991.
King, D., *Opus Anglicanum,* Victoria and Albert Museum, London 1963.
King, D., *Samplers,* Victoria and Albert Museum, London 1960.
King, Donald and Santina Levey, *The Victoria and Albert Museum's Textile Collection: Embroidery in Britain from 1200 to 1750,* Victoria and Albert Museum, 1993.
Krueger, Glee F., *A Gallery of American Samplers,* New York 1980.
Le Moyne de Morgues, Jacques *The Work of Jacques Le Moyne de Morgues,* ed. Paul Hulton, British Museum 1977.
Levey, S. M., 'An Elizabethan Embroidered Cover', *Victoria and Albert Museum Yearbook 3,* 1972.
Levey, Santina M., *An Elizabethan Inheritance: The Hardwick Hall Textiles,* London 1998.
Longfield, Ada K., *Guide to the Collection of Lace,* National Museum of Ireland, Dublin 1970.
Lowes, Mrs, *Chats on Old Lace and Needlework,* London 1908.
Lubell, Cecil (ed.), *Textile Collections of the World,* Vol. 2, United Kingdom and Ireland, 1976.
Macquoid, Percy, *A Record of the Collections of the Lady Lever Art Gallery, Port Sunlight,* Vol. III, London 1928.
Mayorcas, M.J., *English Needlework Carpets,* Leigh-on-Sea 1963.
Meldrum, Alex and Laura Jones, *Irish Patchwork,* catalogue of an exhibition, Kilkenny Design Workshops, Dublin 1979.
Merian, Maria Sybilla, *The Wondrous Transformation of Caterpillars* (Scholar Press 1978). Fifty engravings selected from *Erucarum Ortis* (1718).
Metropolitan Museum of Art, The, 'French Decorative Arts during the reign of Louis XIV' *(Bulletin* 1989).
Millet, G., *Broderies religieuses de style byzantin,* Paris 1947.
Mulliner, H.H., *The Decorative Arts in England, 1660-1780,* 1923.
Morris, Barbara, *Victorian Embroidery,* London 1962.
Nevinson, J.L., *Catalogue of English Domestic Embroidery of the 16th and 17th century,* Victoria and Albert Museum, London 1938.
Nevinson, J.L., 'The Embroidery Patterns of Thomas Trevelyon', *The Walpole Society,* XLI 1966-8, pp.1-38 plus 36 plates.
Parry, Linda (ed.). *William Morris,* London 1996
Pesel, L.F., and Newberry, E.W., *A Book of Old Embroidery,* 1921.
Pjister, R., *Textiles de Palmyre,* Paris 1934.
Pjister, R., *Nouveaux Textiles de Palmyre,* Paris 1937.
Proctor, Molly G., *Victorian Canvas Work,* London 1972.
Ribeiro, Aileen, 'A Paradise of Flowers: Flowers in English Dress in the late sixteenth and early seventeenth centuries', *Connoisseur,* June 1979.

Ring, Betty (ed.), *Needlework, An Historical Survey,* New York, 1975.
Schroeser, Mary and Kathleen Dejardin, *French Textiles from 1760 to the present,* London 1991.
Scott, B., *The Craft of Quilting, with a note on patchwork,* Dryad, Leicester, 1928.
Scott, Philippa, *The Book of Silk,* London 1993.
Sebba, Anne, *Samplers; Five Centuries of Gentle Craft,* London 1979.
Seligman, G., and T. Hughes, *Domestic Needlework,* London, 1926.
Simeon, Margaret, *The History of Lace,* London 1979.
Snook, Barbara, *Embroidery Stitches,* Batsford 1963.
Staniland, Kay, *Medieval Craftsmen: Embroiderers,* British Museum Press 1991.
Stenton, Sir Frank (ed.) *Bayeux Tapestry: a comprehensive survey,* 2nd ed., 1965.
Strong, Roy, *The English Renaissance Miniature,* London 1983 (for Elizabethan costume).
Strong, Roy and Julia Trevelyan Oman, *Elizabeth R,* 1971.
Swain, Margaret, 'A Georgian Mystery: Lady Mary Hog and the Newliston Needlework', *Country Life,* 12 August 1982.
Swain, Margaret, *Figures on Fabric,* London 1980.
Swain, Margaret, *Historical Needlework: a Study of Influences in Scotland and Northern England,* London 1970.
Swain, Margaret, 'Knotting and Stringwork', *Embroidery,* Summer 1982.
Swain, Margaret, *The Flowerers,* 1955.
Swain, Margaret, *The Needlework of Mary Queen of Scots,* London 1973.
Swan, Susan Burrows, *American Needlework,* Winterthur Guide, 1976.
Swan, Susan Burrows, *Plain and Fancy: American Women and their Needlework, 1700-1850,* New York 1977.
Sweerts, Emanuel, *Early Floral Engravings* (Dover 1976). 110 plates from the 1612 Florilegium.
Synge, Lanto (ed.), *The Royal School of Needlework Book of Needlework and Embroidery,* London 1986.
Talbot Rice, David, *Byzantine Art,* Pelican Books 1968.
Talbot Rice, Tamara, *Concise History of Russian Art,* Thames and Hudson 1963.
Tarrant, Naomi, *Samplers in the Royal Scottish Museum,* Edinburgh 1978.
Toller, Jane, *British Samplers: A Concise History,* Chichester (Phillimore and Co Ltd) 1980.
Vulliamy, C.E., *Aspasia, Life and Letters of Mary Granville, Mrs Delany,* London 1935.
Wardle, Patricia, *Guide to English Embroidery,* Victoria and Albert Museum, London 1970.
Watt, James C.Y. and Anne E. Wardell, *When Silk Was Gold, Central Asian and Chinese Textiles,* The Metropolitan Museum of Art, New York 1998.
Webster, M.D., *Quilts: their story and how to make them,* 2nd ed. New York 1928.
Wills, K. C. S., *The Quire Embroideries,* Wells Cathedral 1976.
Wilson, Erica, *Erica Wilson's Embroidery Book,* New York 1973.
Wingfield, Digby G.F., *Elizabethan Embroidery,* London 1963.

Catalogues

Arts Council, The, Great Britain, *Opus Anglicanum,* Victoria and Albert Museum 1963 (exhibition).
Catalogue of the Morris Collection, William Morris Gallery, Walthamstow 1969.
Costume and Textile at Spink, 1990.
Illustrated Catalogue of the Loan Exhibition of English Decorative Art at Lansdowne House, February 1929.
La Mode Du Chale Cachemire en France. Musée de la Mode et du Costume, Paris 1982.
One Man's Samplers, The Goodhart Collection, Orleans House, Twickenham 1983.
Royal Academy of Arts, *Royal Treasures of Sweden 1550-1700,* 1989.
Trésors des Musées du Kremlin, Catalogue of exhibition, Paris 1979.
Treasures in Trust, ed. A.A. Tait, HMSO Edinburgh 1981 in association with the National Trust for Scotland. Article: 'Fabric Furnishings' by Margaret Swain.
Victoria and Albert Museum, London, Picture Books: *English Embroideries;* Part I, Elizabethan, Part II, Stuart, 1928.
Victoria and Albert Museum, London, *Notes on Applied Work and Patchwork,* 1959, and *Notes on Quilting,* 1960.
Victoria and Albert Museum Exhibition, *The Indian Heritage: Court Life and Arts under Mughal Rule,* 1982.

Iguanadon tea cosy by Mrs Arnold, c.1940

Acknowledgements

I am enormously grateful to many people for kindness and help, to owners, curators, experts, authors and photographers, some of whom have also kindly loaned pictures free of charge. Deborah Pope has assisted me greatly coordinating everything.

A number of photographs have been loaned by Malletts and others are acknowledged as follows, with many thanks:

3, 150 Camera Press, **6, 145** V&A picture library/Daniel McGrath, **7, 49, 89, 291** © The British Museum, **8** Sixt Parish Church, Haute-Savoie, France/Bridgeman Art Library, **9** Averbode Abbey, Brabant, **10, 94** Christopher Gibbs Ltd, **11** His Grace the Duke of Buccleuch and Queensbury, K.T., **13** Partridge Fine Arts, **18, 36** Österreichisches Museum für Angewandte Kunst, Vienna, Austria/Bridgeman Art Library, **26, 30, 37, 40, 44, 45, 47, 48, 61, 63, 72, 75, 83, 97, 98, 100, 130, 149, 197, 164, 229, 272, 298, 301, 303, 309, 311, 312, 313** V&A picture library, **27, 280, 282, 283, 284, 285, 286, 287, 288, 289, 290** Linda Wrigglesworth, **28, 58, 104, 209, 212, 245** The Royal Collection © 2001 Her Majesty Queen Elizabeth, **31** Dean & Chapter Library, Durham, **32, 33** Bayeux Museum, **34** © The British Library, **35** Musée National du Moyen Age et des Thermes de Cluny, Paris/Peter Willi/Bridgeman Art Library, **38** Bayerisches National Museum Munich, **39** Videnskapsselskapets Oldsaksamling, Trondheim, **41** Museo Diocesano di Pienza, **42** Museo Civico Medievale di Bologna, **43** Vicar & Church wardens of Steeple Aston/V&A picture library, **46, 105, 153, 237, 281** The Metropolitan Museum, New York, **50** Treasury of San Francesco, Cortona, Italy/Bridgeman Art Library, **51** Museo Nazionale Florence/Bridgeman Art Library, **52, 53, 55** Kunsthistorisches Museum, Vienna, Austria/Ali Meyer/Bridgeman Art Library, **54, 57, 65, 256** Bridgeman Art Library, **56** St Peter's Abbey, Salzburg, **59** V&A picture library, with kind permission from the Rector of Dunstable, **60** Cathedral Treasury, Trento, **64** Traquair House Ltd, **66** © Manchester City Art Galleries, **70** The Bodleian Library, University of Oxford, **71, 147** © Museum of London, **73, 84, 181** The National Trust Photographic Library, **74** The National Trust Photographic Library/John Hammond, **76** Devonshire Collection, Chatsworth, By permission of the Duke of Devonshire and the Chatsworth Settlement Trustees, **80** National Trust Photographic Library/J Whitaker, **81** Parham Park Ltd, **82** National Trust Photographic Library/Ian Shaw, **85** Embroiderers' Guild Museum Collection/Dudley Moss, **86** National Trust Photographic Library/Hawkley Studios, **87, 88** College of Arms, **95** The Royal School of Needlework, **96** Sir Richard Carew Pole, Bt, Antony House, Cornwall, **99, 198** Christie's Photographic Library, **101** Kremlin Museum, **102** Victor Franses Gallery, **103** Sotheby's, **106, 132, (146), 173** Cora Ginsburg Inc (Thaddeus Watkins), **107** National Art Library, Victoria & Albert Museum, **121** The Longridge Collection, **133, 195** Mayorcas Ltd, **137, 295** National Trust Photographic Library/Andreas von Einsiedel, **138** Drayton House, Northamptonshre, **140** Ashmolean Thompson, **141** © Tate, London 2001, **142** Rijksmuseum, The Netherlands, **143** English Heritage Photographic Library, **144** Glasgow Museums: The Burrell Collection, **160** The Trustees of the National Museums of Scotland, 2001, **163** The Trustees of Sir John Soane's Museum, **172** National Museums and Galleries of Wales, **186** Birmingham Museums and Art Gallery, **211** Winterthur Museum, **213** Museum of Fine Arts, Boston © 2001 All rights reserved, **248** Musée Mobilier National, Paris/Bridgeman Art Library, **255** Maureen Morris, **267** Smithsonian Institution, Washington DC/Bridgeman Art Library, **270** Embroiderers' Guild Museum Collection/Joss Reiver Bany, **273** The Castle Howard Collection, **274** Merseyside County Museum 1985, **277** National Gallery of Scotland, **278** Fathers of the London Oratory/Bridgeman Art Library, **292, 293** Jacqueline Simcox/Cleveland Museum of Art, **294** National Trust Photographic Library/Mark Fiennes, **297** Embroiderers' Guild Museum Collection/Dudley Moss, **299** © Houghton Hall and Jarrold Publishing, **306** Francesca Galloway, **314, 322** Beryl Dean Phillips, **317** The Dean and Canons of Windsor, **318** The D-day Museum, Portsmouth, **319** Zara Merrick, The Country Life Picture Library/June Buck, **320, 323, 324** Contemporary Applied Arts: Louise Baldwin, Linda Miller, Alice Kettle, **321** Wells Cathedral.

INDEX
Page numbers in bold refer to illustrations and captions

acupictura, 42
Ackworth, Yorkshire, 256
Adam, Robert, 183, **183**, 192, 200, **217**, 218, 244, 319
Aelgiva, Queen, 35
Aethelflaed, **34-35**, 35
Albert, Prince, **263**, 270
Alexander IV, Pope, 45
Allgood, Lady, 238
Alnwick Castle, Northumberland, 139, 192
altar frontals, 54, 55, **55**, 56, **61**, 70, 221, **278**, 283
Althorp House, Northamptonshire, 107
America, 28, 30, 129, 156, 180-182, 186, 188, 198, 204, 212, 213, 221, **222**, 223, 224, 229, 233, **242-243**, 245, 259, 266, 268-270, **268-269**, 272, 274, 277, 278, 329
  North, Indians, 34
  South, 32, 99
Amies, Sir Hardy, 108
Anagni, 52
Anglesey Abbey, Cambridgeshire, 107, 173
Anne, Queen, **20**, 105, 107, 334
Antony House, Cornwall, 177
Antwerp, 233
appliqué, 84, 86, **88**, 92, 107, 109, 120, **121**, 154, **154, 168-169, 190**, 193, **218-219**, 229, 270, **273**, 278, 321, 328
Arab, 56, 188
arabesques, 67, 68, 69, **69**, 75, 85, 126, **172**
Aragon, Catherine of, 67, 76
Arbury Hall, Warwickshire, 238
Army Museum, 107
Art Institute of Chicago, 58, 91
Art Needlework, 274, **280**
Art Nouveau, 284
Arundel Castle, Sussex, 59, 98, 240
Aston Hall, Birmingham, 192, **200**, 236
Ashmolean Museum, Oxford, 80, 192
Athene, 32
Australia, 212
Austria, **40-41**, 54, 55, 57, 114, **268**
Averbode Abbey, Brabant, **13**, 60, 66
Ayrshire whitework, 28, 225, 271-274, **272**

Baldwin, Louise, **330**
banners, 59, **102, 105**, 106, 108, 117
Barcelona, 58, 59
Bayeux Tapestry, 36-39, **36-37**, 44, 53, 145, 277, 328
beadwork, 113, 130, 131, **139, 143, 214**, 263, 349
beds, **16-17**, 17, 22, 60, 68, 90-94, **90-91**, 106, 114, 118, 120, **145**, 147, **150**, 153, **154, 156-157**, 159, **173**, 201, 226, 228-229, 229, **232-233**, 234, 300

covers/coverlets, **20, 155**, 156, 158, 183, **184-187**, 229, **270, 308, 314**, 321
  curtains, 226
  hangings, **20-21**, 62-63, 90, 98, 110, 182, **188-189**, 328
Belvoir Castle, Lincolnshire, 155
Bengal, **18**, 99, 148, 184, 190, 316
Benningbrough Hall, Yorkshire, 155
Bérain, Jean, 23, 69, 88, 118, **148**, 236
Berkeley Castle, Gloucestershire, 202, 234, 336
Berlin woolwork, 27, **28-29**, 168, 259-260, 261-266, **261**, 268, 274
Berlin work, 19, 245, 255, **265**, 267, 271, 280
Berry, Duke of, 55
Bess of Hardwick – *see* Shrewsbury, Elizabeth
Bethnal Green Museum, 204, 255
Bible, 10, 26, 81, 86, 91, 122, 135, 136, 174, 222, 235, 265, 276, 289
'bizarre' patterns, 173, **234, 335**
Black Death, 52
Black Prince, 60, 61, 63, 102, 106
blackwork, 71, 76-81, **76-77, 80**, 93, **129-131**, 147
Blair Castle, Scotland, 178, 238, 243
Blickling Hall, Norfolk, 105
Boadicea, 34
bobbin lace, 98, 165
Bodleian Library, Oxford, 81, 144
bombyx mori, 34, 286
Boniface VIII, Pope, 47, 51
bookbindings, 81-82, **81**, 143, 144, **143**, 183, 349
Bostocke, Jane, 69, **83-84**
Boston, **221**
  Museum of Fine Arts, 152
Botticelli, Sandro, 17
Boughton House, Northamptonshire, 153, 231, 233
Bowes Museum, Yorkshire, 89, 114, 242, 245
'boxers', 127
Bradford table carpet, **86**, 88
Bristol Orphanage, **256-257**, 258
British Museum, 48, 82, 98, 107, 144, 200
Broderers' Company, The, 24, 63, 70
broderie anglaise, 225, 273
Brooklyn Museum, 173
Broughton Castle, Oxfordshire, 106
Brussels, 57, **57**
Buckingham Palace, 169, 308
Burghley House, Lincolnshire, 155, 222, **222-223**, 245
Burgundy, Dukes of, 55, 58, **58**, 62, 103
Burne-Jones, Sir Edward, 276, 281
Burrell Collection, Glasgow, 67, 91, 113, 188, 236, 245

burses, **104**, 106
Byzantium, 54, 56, 57, 114

cabinets or caskets, 120, 130, **134-135**
Calke Abbey, Derbyshire, 156, 306, **306**
Cambi, Jacopo di, 55, **55**
Cambridge, 283
  King's College, **224**
  Trinity College, **78, 224**
  University of, 58, 80, 82, 103
Canons Ashby, Northamptonshire, **226-227**, 235
Canterbury, 37, 44, 49, 60
  Archbishop of, 47
  Cathedral, 61, 63, 102
canvas work, 25, 191-193
caps, 112
  gentlemen's, 78, **78, 79**, 165
Carlton House, 250
carpets, 19, 27, 67, 68, 70, 86, 87, 88, 126, 156, **175**, 182, 183, 192, 195, 197, 198-201, **199-200, 202-203**, 244, 266-268, **266-269**, 279, 282, 315, 317, 320, 321, 322, 327, 328, 339
Castle Ashby, Northamptonshire, 191
Cavendish family, **87**, 97, **100-101**, 154
chain-stitch, 179
Chambers, Sir William, 194
Charles I, King, 53, 78, 115, 120, 124, 136, **138**, 141, 142, 144, 156, 164, **176-177**, 177, 266, 306
Charles II, King, **105**, 106, 124, 131, 136, 138, 141, 142, 144, 147
Charles V, 62
Charlotte, Queen, **217**, 224, **254**
charter bags, 61
Chastleton House, Oxfordshire, 90, **92**, 156
chasubles, **22, 40-41, 50-51**, 61, **67**, 114, **114**, 229
  Clare, 48
  Melk, 48
Chatsworth House, Derbyshire, **87**, 153
Chaucer, Geoffrey, 18, 24, 45, 60, 73, **277**, 279
chenille, **26**, 250, **252-253**
China, 17, 18, **20-21**, 28, 32, 34, 42, 43, 57, 74, 108, 147, 148, 151, 152, 156, 158, 165, 172, 183, 184, 188, 194, 195, 217, 233, 250, 271, 286-309, **287-288, 290-293, 295-301, 303-312**, 312-313, 315, 318, 320, 321, 327, 328, 332
Chinese exports, 305-309, **305-309**
Chinese robes, **286-287**, 289-299, **289-293, 297-298**
Chinese symbols, 294-299, **295**
chinoiserie, 118, **150**, 151, 173, 174, 186, **192**, 194, 195, 199, 217, **234**, 239, 250, 313, **335**

348

330. A miniature bookbinding of beadwork, French c.1750.

Chippendale, Thomas, 194, 237, 238, 241, 242
Clandon Park, Surrey, **90,** 153, 236
Clement I, Pope, 47
Clement IV, Pope, 47
Cleveland Museum of Art, Ohio, 54, 305
Cogenhoe Church, Northamptonshire, 90
coifs, 76, 78, **80, 164**
Colonial Williamsburg, 148, 183, 188, 321
colours, 283, 332, 339
Commedia dell'Arte, 118, 170, 239
Copenhagen, 158
copes, **58,** 114, 229
    Ascoli Piceno, 46
    Averbode Abbey, **13**
    Bologna, **47,** 47
    Butler Bowden, 49
    Daroca, 48
    Jesse, **10-11,** 16, 48
    Pienza, **46,** 47
    Saint-Betrand-de-Comminges, 47
    Steeple Aston, 48, **48**
    Syon, 48, **49,** 103
    Thanet, **48,** 49
conservation, 30
coronation robes, **5, 30-31,** 167, 169, 177, **248-249**
costume, **14-15,** 18, 25, 60, 67, 68, 73, 75-76, 106, **112,** 120, 160-169, **160-169,** 176, 177, 271, 274, 288, 289, 297, 302
    18th century, 14, 215-218, 225
    Tudor, 14, 17
Cothele House, Cornwall, 146

Crane, Walter, 276, 282
crewelwork, 13, **16-17,** 19, **23,** 110, 113, 145-153, **145, 146, 148-150,** 156, 165, 178-188, **179-182,** 193, 199, 228, **228-229,** 231, 234, 246, 310, 318, 319, 327, 337
Culloden Moor, 204, **205**
Culzean Castle, Ayrshire, 240
cushions, 68, 74, **85,** 87, **87,** 88, 89, 97, 106, 108, 122, 130, **131, 140,** 151, 174, 186, 226, 229, 230, 245, **343**
cutwork, **97,** 126, **162,** 204, 273

Dalemain, Cumberland, 154
darning samplers, 212
Day, Lewis, 326
Dean, Beryl, **324-325,** 328, 330, **332-333**
Deerfield, Massachusetts, 278
Defoe, Daniel, 147
Delany, Mrs, 165, 188, **188,** 193, 215-216, 221, 223, 240, 337
Denmark, 113, 213, 225
Devonshire – *see* Cavendish family
Dickinson, Gary, 290, 338
Doddington Hall, Lincolnshire, 148
Donne, John, 74
Dorney Court, Buckinghamshire, 139, 263
dragons, 291-296, **291-293,** 300
Drayton House, Northamptonshire, **6,** 110, 155, **156-157,** 183, 234, 319, 337
Dresden, 225, 240, 254
Drum Castle, Grampian, 242, 243
Dunstable Priory, 58, **66**

Dunster Castle, Somerset, 242
Dürer, Albrecht, 17
dyes, 289, 315, 338
    aniline, 260, 261, 265

Editha, 35
Edward I, King, 47, 61, 100, 104
Edward II, King, 47, 61, 100, 104
Edward III, King, **39,** 40, 60, 61, 100
Edward VI, King, 90, 226
Edward VII, King, **109**
Edward the Confessor, King, 35, 38
Egypt, 18, **32-33,** 34, 248, 261
Elizabeth I, Queen, 18, 67, 70, 73, **75,** 76, 80, 81, **81,** 90, 93, 96, **102, 104,** 106, 112, 130, 162, 164, 230, 289, 310
Elizabeth II, Queen, **30-31,** 165, 169, **169, 324-325,** 330, **332-333**
Elizabeth the Queen Mother, Queen, **5,** 165, 169
Ely Cathedral, 60
Embroiderers' Guild, 30, 153, 188, 324
embroidery, 13, 34
Emma, Queen, 35
Empire style, **251**
engraving, 27
Erddig, Wrexham, 156, 307, **307**
Euston Hall, Suffolk, 106
Exeter Cathedral, 98

Feltwell, Dr John, 286, 338
Fetternear banner, 59

349

The Art of Embroidery

Field of the Cloth of Gold, 17, **38,** 103
filet, **14** – *see also* lacis
flags, 108, 109
flame stitch, **91, 92**
Flanders, 52, 54, 225
Flemish, 60, 66, **89,** 90, 117, 132, 147, **228**
Florence, 43, 53, 55, 56, 66
Florentine stitch/work, **91,** 92, 156, 233, 332
flowers, 18-19, **23,** 26, 70, 71-74, **71,** 75, **110-111,** 122, 123, 142, 176, 178, **180-181,** 197, 199, **205, 216,** 231, **232, 234, 235, 238, 240, 243, 252-253,** 298
Fontainebleau, 243
France, 13, 16, **16-17,** 22-24, **23, 26,** 38, 53, 57, 62, **68,** 69, 71, 74, 88, **88, 89,** 90, **91, 93,** 95, 99, 103, 112, 114, 115, **121,** 129, 130, 147, **148,** 154, 164, 167, 173, **173,** 174, **174, 182, 192, 193,** 194, **194, 198, 199,** 200, 201, **212-215,** 217, 229, **233,** 236, **238,** 243, 244, 248, 250, **251, 263, 267,** 271, 274, 310, **319, 349**
Francis I, 69
François I, 103
Frick Collection, New York, 235, 236
furniture, 19, **24,** 25, 60, 85-90, **108,** 120, 177, 182, 195, 226-247, **226-247**

George I, **178**
George II, 105, 233
George III, King, 167, **168-169, 220-221,** 224, **254,** 300, 328
George IV, King, 108, 167, 248, **248-249**
George VI, King, **5,** 169, **328-329**
Germany, 28, 43, **43,** 44-45, **45,** 54, **59,** 107, 122, 127, 129, 130, 214, 274
Gheeraerdts, Marcus, **160-161,** 335
Glamis Castle, Angus, 92, 139
Glemham Hall, Suffolk, **245**
gloves, 80, 112-113, 131
Goa, 99, 317, **317**
Goodhart Collection, 126
Göss, Convent of, **40-41,** 55
Gothic, 29, 46, 49, 56, 194, 199, 200, 246
Great Exhibition of 1851, 29, 252, 265, 267, 270, 274, 279
Greece, 32, 114, 192, 217, 221, 248, 288, 301
Greenwich, 18
Grimsthorpe Castle, Lincolnshire, 105
grotesques, 60, 69, 70, 126, 173
guilds, 63,
Gujarat, 99, 147, 179, **313,** 315, 318, 319

Ham House, Surrey, 153, 159, 230, 334
Hampton Court Palace, 22, **30,** 104, **118,** 120, 153, 159, 182, 229, 324
handkerchiefs, 273, 274
hangings, 68, 70, **94-95,** 96, **116-117, 118,** 124, **189**
Hardwick Hall, Derbyshire, 74, 75, **84, 85,** 86, 87, 88, 89, 93, 96, 107, 120, 122, 230, 316, 339
Bess of – *see* Shrewsbury, Elizabeth

Harrison, Edmund, 142
Hartnell, Norman, 169, **169**
Hastings, Battle of, 37-38
Hatfield House, Hertfordshire, 75, 76, 306, 328
Henri II, 69
Henry III, King, 16
Henry IV, King, 71
Henry V, King, 103
Henry VI, King, 63, 102
Henry VII, King, 63, 90, 104, 162, 336
Henry VIII, King, 17, **64-65,** 67, 68, 76, 80, 90, 104, 106, 162, 230
heraldry, 14, 36, 48, 61, 62, 70, 82, 100-109, 129, **129,** 132, 142, 144, **144,** 229, 273
Holkham Hall, Norfolk, 223
Holland, 22, 71, 112, 122, 129, 130, 132, 142, 159, 213, 214, 310, 314, **320**
hollie-point, 204
Holyrood, Palace of, Edinburgh, 17, 96, 107, 234, 335
Hornby Castle, Lancashire, 237
Houghton Hall, Norfolk, 108, 151, 185, 230, **232-233,** 246, 307, **310-311,** 312-313
House of Lords, 105, 246
Höylander, 44

Iceland, 58
India, **20-21,** 28, 34, 74, 99, 147, 148, **150,** 151, **155,** 156, 158, 165, 172, 178, 183, 184, 185, **186,** 188, 190, 194, 197, 225, **235,** 251, 271, 277, 301, 302, 307, 308, 310-121, **310-323,** 327
Indians, North American, 34
Innocent IV, Pope, 45, 334
insects, 74, 129
Ireland, 127, 188, **188,** 203, **209,** 222, 233, 237, 270, 271, 272, 273, 274, 276
Irish stitch, **242-243**
Islam, 67, 69, 114, **274-275,** 279, 320, 321, 322
Italy, 16, **23,** 52, 63, 64, 66, **67, 69,** 70, 71, 114, 117, **116-117,** 126, 129, 130, 147, **158, 162,** 173, **175,** 180, 192, 201, 213, 272

Jacob at the Well, **25**
James I, King, 70, 95, 98, 106, 110, 112, 115, 120, 142, 174, 229, 230
James II, King, 107, 113, 136, 164, **165,** 230, 274, 334
Japan, **29,** 164, 276, 302
japanning, 151
Jennens, Mrs, 238, 337
Jewish needlework, 174
John XXII, Pope, 47

Kashmir, 322, **323,** 327
Kay-Shuttleworth, The Hon. Mrs Rachel, 329
Kempe, Charles, **278**
Kensington Palace, London, 102, 108, 167, 169, 266
Kettle, Alice, **333**
Kew Palace, 224
Kings College, Cambridge, **224**

Knebworth House, Hertfordshire, 180
Knole, Kent, 153, **154,** 155, 230
knotting, **81,** 159, 188, **188,** 215, 252
Knowles, Mary, **220-221,** 224

lace, 29, 85, 172, 216-217, 225
lacis, **14,** 95, **97,** 98
Lady Lever Art Gallery, Port Sunlight, 90, 132, 140
Landseer, Sir Edwin, **261-263,** 265, 266
Laton, Margaret, 76, 80, 112, **112-113,** 163
Le Brun, Charles, 23
Leeds Castle, Kent, 183
Leicester Museum, 238
Leixlip Castle, Co. Kildare, 243
leopards of England, **39,** 61
Lincoln Cathedral, 42
Linwood, Mary, 224, 225, 252
Little Gidding Community, 144
London, City of, 61, 107, 129
  livery companies, 58, 104
London Museum, 85, 146
Longleat House, Somerset, 185
Louis XIV, 22, 113, 115, 118, **118-119**
Louis XV, 170, 173, 174
Ludwig II, 251
Lyons, 54, 167, 215

Maaseik, 35
Macbeth, Ann, 328
Maintenon, Madame de, 22, 173
mantles
  of Charlemagne, 57
  of St Kunigund, 54
  of the Holy Roman Emperors, **56**
Mapledurham House, Oxfordshire, 245
maps, 259
Marble Hill House, London, 239
Margaret, Queen, 35
Marot, Daniel, **16-17, 118,** 120, 153, 230
Mary, Queen, 22, 63, 159, 306, 337
Mary, Queen (late), 169, 308, 327
Mary Queen of Scots, 17, 20, 69, 74, 76, 88, 91, 92, **94-95,** 95-98, 163, 229, 265, 266
Mary Tudor, Queen, 82
Matisse, Henri, 328
Medici, Catherine de, 17, 69, 95, 99
Mellerstain, Berwickshire, 176-177, 243
Merrick, Zara, **328-329**
metal thread embroidery, **6,** 143, 144, 165, 166, 167, **168-169,** 172, **186-187, 216,** 228
Metropolitan Museum, 49, 54, 70, 91, 117, 118, 122, 139, 141, 156, 159, 177, 195, 199, 201, 233, 236, 239, 241, 243, 305, 328
Milan Cathedral, 117
Miller, Linda, **332-333**
Milton, Peterborough, 92
mirrors, 130, 132, **132,** 141
mitres, **13,** 42, **43**
Mompesson House, Salisbury, 236
Montacute House, Somerset, 191, 238
Montague, Belinda, Lady, 329

350

Index

Monymusk, Aberdeen, 192
Moors, 67, 68
Morris, Anne Elizabeth, 338
Morris, William, 29, 274, **274-275**, 277, **277**, 278-283, 326
Morritt, Miss, 224
Mughal period, 28, 42, 114, 147, 148, 156, 310, **313**, 315, **315**, 316, 317, **319**, 320, **321**, **322**
Muncaster Castle, Cumbria, 91
Murray, Lady Evelyn **326**
Musée de Cluny, 42, 61
Musée Historique des Tissus, Lyons, 167
Musée Nissim de Camondo, 117, 200, 243
muslin, 188, 217, 225, 271

Napoleon, 167, 225, 248, **248**
National Gallery of Canada, Ottawa, 67
National Gallery of Scotland, 282
National Museum, Dublin, 127
National Museum of Ireland, 273
National Museums of Scotland, 59, 91-92, 104, 126, 178
National Trust, 307
 See also properties – Anglesey Abbey, Antony House, Benningborough, Blickling, Calke Abbey, Canons Ashby, Chastleton, Clandon, Cothele, Dunster Castle, Ham House, Hardwick Hall, Mompesson House, Osterley Park, Oxburgh Hall, Saltram, The Vyne, Waddesdon Manor, Wallington Hall
National Trust for Scotland, 193, 204, 240
 See also properties – 28 Charlotte Square, Culloden Moor Visitors' Centre, Culzean Castle, Drum Castle
needlepainting, 42, 52, 142, 224, 252, **253**, **264-265**, 279
needlepoint, 13
 lace, 29, 76, **97**, 126, 127, 130, 204, 216
needlework, 13
 lace, 165
neo-classicism, 170, **172**, 174, 183, 192, 217, **217**, **218**, **222-223**, 244, 248, **248-249**, 250
Netherlands, **13**, **58**, 60, 62
Newliston, Midlothian, 192, 193, 328
Nicholas IV, Pope, 46
Northern Ireland, 28
Norway, **44**
Nostell Priory, Yorkshire, 308
Nunwick, Northumberland, 238

Old Pretender, 178, **180**
opus anglicanum, **10-11**, **12-13**, 16, 17, 18, 40, 45-52, **47**, 160, 225, **288-289**, 328
opus teutonicum, 54
or de chypre, 43
or nué, 52, **54**, 57, 66, 142, 143
Orange, William of – *see* William III
Order of the Garter, 107, **107**, 144, 165, 183
Order of the Golden Fleece, 57, **57**, 59
Order of the Thistle, 107
Orléans, Duke of, 62

orphreys, 54
Osborne House, **262**, 266
Osterley Park, London, 183, **183**, 244, 246, 319, 320
Ottoman, 147
Overlord Embroidery, 328, **328-329**
Ovid, 70, 87
Oxburgh Hall, Norfolk, 20, 92, **94-95**, 96, 114, 124
 hangings, 70
Oxford, 81, 131

painting, 27
Palermo, 56, 57
palls, 58, **66**, 70, 103, 104
Parham Park, Sussex, **91**, 92, 113, 233, 244
Parry, Linda, 281
patchwork, 186, 229, 268-271, **270**
pattern books, 17, 70, 71, 120, 121-124, **122**, 176, 223
pattern drawers, 176
patterns, 82, 85, 197, 198, 241
Penshurst Place, Kent, 120
Pepys, Samuel, 147
Persia, **20**, 29, 42, 43, 73, 148, 156, 172, 183, 184, 188, 194, 279, 297, 315, 318, 320
Pesel, Louisa, 330
Philippa, Queen, 60, 62
phoenix (*simurgh*), 297, 300, 305, 313, 320
Piedmont, **172**
plush stitch, **271**
Pollaiuolo, 53, 66
Portugal, **18**, 58, 99, 147, 153, 156, 158, 184, 190, 213, 310, 314, 316, **316**, 317, **317**
pouncing, 52, 73, **122**
professional embroiderers, 40, 45, 58, 70, 71, 85, 88, 89, 90, 143, 144, 166, 167, 173, 184, 194, 195, 198, 225, 241, 243, 248, 271
Pugin, Augustus W.N., 246, 283
purses, **6**, 62, 70, 81, 106, 107, **113**

quilting, **20**, 25, 43, 102, **155**, 156, 158, **166**, 183, 184, **184**, 185, 186, **186-187**, 197, 229, 268-271, **269**, 313, 316, 317, 318, 321, 337

Raby Castle, Co. Durham, 200
Raphael, 69, 118, 126, 132, 224, 278
Reformation, 17, **46**, 59, 63, 64, 70, 99
Régence period, 170, **182**, **192**, 200, 235, 236
Regency period, 168, 224, 248, 250, 255, 269
Renaissance, 17, 59, 64, 67, **67**, 68, **68**, 88, 99, 147, 273, **278**, 323
Richard II, King, 61, 62, 106, 160, **210**
Roberts, Hugh, 105
rococo, 170, 194-198, 199, 217, 241, **331**
Roger II, 56, **56**
Rokeby, Yorkshire, 224
Rome, 51, 52, 69, 173, 192, **201**, 202, 286, 288, 314
Roosevelt, Mrs Theodore, 329
Royal Collection, 108, 117, 234
Royal Ontario Museum, Toronto, 235

Royal Pavilion, Brighton, 250
Royal School of Needlework, **5**, 30, **30-31**, **109**, 169, 274-277, **281**, 282, 328, 330, 334
Russia, 32, 99, 114, **115**, 180, 266

saddles, 113, 143
St Augustine, 34
St Cuthbert, 34-35, **34-35**
St Cyr, 173, 194, **234**, 239, 241, **335**
St Dunstan, 35
St Etheldreda, 34, 284, 334
St Fagan's Castle, Wales, 180, 191, 258, 271
St Kunigund, 54
St Louis, 53
St Martin, 54
St Paul's Cathedral, 63, 98, 330, **332-333**
St Thomas, **43**, 44, 47
Saltram, Devon, 318, 319
samplers, 14, 25, 69, **81-82**, 82-85, 113, 120, 124-130, **124-131**, 203-214, **204-211**, 248, 252, 253-260, **254-257**, **259-260**
Sarto, Andrea del, **54**
Saxony, 263 Scandinavia, 36
scarves, 164
Scone Palace, Perth, 87, 92, 96, 235, 241
Scotland, 28, 34, 35, 59, 70, 91, 95, 153, 188, 192, 203, **204**, **205**, 225, 229, 263, 271, 272
Seaton Delaval, Northumberland, 235
secular embroidery, 60-63
Sens Cathedral, 44
Seville, 58
Sforza, Beatrice d'Este, 67, 162
shawls, 322, **323**
Shorleyker, Richard, 122, **122**
Shrewsbury, Elizabeth, Countess of (Bess of Hardwick), 20, 86, 92, 96, 121, 316
Sicily, **42**, 43, 56, **56**, 57
silk, 34, 286-309
Simcox, Jacqueline, 303, 339
slips, 71, 75, 176
smocking, 271
smocks, 168
Soane Museum, 200
Spain, 56, 58, 68, 82, **97**, 99, 114, **114**, 117, 173, 213
'spot' motifs, 26, **124-125**, 129, **131**
Squerryes Court, Kent, 108
stitches, 113, 280, **352**
Stoke Edith, Herefordshire, 191, 197
Stoneleigh Abbey, Warwickshire, 235
Stowe, Buckinghamshire, 239, **244**
strapwork, 68, **68**, 70, **76-77**, **81**, 87, **154**, 192, 328
Street, G.E., 279, 282-283
Strong, Roy, 93, 162, 336, 337
Stubbs, George, **27**, 225
stumpwork, **19**, 54, 112, 113, 130-143, **134-137**
Swain, Margaret, 86, 228
Sweden, 63, 158, 174
 Royal Collection, 113, 164
Switzerland, 213, 274

The Art of Embroidery

Syon House, London, 244
tabards, **103**
Tabernacle, 10
table carpets, 88, 89, 106
tambour embroidery, 217, 225, 243, 244
tapestry, 13, 34, 36, 42, 53, 106, 115, 132, 202, 234, 242, 279, 282, 288
Temple Newsam, Leeds, 233, 242
tents, **38**
Textile Conservation Centre, The, 324
thanka, **303,** 305, **305**
Tibet, 17, 301, 302-305 **303-305,** 328
Tiffany, 277, 278
Toledo, 58
Topsell, Edward, 32
Tower of London, 17, 40
Traquair House, Peeblesshire, 63, **72-73,** 108, 121
Traquair, Phoebe Anna, 282, **282-283**
Trinity College, Cambridge, 222, **224**
Tristan, **42,** 43, 45
Tudor, House of, 64, 68
Turkey, 68

Untermyer Collection, 122, 138, 159, 201, 241
Urban IV, Pope, 45

valances, 68, 69, **69,** 88, **88, 89,** 90, 91, 105, 106, 132, 151, **173,** 186, 201, 228, 229
Vallet, Pierre, 71
Vatican, 51, 69

Vence, 328
Venice, 29, 57, 147, **162,** 172
Vernon, Elizabeth, Countess of Southampton, **14-15**
Versailles, 22, 115, 117, 118, 248, 251
vestments, 16, 42, 53-55, 63, **84,** 93, 103, 114, 160, 173, 226, 229, 281, 282, 283, 289, 305
Victoria, Princess/Queen, 165, 225, 262, 266, 267, 270, 276
Victoria and Albert Museum, 17, 40, 43, 44, 45, 48, 70, 76, 81, 82, 88, 91, 92, 96, 102, 103, 106, 108, 110, 114, 120, 126, 127, 129, 136, 141, 144, 148, 151, 152, 158, 159, 164, 165, 173, 174, 180, 183, 188, 206, 213, 224, 238, 252, 258, 300, 301, 309, 315, 317, 318, 320, 321, 322, 323
Victorian age, 261, 279
Victorian needlework, 29, **270**
Vienna, **22,** 48, 55, 56
Vinci, Leonardo da, 67
Vinciolo, Frederico di, 17, 67, 126, 272
Virgil, 178, 191, 202
Vollmer, John, 292, 338
Vyne, The, Hampshire, 70

Waddesdon Manor, Buckinghamshire, 70, 235, 243, 322, 337, 338
Wales, 153
  Prince of, 165, **261,** 266, 268, 282
Wallington Hall, Northumberland, 191, 202, 240, 245

Walpole, Horace, **6**
weaving, 13, 52, 117, 282, 289
Wells Cathedral, 329, **330-331**
Wemyss Castle, Fife, 192, 276
Wemyss, Lady Victoria, 246
Westminster, 38, 39, 59
  Abbey, 16, 39, 61, 63, 104, 226
  Palace of, 246
Weston Hall, Northamptonshire, 238, 337 (Note 5, Chapter 7)
white hart, 62
Whitehall Palace, **64-65,** 155
whitework, 28, 54, **81-82,** 85, 95, 98, 126, 127, **128-129,** 130, 188-191, 204, 217, 225, 254, 271-274, 276, **326**
Whitworth Art Gallery, Manchester, 114, 131
William I (the Conqueror), King, 37-39, **37**
William III (of Orange), King, 22, 63, 104, 107, 112, 120, 129, 159, 306
William IV, King, 262
Winchester, 35, 39
  Cathedral, 330
Windsor Castle, 90, 144, 159, 182, 215, 266, 320, **328**
Winterthur Museum, Delaware, 107
wool, **27,** 37, 53, **92,** 145, **146, 152,** 176, 186, 188, 224, 229, 259, **264-265,** 279, 286
woolwork, **259**
Worcester Cathedral, 48
workshops, 56, 58, 62
Worksop Manor, Nottinghamshire, 240
Wrigglesworth, Linda, 290, 338

331. A small silkwork picture worked in rococo stitch, with a white diaper background. English, c.1710.

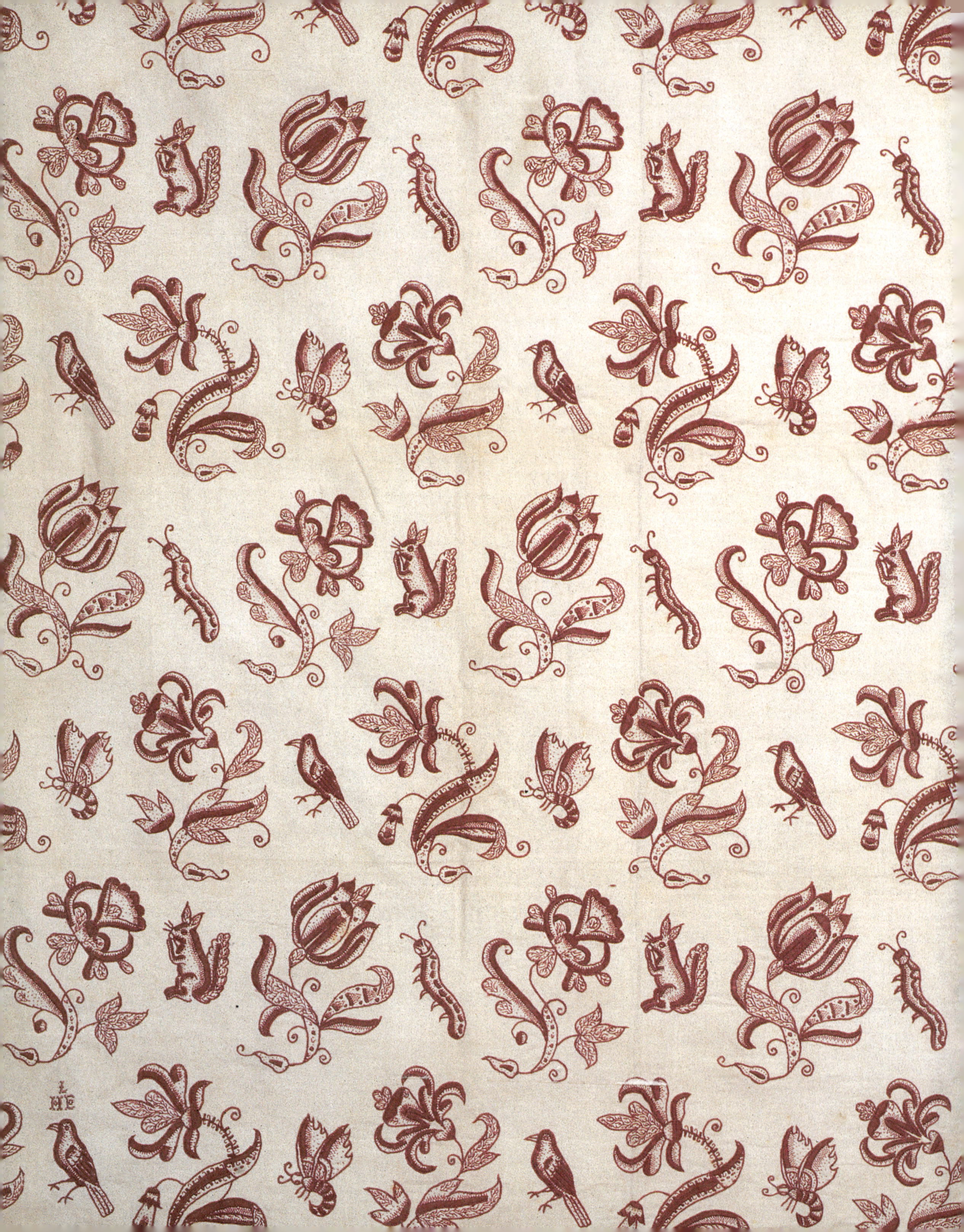